SPECIAL REPORT

ON

SURNAMES IN IRELAND

[TOGETHER WITH]

VARIETIES AND SYNONYMES

OF

SURNAMES AND CHRISTIAN NAMES
IN IRELAND

BY

SIR ROBERT E. MATHESON, LL.D.,
Barrister-at-Law,
Registrar-General for Ireland.

Two Volumes In One

Originally published as *Varieties and Synonymes of Surnames and Christian Names in Ireland*, Dublin, 1901, and *Special Report on Surnames in Ireland*, Dublin, 1909
Reprinted in one volume by
Genealogical Publishing Co., Inc.
1001 N. Calvert St., Baltimore, Md. 21202
1968, 1975, 1982, 1988, 1994, 2003
Library of Congress Catalogue Card Number 68-54684
International Standard Book Number 0-8063-0187-2
Made in the United States of America

SPECIAL REPORT

ON

SURNAMES IN IRELAND,

WITH

NOTES AS TO NUMERICAL STRENGTH, DERIVATION, ETHNOLOGY, AND DISTRIBUTION;

BASED ON INFORMATION EXTRACTED FROM THE INDEXES OF THE GENERAL REGISTER OFFICE.

BY

SIR ROBERT E. MATHESON, LL.D.,

BARRISTER-AT-LAW,

Registrar-General for Ireland.

DUBLIN:

PRINTED FOR HIS MAJESTY'S STATIONERY OFFICE,

BY ALEX. THOM & CO. (LIMITED), ABBEY-STREET.

And to be purchased, either directly or through any Bookseller, from
E. PONSONBY, 116, GRAFTON-STREET, DUBLIN ; or
WYMAN & SONS (LIMITED), FETTER-LANE, LONDON, E.C.; or
OLIVER & BOYD, TWEEDDALE-COURT, EDINBURGH.

1909.

PREFACE.

THE following Special Report was originally prepared by me and issued as an Appendix to the Twenty-ninth Annual Report of the Registrar-General for Ireland. It has been for some years out of print, but a motion having been made in the House of Commons by Mr. Jeremiah MacVeagh, M.P., for its re-printing, the Government have now sanctioned its issue as a Stationery Office Publication.

In re-issuing the Report, I have inserted, as an Addendum, the List of the Names of Irish Septs given in the Book of Arms, compiled by Sir James Terry, Athlone Herald (1690), now pre-served in the British Museum.

ROBERT E. MATHESON.

General Register Office,
    Charlemont House,
        Dublin, *November*, 1909.

TABLE OF CONTENTS.

SPECIAL REPORT

ON

SURNAMES IN IRELAND,

WITH

NOTES AS TO NUMERICAL STRENGTH, DERIVATION, ETHNOLOGY, AND DISTRIBUTION.

CHAPTER I.

INTRODUCTORY REMARKS.

The investigation into the personal names of the people of any country is a subject surrounded with very great interest. By means of family nomenclature much light can be thrown on the early employments and customs of a people, as well as the sources from which they have sprung. In fact, the history of our country lies enshrined in its Surnames; and on our shop fronts and in our graveyards may be found side by side the names of the descendants of the Milesian Prince, of the Scandinavian Viking, and of the Norman Knight.

So far back as 1851 the Census Commissioners for that year attempted to arrange the Surnames of the country in such a way as to show their distribution. The effort, however, proved unsuccessful, owing to the difficulties met with, and when the names were partially extracted the task was abandoned.

At the termination of the Census of 1881, the late Dr. Lyons, then M.P. for Dublin, pressed the Government to institute an inquiry into names, such as had been attempted in 1851, and his proposal was very favourably entertained, but as the work of the Census Department was then about to close, the Commissioners were unable to comply with his request.

It may be observed that as a preliminary to any successful effort to tabulate the Surnames in the country, some codification of the variations in form and spelling was necessary. With this and other objects in view, from the materials collected during many years in the General Register Office, as well as special reports obtained from local officers in the Registration Service, I prepared in 1890 a treatise entitled "Varieties and Synonymes of Surnames and Christian Names in Ireland," which was issued by the Registrar-General for use in connection with searches in his Office, and in those of the Superintendent Registrars and Registrars throughout the country.

That book set forth the principal orthographical changes in Surnames, exhibiting the varieties in spelling; the use of prefixes and affixes; spelling according to usual pronunciation; older forms of names showing the alterations they have undergone in course of time; local variations in spelling and form, exhibiting the tendency of names to assume different forms in different localities; variations in spelling at pleasure; and changes owing to illiteracy and other causes.

It further contained examples of the use of entirely different names interchangeably by the same person, a practice which pre-

vails in some parts of Ireland, many being cases of translation of
Irish names into English, or *vice versa,* or equivalents, modifications, or corruptions of them. A table was also given showing
cases of English names and their Irish equivalents met with in
the Registration Records. The work also contained an Alphabetical List of Surnames, with their Varieties and Synonymes,
and a Table showing the respective Poor Law Unions and
Districts in which many of the peculiarities had been found.

The reception which that book met with at the hands of the
Press and the Public was very gratifying, and I determined to
attempt, in connection with the Census of 1891, the interesting
work of extracting and classifying the Surnames of the population generally on the lines unsuccessfully followed in 1851. An
unexpected occurrence, however, prevented this. The Census
Records which previously afforded complete data for the purpose were, in 1891, rendered imperfect in this respect, owing to
the insertion of a clause in the Act of Parliament, directing that
in the case of Inmates of Public Institutions, initials only should
be given in the Enumeration Forms.

The Surnames of a considerable number of persons were thus
omitted from these Records, and the question arose whether with
these imperfect data, the work should be abandoned, or whether
the general results could not be obtained with sufficient accuracy
from other sources.

The Indexes of the General Register Office afford a reliable
basis on which to found general conclusions regarding Surnames,
and though in the Index for any one year all the Surnames in the
country will not be found, yet if a name be of frequent occurrence
it is certain to be represented in the Index, the number of entries
opposite the name indicating its relative frequency with respect
to other Surnames.

The Indexes further afford facilities for distributing the Surnames over the country, as in the case of each entry the Poor
Law Union is given.

In view of these facts, I decided to take these Indexes as the
basis of my inquiries, and I was confirmed in my determination
by the opinion of that eminent scholar, the late Right Rev. Dr.
Reeves, Lord Bishop of Down, Connor, and Dromore, and President of the Royal Irish Academy, who encouraged me to under-
take the task, and promised me his cordial assistance. His
lamented death, however, unhappily deprived me of the benefit
of his valuable aid and advice.

I may mention that both in England and Scotland the subject
of personal nomenclature has received attention, and statistics
relating thereto, derived from the Indexes of Births, Deaths,
and Marriages, have been published by the respective Registrars-
General, to which I shall further refer.

I have divided the consideration of the subject as follows :—

1st. The principal Surnames in Ireland compared with those
    in other portions of the United Kingdom.
2nd. The Derivation of Surnames in Ireland.
3rd. Surnames in Ireland Ethnologically considered.
4th. The Local Distribution of Surnames in Ireland.

CHAPTER II.

PRINCIPAL SURNAMES IN IRELAND COMPARED WITH THOSE IN OTHER PORTIONS OF THE UNITED KINGDOM.

The following Table exhibits One Hundred of the Principal Surnames in Ireland (including varieties) arranged in order of numerical strength, together with the Estimated Number of Persons bearing each Name.

TABLE showing One Hundred of the principal Surnames in Ireland (including varieties) taken from the Births Index of 1890, together with the Estimated Population bearing each Surname.

Population of 1890, estimated at 4,717,959 persons.

No. on List.	SURNAMES.	Estimated Population bearing each Surname.	No. on List.	SURNAMES.	Estimated Population bearing each Surname.
1	Murphy,	62,600	38	Martin,	14,600
2	Kelly,	55,900	39	Maguire,	14,400
3	Sullivan,	43,600	40	Nolan,	14,300
4	Walsh,	41,700	41	Flynn,	14,300
5	Smith,	33,700	42	Thompson,	14,200
6	O'Brien,	33,400	43	Callaghan,	14,000
7	Byrne,	33,300	44	O'Donnell,	13,900
8	Ryan,	32,000	45	Duffy,	13,600
9	Connor,	31,200	46	Mahony,	13,500
10	O'Neill,	29,100	47	Boyle,	13,000
11	Reilly,	29,000	48	Healy,	13,000
12	Doyle,	23,000	49	Shea,	13,000
13	McCarthy,	22,300	50	White,	13,000
14	Gallagher,	21,800	51	Sweeney,	12,500
15	Doherty,	20,800	52	Hayes,	12,300
16	Kennedy,	19,900	53	Kavanagh,	12,200
17	Lynch,	19,800	54	Power,	12,100
18	Murray,	19,600	55	McGrath,	11,900
19	Quinn,	18,200	56	Moran,	11,800
20	Moore,	17,700	57	Brady,	11,600
21	McLaughlin,	17,500	58	Stewart,	11,400
22	Carroll,	17,400	59	Casey,	11,300
23	Connolly,	17,000	60	Foley,	11,200
24	Daly,	17,000	61	Fitzpatrick,	11,100
25	Connell,	16,600	62	Leary,	11,000
26	Wilson,	16,300	63	McDonnell,	11,000
27	Dunne,	16,300	64	McMahon,	10,700
28	Brennan,	16,000	65	Donnelly,	10,700
29	Burke,	15,900	66	Regan,	10,500
30	Collins,	15,700	67	Donovan,	9,900
31	Campbell,	15,600	68	Burns,	9,800
32	Clarke,	15,400	69	Flanagan,	9,800
33	Johnston,	15,200	70	Mullan,	9,800
34	Hughes,	14,900	71	Barry,	9,700
35	Farrell,	14,700	72	Kane,	9,700
36	Fitzgerald,	14,700	73	Robinson,	9,700
37	Brown,	14,600	74	Cunningham,	9,600

TABLE showing One Hundred of the principal Surnames in Ireland (including varieties) taken from the Births Index of 1890—*continued.*

No. on List.	SURNAMES.	Estimated Population bearing each Surname.	No. on List.	SURNAMES.	Estimated Population bearing each Surname.
75	Griffin, ...	9,600	88	McKenna, ...	9,000
76	Kenny, ...	9,600	89	Bell, ...	8,800
77	Sheehan, ...	9,600	90	Scott, ...	8,700
78	Ward, ...	9,500	91	Hogan, ...	8,600
79	Whelan, ...	9,500	92	Keeffe, ...	8,600
80	Lyons, ...	9,400	93	Magee, ...	8,600
81	Reid, ...	9,200	94	McNamara, ..	8,600
82	Graham, ..	9,100	95	McDonald, ...	8,500
83	Higgins, ..	9,100	96	McDermott, ..	8,400
84	Cullen, ...	9,000	97	Moloney, ...	8,300
85	Keane, ...	9,000	98	Rourke, ...	8,300
86	King, ...	9,000	99	Buckley, ...	8,200
87	Maher, ...	9,000	100	Dwyer, ...	8,100

The following Table sets forth the Fifty most common Surnames in England, deduced from the Indexes of 1853; showing also the estimated Population holding each Surname in 1853. [Extracted from the 16th Annual Report of the Registrar-General for England.]

N.B.—Population of 1853 estimated at 18,404,421 persons.

No. on List.	SURNAMES.	Estimated Population holding each Surname.	No. on List.	SURNAMES.	Estimated Population holding each Surname.
1	Smith, ...	253,600	26	Harris, ...	51,900
2	Jones, ...	242,100	27	Clark, ...	50,700
3	Williams, ...	159,900	28	Cooper, ...	48,400
4	Taylor, ...	124,400	29	Harrison, ...	47,200
5	Davies, ...	113,600	30	Ward, ...	45,700
6	Brown, ...	105,600	31	Martin, ...	43,900
7	Thomas, ...	94,000	32	Davis, ...	43,700
8	Evans, ...	93,000	33	Baker, ...	43,600
9	Roberts, ...	78,400	34	Morris, ...	43,400
10	Johnson, ...	69,500	35	James, ...	43,100
11	Wilson, ...	66,800	36	King, ...	42,300
12	Robinson, ...	66,700	37	Morgan, ...	41,000
13	Wright, ...	62,700	38	Allen, ...	40,500
14	Wood, ...	61,200	39	Moore, ...	39,300
15	Thompson, ..	60,600	40	Parker, ...	39,100
16	Hall, ...	60,400	41	Clarke, ...	38,100
17	Green, ...	59,400	42	Cook, ...	38,100
18	Walker, ...	59,300	43	Price, ...	37,900
19	Hughes, ...	59,000	44	Phillips, ...	37,900
20	Edwards, ...	58,100	45	Shaw, ...	36,500
21	Lewis, ...	58,000	46	Bennett, ...	35,800
22	White, ...	56,900	47	Lee, ...	35,200
23	Turner, ...	56,300	48	Watson, ...	34,800
24	Jackson, ...	55,800	49	Griffiths, ...	34,800
25	Hill, ...	52,200	50	Carter, ...	33,400

The following Table exhibiting the Fifty most common Surnames in Scotland, as ascertained from the General Index to the Birth Registers for the year 1863, is extracted from the 12th Annual Report of the Registrar-General for Scotland.

N.B.—Population of 1863 estimated at 3,101,345 persons.

No. on List.	SURNAMES.	Estimated Number in entire Population in 1863.	No. on List.	SURNAMES.	Estimated Number in entire Population in 1863.
1	*Smith, ...	44,200	26	Cameron, ...	15,300
2	*M'Donald.	36,600	27	Watson, ...	15,000
3	*Brown, ...	33,800	28	Walker, ...	14,600
4	*Thomson, ...	31,200	29	Taylor, ...	14,400
5	Robertson, ..	31,200	30	M'Leod, ...	14,300
6	*Stewart, ...	30,600	31	*Ferguson, ...	13,200
7	Campbell, ...	30,200	32	Duncan, ...	12,900
8	Wilson, ...	29,300	33	Gray, ...	12,700
9	Anderson, ...	26,500	34	Davidson, ...	12,600
10	Scott, ...	22,400	35	Hunter, ...	12,200
11	*Miller, ...	21,400	36	Hamilton, ...	12,000
12	McKenzie, ...	21,300	37	*Kerr, ...	11,700
13	*Reid, ...	19,700	38	Grant, ...	11,400
14	Ross, ...	19,000	39	M'Intosh, ...	11,400
15	M'Kay, ...	18,700	40	*Graham, ...	11,200
16	*Johnston, ...	18,000	41	*White, ...	11,100
17	*Murray, ...	17,900	42	*Allan, ...	10,900
18	*Clark, ...	17,800	43	*Simpson, ...	10,700
19	*Paterson, ...	17,700	44	M'Gregor, ...	10,400
20	Young, ...	17,600	45	*Munro, ...	10,300
21	*Fraser, ...	17,500	46	Sinclair, ...	10,200
22	*M'Lean, ...	16,800	47	Bell, ...	10,100
23	Henderson, ..	16,500	48	Martin, ...	10,000
24	Mitchell, ...	16,100	49	*Russell, ...	9,500
25	*Morrison, ...	15,700	50	Gordon, ...	9,500

*NOTE.—The Surnames indicated by an asterisk occur under two or more different spellings.

It will be seen from the foregoing Tables that the name " Murphy " stands first in Ireland, in order of numerical strength, representing an estimated number of 62,600 persons (or 13·3 per thousand of the population), and that in both England and Scotland the name " Smith " occupies the first place, representing, it is estimated, in England and Wales (in the year 1853) 253,600 persons (or 13·8 per thousand of the population), and in Scotland (in the year 1863) 44,200, or 14·2 per thousand of the population.

The second place on the Irish List is held by the name " Kelly," representing 55,900 persons (or 11·8 per thousand of the population). In the English Tables " Jones " has the second place, representing, it is estimated, 242,100 people (or 13·2 per thousand). It is the most common name in the Principality of Wales, and its prevalence there has given it the high place it occupies on the List for the country generally. The Registrar-General for England states that in some years the

Joneses contributed to the registers a larger number of Births than even the Smiths. In Scotland the second place is held by " M'Donald," the estimated population bearing the name being 36,600, or 11·8 per thousand.

The third place in Ireland is filled by " Sullivan," the number of persons of which name it is estimated amounts to 43,600 (or 9·2 per thousand). In England " Williams " is the third name in numerical importance, representing 159,900 persons (or 8·7 per thousand). In Scotland " Brown " stands third, reckoning 33,800 (or 10·9 per thousand).

Several names among the first Fifty on the Irish List appear on the Lists for one or both of the other Divisions of the Kingdom. Thus " Smith " is 5th in Ireland and 1st in England and Scotland ; " Murray " is 18th in Ireland, and 17th in Scotland ; " Moore " is 20th in Ireland, and 39th in England ; " Wilson " is 26th in Ireland, 11th in England, and 8th in Scotland ; " Campbell " is 31st in Ireland, and 7th in Scotland ; " Clarke " (or " Clark ") is 32nd in Ireland, 9th (taking both spellings) in England, and 18th in Scotland ; " Johnston " appears 33rd in Ireland, and 16th in Scotland ; " Hughes " appears 34th in Ireland, and 19th in England ; " Brown " is 37th in Ireland, 6th in England, and 3rd in Scotland ; " Martin " is 38th in Ireland, 31st in England, and 48th in Scotland ; " Thompson " or " Thomson " is 42nd in Ireland, 15th in England, and 4th in Scotland ; " White " is 50th in Ireland, 22nd in England, and 41st in Scotland.

It will also be observed that among the second fifty names on the Irish List, several appear in the first fifty of England or Scotland. Thus,—" Stewart " is 58th in Ireland, and 6th in Scotland ; " Robinson," 73rd in Ireland, and 12th in England ; " Ward," 78th in Ireland, and 30th in England ; " Reid," 81st in Ireland, and 13th in Scotland ; " Graham," 82nd in Ireland, and 40th in Scotland ; " King," 86th in Ireland, and 36th in England ; " Bell," 89th in Ireland, and 47th in Scotland ; " Scott," 90th in Ireland, and 10th in Scotland ; and " M'Donald," which is 95th in Ireland, is 2nd in Scotland.

It will be perceived, however, that most of the names in Ireland with the larger numbers are peculiar to this country, representing the names of Irish Clans and Septs, such as the Murphys, Kellys, Sullivans, O'Briens, Byrnes, Ryans, Connors, O'Neills, Reillys, Doyles, McCarthys, Gallaghers, Dohertys, &c.

The Scotch Clans are similarly represented in the List for Scotland, such as the M'Donalds, M'Kenzies, M'Gregors, M'Leods, M'Kays, Campbells, Stewarts, Camerons, &c.

CHAPTER III.

DERIVATION OF SURNAMES.

The consideration of the Derivation of Surnames forms an interesting branch of study, but it would be impossible within the limits of this Report to enter fully into the subject, and all that can be attempted is to give a brief summary of its main sub-divisions as applicable to this Country.

Surnames in Ireland may be divided with reference to their derivation into six classes, viz. :—

1. FROM PERSONAL NAMES.
2. FROM RANK OR OCCUPATION.
3. FROM THE ANIMAL, VEGETABLE, AND MINERAL KINGDOMS.
4. FROM LOCALITY.
5. FROM PERSONAL PECULIARITIES OR ATTRIBUTES.
6. OTHER SURNAMES.

1. The following examples may be given of Surnames derived from Personal names :—

CELTIC NAMES.

McShane,	(*MacShawn*—Irish. Son of John).	O'Ferrall,	(*O'Feargail*—Irish. The descendant of Feargal).
McFadden,	(*MacPaidin*—Irish. Son of little Patrick).	O'Toole,	(*O'Tuathail*—Irish. The descendant of Tuathal)
McAndrew,	(*MacAindris*—Irish. Son of Andrew).	McDonnell,	(*MacDomhnaill*—Irish. Son of Donall).
McHugh,	(*MacAedha*—Irish. Son of Hugh).	McKeown,	(*MacEoghain*—Irish. Son of Eoghan or Owen).
McDermott,	(*MacDiarmada*—Irish. Son of Diarmaid).	McRory,	(*MacRuadhri*—Irish. Son of Ruadhri) (Rory).

Many Surnames derived from Celtic Names are compounded with the word "*Giolla*"—a servant (or disciple) of—such as—

Kilbride,	(*GiollaBridghid*—The Servant of *St. Bridget*).	Gildea,	(*GiollaDé*—the Servant of God).
Gilpatrick,	(*GiollaPadraic*—the Servant of *St. Patrick*).	Gilfoyle,	(*GiollaPhoil*—the Servant of *St. Paul*).
Gilchrist,	(*GiollaChriosd*—the Servant of *Christ*).		

Maol is also prefixed to the names of Saints, signifying a bald or tonsured person who became the spiritual servant of such Saint, as—

Maol-Dubhan [Maoldun],—the Servant of St. Dubhan. Anglicised—Muldoon.

ENGLISH NAMES.

Abraham.	Fergus.	Jacob.	Lawrence.	Roberts.	Thomas.
Adams.	Ferguson.	James.	Mathews.	Robinson.	Thompson.
Adamson.	Henry.	Jameson.	Paul.	Rodgers.	Williams.
Davidson.	Jackson.	Johnson.	Peters.	Stevenson.	Williamson.

2. Surnames from Rank or Occupation.—The following may be selected by way of illustration :—

CELTIC NAMES.

McGowan, · (*Gobha*—Irish—a Smith, son of the Smith).
Breheny, · (*Breathamh*—Irish—a Judge).
Cleary, · (*Cleireach*—Irish—a Clerk)
Ward, · (*Bhard*—Irish—a Bard).
Colgan, · (*Colg*—Irish—a sword, a Swordsman).

McCraith, · (*Craith*—Irish—to weave, son of the Weaver).
Davin, · (*Daimh*—Irish—a Poet).
McIntyre, · (*Mac-an-t-Saoir*—Irish— the son of the Work-man).

ENGLISH NAMES.

Abbott.	Butler.	Deacon.	Fuller.	Mason.	Prior.
Archer.	Carpenter.	Draper.	Gardiner.	Mercer.	Sexton.
Baker.	Chandler.	Farmer.	Gardner.	Naylor.	Sheppard.
Barber.	Clarke.	Forrester.	Glover.	Page.	Smith.
Bishop.	Cooke.	Forster.	Harper.	Porter.	Taylor.
Butcher.	Cooper.	Fowler.	Hunter.	Potter.	Usher.

3. Many Surnames are taken from natural objects in the Animal, Vegetable, and Mineral Kingdoms, such as :—

CELTIC NAMES.

Carrick, · (from *carraicc*—a rock).
Clough. · (from *cloch*—a stone).
Columb, · (from *colum*—a dove).
Cunneen, · (from *coinin*—a rabbit).

Darragh, · (from *dair*—an oak).
Mullally, · (from *eala*—a swan).
Quilty, · (from *coillte*—woods).
Sheedy, · (from *sioda*—silk).

ENGLISH NAMES.

Ashe.	Clay.	Fox.	Moss.	Silver.	Veale.
Bird.	Crowe.	Hare.	Peacock.	Spratt.	Waters.
Buck.	Deer.	Heron.	Pidgeon.	Sturgeon.	Woods.
Bull.	Dove.	Hogg.	Rabbit.	Swan.	Woulfe.
Chestnutt.	Forrest.	Lamb.			

4. *Surnames derived from Locality.*—Surnames derived from locality, which in England and Scotland form a large class, are but rarely met with in this country, and in most of these cases considerable doubt exists as to whether the surname has been acquired from the locality.

The following surnames amongst others are the names of localities in Ireland :—

Adair (Adare).	Borris.	Galway.	Kilkenny.	Monaghan.
Ardagh.	Cashell, (Cashel).	Kells.	Limerick.	Monahan.
Athy.	Cavan.	Kilcullen.	Longford.	Pallas.

The following names of localities in England and Scotland are also found amongst surnames in this Country :—

Bermingham. }	Carlisle. }	Galloway.	Glasgow.	Lincoln.	Peebles.
Birmingham. }	Carlile. }	Girvan.	Hastings.	Paisley.	Sherwood.
Cambridge.					

5. *Surnames derived from Personal Peculiarities or Attributes,* such as :—

CELTIC NAMES.

Roe,	·	(*Ruadh*—red).	Casey,	·	(*Cathaiseach*—valiant).
Duff,	·	(*Dubh*—black).	Dempsey,	·	(*Diomusach*—arrogant).
Lauder,	·	(*Laidir*—strong).	Brody,	·	(*Brodach*—proud).
Daly,	·	(*Dall*—blind).	Corcoran,	·	(*Corcurach*—purple or red)
McGirr,	·	(*Gor*—short).			

ENGLISH NAMES.

Black.	Gray.	Long.	Short. ⎫	Strong.	Wise. ⎫
Brown. ⎫	Jolly.	Meek.	Shortt. ⎭	Swift.	Wyse. ⎭
Browne. ⎭	Little. ⎫	Merry.	Small.	White.	
Fair.	Lyttle. ⎭				

6. *Other Surnames.*—There are many surnames not falling in any of the above classes, such as those from :—

> *Parts of the Body* (Celtic Names)—Kinnavy (*cnamh*—Irish—a bone) ; McCosh (*cos*—Irish—a foot) ; McClave (*lamh*—Irish—the hand) ; (English Names)—Beard, Foote, Head, Legge.
>
> *Names of the Seasons, as* Spring, Summers, Winter.
> *Points of the Compass, as* North, South, East, West.
> *Natural Objects, as* Field, Flood, Hill, Snow.
> *Other Sources, as* Church, Ferry, Hood, Hunt, Kirk.

It may be interesting to quote here the remarks of the Registrar-General for England and Wales regarding the derivation of Family Names found in those countries.

Major Graham remarked in his 16th Annual Report, already referred to :—" The most striking circumstance presented by the Indexes is the extraordinary number and variety of the surnames of the *English* people. Derived from almost every imaginable object, from the names of places, from trades and employments, from personal peculiarities, from the Christian name of the father, from objects in the Animal and Vegetable **kingdoms**, from things animate and inanimate ; their varied character is as remarkable as their singularity is often striking. Some of the terms which swell the list are so odd, and even ridiculous, that it is difficult to assign any satisfactory reason for their assumption in the first instance as family names, unless indeed, as has been conjectured, they were nicknames or *sobriquets,* which neither the first bearers nor their posterity could avoid."

Referring to Welsh surnames he stated :—" In Wales, however, the surnames, if *surnames* they can be called, do not present the same variety, most of them having been formed in a simple manner from the Christian or fore-name of the father in the Genitive case, *son* being understood. Thus, Evan's son became *Evans,* John's son *Jones,* &c. Others were derived from the father's name coalesced with a form of the word ap or hab (son of), by which Hugh ap Howell became *Powell,* Evan ap Hugh became *Pugh,* and in like manner were formed nearly all the Welsh surnames beginning with the letters B and P. Hereditary surnames were not in use even amongst the gentry of Wales until the time of Henry VIII., nor were they generally established until a much later period ; indeed, at the present day they can scarcely be said to be adopted amongst the lower classes in the wilder districts, where, as the marriage registers show, the Christian name of the father still frequently becomes the patronymic of the son in the manner just described."

With respect to Cornish names the Report states :—" From the circumstance of their common British origin it might be supposed that the Welsh people and the inhabitants of Cornwall would exhibit some analogous principles in the construction of their surnames; such, however, is not the case. The Cornish surnames are mostly local, derived from words of *British* root, and they are often strikingly peculiar. A large number have the prefix *Tre*, a town; the words *Pol*, a pool, *Pen*, a head, *Ros*, a heath, and *Lan*, a church, are also of frequent occurrence in surnames."

With regard to the derivation of names in Scotland, the Registrar-General for that country in his 6th Report, remarks :— " Almost all the names of our Border and Highland Clans belong to the first class " [Surnames derived from Patronymics], " and they are peculiarly Scottish, neither belonging to England nor to Ireland. These Surnames include all those beginning with Mac, as Macgregor, Mactaggart, etc., besides those simple ones, as Fraser, Douglas, Cameron, Kerr, Grant, &c." . . . " The Surnames derived from rank and occupation are very numerous, but are equally common to England as to Scotland." . . . " Surnames taken from the locality in which the persons originally resided form a very numerous class, and they also are, to a great extent, peculiar to Scotland, seeing that there is scarcely a county, parish, town, river, or remarkable locality but has its name perpetuated in the Surnames." . . . " The sobriquets perpetuated as Surnames are, perhaps, the most varied of all, and embrace every personal or mental quality supposed to reside in the different individuals to whom they were originally given."

The personal Names in the Isle of Man are of considerable interest in connection with Irish Surnames, as that Island has passed through phases of occupancy somewhat similar to those of this country. Its history may be divided into three periods : the first, when it was inhabited by Celts similar in race and language to the Irish; the second, the period of Scandinavian domination; and the third, the time during which it has been under English dominion. The names in the Island represent each of these periods. As in Ireland, the largest number of names are derived from words of Celtic origin; some are from Scandinavian roots, and there are now a large number of names traceable to English sources.

On visiting the Island, I was much struck by the peculiar forms many names had assumed there differing from those found in Ireland, though evidently derived from the same source. Thus, the name " Clucas " is the Manx form of Lucas, both names being derived from the Celtic MacLucais—son of Luke. " Cannell," a name peculiar to the Isle of Man, is derived from the Celtic MacConaill—son of Conall. The Irish modern form is M'Connell.

" Kermode," another Manx name, is contracted from the Celtic name MacDiarmaid, son of Diarmaid—Irish modern form M'Dermott. " Mylchreest " is derived from the Celtic MacGiolla Chriosd—the son of the servant of Christ. The modern Irish form is Gilchrist. Many other instances could be adduced.

CHAPTER IV.

SURNAMES IN IRELAND ETHNOLOGICALLY CONSIDERED.

CELTIC NAMES.

The present population of Ireland is a mixture of a number of different races in which the Celtic is the predominant element.

The great bulk of the most common names in the country are undoubtedly of Celtic origin. Many of them still retain the prefixes O and Mac, the former peculiar to Ireland and the latter used both in Ireland and Scotland. In many cases, however, these prefixes have been dropped. It is a matter of common occurrence to find in the same record Celtic names written with the prefixes O and Mac and without them.

It is impossible now, in some cases, to trace whether families are of Celtic or English descent, as some of the English settlers took Irish names, and Irish families were compelled to adopt English surnames.

By a Statute of 1366, it was provided, *inter alia,* that " Every Englishman do use the English language, and be named by an English name, leaving off entirely the manner of naming used by the Irish " ; and in 1465 (5 Ed. IV., cap. 3), a law was passed enacting " that every Irishman that dwells betwixt or amongst Englishmen in the County of Dublin, Myeth, Vriell, and Kildare . . . shall take to him an English Surname of one town, as Sutton, Chester, Trym, Skryne, Corke, Kinsale ; or colour, as white, blacke, browne ; or arte or science, as smith or carpenter ; or office, as cooke, butler . . ."

The existence of the two languages in the country accounts for the practice which prevails in some parts of Ireland of using English names with their Irish translations or equivalents interchangeably, some particulars regarding which will be found in my Book of Varieties and Synonymes of Surnames and Christian Names in Ireland already referred to.

The Annals of the Four Masters, and other eminent Authorities, afford information whereby the ancient location of the principal Irish Tribes and Septs can be approximately ascertained, and Tribal Maps of Ireland have been published from time to time, among which the following may be mentioned :—

1. A Map showing the territories of the Irish Princes and Chiefs—the various Septs subordinate to them, etc., also the Districts in possession of the English Lords, their armorial bearings, etc., A.D. 1567.

[A copy of this Map will be found appended to State Papers of Henry VIII., Vol. 2, Part 3, and another copy in National Manuscripts of Ireland, Part IV.-1 ; No. 5.]

2. Hiberniæ, Britanniæ Insulæ, Nova Descriptio, by Abraham Ortelius, 1572.

3. Ortelius improved, or a new Map of Ireland wherein are inserted the principal Families of Irish and English Extraction, who possessed that kingdom on the commencement of the 17th Century. Published according to Act of Parliament by P. Wogan, Old Bridge No. 23, Dublin.

4. A Topographical and Historical Map of Ancient Ireland by Baronies, by Philip MacDermott, M.D., attached to Connellan's Annals of the Four Masters. Published in 1846. (This Map has since been reproduced both in Ireland and in America.)

From these sources the following list of the principal Ancient Celtic Families, with the Counties in which they were located, has been compiled :—

NAMES with the PREFIX MAC.*

NAME.	COUNTY.	NAME.	COUNTY.
MacAlister,	Antrim.	MacCraith or	Clare, Fermanagh,
MacArdell,	Monaghan.	Magrath.	Kerry, Tipper-
MacArthur,	Limerick.		ary, Waterford.
MacAuley,	Westmeath.	MacCrehan,	Kerry.
MacAuliffe,	Cork.	MacCrossan,	Donegal, Tyrone.
MacBrady,	Cavan.	MacDavett,	Donegal, Mayo.
MacBreen,	Kilkenny, Tyrone.	MacDermott,	Roscommon, Sligo.
MacBrennan,	Roscommon.	MacDonnell,	Antrim, Clare, Fer-
MacBride,	Donegal.		managh, Kildare,
MacBrodin,	Clare.		Londonderry,
MacCabe,	Cavan, Monaghan.		Monaghan,
MacCaffrey,	Fermanagh.		Queen's.
MacCafney,	Cavan.	MacDonough,	Cork, Sligo.
MacCaghwell,	Tyrone.	MacDorchy,	Leitrim.
MacCann,	Armagh, Louth.	MacDougall,	Antrim.
MacCartan,	Down.	MacDowell,	Roscommon.
MacCarthy,	Cork, Kerry, Tip-	MacDuvan,	Donegal.
	perary.	MacEgan,	Galway, Kerry,
MacCashin,	Queen's.		Tipperary.
MacClancy,	Clare, Cork, Kerry,	MacElligot,	Kerry.
	Leitrim.	MacEneiry,	Limerick.
MacClean,	Antrim, Donegal.	MacEnteggart,	Fermanagh.
MacCloskey,	Donegal, London-	MacEvoy,	Armagh, Queen's,
	derry.		Westmeath.
MacCogan,	Queen's.	MacFadden,	Donegal.
MacCoggan,	Leitrim.	MacFergus,	Leitrim.
MacCoghlan,	King's.	MacFineen,	Kerry.
MacColreavy,	Leitrim.	MacFinnevar,	Leitrim.
MacConmee,	Tyrone.	MacFirbis,	Sligo.
MacConnell,	Londonderry,	MacGargan,	Cavan.
	Tyrone.	MacGarrahan,	Fermanagh.
MacConry,	Galway.	MacGarry,	Mayo.
MacConsnava or	Leitrim.	MacGauran,	Cavan.
Ford.		MacGavan,	Longford, Mayo.
MacConway,	Longford, Sligo.	MacGennis,	Down.
MacCormac,	Longford, Tip-	MacGeoghegan,	Westmeath.
	perary.	MacGeraghty,	Mayo, Sligo.
MacCoskley,	Tyrone.	MacGettigan,	Donegal.
MacCourt,	Tyrone.	MacGibbon,	Mayo.
MacCracken,	Londonderry.	MacGilbride,	Donegal.

* Some of the names given in this Table are represented also in Scotland, and are stated to have been borne by followers of the Three Collas who returned to Ireland from that country in the fourth century.

Names with the Prefix Mac*—continued.

Name.	County.	Name.	County.
MacGilchrist, ..	Longford.	MacKeon, ..	Leitrim.
MacGilduff, ..	Galway.	MacKiernan, ..	Cavan.
MacGilfinnen or Leon.	Fermanagh.	MacLennon, ..	Fermanagh.
		MacLoghlin, ..	Donegal.
MacGilfoyle, ..	Tipperary.	MacLoughlin, ..	Londonderry.
MacGillicuddy, ..	Kerry.	MacLysaght, ..	Clare.
MacGilligan, ..	Londonderry, Longford.	MacMahon, ..	Clare, Monaghan.
		MacManus, ..	Fermanagh, Roscommon.
MacGillikelly, ..	Clare, Galway.		
MacGilmartin, ..	Leitrim.	MacMurrough, ..	Carlow, Wexford; Wicklow.
MacGilmichael, ..	Monaghan.		
MacGilmore, ..	Down.	MacNally, ..	Antrim, Mayo,
MacGilpatrick or Fitzpatrick.	Kilkenny, Queen's.	MacNamara, ..	Clare.
		MacNamee, ..	Londonderry.
MacGilroy, ..	Monaghan.	MacNeney, ..	Monaghan.
MacGinty, ..	Donegal.	MacNevin, ..	Galway.
MacGiollamoholmoge,	Dublin.	MacNulty, ..	Cavan, Donegal, Mayo.
MacGloin, ..	Leitrim.	MacOiraghty, ..	Roscommon.
MacGolrick, ..	Tyrone.	MacOscar, ..	Monaghan.
MacGonigal, ..	Donegal.	MacOwen, ..	Tyrone.
MacGorman, ..	Queen's.	MacPartlan, ..	Leitrim.
MacGourty, ..	Leitrim.	MacQuade, ..	Monaghan.
MacGowan or Smith	Cavan, Donegal, Down, Leitrim.	MacQuillan, ..	Antrim.
		MacRannall or Reynolds.	Leitrim.
MacGrane, ..	Meath.	MacRory, ..	Down, Tyrone.
MacGreal, ..	Mayo.	MacRuarc, ..	Westmeath.
MacGuire, ..	Fermanagh.	MacShane, ..	Tyrone.
MacGulshenan, ..	Fermanagh.	MacShanley, ..	Leitrim. [rick.
MacHale, ..	Mayo.	MacSheehy, ..	Cork, Kerry, Lime-
MacHugh, ..	Cavan, Donegal, Galway, Longford.	MacSherry, ..	Cork.
		MacSweeney, ..	Cork, Donegal.
Mac-I-Brien, or O'Brien.	Tipperary.	MacSweeny, ..	Kerry.
		MacTaggart, ..	Tyrone.
MacIntire, ..	Donegal.	MacTeige, ..	Donegal.
MacIntyre, ..	Tyrone.	MacTeigue, ..	Leitrim, Queen's.
MacKenna, ..	Kerry, Monaghan.	MacTiernan, ..	Cavan, Fermanagh
MacKenney, ..	Leitrim.	MacTully, ..	Cavan, Fermanagh, Galway.
MacKenny, ..	Louth.		
MacKeogh, ..	Roscommon, Wexford.	MacWard, ..	Donegal, Galway.

* Some of the names given in this Table are represented also in Scotland, and are stated to have been borne by followers of the Three Collas who returned to Ireland from that country in the fourth century.

Names with the Prefix O.

Name.	County.	Name.	County.
O'Ahern, ..	Cork.	O'Boyle, ..	Donegal.
O'Baire, ..	Cork.	O'Bradley, ..	Cork, Donegal.
O'Bannan, ..	King's, Mayo.	O'Branagan, ..	Louth.
O'Begley, ..	Cork, Donegal.	O'Bree, ..	Kilkenny.
O'Behan, ..	King's.	O'Brennan, ..	Kerry, Kilkenny.
O'Beirne, ..	Roscommon.	O'Breslin, ..	Donegal, Fermanagh, Tipperary.
O'Billry, ..	Limerick.		
O'Birn, ..	Mayo.	O'Bric, ..	Waterford.
O'Bligh, ..	Mayo.	O'Brien, ..	Clare, Cork, Limerick, Tipperary, Waterford.
O'Bolger, ..	Carlow, Kilkenny.		
O'Boylan, ..	Monaghan.		

Names with the Prefix O—*continued.*

Name.	County.	Name.	County.
O'Brien or Mac-I-Brien.	Tipperary.	O'Connolly, ..	Galway, Monaghan.
O'Brigan, ..	Cork.	O'Connor, ..	Kildare, Roscommon.
O'Brodar, ..	Donegal, Kilkenny.	O'Conolly, ..	Meath.
O'Brody, ..	Mayo.	O'Conor, ..	Clare, Galway, Kerry, King's, Londonderry, Mayo, Roscommon, Sligo.
O'Brogan, ..	Cavan, Mayo, Queen's, Sligo.		
O'Brolchan, ..	Londonderry.		
O'Brosnaghan, ..	Kerry.	O'Conran, ..	Waterford.
O'Byrne, ..	Wicklow.	O'Considine, ..	Clare.
O'Cahaney, ..	Mayo.	O'Cooney, ..	Tyrone.
O'Cahill, ..	Carlow, Clare, Galway, Kerry, Tipperary.	O'Corcoran, ..	Fermanagh, Tipperary.
O'Callaghan, ..	Clare, Cork, Mayo, Tipperary.	O'Corley, ..	Sligo.
		O'Cormac, ..	Down.
		O'Corr, ..	Roscommon.
O'Callan, ..	Armagh, Kilkenny	O'Corran, ..	Tyrone.
O'Callanan, ..	Cork, Galway.	O'Corrigan, ..	Fermanagh, Westmeath.
O'Canavan, ..	Galway.		
O'Cannanan, ..	Donegal.	O'Cosgry, ..	Wexford.
O'Carberry, ..	Westmeath.	O'Cowhy, ..	Cork.
O'Carey, ..	Kildare.	O'Coyle, ..	Cavan, Donegal.
O'Carmody, ..	Clare.	O'Creagh, ..	Clare, Cork, Kerry.
O'Carolan. ..	Londonderry, Meath.	O'Crean, ..	Sligo.
		O'Criocan, ..	Tyrone.
O'Carragher, ..	Louth.	O'Criodan, ..	Antrim.
O'Carroll, ..	Kerry, Kilkenny, King's, Leitrim, Louth, Tipperary	O'Cronin, ..	Kerry.
		O'Cronly, ..	Cork.
		O'Crossan, ..	Tyrone.
O'Casey, ..	Cork, Fermanagh, Kerry, Limerick, Westmeath.	O'Crotty, ..	Waterford.
		O'Crowly, ..	Cork.
		O'Cuire, ..	Tipperary.
O'Cashin, ..	Galway.	O'Cuirneen, ..	Leitrim.
O'Cassidy, ..	Fermanagh, Londonderry, Monaghan.	O'Cullen, ..	Cork, Galway, Kildare, Limerick, Tipperary, Wicklow.
O'Cavanagh, ..	Carlow, Wexford.		
O'Cawley, ..	Galway.	O'Cullenan, ..	Clare, Cork, Tipperary.
O'Claisin, ..	Cork.		
O'Clerkin, ..	Limerick.	O'Culligan, ..	Clare.
O'Clery, ..	Cavan, Clare, Donegal, Galway.	O'Cummin, ..	Mayo.
		O'Curran, ..	Clare, Donegal.
O'Coffey, ..	Galway, Westmeath.	O'Curry, ..	Cavan, Cork, Westmeath.
O'Coigley, ..	Donegal, Fermanagh.	O'Daly, ..	Cavan, Clare, Cork, Galway, Kerry, Westmeath.
O'Coleman, ..	Cork, Louth, Sligo.		
O'Colgan, ..	Armagh, Down, Kildare.	O'Danaher, ..	Cork.
		O'Davoren, ..	Clare.
O'Colman, ..	Louth.	O'Dea, ..	Clare, Cork, Tipperary.
O'Coltaran, ..	Down.		
O'Conaghty, ..	Cavan, Sligo.	O'Deasey, ..	Cork.
O'Concannon, ..	Roscommon.	O'Deegan, ..	Clare.
O'Conealy, ..	Galway.	O'Delany, ..	Kerry, Kilkenny.
O'Conlan, ..	Limerick.	O'Dempsey, ..	Kildare, King's, Queen's.
O'Connegan, ..	Mayo.		
O'Connelan, ..	Tyrone.	O'Dennehy, ..	Waterford.
O'Connell, ..	Clare, Down, Galway, Kerry, Limerick.	O'Dennery, ..	Cork.
		O'Dermody, ..	Clare, Tipperary.
		O'Devin, ..	Fermanagh.
O'Connellan, ..	Galway, Mayo, Roscommon.	O'Devir, ..	Donegal.
		O'Devlin, ..	Londonderry, Sligo

NAMES WITH THE PREFIX O—*continued.*

NAME.		COUNTY.	NAME.		COUNTY.
O'Dinan,	..	Tipperary.	O'Feeney,	..	Galway, Sligo.
O'Dinane,	..	Cork.	O'Felan,	..	Fermanagh, Water-ford.
O'Dineen,	..	Cork.			
O'Dinerty,	..	Tipperary.	O'Ferral,	..	Longford.
O'Dinnahan,	..	Limerick.	O'Fihelly,	..	Cork, Roscommon.
O'Dogherty,	..	Donegal, Mayo.	O'Finan,	..	Mayo.
O'Dolan,	..	Cavan, Mayo.	O'Finegan,	..	Mayo, Roscom-mon.
O'Donaghey,	..	Galway.			
O'Donegan,	..	Cork.	O'Finn,	..	Leitrim.
O'Donelly,	..	Donegal.	O'Finnelan,	..	Westmeath.
O'Donevan,	..	Limerick.	O'Flahavan,	..	Waterford.
O'Donlevy,	..	Donegal, Down, Tyrone.	O'Flaherty,	..	Galway.
			O'Flanagan,		Fermanagh.
O'Donnegan,	..	Armagh, Ferman-agh, Tipperary, Tyrone.	O'Flannagan,	..	Roscommon, Waterford.
			O'Flannelly,	..	Sligo.
O'Donnelan,	..	Roscommon.	O'Flannery,	..	Limerick, Mayo.
O'Donnell,	..	Donegal, Galway, Mayo, Sligo.	O'Flattery,	..	Clare.
			O'Florry,	..	Down.
O'Donnellan,	..	Antrim, Galway.	O'Flynn,	..	Antrim, Cork, Kerry, Mayo, Roscommon.
O'Donnelly,	..	Tipperary, Tyrone.			
O'Donoghoe,	..	Kerry, Kilkenny.			
O'Donohoe,	..	Tipperary.	O'Fogarty,	..	Tipperary.
O'Donovan,	..	Cork, Limerick.	O'Foley,	..	Kerry.
O'Dooley,	..	Westmeath.	O'Foran,	..	Galway.
O'Doolin,	..	Kerry.	O'Forranan,	..	Donegal.
O'Dooyarma,	..	Donegal.	O'Fox,	..	Longford, Meath.
O'Doran,	..	Queen's, Wexford.	O'Freel,	..	Donegal, London-derry.
O'Dorchy,	..	Mayo.			
O'Dornin,	..	Donegal.	O'Furey,	..	Tipperary.
O'Dorrian,	..	Donegal.	O'Furry,	..	Antrim.
O'Dowd,	..	Mayo, Sligo.	O'Fynn,	..	Clare.
O'Dowling,	..	Queen's, Wicklow.	O'Gahan,	..	Wicklow.
O'Doyle,	..	Carlow, Galway, Kilkenny, Wex-ford, Wicklow.	O'Gallagher,	..	Donegal.
			O'Gallivan,	..	Kerry.
			O'Gara,	..	Sligo.
O'Doyne,	..	Carlow.	O'Garvey,	..	Armagh, Down, Wexford.
O'Dreenan,	..	Galway.			
O'Drinan,	..	Clare.	O'Gavagan,	..	Mayo, Sligo.
O'Driscoll,	..	Cork.	O'Gearan,	..	Mayo.
O'Drom,	..	Cavan.	O'Geary,	..	Waterford.
O'Duane,	..	Galway.	O'Gevany,	..	Galway.
O'Duff,	..	Queen's.	O'Gleeson,	..	Tipperary.
O'Duffy,	..	Donegal, Galway, Mayo, Monaghan.	O'Glennon,	..	Roscommon.
			O'Gloran,	..	Kilkenny.
O'Dugan,	..	Cork, Mayo, Ros-common, Wexford.	O'Gogarty,	..	Meath.
			O'Gorman,	..	Carlow, Clare, Fer-managh.
O'Duigenan,	..	Roscommon.			
O'Dunn,	..	Kildare, Meath, Queen's.	O'Gormley,	..	Donegal, Mayo.
			O'Gormoge,	..	Mayo.
O'Dunnady,	..	Kerry.	O'Grady,	..	Clare, Kerry, Lime-rick, Mayo.
O'Durkan,	..	Sligo.			
O'Duvan,	..	Meath.	O'Griffin,	..	Clare, Kerry.
O'Duvany,	..	Armagh, Tyrone.	O'Hagan,	..	Tyrone.
O'Dwyer,	..	Tipperary.	O'Hagarty,	..	Kerry, London-derry.
O'Eire,	..	Antrim.			
O'Etigan,	..	Tyrone.	O'Hagerty,	..	Donegal.
O'Fahy,	...	Galway.	O'Halahan,	..	Cork.
O'Fallon,	..	Roscommon.	O'Halligan,	..	Meath.
O'Falvey,	..	Cork, Kerry.	O'Hallinan,	..	Limerick.
O'Farrelly,	..	Cavan.	O'Halloran,	..	Clare, Galway.
O'Fay,	..	Westmeath.	O'Hamill,	..	Antrim, Tyrone.
O'Feenaghty,	..	Kerry, Roscom-mon.	O'Hand,	..	Meath.
			O'Hanley,	..	Roscommon.

NAMES WITH THE PREFIX O—*continued.*

NAME.	COUNTY.	NAME.	COUNTY.
O'Hanlon,	Armagh.	O'Kelleher,	Cork, Kerry, Tipperary.
O'Hanrahan,	Westmeath.		
O'Hanratty,	Armagh.	O'Kelly,	Down, Dublin, Galway, Kildare, Louth, Meath, Queen's, Roscommon, Tyrone, Wicklow.
O'Hanvey,	Down, Westmeath.		
O'Hara,	Antrim, Londonderry, Mayo, Sligo.		
O'Harkan,	Donegal.		
O'Harney,	Kerry.		
O'Hart,	Meath, Sligo.	O'Kennedy,	Kerry, Tipperary.
O'Hartigan,	Cork, Limerick.	O'Kenny,	Donegal, Roscommon.
O'Haverty,	Galway.		
O'Hea,	Cork, Limerick, Meath.	O'Kernaghan,	Donegal, Sligo.
		O'Kerrigan,	Mayo.
O'Healy,	Cork, Kerry.	O'Keveny,	Kilkenny.
O'Heaney,	Fermanagh.	O'Killeen,	Mayo.
O'Heffernan,	Clare, Tipperary.	O'Kindellan,	Meath.
O'Hehir,	Clare.	O'Kinealy,	Limerick.
O'Heir,	Armagh.	O'Kinsellagh,	Carlow.
O'Hely,	Kilkenny, Limerick.	O'Kirwan,	Galway.
		O'Kirwick,	Limerick.
		O'Kissane,	Kerry.
O'Hennesey,	King's, Westmeath.	O'Lanigan,	Tipperary.
		O'Largnan,	Down.
O'Hennigan,	Cork.	O'Larkin,	Armagh, Galway, Wexford.
O'Heoghy, or Hoey,	Down.		
O'Herlihy,	Cork.	O'Larrisey,	Mayo.
O'Heyne,	Clare, Cork, Galway.	O'Laverty,	Donegal, Tyrone.
		O'Lavett,	Mayo.
O'Hickey,	Clare, Tipperary.	O'Lawlor,	Down, Queen's.
O'Higgin,	Longford, Mayo, Westmeath.	O'Lawry,	Down.
		O'Leahan,	Galway.
O'Hoey,	Monaghan.	O'Leahy,	Kerry.
O'Hogan,	Clare, Tipperary.	O'Leaney,	Donegal.
O'Honan,	Limerick.	O'Leary,	Cork.
O'Honeen,	Clare.	O'Lee,	Galway.
O'Hoolaghan,	Cork, King's.	O'Lehan or Lyons,	Cork.
O'Hoollaghan,	Galway.	O'Lenahan,	Tipperary.
O'Horan,	Galway, Wicklow.	O'Lennon,	Galway, Mayo.
O'Horgan,	Cork.	O'Leyne,	Kerry.
O'Hosey,	Fermanagh, Tyrone.	O'Liddy,	Clare.
		O'Loan,	Tyrone.
O'Howley,	Clare, Sligo.	O'Loghlin,	Clare.
O'Hugh,	Donegal.	O'Loman,	Galway, Roscommon.
O'Hurley,	Cork, Limerick, Tipperary.		
		O'Lomasey,	Cork.
O'Hynes,	Galway.	O'Lonergan,	Roscommon, Tipperary.
O'Kane,	Antrim, Londonderry.		
		O'Longan,	Down.
O'Kean,	Galway, Tipperary.	O'Looney,	Cork.
		O'Loughnan,	Down, Kilkenny, Mayo.
O'Kearney,	Clare, King's, Tipperary, Westmeath.		
		O'Luinin,	Fermanagh.
		O'Lunney,	Tyrone.
O'Kearny,	Cork, Mayo.	O'Lynch,	Cavan, Clare, Cork, Down, Tipperary.
O'Keefe,	Cork.		
O'Keeley,	Clare.		
O'Keely,	Kilkenny, Tipperary.	O'Lynchy,	Donegal.
		O'Macken,	Down.
O'Keenan,	Fermanagh, Londonderry.	O'Mackesey,	Limerick.
		O'Mackey,	Tipperary.
O'Keerin,	Mayo.	O'Madden,	Galway, King's.
O'Keevan,	Antrim, Sligo.	O'Maginn,	Galway.
O'Keiran,	Armagh.	O'Mahon,	Down.

NAMES WITH THE PREFIX O—*continued.*

NAME.	COUNTY.	NAME.	COUNTY.
O'Mahony,	Cork, Kerry.	O'Mulroy,	Mayo.
O'Malbride,	Roscommon.	O'Mulvany,	Donegal, King's,
O'Malley,	Mayo.		Sligo.
O'Malone,	Westmeath,	O'Mulvey,	Leitrim.
O'Malquiney,	Tipperary.	O'Mulvihil,	Roscommon.
O'Manning,	Galway.	O'Mureedy,	King's.
O'MaolConry,	Roscommon.	O'Murphy,	Cork, Wexford.
O'Markey,	Louth.	O'Murray,	Cavan, Donegal,
O'Marron,	Armagh. Monaghan.		Londonderry, Mayo.
O'Meagher,	Tipperary.	O'Murrigan,	Kildare.
O'Meaney,	Roscommon.	O'Murtagh,	Meath.
O'Meara,	Tipperary.	O'Naghtan or Norton.	Galway.
O'Meechan,	Leitrim.		
O'Meehan,	Fermanagh, Sligo, Tipperary.	O'Neil, or Nihil,	Clare.
		O'Neill,	Antrim, Armagh,
O'Melaghlin,	Meath, Westmeath.		Donegal, Down,
O'Mellan,	Tyrone.		Tyrone.
O'Milford,	Mayo.	O'Neney,	Tyrone.
O'Moghan,	Mayo.	O'Neny,	Monaghan.
O'Molloy,	King's.	O'Neylan,	Armagh, Clare.
O'Moloney,	Clare.	O'Nolan,	Carlow.
O'Monahan,	Roscommon.	O'Noonan,	Cork.
O'Mongan,	Sligo.	O'Norton,	Roscommon.
O'Mooney,	King's. Queen's.	O'Quigly,	Londonderry.
O'Moore,	Down, Kerry, Queen's.	O'Quill,	Kerry.
		O'Quinlan,	Kerry, Tipperary.
O'Moran,	Down, Galway, Kerry, Mayo, Roscommon, Sligo.	O'Quinlevan,	Clare, Tipperary.
		O'Quinn,	Clare, Donegal,
O'Moriarty,	Kerry.		Limerick, Londonderry, Long-
O'Morony,	Clare, Cork, Limerick.		ford, Mayo, Tyrone.
O'Morrison,	Donegal, Sligo.		
O'Morrissey,	Sligo, Tipperary.	O'Rafferty,	Donegal, Tyrone.
O'Moynagh,	Sligo.	O'Regan,	Cork, Meath, Queen's.
O'Mulcahy,	Limerick, Tipperary.	O'Reilly,	Cavan, Longford,
O'Mulclohy,	Sligo.		Meath, West-
O'Muldoon,	Fermanagh.		meath.
O'Muldorry,	Donegal.	O'Riordan,	Cork.
O'Mulfinny,	Longford.	O'Roddan,	Mayo.
O'Mulgee,	Donegal.	O'Roddy,	Donegal.
O'Mulhall,	Queen's.	O'Rodoghan,	Leitrim.
O'Mulhollan,	Londonderry.	O'Rogan,	Down.
O'Mulholland,	Antrim.	O'Ronan,	Longford, Mayo.
O'Mulkerrin,	Galway.	O'Ronayne,	Cork.
O'Mullally,	Galway.	O'Rooney,	Down.
O'Mullane,	Cork, Kerry.	O'Rory,	Meath.
O'Mullany,	Sligo, Waterford.	O'Rothlan,	Mayo.
O'Mullarky,	Galway.	O'Rourke,	Leitrim.
O'Mulledy,	Westmeath.	O'Ryan,	Carlow, Kilkenny,
O'Mulleeny,	Mayo.		Limerick, Tipperary.
O'Mullen,	Londonderry.		
O'Mulligan,	Cavan, Londonderry.	O'Scanlan,	Kerry, Limerick.
		O'Scanlon,	Louth.
O'Mullins,	Clare.	O'Scannell,	Cork.
O'Mulloy,	Roscommon.	O'Scullan,	Londonderry.
O'Mulmoghery or Early.	Donegal.	O'Scully,	Tipperary, Westmeath.
O'Mulrenin,	Mayo, Roscommon.	O'Scurry,	Galway.
		O'Sexton,	Tipperary.
O'Mulrooney,	Fermanagh, Galway.	O'Shanahan,	Tipperary.
		O'Shaughnessy,	Clare, Galway.

NAMES WITH THE PREFIX O—*continued.*

NAME.	COUNTY	NAME.	COUNTY.
O'Shea, ..	Cork, Kerry, Kilkenny, Tipperary	O'Talcharan, ..	Mayo.
		O'Tarcert, ..	Donegal.
O'Sheehan, ..	Galway, Kerry, Limerick.	O'Teige or Tighe,	Wicklow.
		O'Teigue, ..	Tyrone.
O'Sheeran, ..	Donegal.	O'Tierney, ..	Armagh, Mayo.
O'Sheridan, ..	Cavan, Longford.	O'Tolarg, ..	Westmeath.
O'Shiel, ..	Antrim, Westmeath.	O'Tomalty, ..	Tyrone.
		O'Toole, ..	Galway, Kildare, Mayo, Wicklow.
O'Sionagh, or Fox,	King's.		
O'Slattery, ..	Kerry, Tipperary.	O'Tormey, ..	Galway.
O'Slevin, ..	Longford.	O'Tracey, ..	Galway.
O'Spillan, ..	Tipperary.	O'Tracy, ..	Fermanagh.
O'Spillane, ..	Sligo.	O'Traynor, ..	Meath.
O'Sullivan, ..	Cork, Galway, Kerry, Tipperary.	O'Tully, ..	Fermanagh.
		O'Tuohy, ..	Cork.
		O'Tuomey, ..	Cork.

By comparing the foregoing Lists with the Table at the end of this Report, it can be seen how far these families are at present represented in the localities formerly inhabited by them and in the country at large. The above Tables, however. exhibit the information for counties proper, whereas the Tables on pages 32-34 and 37-75 are compiled by Registration Counties, *i.e.*, groups of entire Poor Law Unions most nearly representing the area of the county proper. The differences are for the most part slight, but in a few instances the name may be found in the county proper immediately adjoining.

It will be seen that some of these names have spread all over Ireland, such as Murphy, Kelly, Kennedy, Maguire, Quinn, &c. Some of these Families have disappeared, or have migrated to another part of the country, or their names have become so altered in process of time as to be incapable of identification.

In many cases, however, the descendants of the ancient families are still domiciled in the same tracts as their forefathers, as shown in the following instances :—

The MacCabes were a warlike clan originally from County Monaghan, but subsequently settled in County Cavan. At the present time they are largely represented in the population of each of these counties.

The MacCarthys were anciently Kings and Princes of Desmond, Southern Munster, *i.e.*, County Cork, the greater part of Kerry, and portions of Waterford and Tipperary. The MacCarthys are now resident principally in the Counties of Cork, Kerry, and Limerick, more than half of them being found in County Cork.

The MacDermotts were ancient Princes of Moylurg, having their territories in the Barony of Boyle, County Roscommon, and parts of the Parishes of Islandeady, Turlough, and Breaffy, in Counties Sligo and Mayo. Their chief fortress was on an island in Lough Key, near Boyle, and they were hereditary Marshals of Connaught. At the present time Connaught is the province in which the MacDermotts are principally found, and half of the persons of the name in that province belong to County Roscommon.

The Munster MacMahons formerly possessed the greater part of the Baronies of Moyarta and Clonderalaw, in the County Clare, in which county the predominant name now is McMahon.

The O'Byrnes anciently possessed the greater part of the Barony of Ballinacor, County Wicklow, and were powerful Chiefs in that part of the country. Byrne is the leading name now in the Counties of Wicklow, Dublin, and Louth.

The original habitat of the O'Driscolls was the Barony of West Carbery, in County Cork, where O'Driscoll was Lord of Baltimore, and possessed the Island of Cape Clear and adjacent territory. The great majority of the present Driscolls are to be found there.

The O'Doghertys were a powerful Sept in County Donegal, and were located in Inishowen Barony, of which O'Dogherty was Lord. The Doghertys or Dohertys are numerously represented there at the present time.

The O'Flahertys were originally located in the Barony of Clare, County Galway, but in the thirteenth century, having been expelled from this territory, they settled in the Barony of Moycullen, and were styled Lords of Iar Conacht or West Connaught. A large number of the Flahertys are now to be found in the Baronies of Moycullen, Ross, and Ballinahinch, in County Galway.

The O'Gallaghers were a warlike Clan in the Baronies of Raphoe and Tirhugh, County Donegal. As will be seen from the Table on page 33, Gallagher is now the most numerously represented name in County Donegal.

In ancient times the O'Keeffes were Marshals and chief military leaders of Desmond. They possessed several castles, and were styled Princes of Fermoy. The principal county for the Keeffes and O'Keeffes at present is Cork.

The O'Mahonys were anciently located in Cork and Kerry, where they were powerful Chiefs and sometimes styled Princes. They had several castles along the sea-coast. In County Cork an O'Mahony was Lord of Ivaugh, in the Barony of West Carbery, and an O'Mahony was Chief in Kinalea Barony. In County Kerry there was a Chief of the name in the Barony of Iveragh, and there were O'Mahonys in the Barony of Clanmaurice. The majority of persons of the name of Mahony or O'Mahony are still found in these two counties.

The O'Malleys were celebrated Chiefs whose territory comprised the present Baronies of Murrisk and Burrishoole in the County Mayo. The Malleys and O'Malleys are now located principally in the two baronies named, and in that of Erris, in County Mayo.

The O'Meaghers were formerly powerful Chiefs possessing the Barony of Ikerrin, in County Tipperary, of which O'Meagher was Lord. The Meaghers or Mahers are principally found in the County Tipperary at present.

The O'Mearas had an extensive territory in the Barony of Upper Ormond, County Tipperary, in which O'Meara was a Chief. The name of their principal residence, Tuam-ui-Meara, is still retained in the town of Toomyvara. The Mearas or O'Mearas are still numerous in that locality.

The name Moriarty is now largely represented in County Kerry, in which county the O'Moriartys were Chiefs in the Barony of Dunkerron.

O'Mulvey was a Chief in the Barony of Mohill, County Leitrim, in which county about 50 per cent. of persons bearing the name Mulvey are now found.

The name Noonan occurs chiefly in Cork, in which county the O'Noonans formerly dwelt. O'Noonan was a Chief in Duhallow Barony, and there were O'Noonans in Barrymore and Kinalea Baronies.

There were two branches of the O'Ryans or O'Mulrians—the Carlow branch, in which county O'Ryan was Prince of Idrone—and the Tipperary branch, in which county one O'Ryan was Lord of Owney and Arra, and another Chief of Borrisoleigh. They also had possessions in County Limerick. The Ryans are now found in the Counties of Carlow, Kilkenny, Limerick, and Tipperary, the last county having by far the largest number. The Ryans of Tipperary are in some places so numerous that they are distinguished in the records by additional names appended to the surnames, such as—Ryan (Bawn); Ryan (Buckly); Ryan (Cooper); Ryan (Cormack); Ryan (Corney); Ryan (Dalton); Ryan (Dan); Ryan (Jack); Ryan (James); Ryan (Larry); Ryan (Ned); Ryan (Owen); Ryan (Russell); Ryan (Tim Daniel).

There were several branches of the O'Sullivan family; one was located in County Cork, where they were Princes of Beara, now Bere and Bantry Baronies, and were called O'Sullivan (Beara). Another (O'Sullivan Mor), occupied portion of County Kerry, where they were Lords of Dunkerron. At the present time the Sullivans and O'Sullivans are most numerous in the Counties of Cork and Kerry.

The O'Tooles were celebrated Princes of Imaile, in County Wicklow, and had their seat in the Glen of Imaile, which still retains that name. Their power extended into County Kildare. A considerable number of Tooles are still resident in the County Wicklow.

DANISH NAMES.

From the Ninth to the Twelfth Centuries the Ostmen or Danes came to Ireland and established themselves on the seaboard. They founded the Kingdom of Dublin A.D. 852, and their chief towns were Dublin, Wexford, Waterford, Cork, and Limerick. Some of the surnames now in use are traceable to Danish origin. Amongst these may be mentioned Betagh, Coppinger, Dowdall, Dromgoole or Drumgoole, Gould, Harold, Palmer, Plunkett, Skiddy, Sweetman (Swedeman), Trant, &c. The name " Ost " is met with in County Wicklow.

Dr. MacDermott, in his annotations to the Annals of Ireland by the Four Masters, states :—" Many families of Danish origin took Irish surnames, prefixing O and Mac, so that their descent cannot now be ascertained, and several of their chiefs took Irish Christian names, particularly that of Patrick in honour of the patron saint of Ireland. The Danes and Norwegians being in possession of Dublin and some other parts of the country, and having maintained their colonies there for more than 300 years, there is consequently much of Danish blood in the Counties of Dublin and Meath, particularly in Fingall, and there are many families of Danish descent mixed by intermarriages with the old Milesian Irish."

ANGLO-NORMAN NAMES.

The circumstances connected with the Anglo-Norman invasion need not be referred to here. It suffices to say that through it the second great graft on our Celtic stock took place, many of our present surnames, notwithstanding the changes in form and spelling which time has wrought in them, being traceable to an Anglo-Norman source. As examples the following may be given :—

Barry, Bellew, Bermingham, Burke, Carew, Clare, Cogan, Dalton, Darcy, De Courcy, Delamere, Dillon, FitzEustace (Eustace), Fitzgerald, Fitzhenry, Fitzmaurice, Fitzsimons, Fitz-stephen, Gernon, Grace, Hussey, Keating, Lacy, Le Poer, Mar-shall, Montmorency, Mortimer, Nangle, Nugent, Petit, Prendergast, Purcell, Roche, Staunton, Taaffe, Talbot, Tuite, Tyrrell, Verdon, Vesey.

Dr. MacDermott, in a note to the "Annals of the Four Masters," states :—" The following Anglo-Norman or English families adopted Irish surnames :—The de Burgos or Burkes, of Connaught, took the name of MacWilliam, and some of them that of MacPhilip ; the de Angulos or Nangles, of Meath and Mayo, changed the name to MacCostello ; the de Exeters, of Mayo, to MacJordan ; the Barretts, of Mayo, to MacWattin ; the Stauntons, of Mayo, to M'Aveeley ; . . . . the de Ber-minghams, of Connaught and other places, to MacFeorais, or Peorais ; . . . . the Fitzsimmons, of the King's County, to MacRuddery ; . . . . the Poers, of Kilkenny and Water-ford, to MacShere ; the Butlers, to MacPierce ; the Fitzgeralds, to MacThomas and MacMaurice ; the de Courcys, of Cork, to MacPatrick ; the Barrys, of Cork, to MacAdam ; and many others, in like manner."

ENGLISH NAMES.

Large numbers of English came to Ireland from the 12th to the 18th century, and from these sources the great bulk of the English names now found in Ireland are derived. These names are very numerous, though in many cases, as compared with the old Celtic names, they represent but a small number of persons.

The following are a few specimens of English names numerously represented :—

Adams ; Andrews ; Arnold ; Ashe ; Atkinson ; Baker ; Barr ; Barton ; Bates ; Bennett ; Berry ; Bingham ; Bolton ; Bradshaw ;

Brooks; Canning; Carlisle; Carter; Christy; Cooper; Cox; Crowe; Downes; Edwards; English; Field; Fisher; Freeman; Goodwin; Hall; Harper; Harris; Harrison; Hawthorne; Henry; Hewitt; Hill; Holmes; Hopkins; Hunt; Hunter; Jackson; Jenkins; Johnson; Johnston; Kidd; King; Lamb; Lane; Little; Long; Mitchell; Morton; Nash; Osborne; Pearson; Richardson; Roberts; Robinson; Salmon; Shaw; Short; Simpson; Small; Somers; Swan; Taylor; Thornton; Turner; Walker; Wall; Waters; Watson; Webb; Webster; West; White; Woods; Wright.

CORNISH·NAMES.

Some Cornish or Briton names are also found in Ireland, such as Jagoe, Lanyon, Pascoe, Pender, Pendred, Penrose, Tredennick, Tresilian, Trevelyan, Vivian, &c.

WELSH NAMES.

Welsh immigrants also found their way into Ireland. The name "Walsh"—Irish, Brannagh or Breathnach, a Briton or Welshman—occurs in early times in the counties of Cork, Dublin, Kerry, Kilkenny, Tipperary, Waterford, Wexford, and Wicklow; and at the present day the name is largely represented in nearly every county in Ireland, especially in Cork, Mayo, Waterford, Galway, Dublin, and Wexford. According to some ancient authorities, Welshmen of the following names settled in Ireland after the English Invasion: Howell, Lawless, Lillis, Lynagh, Lynnott, and Merrick.

A remarkable colony from Wales, yet not consisting solely or even mainly of Welsh, was formed at any early date in the Baronies of Forth and Bargy, county Wexford. It is supposed to have been a settlement made at the time of the Norman Invasion. The interest in this colony is centred in the fact that it continued to exist separate from the native Irish, and maintained its peculiarities, character, and language down to a recent period; and traces of its special characteristics are still to be found.

Reference is made to this colony in a series of returns supplied to Sir William Petty, written about 1680. In them it is stated "they preserve their first language and almost only understand the same unless elsewhere educated." Also that "they observe the same form of apparel their predecessors first used," which is, "according to the English mode, of very fine exquisitively dressed frieze, comlie, but not costlie; that they invioblie profess and maintain the same faith and form of religion," and that "they seldom dispose of their children in marriage but unto natives or such as will determine to reside in the Barony." Several peculiar customs and usages of the colony are also detailed in the returns referred to.

In 1788 General Vallancey visited the colony and embodied the result of his researches in a paper which is printed in the Second Volume of the *Transactions of the Royal Irish Academy*, and in which he gives a specimen of the old dialect of the colony.

He remarks:—"This Colony have preserved their ancient "manners, customs, and language; and fully occupying every

" inch of ground, the natives could never obtain a re-establish-
" ment therein. As population increased some of the English
" have been obliged to remove into the neighbouring baronies
" within these fifty years, and by an intercourse with the Irish
" the language of these emigrants became corrupted, and these
" by their connections with their kindred remaining in the
" baronies of Bargie and Forth have in some measure introduced
" this corrupted dialect there."
He mentions, amongst the names of the old colonists at that
date—" Hore," " Cod," " Stafford," " Whitty," " Rossiter,"
" Sinnott," " Stephen," " Quiney," and " Walsh."
In Hall's Ireland also (published in 1841), there are references
to this interesting colony.
Mr. and Mrs. S. C. Hall observe :—" The baronies of Bargy
" and Forth, which extend along the coast from the Bay of Ban-
" now to the Bay of Wexford, form perhaps the most singular
" and remarkable district of Ireland, its inhabitants being to this
" day ' a peculiar people.' . . . The peninsular position of
" these baronies—the sea on the one side, and the mountain of
" Forth on the other—contributed, no doubt in a great degree,
" to the safety and stability of the Colony ; yet had it not been
" for the numerous castles, or, more properly speaking,
" ' fortalices,' the ruins of which form so remarkable a feature in
" the landscape, the courage and daring of the native Irish would
" have caused their extermination. Over a surface of about
" 40,000 acres there are still standing the remains of fifty-nine
" such buildings ; and the sites of many more can be still pointed
" out."
A paper on the subject of the dialect of the Barony of Forth
was read by the Right Rev. Dr. Russell, late President of May-
nooth College, at the Dublin Meeting of the British Association
in August, 1857.
After an examination of the fragments of the language extant,
he states :—" I venture, therefore, to conclude that the barony
" of Forth language is a lineal descent of the English introduced
" by the first settlers, modernized in its forms, and also, though
" in a less degree, in its vocabulary."
Dr. Russell also remarks—" Like Irish in what used to be
the Irish-speaking districts, the Forth language has become un-
fashionable in Forth itself, and the young generation are unwill-
ing even to acknowledge an acquaintance with it, much less to
employ it as a medium of ordinary intercourse."
Dr. Mitchell, Inspector of Registration, who visited the locality
in June last, states :—" There is a very great change over the
" face of this district since Mr. and Mrs. S. C. Hall—50 years
" ago—described its inhabitants as still ' a peculiar people.'
" The change is easily explained by the opening up of
" the whole country—the district markets—and the facilities
" for travel afforded by railway train and steamboat. There is
" no doubt, I think, that the present inhabitants are largely the
" offspring of intermarriage with native Irish. It is only among
" the most illiterate that any considerable number of words of
" their old dialect is now used. Of the surnames given by
" **Vallancey two, viz., Stephen and Quiney, appear to have** died

"out in these Baronies, and others have spread all over the
"county and beyond. The names Codd, Stafford, Sinnott, Hore,
"Rossiter, and Walsh are very common in the town of Wex-
"ford."

SCOTTISH NAMES.

From an early period there were migrations of Scotch from
Scotland to Ireland where they settled in Ulster, but the formal
Plantation of Ulster took place in the seventeenth century. The
majority of these settlers were Scotch.

On reference to the Table at the end of this Report the very
frequent occurrence of Scotch names in the Province of Ulster
will be seen. The following may be given as examples—Stewart,
Campbell, Scott, Miller, McKenzie, Ross, McKay, Paterson,
Fraser, Morrison, Cameron, McIntosh, McGregor, Kerr,
Graham, Sinclair, Gordon.

HUGUENOT NAMES.

Representatives of other races have from time to time settled
in this country; prominent amongst these may be mentioned the
French and Flemish Huguenots. The Irish Parliament in 1674
passed an Act granting letters of naturalization to the refugees.
The Duke of Ormonde, then Viceroy, patronized them, and
through his instrumentality, colonies of them were founded at
Dublin, Kilkenny, Portarlington, Waterford, Cork, and Lisburn.

They started manufactures of silk, gloves, lace, cloth, and linen.
The manufacture of "Irish Poplin" in the Liberties of Dublin
had its origin with these industrious foreigners, and in the north
of Ireland they established the manufacture of linen and cambric.

Many Huguenot names are still amongst us; the following may
be given as examples—Barré, Blacquiere, Boileau, Chaigneau,
Du Bedat, Champion, Chenevix, Corcellis, Crommelin, Dela-
cherois, Drelincourt, Dubourdieu, Du Cros, Fleury, Gaussen,
Logier, Guerin, Hazard (Hassard), La Touche, Le Fevre,
Lefroy, Lefanu, Maturin, Perrin, Saurin, Trench, Des Vignolles.

I have been furnished by Dr. Mitchell with the following notes
regarding the Huguenot settlement in Portarlington at present :—

"There is at the present time (June, 1893) in the Townland of
'Deerpark' near Portarlington, a colony of men of pure Huguenot
descent."

"Mr. Smiles, in his book on 'The Huguenots' (1867), states,
the Blancs, butchers, transmitted the business fror father to son
for more than 150 years, and they are still recognisable at Portarlington under the name of 'Blong.' Not only is this so, but
there are three families of them there now, two of which have
retained (or returned to) the original spelling of the surname
Blanc—as can be seen in our Register Books, and the trade of
butchering is still followed by the family."

"The Medical Officer of Cloneygowan Dispensary District,
Dr. Tabuteau, represents another Portarlington Huguenot
family, and his father, the late Dr. Tabuteau (now eighteen years
dead), remembered the time when Divine service was conducted

in French. The surnames Boileau and Des Voeux have disappeared from this locality only a few years ago, General Boileau and Major Des Voeux with their families having left Portarlington. There is an aged carpenter here, ' La Combre,' of pure Huguenot descent, so that this name also, as well as another, ' Champ.' may be added to the list. The ' Corcellis ' family now spell it Corsellis, and the full surname ' Des Vignolles ' still occurs."

GERMAN PALATINATE NAMES.

In the Eighteenth Century there was a German migration into Ireland from the Palatinate of the Rhine. In 1709 a fleet was sent to Rotterdam by Queen Anne, which brought over about 7,000 of these refugees to England. About 3,000 were sent to North America, where they settled in Pennsylvania and North Carolina. The remainder, except a few families which remained in England, came over to Ireland, and settled principally in the County of Limerick. They were allowed eight acres of land for each man, woman, and child, at 5s. an acre, and the Government engaged to pay their rent for twenty years. They were an industrious and frugal race, but their numbers were subsequently largely reduced by emigration to America, and at the present day but few, comparatively, remain.

Ferrar, the historian of Limerick, describes thus this German Colony as it existed in 1780 :—" The Palatines preserve their " language, but it is declining ; they sleep between two beds ; " they appoint a burgomaster to whom they appeal in all dis- " putes. They are industrious men, and have leases from the " proprietor of the land at reasonable rents ; they are, conse- " quently, better fed and clothed than the generality of Irish " peasants. Besides, their mode of husbandry and crops are " better than those of their neighbours. They have by degrees " left off their sour krout, and feed on potatoes, milk, butter, " oaten and wheaten bread, some meat and fowls, of which they " rear many. * * * The women are very industrious " * * *. Besides their domestic employments and the care " of their children, they reap the corn, plough the ground, and " assist the men in everything. In short the Palatines have " benefited the county by increasing tillage, and are a laborious, " independent people, who are mostly employed on their own " small farms."

Mr. and Mrs. S. C. Hall describe the " Palatines " in 1840 as " different in character, and distinct in habits from the people of " the country." They state :—" The elders of the family pre- " serve in a great degree the language, customs, and religion of " their old country ; but the younger mingle and marry with their " Irish neighbours."

Dr. Mitchell has kindly furnished me with the following remarks regarding the present condition of this colony :—

" I find by personal inquiries made on the spot (May, 1893), that Palatines bearing the following surnames at the present time occupy farms in and round Court Matrix, Ballingran, and Killiheen :—Baker, Bovanizer, Bowen (Adam Bowen was one of my informants, interviewed on his own 8 (Irish) acre farm near Court Matrix), Doube (pronounced 'Dobe'), Delmege (or 'Delmage'—as they themselves pronounce it), Gilliard, Latchford, Ligier (pronounced 'Leg-iar,' with the 'g' hard), Millar, Lodwig, Modlar, Pyper, Reynard (pronounced 'Reinart'); Ruttle, Shire, Stark, Switzer (Jacob Switzer was another of my informants, whom I interviewed on his own 24-acre farm at Court Matrix), Teskey.

" The above 18 names undoubtedly represent more than double that number of families in the localities specified above; several of them also occur at Adare. There are several families of the name 'Switzer,' several of the name 'Delmege,' and 'Ruttle,' and so on.

" When I got to Askeaton District, 1 found a Palatine name, 'Ruttle,' on a signboard (a very unusual circumstance). Generally, Palatine sons succeed their fathers on the same farms originally allotted to their ancestors in 1709. And however those may have fared who have since left Co. Limerick for America, the Palatines here at present are tenant farmers, as a rule, like the original settlers, many of the 8-acre lots having been consolidated into larger farms.

" At Court Matrix, I saw the house of the Rev. Mr. Doube—a Palatine Clergyman at present stationed in Co. Wicklow. When I got to Pallaskenry, I found along with some of the surnames already given, others, viz. :—Neazor, Heavenor, Smyth (spelled with a 'y' and originally 'Schmidt').

" The Christian names for males, Nehemiah, Christopher, Adam, Jacob, Jethro, Julius, Ebenezer, and for females—Dorothy, &c., are still of common occurrence.

" Differing originally in language (though even the oldest of the present generation know nothing of the German tongue, spoken or written), as well as in race and religion from the the natives among whom they were planted, these Palatines still cling together like the members of a clan, and worship together. Most of them have a distinctly foreign type of features, and are strongly built, swarthy in complexion, dark-haired and brown-eyed. The comfortable houses built in 1709 are in ruins now. I traced, with Jacob Switzer's aid, the original 'Square' of Court Matrix in the ruined walls still standing; I also traced in the very centre of this square the foundations of the little Meeting House in which John Wesley occasionally preached to them in the interval, 1750-1765. Modern houses stand there now, but not closely grouped together. They are all comfortable in appearance, some thatched, some slated, some of one storey, others of two. Nearly all have a neat little flower garden in front, and very many have an orchard beside, or immediately behind the house. There is all the appearance of thrift and industry among them."

JEWISH NAMES.

The last colony to which attention need be called is that resulting from the recent Jewish immigration. For many years Jews have been resident in Dublin and other chief cities in Ireland, but during the decade 1881-90, their numbers were largely increased by the arrival of Russian and Polish Jews. Most of these have settled in Dublin, where, on the south side of the city, they have formed a Jewish Quarter, and opened several Synagogues. The Marriage and Birth Indexes of this Office now afford abundant evidence of their presence in our midst.

As shown by the Census Returns, they principally follow the occupations of—Commercial Clerks, Commercial Travellers, Drapers, Dressmakers, General Dealers, Merchants, Pedlars, Shop Assistants, Tailors, and Tailoresses.

The following may be given as examples of the names of the Jewish Settlers :—

Coplan.	Maisell.	Statzumsky.	Wedeclefcky.
Fridberg.	Matufsky.	Stuppel.	Weiner.
Greenberg.	Rabinovitch.	Wachman.	Winstock.
Hesselberg.	Rossin.		

In addition to the foregoing there are a number of foreigners who have settled in Ireland from France, Germany, Italy, and other countries, and whose names appear in our Indexes.

Though "Birthplace" is not an accurate test of nationality, it may be of interest to attach the following Table extracted from the Census of 1891, which shows the Birthplaces of the persons enumerated in Ireland according to each Census from 1841 to 1891 :—

CENSUS PERIODS.	BIRTHPLACE.						
	Province of Leinster.	Province of Munster.	Province of Ulster.	Province of Connaught.	Great Britain.		Born Abroad.
					England and Wales.	Scotland.	
1841, ..	1,932,243	2,394,988	2,390,028	1,423,257	21,552	8,585	4,471
1851, ..	1,614,160	1,853,628	2,015,424	1,018,446	34,454	12,312	9,961
1861, ..	1,398,956	1,502,669	1,905,886	913,052	50,761	16,861	10,379
1871, ..	1,266,010	1,375,600	1,815,901	849,246	67,881	20,318	17,010
1881, ..	1,203,364	1,316,273	1,720,742	821,908	69,382	22,328	19,535
1891, ..	1,113,585	1,154,803	1,587,271	725,722	74,523	27,323	21,330

From this Table it will be seen that the number of persons resident in Ireland at the time of each Census, but born elsewhere, has largely increased at each decennial period.

CHAPTER V.

DISTRIBUTION OF SURNAMES.

In the Table at the end of this Report, will be found the Surnames in Ireland represented by five Entries and upwards in the Births Index for 1890, and the number of such Entries in each Province, together with notes as to their distribution by Counties.

It was not deemed advisable to exhibit in tabular form the details in that Table by Counties, but the relative numerical strength of the principal Surnames in each Registration County is as follows* : —

REGISTRATION PROVINCE OF LEINSTER.

REGISTRATION COUNTY.	SURNAMES AND NUMBER OF ENTRIES IN BIRTHS INDEX FOR 1890.
Carlow,	MURPHY, 41, Byrne 33, Doyle 32, Nolan, 28, Neill 27, Brennan 24, Kelly 15, McDonald 15, Kavanagh 14, Whelan 12, Ryan 10.
Dublin,	BYRNE 301, Kelly 194, Doyle 162, Murphy 132, Smith 106, O'Brien 105, Kavanagh 97, Dunne 93, O'Neill 93, Reilly 93, Nolan 89, Connor 82, Walsh 77, Farrell 73, Carroll 71, Ryan 65, Moore 63, Cullen 62, Keogh 60, Murray 60, Whelan 59, Brady 52, Kennedy 51.
Kildare,	KELLY 40, Murphy 34, Dunne 32, Byrne 28, Nolan 20, Connor 18, Smith 18, Farrell 15, Ryan 15, Moore 14, Carroll 13, Neill 13, Bolger 12, Doyle 12.
Kilkenny,	BRENNAN 49, Walsh 45, Murphy 35, Ryan 34, Carroll 25, Byrne 22, Butler 22, Maher 21, Dunne 20, Phelan 18, Kelly 17, Neill 17, Power 17, Purcell 17, Brien 15, Shea 15, Delany 14, Dowling 14.
King's,	KELLY 34, Dunne 23, Daly 20, Egan 17, Molloy 16, Mooney 16, Carroll 12, Walsh 12, Kenny 11, Murray 11, Dempsey 10, Kennedy 10, Maher 10.
Longford,	REILLY 78, Farrell 36, Kiernan 24, Kelly 23, Donohoe 19, Murphy 14, Brady 13, Quinn 12, Smith 12.
Louth,	BYRNE 36, Kelly 30, Murphy 30, Smith 26, Clarke 23, Duffy 21, McArdle 20, Reilly 20, Carroll 19, Mathews 16, Martin 14, Donnelly 13, Farrell 13, Morgan 13, Rice 13, Hanratty 12, McCourt 12, McKenna 12, Boyle 11, Connor 11, Lynch 11, O'Hare 11.
Meath,	REILLY 53, Smith 30, Lynch 17, Brady 16, Farrell 14, Farrelly 14, Kelly 14, Brien 13, Daly 11, Maguire 11, Duffy 9, Dunne 9, Byrne 8, Connor 8, Mahon 7, Clarke 7, Martin 7, Mathews 7.
Queen's,	DUNNE 34, Delany 30, Conroy 19, Lalor 18, Phelan 18, Fitzpatrick 17, Ryan 13, Carroll 12, Whelan 12, Byrne 11, Kavanagh 11, Kennedy 11, Brennan 10, Kelly 10, Murphy 10.
Westmeath,	LYNCH 14, Farrell 13, Reilly 12, Daly 11, Murray 10, Duffy 9, McCormick 9, Walsh 9, Dalton 8, Kelly 8, Smith 8, Byrne 7, Carey 7, Dunne 6, Fagan 6, Flynn 6, Leavy 6, Murtagh 6, O'Neill 6.
Wexford	MURPHY 137, Doyle 102, Walsh 56, Byrne 46, Cullen 34, Kavanagh 34, Brien 32, Roche 31, Kelly 30, Nolan 30, Redmond 30, Connor 28, Kehoe 28, Ryan 26, Bolger 25, Whelan 25.
Wicklow,	BYRNE 87, Doyle 53, Murphy 26, Kelly 25, Kavanagh 24, Nolan 21, Brien 18, Kehoe 16, Lawler 15, Toole 14, Dunne 13, Farrell 11, Redmond 10.

* The figures inserted represent the number of entries in the Births Index, under each name (including varieties), and thus afford material for comparison as to the relative number of persons of each name. Names where the prefixes " O " and " Mac " have been retained have been combined in this Table with those in which these prefixes have been dropped, the form given in each case being that most numerously represented.

REGISTRATION PROVINCE OF MUNSTER.

REGISTRATION COUNTY.	SURNAMES AND NUMBER OF ENTRIES IN BIRTHS INDEX FOR 1890.
Clare, ..	McMAHON 74, McNamara 61, Moloney 50, O'Brien 47, McInerney 39, Kelly 38, Keane 33, Murphy 29, Griffin 27, Halloran 26, Ryan 23, Lynch 22, Clancy 21.
Cork, ..	SULLIVAN 418, Murphy 390, McCarthy 277, Mahony 193, Donovan 182, Walsh 143, O'Brien 139, Callaghan 134, Leary 134, Crowley 116, Collins 115, Driscoll 110, Connell 109, Barry 108, Cronin 102, Buckley 100, Daly 97, Sheehan 97, Riordan 94, Kelleher 92, O'Connor 91, Hurley 86, Regan 85, O'Keeffe 84, Harrington 82, Fitzgerald 81, O'Neill 75.
Kerry, ..	SULLIVAN 349, Connor 188, Shea 146, Murphy 95, McCarthy 88, Moriarty 74, Fitzgerald 72, Griffin 58, Connell 56, Brosnan 55, Foley 55, Leary 47, Clifford 45, Walsh 45, Cronin 43, Lynch 41, Mahony 38, Daly 34.
Limerick, ..	RYAN 91, O'Brien 78, Fitzgerald 58, Sullivan 50, Hayes 45, Walsh 45, Collins 40, O'Connell 39, Murphy 38, Moloney 38, O'Connor 37, Lynch 31, McNamara 31, O'Donnell 28, Ahern 25.
Tipperary, ..	RYAN 277, Maher 74, O'Brien 74, Kennedy 70, Dwyer 64, Hogan 46, Hayes 38, Gleeson 38, McGrath 38, Walsh 38, Kelly 31, Lonergan 31.
Waterford, ..	POWER, 125, Walsh 97, O'Brien 47, Murphy 35, Ryan 35, McGrath 31, Foley 30, Flynn 28, Morrissey 27, Kelly 26, Phelan 25, Sullivan 25, Whelan 23, McCarthy 22, Butler 21, Tobin 20.

REGISTRATION PROVINCE OF ULSTER.

Antrim, ..	SMITH 134, Johnston 126, Stewart 126, Wilson 119, Thompson 101, O'Neill 98, Campbell 96, Moore 96, Bell 90, Robinson 89, Millar 86, Brown 82, Boyd 81, Scott 66, Graham 64, Reid 63, Martin 61, Kerr 60, Hamilton 50.
Armagh, ..	MURPHY 50, Hughes 47, Wilson 45, Campbell 42, O'Hare 37, Smith 31, McCann 29, Donnelly 28, Watson 28, Quinn 26, Johnston 25, Kelly 25, Thompson 23.
Cavan, ..	REILLY 137, Smith 108, Brady 85, Lynch 51, McCabe 36, Clarke 30, Farrelly 29, Maguire 26, Sheridan 26, Galligan 20, Fitzpatrick 19, Dolan 18, McGovern 18, Donohoe 17, Martin 15, McMahon 15.
Donegal, ..	GALLAGHER 196, Doherty 160, Boyle 102, O'Donnell 102, McLaughlin 81, Sweeney 50, Ward 40, Kelly 37, McGinley 37, McFadden 33, McGowan 33, Duffy 29, Campbell 28.
Down, ..	THOMPSON 55, Smith 53, Campbell 45, Patterson 41, Martin 35, Wilson 35, Graham 34, Johnston 34, Murray 33, Brown 31, Robinson 29, Hamilton 28, Bell 27, Scott 27, Boyd 25.
Fermanagh,	MAGUIRE 44, McManus 30, Dolan 23, McGovern 23, Johnston 22, McHugh 20, Cassidy 17, Wilson 15, Thompson 14, Elliott 13, Irvine 13, McLoughlin 12, Gallagher 11, Murphy 11, Reilly 11, Fitzpatrick 10, Flanagan 10.
Londonderry,	DOHERTY 80, McLaughlin 68, Kelly 50, Bradley 40, Brown 36, McCloskey 36, Campbell 33, Mullan 33, Smith 31, O'Neill 29, Kane 26, Moore 25, Gallagher 23.

REGISTRATION PROVINCE OF ULSTER—*continued.*

REGISTRATION COUNTY.	SURNAMES AND NUMBER OF ENTRIES IN BIRTHS INDEX FOR 1890.
Monaghan, ..	DUFFY 38, Connolly 36, McMahon 33, M'Kenna 32, Hughes 25, Murphy 24, McCabe 22, Martin 19, Smith 19, Keily 18, Quinn 18, Maguire 17, Murray 17, Woods 14.
Tyrone, ..	QUINN 40, Mullan 39, Kelly 38, Donnelly 34, Gallagher 34, McKenna 33, Campbell 32, Hughes 31, Wilson 30, McLaughlin 29, O'Neill, 29, Doherty 27, Smith 25, Hamilton 23.

REGISTRATION PROVINCE OF CONNAUGHT.

Galway, ..	KELLY 119, Burke 89, Conneely 89, Joyce 85, McDonagh 80, Walsh 80, Fahy 63, Mannion 59, Flaherty 48, Murphy 47, Connolly 46, Keane 40, King 36, Forde 35, Connor 33, Lyons 30, Mullin 30, Egan 28, Kenny 27, Toole 25.
Leitrim, ..	KELLY 30, Reynolds 30, Flynn 20, McLoughlin 20, McHugh 19, Rooney 18, McMorrow 18, McTernan 17, Keany 16, McGowan 16, Moran 16, Reilly 16, Maguire 15, Dolan 14, Beirne 13, Gallagher 13, McDermott 13, McGovern 13, McSharry 13, Mulvey 13.
Mayo, ..	WALSH 134, Gallagher 92, Kelly 89, Malley 78, Moran 77, Duffy 55, McHale 50, Gibbons 47, Joyce 46, Connor 45, Conway 40, Higgins 39, Murphy 39, Burke 36, Reilly 36, Durkan 35, Doherty 34, McHugh 34, Sweeney 33, Lyons 32.
Roscommon, ..	KELLY 68, McDermott 45, Beirne 38, Regan 35, Flanagan 32, Connor 30, McDonagh 26, Quinn 25, Murray 24, Brennan 22, Higgins 22, Towey 22, Kenny 21, Flynn 20.
Sligo, ..	BRENNAN 31, McLoughlin 28, Gallagher 26, Kelly 23, Harte 20, McGowan 18, Walsh 18, Kennedy 16, Durkan 15, Henry 15, Flynn 14, Gilmartin 14, Leonard 14, Scanlon 14, Connolly 13, O'Hara 13, Feeney 11, Stenson 11, Conway 10, Sheridan 10.

It will be seen that although the name " Murphy " is the most numerous in the country at large, it does not occupy the leading place in many of the counties. In the Province of Leinster in two Counties only—Wexford and Carlow—does it stand first. With regard to this name in the former County, the Earl of Courtown in a recent paper on the " Celts and Teutons in Ireland," remarks as follows :—

" Murphy is the Anglicised form of MacMurrough, the old regal family of Leinster. On the death of Dermot MacMurrough, the last acknowledged King of Leinster, his rights, by English law, passed to his only legitimate child, Eva, wife of Richard de Clare, Earl of Pembroke, known as Strongbow. The legitimate male line was continued in the descendants of Dermot's brother Morrogh, who continue to hold lands in North Wexford. This name is by far the most numerous in the county, and is found in every part of it."

In the counties of Dublin, Louth, and Wicklow, " Byrne " is the most common name, whereas in Kildare and King's County, " Kelly " heads the list. In Longford and Meath, " Reilly " is the principal name, and in Kilkenny, "Brennan." In Queen's County, "Dunne" appears at the head of the list, and in West-meath, "Lynch."

In the Province of Munster, "Sullivan" is the predominant name in Cork and Kerry, followed, in the former county, very closely by the name "Murphy." "Ryan" heads the list in Limerick and Tipperary, while "McMahon" and "Power" are the leading names, respectively, in the counties of Clare and Waterford.

In the Province of Ulster in one county only, namely, Armagh, is the name "Murphy" in excess of the others. In Antrim, "Smith" appears first; in Cavan, "Reilly"; in Donegal, "Gallagher"; and in Down, "Thompson." The leading name in Fermanagh is "Maguire," and in Londonderry, "Doherty" stands at the head of the list. The principal names in Monaghan and Tyrone are "Duffy" and "Quinn," respectively.

In the Province of Connaught, in no one county does the name "Murphy" occupy the principal position. In Galway and Ros-common the name "Kelly" takes precedence, and in Leitrim that name and "Reynolds" are the first two on the list and equally represented. "Walsh" stands first in the county of Mayo, and "Brennan" heads the list in Sligo.

An interesting feature connected with the Table on pages 37 to 75, is the fact that it exhibits certain names as peculiar to par-ticular provinces or counties. Some of these names may be found in other parts of the country, though not so represented in the Births Index for 1890.

Thus the following names, amongst others, are principally found in the Province of Leinster :—

Behan.	Condron.	Doyle.	Furlong.	Kinsella.	Sinnott.
Bolger.	Curtis.	Ennis.	Harford.	Mulhall.	Tallon.
Brophy.	Deegan.	Fagan.	Kavanagh.	Plunkett.	Tyrrell.
Byrne.	Dowdall.	Fenlon.	Keogh.	Redmond.	Whitty.

The Province of Munster is the chief seat of the undermen-tioned names :—

Ahern.	Crowley.	Harrington.	Lehane.	Moynihan.	Shea.
Barry.	Curtin.	Hartnett.	Lucey.	Mulcahy.	Sheehan.
Brosnan.	Dennehy.	Herlihy.	Mahony.	Noonan.	Sheehy.
Carmody.	Desmond.	Horgan.	M'Auliffe.	O'Connell.	Slattery.
Condon.	Dinneen.	Hurley.	M'Carthy.	O'Sullivan.	Spillane.
Cotter.	Donovan.	Kelleher.	Moloney.	Riordan.	Stack.
Cremin.	Driscoll.	Kingston.	Moriarty.	Scannell.	Sullivan.
Cronin.	Enright.	Leary.	Moroney.	Shanahan.	Twomey.

The following names are confined principally to the Province of Ulster :—

Adair.	Campbell.	Houston.	M'Kee.
Adams.	Carson.	Hunter.	M'Mullan.
Alexander.	Cowan.	Kerr.	Montgomery.
Armstrong.	Craig.	Lavery.	Morrow.
Barr.	Davidson.	M'Allister.	Mulholland.
Bell.	Donaghy.	M'Auley.	Porter.
Blair.	Ferguson.	M'Connell.	Steele.
Bonar.	Gillespie.	M'Dowell.	Stevenson.
Boyd;	Graham.	M'Fadden.	Stewart.
Cairns.	Greer.	M'Farland.	Watson.
Caldwell.	Hamilton.	M'Ginley.	Weir.
Cameron.	Hanna.	M'Gonigle.	Wylie.

The Province of Connaught is the chief habitat of the Names :—

Beirne.	Faherty.	Hession.	Mannion.
Cafferky.	Frain.	Joyce.	M'Nicholas.
Conneely.	Gaughan.	Keaveny.	Mullarkey.
Cunnane.	Giblin.	Kyne.	Noone.
Cunniffe.	Gilmartin.	Lavin.	Ruane.
Durkan.	Ginty.	Malley.	Spelman.

Passing from Provinces to Counties, it will be seen from the Table that, in the Births Index for 1890, the following names appear only in particular Counties :—

Thunder appears in Dublin only.

Howlin, Parle, Rossiter, in Wexford ; and Kearon in Wicklow.

M'Guane is found only in Clare. Anglin, Bohane, Bransfield, Brickley, Bullman, Dullea, Hornibrook, Keohane, Kidney, Lombard, Lordan, Lowney, Motherway, Northridge, Santry, Twohig, appear in the Index for Cork only ; and Bowler, Brick, Cournane, Culloty, Currane, Kerrisk, M'Crohan, M'Gillicuddy for Kerry. The surname Leo is peculiar to Limerick, and Dahill to Tipperary.

The following are found exclusively in Antrim—Buick, Drain, Esler, Gaston, Kernohan, M'Killen, M'Murtry, M'Ninch, Meharg, Miskelly, Mulvenna, O'Rawe, Picken, Quee, Richmond, Snoddy, Warwick, Weatherup, and Wharry.

Cartmill and M'Polin appear in Armagh only, and M'Givney in Cavan.

The names M'Geady, M'Gettigan, and M'Nelis have representatives in Donegal only ; Jess and Lightbody in Down ; M'Eldowney in Londonderry, and M'Aneny in Tyrone.

Cloherty, Dirrane, Diskin, Faherty, Gorham, Grealish, Hara, and Welby, are found only in Galway ; Dever, Forkin, Heffron, Kilbane, Kilgallon, Kirrane, Kitterick, M'Andrew, M'Manamon, M'Nicholas, Mea, O'Hora, Ractigan, and Tougher, in Mayo only ; and Guihen in Roscommon only.

[TABLE

TABLE Showing the SURNAMES IN IRELAND having Five Entries and upwards in the Birth Indexes of 1890, together with the Number in each Registration Province, and the Registration Counties in which these Names are principally found arranged according to the Number of the Names in each.

The Number of Entries opposite Names marked (*) includes varieties in spelling. The figures within brackets after the names denote the number returned according to the spelling here given. Names where the prefixes "Mac" and "O" have been dropped, are shown separately, in this Table, from those in which these prefixes have been retained.

NOTE.—The Estimated Number of Persons of each Surname in the Population can be ascertained by multiplying the Number of Entries in the Table by the Average Birth-rate, which for the Year 1890 is 1 in 44.8 persons.

Names.	NUMBER OF ENTRIES IN BIRTH INDEXES FOR 1890.					Counties in which principally found.
	IRELAND.	Leinster.	Munster.	Ulster.	Connaught.	
*Abbott (10),	11	5	1	3	2	—
Abernethy,	6	-	-	6	-	—
*Abraham (8),	9	4	-	4	1	Armagh.
*Acheson (17),	27	1	2	23	1	Antrim, Armagh, and Down.
Adair,	29	1	1	27	-	19 in Antrim, 6 in Down, and 2 in Londonderry.
Adams,	77	6	5	62	4	Antrim and Londonderry.
Adamson,	9	-	-	9	-	Armagh and Down.
Agnew,	39	2	-	37	-	25 in Antrim, 6 in Armagh, and 4 in Down.
*Ahern (92)- Aherne (15) —Ahearn (9).	122	4	117	1	-	Nearly all in Cork and Limerick.
*Aiken (15),	19	-	1	18	-	Antrim.
Alcock,	5	2	2	1	-	—
Alcorn,	6	-	-	6	-	Donegal and Londonderry.
Alderdice	6	-	-	6	-	Antrim and Armagh.
Alexander,	53	3	-	49	1	Antrim and Down.
*Allen (158),	163	37	15	102	9	A scattered name—chiefly found in Antrim, Armagh, and Dublin.
Allingham	5	-	1	-	4	4 in Leitrim.
Allison,	5	1	-	4	-	Antrim.
Ambrose,	12	-	11	1	-	6 in Cork and 5 in Limerick.
Anderson,	175	36	14	120	5	Antrim, Dublin, Down, and Londonderry.
Andrews,	42	11	2	29	-	Antrim and Down.
Anglin,	5	-	5	-	-	All in Cork.
Angus,	10	1	-	9	-	Down and Antrim.
Annett,	8	-	-	8	-	7 in Down and 1 in Antrim.
Archbold,	8	8	-	-	-	5 in Dublin and 3 in Kildare.
Archer,	15	5	-	10	-	Armagh, Antrim, and Dublin.
Archibald,	8	-	-	7	1	Londonderry.
Armour,	10	1	-	9	-	Antrim.
Armstrong,	140	15	2	110	13	Antrim, Fermanagh, Cavan, and Tyrone.
Arnold,	22	8	2	11	1	Antrim and Dublin.
Arnott,	5	1	3	1	-	Cork.
Arthur,	9	3	4	2	-	—
Arthurs,	11	1	1	9	-	Antrim and Tyrone.
*Ashe (18),	22	4	9	6	3	Kerry and Antrim.
*Aspel (8),	11	9	-	1	1	Wexford.
Atkins,	6	1	3	1	1	Cork.
Atkinson,	37	6	1	28	2	Antrim, Armagh, and Down.
Auld,	6	-	-	6	-	3 in Antrim and 2 in Monaghan.
*Austin (19),	20	7	3	9	1	Antrim and Dublin.
Aylward,	14	6	7	-	1	Waterford and Kilkenny.
Bacon,	7	4	1	2	-	—
*Bagnall (6),	9	7	-	-	2	King's.
*Bailey (34), Bailie (29), Bayley (7).	80	15	16	44	5	"Bailey," Antrim and Wexford; "Bailie," Antrim and Down; "Bayley," Tipperary and Dublin.
Baird,	39	4	1	34	-	Antrim and Down.
Baker,	30	10	10	8	2	Dublin and Antrim.
Baldwin,	10	3	7	-	-	Waterford.
*Balfe (7),	9	7	-	-	2	—
Balfour,	5	-	-	5	-	Antrim.
Ball,	16	9	2	5	-	Antrim, Meath, and Dublin.
*Ballantine (8), Ballentine (8).	19	-	-	17	2	Antrim.
Balmer,	8	1	-	7	-	Down.
Bamford,	9	1	-	8	-	7 in Antrim.
Banks,	8	-	2	2	4	—

TABLE showing the SURNAMES IN IRELAND having Five Entries and upwards in the Birth Indexes of 1890, together with the Number in each Registration Province, and the Registration Counties in which these Names are principally found—*continued.*

Names.	NUMBER OF ENTRIES IN BIRTH INDEXES FOR 1890.					Counties in which principally found.
	IRELAND.	Leinster.	Munster.	Ulster.	Connaught.	
Bannister,	5	1	1	3	–	—
*Bannon (21),	23	6	9	5	3	Tipperary.
*Barber (15),	18	2	1	11	4	Antrim.
Barclay,	6	–	–	4	2	Antrim and Galway.
Barker,	7	4	–	3	–	—
*Barkley (6),	9	–	1	8	–	8 in Antrim.
Barlow,	7	3	–	–	4	—
*Barnes (22),	26	7	2	14	3	Antrim.
Barnett,	15	3	2	9	1	—
Barr,	60	3	–	57	–	Antrim, Londonderry, and Down.
*Barrett (141),	146	17	74	11	44	Dublin, Cork, Kerry, Limerick, Galway, and Mayo.
Barrington,	7	4	2	–	1	—
*Barron (41),	43	12	11	20	–	Antrim, Donegal, Wexford, and Waterford.
Barry,	217	22	173	12	10	Cork, Limerick, Waterford—Cork alone containing about half the entries in all Ireland.
*Bartley (8),	10	3	2	3	2	—
Barton,	20	6	4	10	–	Fermanagh and Dublin.
*Bassett (6),	9	1	4	4	–	—
Bateman,	19	5	10	4	–	Cork and Dublin.
Bates,	22	12	1	9	–	Dublin.
Battersby,	5	3	–	2	–	Dublin.
Battle,	6	–	–	–	6	Sligo.
Baxter,	31	4	–	26	1	Antrim.
Beamish,	5	1	4	–	–	4 in Cork.
*Beattie (61), Beatty 36),	101	13	3	80	5	"Beattie," Antrim and Down; "Beatty," Dublin, Armagh, and Tyrone.
Beck,	7	1	–	6	–	Antrim and Down.
Beckett,	6	–	1	5	–	Antrim.
*Beggan (5),	7	1	1	5	–	Monaghan.
Beggs,	30	6	–	24	–	17 in Antrim, 6 in Dublin.
*Begley (36),	39	2	20	12	5	Kerry and Donegal.
*Behan (37),	46	38	6	1	1	Dublin and Kildare.
Beirne,	64	3	3	–	58	38 in Roscommon and 13 in Leitrim.
Bell,	197	22	3	169	3	Antrim, Down, Tyrone, Armagh, and Dublin.
Bellew,	8	6	–	2	–	Louth.
Belton,	12	6	1	–	5	Longford and Louth.
*Bennett (79),	81	26	20	34	1	Cork, Dublin, Antrim, Armagh, and Down.
*Benson (15),	16	3	2	7	4	—
Beresford,	6	2	1	3	–	—
*Bergin (40),	45	29	15	1	–	Tipperary, Queen's, and Dublin.
Berkery,	6	–	6	–	–	4 in Tipperary and 2 in Limerick.
Bermingham (23), Birmingham (17),	40	22	13	–	5	Dublin, King's, and Cork.
Bernard,	6	2	4	–	–	—
Berry,	30	10	2	12	6	Antrim, King's, and Mayo.
Best,	21	–	1	19	1	Armagh and Tyrone.
Bickerstaff,	5	–	–	5	–	3 in Down and 2 in Antrim.
Biggins,	6	1	–	2	3	Mayo.
Bill,	5	1	–	4	–	4 in Antrim.
Bingham,	30	2	–	27	1	12 in Down and 11 in Antrim.
Birch,	9	4	2	3	–	—
*Bird (21),	22	7	8	5	2	Dublin and Cork.
*Birney (6),	7	2	–	5	–	—
Bishop,	9	6	2	1	–	Dublin.
Black,	116	15	1	96	4	Antrim, Armagh, Tyrone, and Down.
*Blackburn (6),	8	4	1	3	–	Antrim.
Blackstock,	5	–	–	5	–	Antrim and Armagh.
Blackwood,	7	–	–	7	–	Antrim.
*Blain (6),	8	–	–	8	–	5 in Antrim and 3 in Down.
Blair,	78	2	2	74	–	47 in Antrim, 12 in Londonderry, and 8 in Tyrone.
Blake,	58	18	20	8	12	Cork, Galway, Clare, Antrim, and Dublin.
*Blaney (7),	9	1	–	6	2	Antrim.
*Bleakley (7),	11	1	–	9	1	Antrim.
Bloomer,	6	1	–	5	–	3 in Antrim and 2 in Tyrone.
*Boal (12),	17	–	–	17	–	12 in Antrim and 4 in Down.
*Bogan (7),	12	7	2	3	–	Wexford.
Bogue,	9	2	–	7	–	Fermanagh.
*Bohan (27),	30	4	4	4	18	Leitrim and Galway.

TABLE showing the SURNAMES IN IRELAND having Five Entries and upwards in the Birth Indexes of 1890, together with the Number in each Registration Province, and the Registration Counties in which these Names are principally found—*continued.*

Names.	NUMBER OF ENTRIES IN BIRTH INDEXES FOR 1890.					Counties in which principally found.
	IRELAND.	Leinster.	Munster.	Ulster.	Connaught.	
Bohane,	5	–	5	–	–	All in Cork.
Boland	57	16	24	3	14	Clare, Kildare, and Roscommon.
Boles (7)—Bowles (5),	12	5	1	–	6	—
*Bolger (64),	70	64	3	1	2	Wexford, Kildare, and Wicklow.
Bollard,	7	7	–	–	–	Dublin.
Bolton,	22	10	6	5	1	—
*Bonar (22),	38	–	–	38	–	29 in Donegal.
Bond,	18	9	4	5	–	Dublin.
Bones,	7	–	–	3	4	—
*Booth (14),	17	7	1	7	2	Antrim and Dublin.
Bothwell,	7	1	–	6	–	—
*Boucher (5),	7	2	4	1	–	—
Bourke,	140	20	84	4	32	Tipperary, Limerick, Mayo, Kerry, and Cork.
Bowden,	8	4	–	4	–	—
Bowe,	14	12	2	–	–	Kilkenny.
Bowen,	14	1	11	1	1	Cork.
Bowers,	5	2	–	3	–	—
Bowes,	10	7	2	1	–	Dublin.
Bowler,	14	–	14	–	–	All in Kerry.
Bowman,	11	1	2	8	–	Antrim and Down.
*Boyce (39),	40	7	2	31	–	Donegal, Down, and Londonderry.
*Boyd (154),	155	10	1	141	3	Antrim, Down, and Londonderry.
Boylan,	49	22	4	16	7	Dublin, Monaghan, Cavan, and Meath.
Boyle,	273	27	23	189	34	Donegal, Antrim, Mayo, Tyrone, Armagh, and Louth.
Boyne,	7	6	–	1	–	Dublin.
Brabazon,	5	2	1	1	1	—
*Bracken (24),	26	18	–	4	4	Dublin and King's.
*Bradley (132),	135	21	16	89	9	Londonderry, Antrim, Tyrone, Donegal, Dublin, and Cork.
Bradshaw,	25	6	6	11	2	Antrim, Tipperary, and Dublin.
Brady,	261	105	10	125	21	Cavan, Dublin, Antrim, Meath, and Longford.
Brandon,	8	–	1	6	1	—
*Brannan (8)—Brannon (7),	18	1	–	14	3	Donegal.
*Brannigan (20)—Branagan (7),	38	16	2	20	–	"Brannigan" Armagh and Monaghan—"Branagan" Dublin.
Bransfield,	5	–	5	–	–	All in Cork.
Bray,	14	5	5	4	–	Cavan and Dublin.
*Brazil (10),	19	8	9	–	2	Dublin and Waterford.
*Breadon (7),	13	1	–	11	1	Fermanagh and Tyrone.
*Breen (110),	112	57	32	23	–	Wexford, Dublin, and Kerry.
*Breheny (7),	16	–	–	–	16	Roscommon and Sligo.
*Brennan (336)	358	178	50	36	94	Kilkenny, Dublin, Sligo, Mayo, Carlow, and Roscommon.
*Brereton (8),	15	12	1	2	–	Dublin and King's.
*Breslin (42),	43	13	1	29	–	Donegal.
Brett,	20	7	4	–	9	Sligo and Dublin.
Brew,	9	–	9	–	–	6 in Clare.
*Brick (9),	10	–	10	–	–	"Brick," all in Kerry.
Brickley,	5	–	5	–	–	All in Cork.
*Bridget (5),	7	2	–	5	–	—
Brien,	246	110	122	5	9	Cork, Dublin, Tipperary, Wexford, and Waterford.
*Briggs (16),	17	1	–	15	1	Antrim and Down.
Bright,	7	5	1	1	–	Dublin.
Briody,	13	9	–	4	–	6 in Longford and 4 in Cavan.
Britt,	12	1	10	1	–	6 in Tipperary and 4 in Waterford.
*Britton (9),	13	6	2	4	1	—
Brock,	6	6	–	–	–	—
Broder,	11	–	10	–	1	6 in Kerry and 4 in Limerick.
*Broderick (37),	39	10	14	–	15	Galway, Cork, Kerry, and Dublin.
*Brody (6),	7	–	7	–	–	6 in Clare.
Broe,	8	7	1	–	–	4 in Kildare and 3 in Dublin.
Brogan,	33	5	2	16	10	Mayo and Donegal.
*Brolly (7),	8	–	–	8	–	7 in Londonderry and 1 in Tyrone.
*Brooks (20),	25	7	12	6	–	Cork and Dublin.
Brophy,	50	41	8	–	1	Dublin, Kilkenny, Queen's, and Tipperary.
*Brosnan (47),	66	–	66	–	–	55 in Kerry.
Brown,	327	58	39	214	16	Antrim, Londonderry, Down, and Dublin.
Browne,	146	36	51	30	29	Cork, Mayo, Wexford, and Dublin.

TABLE showing the SURNAMES IN IRELAND having Five Entries and upwards in the Birth Indexes of 1890, together with the Number in each Registration Province, and the Registration Counties in which these Names are principally found—*continued*.

Names.	NUMBER OF ENTRIES IN BIRTH INDEXES FOR 1890.					Counties in which principally found.
	IRELAND.	Leinster.	Munster.	Ulster.	Connaught.	
Brownlee,	19	1	–	18	–	Antrim and Armagh.
Bruce,	7	2	–	5	–	—
Bruen,	10	–	–	1	9	Roscommon.
Bruton,	9	8	–	–	1	Dublin.
*Bryan (38),	47	31	8	4	4	Dublin, Kilkenny, Wexford, Cork, and Down.
Bryans,	16	1	–	15	–	Antrim and Down.
Bryson,	9	–	–	9	–	Londonderry.
*Buchanan (20),	24	–	1	21	2	Tyrone.
*Buckley (176),	184	31	144	5	4	Cork, Kerry, Dublin, Kilkenny, and Tipperary. Very few in any other County.
Buggy,	12	10	2	–	–	Kilkenny and Queen's.
Buick,	7	–	–	7	–	All in Antrim.
Bullman,	5	–	5	–	–	All in Cork.
Bunting,	17	–	1	16	–	11 in Antrim and 4 in Armagh.
*Burchill (6),	7	2	5	–	–	Cork.
Burgess,	19	8	3	7	1	Dublin.
*Burke (353),	357	76	107	32	142	Galway, Cork, Dublin, Mayo, Tipperary, and Waterford.
*Burnett (7),	8	3	–	5	–	—
*Burns (215),	219	18	49	140	12	Antrim, Down, and Armagh. The Munster entries are chiefly in Clare, Cork, Kerry, and Tipperary.
Burnside,	8	1	1	6	–	Londonderry and Antrim.
Burrell,	5	1	–	4	–	Armagh.
*Burrows (15),	19	2	5	10	2	Down.
Burton,	10	5	1	4	–	Dublin and Antrim.
Bustard,	7	–	–	7	–	Donegal.
*Butler (168),	172	72	66	9	25	Dublin, Kilkenny, Tipperary, and Waterford
Butterfield,	7	5	1	1	–	Dublin and Kildare.
Byers,	10	1	–	9	–	Cavan.
*Byrne (715),	734	583	52	53	46	Dublin, Wicklow, Wexford, and Louth. Many are also found in Carlow, Kildare, and Kilkenny; in Cork and Waterford; Donegal; Galway, Mayo, and Roscommon.
Byron,	10	3	2	4	1	Dublin and Antrim.
*Caddell (5),	6	3	1	2	–	—
Cadden,	5	–	–	5	–	—
*Cadogan (6),	8	–	8	–	–	Cork.
Cafferky (19),	25	–	–	–	25	22 in Mayo and 3 in Roscommon.
Cafferty,	6	–	–	4	2	Cavan.
*Caffrey (32),	35	25	1	6	3	Dublin, Meath, and Cavan.
*Cahalane (13),	27	1	22	–	4	Cork and Kerry.
Cahill,	147	54	73	8	12	Cork, Kerry, Dublin, Kilkenny, and Tipperary.
*Cain (23),	31	8	4	3	16	Mayo.
*Cairns (43),	44	3	1	39	1	Antrim, Down, and Armagh.
Calderwood,	12	–	–	12	–	10 in Antrim.
*Caldwell (40),	42	5	–	37	–	Antrim, Londonderry, and Tyrone.
*Callaghan (243),	250	40	133	48	29	Cork, Kerry, and Dublin.
Callan,	33	18	–	15	–	Louth and Monaghan.
*Callanan (18)—Callinan (13),	41	–	32	1	8	"Callanan" Galway and Cork: "Callinan" Clare.
Calvert,	15	–	–	15	–	Antrim, Armagh, and Down.
*Calvey (7),	9	–	–	–	9	Sligo.
Cambridge,	5	–	3	2	–	3 in Cork and 2 in Antrim.
Cameron,	30	1	–	28	1	17 in Antrim and 7 in Londonderry.
Campbell,	349	39	8	279	23	Antrim, Down, Armagh, Tyrone, Londonderry, and Donegal.
Campion,	13	11	2	–	–	Kilkenny and Queen's.
*Canavan (22),	26	2	7	13	4	Cork.
*Canniff (5),	6	–	5	1	–	Cork.
Canning,	25	3	2	15	5	Londonderry.
Cannon,	49	7	1	21	20	Donegal, Leitrim, and Mayo.
Canny,	8	–	–	3	5	Clare and Mayo.
Cantwell,	15	8	7	–	–	Tipperary and Dublin.
Canty,	23	2	21	–	–	Cork and Limerick.
*Carberry (15),	26	11	4	10	1	Antrim.
Cardiff,	5	5	–	–	–	—
Cardwell,	9	–	–	9	–	Antrim.
Carew,	12	1	10	–	1	9 in Tipperary.

TABLE showing the SURNAMES IN IRELAND having Five Entries and upwards in the Birth Indexes of 1890, together with the Number in each Registration Province, and the Registration Counties in which these Names are principally found—*continued.*

Names.	NUMBER OF ENTRIES IN BIRTH INDEXES FOR 1890.					Counties in which principally found.
	IRELAND.	Leinster.	Munster.	Ulster.	Connaught.	
Carey, ...	118	36	59	10	13	Cork, Dublin, Tipperary, Mayo, and Kerry.
Carleton,	15	3	1	11	–	Antrim.
*Carley (6), ..	8	4	3	–	1	Wexford.
*Carlin (17), ..	20	3	–	15	2	Tyrone and Londonderry.
*Carlisle (22), ..	24	–	–	24	–	16 in Antrim and 5 in Down.
Carmichael, ..	19	2	–	17	–	Antrim.
Carmody,	33	1	32	–	–	Clare, Kerry, and Limerick.
*Carney (48), ..	49	7	4	8	30	21 in Mayo.
*Carolan (39), ..	47	19	1	13	14	Mayo and Cavan.
Carpenter, ..	10	8	1	1	–	Dublin.
*Carr (85), ..	90	21	10	35	24	Donegal, Galway, and Dublin.
*Carrick (7), ..	12	2	6	2	2	—
Carrigan, ..	9	2	2	4	1	Fermanagh.
*Carroll (374), ..	386	181	125	26	54	Dublin, Kilkenny, Cork, Tipperary, and Limerick, but found in every County of Leinster, Munster, and Connaught.
*Carruthers (7),	11	1	–	10	–	
Carry, ..	5	5	–	–	–	Louth.
Carson, ..	77	3	2	71	1	Antrim, Down, and Tyrone.
Carter, ..	38	17	4	7	10	Dublin and Galway.
Carthy, ..	25	13	9	2	1	Wicklow, Waterford, and Cork
Cartmill, ..	5	–	–	5	–	All in Armagh.
*Carton (27), ..	32	24	1	7	–	Dublin, Wexford, and Londonderry.
Carty, ..	68	33	6	3	26	Roscommon, Wexford, Galway, and Longford
*Carvill (8), ..	14	2	–	12	–	Armagh and Down.
*Casey (252), ..	254	61	134	17	42	Cork, Kerry, Dublin, and Limerick.
Cash, ..	12	6	4	2	–	Tipperary and Wexford.
*Cashin (11),	21	9	10	–	2	—
Cashman,	16	–	16	–	–	13 in Cork.
Caskey, ..	6	–	–	6	–	Antrim.
*Cassells (16), ..	17	2	–	11	4	Armagh.
Casserly, ..	16	4	–	3	9	Roscommon.
*Cassidy (140), ..	141	26	3	96	16	Donegal, Dublin, Antrim, and Fermanagh.
Cassin, ..	5	3	1	–	1	—
Cathcart,	16	2	–	13	1	Antrim.
Catherwood,	9	–	–	9	–	Antrim.
*Caughey (12), ..	13	–	–	13	–	7 in Down and 6 in Antrim.
*Caulfield (55), ..	59	16	4	21	18	Mayo, Antrim and Monaghan.
Cawley, ..	17	–	2	–	15	10 in Mayo, and 4 in Sligo.
Chambers,	69	11	6	39	13	Antrim, Mayo, Down, and Armagh.
Chandler,	7	5	1	–	1	Dublin.
Chapman,	19	8	1	10	–	Dublin, Down, and Antrim.
*Charles (7), ..	8	–	2	5	1	—
Charleton (7)—Charlton (7),	14	2	–	10	2	Tyrone and Antrim.
*Charters (8), ..	10	2	–	8	–	—
Cherry, ..	10	1	–	9	–	Down.
Christian, ..	12	4	–	6	2	—
Christopher,	6	–	5	–	1	5 in Waterford and 1 in Leitrim.
Christy (17)—Christie (16),	33	6	–	26	1	Antrim.
Church, ..	7	1	–	4	2	—
Claffey, ..	7	4	–	–	3	—
Clancy (95), ..	100	18	43	11	28	Clare, Leitrim, Galway, and Tipperary.
Clare, ..	9	8	1	–	–	Dublin.
*Clarke (327), ..	345	99	17	176	53	Antrim, Dublin, Mayo, Cavan, and Louth Generally distributed through the Counties of Ulster.
Clarkson, ..	5	2	3	–	–	—
Clay, ..	5	–	1	3	1	—
Clayton, ..	12	2	2	5	3	—
*Clear (11), ..	12	9	2	–	1	Queen's and Wexford.
*Cleary (122), ..	127	47	59	12	9	Dublin, Tipperary, Clare, Limerick, and Waterford.
Clegg, ..	12	1	–	11	–	Down and Antrim.
*Cleland (9), ..	14	1	–	13	–	Down and Antrim.
Clements,	25	2	–	23	–	17 in Antrim.
Clenaghan,	5	–	–	5	–	—
*Clendinning (8),	10	1	–	9	–	Antrim.

TABLE showing the SURNAMES IN IRELAND having Five Entries and upwards in the Birth Indexes of 1890, together with the Number in each Registration Province, and the Registration Counties in which these Names are principally found—*continued.*

Names.	NUMBER OF ENTRIES IN BIRTH INDEXES FOR 1890.					Counties in which principally found.
	IRELAND.	Leinster.	Munster.	Ulster.	Connaught.	
*Clerkin (11), ...	15	6	–	4	5	—
*Clifford (82), ...	83	10	58	9	6	45 in Kerry.
Clinton, ...	18	10	1	5	2	Dublin and Louth.
*Cloherty (12), ..	13	–	–	–	13	All in Galway.
*Clohessy (10), ..	12	2	10	–	–	Clare and Limerick.
*Cloonan (7), ...	8	1	1	–	6	" Cloonan," 6 in Galway.
Close, ...	16	3	–	13	–	Antrim.
Clune, ...	10	1	9	–	–	Clare.
Clyde, ...	7	–	–	7	–	Antrim and Londonderry.
Clyne, ...	11	6	–	–	5	Leitrim and Longford.
*Coakley (31), Colclough (4),	36	5	29	–	2	" Coakley," 26 in Cork ; " Colclough," all in Leinster.
*Coates (14), ...	15	3	3	9	..	Antrim.
*Coburn (9), ...	10	2	–	8	–	Down, Armagh, and Louth.
*Cochrane (38), ..	42	2	1	37	2	Antrim, Londonderry, Down, and Tyrone.
Codd, ...	10	10	–	–	–	8 in Wexford.
*Code (8), ...	10	7	2	–	1	—
Cody (23), Coady (12), ..	35	19	13	–	3	Kilkenny, Tipperary, Galway, and Cork.
*Coen (21), ...	27	1	2	3	21	Galway and Roscommon.
Coey, ...	6	–	–	6	–	3 in Antrim and 3 in Down.
*Coffey (90), ...	98	22	60	5	11	Kerry, Tipperary, Dublin, Cork, and Roscommon.
Cogan, ...	14	8	5	1	–	Cork and Kildare.
Colbert, ...	11	1	10	–	..	Cork and Waterford.
*Cole (36), ...	57	15	6	13	3	Dublin, Londonderry, Armagh, Down, and King's.
*Coleman (128), ..	138	31	63	14	30	Cork, Roscommon, Dublin, and Waterford.
*Colgan (31), ...	32	17	1	11	3	Dublin, King's, and Antrim.
*Colhoun (20), ..	22	2	–	20	–	8 in Londonderry and 8 in Tyrone.
Coll, ...	28	2	2	21	3	17 in Donegal.
Colleran, ...	7	–	–	–	7	5 in Mayo and 2 in Galway.
Collier, ...	7	6	1	–	–	Wexford.
Colligan, ...	5	2	–	2	1	
*Collins (350), ...	352	60	200	49	43	Cork, Limerick, Dublin, Galway, and Antrim. A good many are also found in Kerry and Clare.
Colvin, ...	6	1	1	4	..	—
Comber	5	–	1	–	4	Mayo.
*Comerford (28), ..	30	21	8	1	–	Kilkenny and Dublin.
*Commins (17), ..	20	4	4	2	10	Mayo and Waterford.
*Commons (13), ..	14	7	1	–	6	Kilkenny, Galway, and Mayo.
Compton, ...	5	1	–	3	1	Antrim.
Conaghan, ...	7	–	–	6	1	Donegal and Londonderry.
*Conaty (12), ...	14	1	–	12	1	10 in Cavan.
*Conboy (11), ...	12	1	1	1	9	Roscommon and Sligo.
*Concannon (17), ..	18	..	..	..	18	11 in Galway, 4 in Mayo, and 3 in Roscommon.
*Condon (63), ...	64	9	53	1	1	22 in Cork, 17 in Tipperary, and 9 in Kerry.
*Condron (19), ..	23	22	–	1	–	Carlow, Dublin, Kildare, and King's.
Condy, ...	5	–	–	5	–	4 in Tyrone and 1 in Fermanagh.
*Conefry (6), ...	7	1	–	–	6	6 in Leitrim.
*Conlon (66)—Conlan (36),	107	31	9	25	42	Roscommon, Mayo, and Sligo. Generally distributed in Leinster and Ulster.
Conn, ...	9	1	..	8	..	Down and Armagh.
*Connaughton (9), ..	10	1	2	–	7	Galway and Roscommon.
*Conneely (81), ..	92	–	–	..	92	89 in Galway.
*Connell (236), ...	242	40	145	23	34	Cork, Kerry, Limerick, Tipperary, and Galway.
*Connellan (6), ..	8	1	3	3	1	—
Conney, ...	5	–	2	1	2	—
* Connolly (303)— Connelly (43),	381	81	66	146	88	" Connolly," Cork, Monaghan, Galway, Antrim and Dublin ; " Connelly," Galway.
*Connor (423), ...	432	110	162	68	92	Kerry, Dublin, Mayo, and Cork ; also found to a large extent in Roscommon and Galway and in Antrim and Londonderry.
*Connors (141), ...	142	42	87	5	8	Cork, Wexford, and Tipperary.
Conroy, ...	78	45	9	1	23	Nearly all in Galway, Queen's, and Dublin.
*Conry (36), ...	52	4	11	5	32	Mayo and Roscommon
Considine, ...	21	1	19	1	..	Clare and Limerick.
*Convery (10), ...	11	–	–	11	..	10 in Londonderry.
Convey, ...	5	–	..	2	3	3 in Mayo and 2 in Down.
Conway	169	34	48	29	58	Mayo, Tyrone, and Dublin, and generally in Munster.

TABLE showing the SURNAMES IN IRELAND having Five Entries and upwards in the Birth Indexes of 1890, together with the Number in each Registration Province, and the Registration Counties in which these Names are principally found—*continued.*

Names.	IRELAND.	Leinster.	Munster.	Ulster.	Connaught.	Counties in which principally found.
			NUMBER OF ENTRIES IN BIRTH INDEXES FOR 1890.			
Coogan, ...	23	13	1	7	2	Dublin, Kilkenny, and Monaghan.
*Cooke (74), ..	89	21	18	33	17	Antrim, Dublin, Cork, Limerick, Galway, and Sligo.
*Cooley (8), ..	9	–	1	5	3	Antrim and Galway.
Cooney, ..	76	20	21	9	26	Mayo and Dublin.
Cooper, ...	36	17	4	15	–	Antrim and Dublin.
Coote, ...	6	3	–	3	–	Dublin.
Copeland, ..	17	1	1	15	–	Armagh and Antrim.
Copley, ...	5	–	4	–	1	Cork.
*Corbett (54), ..	64	4	34	19	7	Cork, Tipperary, and Galway.
*Corcoran (127), ..	132	41	40	2	40	Mayo, Cork, Tipperary, Dublin, and Kerry.
Cordner, ...	5	1	–	4	–	Armagh.
Corish, ..	5	3	1	–	1	—
*Corkery (12), ..	15	–	15	–	–	9 in Cork, 3 in Limerick, and 2 in Kerry.
Corkin, ...	5	–	–	5	–	4 in Down.
*Corless (5), ..	6	2	–	–	4	Galway.
Corley, ...	6	2	–	1	3	—
Cormack, ..	18	11	4	1	2	Kilkenny and Tipperary.
*Cormican (8), ..	10	–	–	2	8	6 in Galway.
Corr, ...	55	16	3	31	5	Dublin and Tyrone. [Louth.
Corrigan, ..	74	31	3	26	14	Dublin, Mayo, Fermanagh, Monaghan, and
*Corry (42), ..	44	5	13	23	3	17 in Antrim, and 12 in Clare.
*Cosgrave (33), ..	34	17	9	3	5	Dublin and Wexford.
Cosgrove, ...	40	6	3	16	15	Mayo and Galway. Scattered in Ulster.
*Costello (80)—Costelloe (58), ..	147	32	45	3	67	"Costello," Mayo, Dublin, and Galway— "Costelloe," Limerick, Galway, and Clare.
Costigan, ...	8	7	1	–	–	Dublin, Kilkenny, and Queen's.
Cotter, ...	64	–	58	6	–	43 in Cork.
*Cotton (8), ..	9	3	1	3	2	—
Coughlan (65)— Coghlan (49), ..	125	34	81	5	5	"Coughlan," Cork—"Coghlan," Cork and Dublin.
*Coulter (44), ..	45	2	–	42	1	Antrim, Down, and Fermanagh.
Counihan, ..	8	–	7	–	1	Kerry.
*Cournane (8), ..	9	1	8	–	–	"Cournane," all in Kerry.
Courtney (55), ..	59	16	27	10	6	Kerry, Antrim, and Dublin.
Cousins, ...	18	8	2	8	–	—
*Cowan (31), ..	33	3	–	30	–	Antrim, Down, and Armagh.
*Cowley (14), ..	15	5	1	2	7	Mayo.
Cox, ...	75	27	11	15	22	Roscommon and Dublin.
Coy, ...	5	2	–	1	2	—
Coyle, ...	90	23	–	52	15	Donegal, Cavan, Londonderry, Dublin, Tyrone, and Longford.
Coyne, ...	54	13	1	1	39	27 in Galway and 8 in Mayo.
Craig, ...	120	7	1	111	1	Antrim, Londonderry, and Tyrone.
*Crampsy (5), ..	9	–	–	9	–	Donegal.
Crampton, ..	7	7	–	–	–	—
Crane, ...	8	2	–	4	2	—
Cranny, ...	6	3	1	2	–	—
Cranston, ..	9	1	–	8	–	Armagh and Antrim.
*Craven (9), ..	10	5	–	3	2	—
Crawford, ..	96	8	7	79	2	Antrim, Down, Londonderry, and Tyrone.
Crawley, ..	19	10	1	3	5	Louth and Roscommon.
Creagh, ...	17	6	8	1	2	—
*Crean (24), ..	27	4	16	–	7	9 in Kerry, 7 in Cork, and 4 in Wexford.
Creaney, ..	5	–	–	5	–	4 in Armagh and 1 in Down.
Creaton, ..	8	2	1	1	4	—
*Creed (7), ..	9	4	5	–	–	Cork.
*Creedon (14), ..	15	–	15	–	–	12 in Cork.
Cregan (20), Creegan (13),	33	10	12	4	7	"Cregan" Limerick and Meath ; "Creegan," Leitrim and Sligo.
Cregg, ...	13	1	1	–	11	Roscommon.
*Crehan (15), ..	17	–	1	1	15	"Crehan," 14 in Galway.
*Creighton (20), ..	23	6	–	15	2	Antrim and Dublin.
*Cremin (20), ..	25	–	25	–	–	11 in Cork and 11 in Kerry.
*Crilly (18), ..	23	5	–	18	–	Antrim, Londonderry, and Louth.
*Croghan (6), ..	9	3	3	1	2	—
Croke, ...	12	1	11	–	–	Tipperary and Waterford.
Cromie (20), ..	21	–	–	21	–	Armagh and Down.
Crone, ...	9	1	4	3	1	3 in Cork and 3 in Antrim.
*Cronin (168), ..	176	6	161	3	6	102 in Cork, 43 in Kerry, and 11 in Limerick
Crooks, ...	15	–	–	15	–	Antrim and Londonderry.

TABLE showing the SURNAMES IN IRELAND having Five Entries and upwards in the Birth Indexes of 1890, together with the Number in each Registration Province, and the Registration Counties in which these Names are principally found—*continued.*

Names.	IRELAND.	Leinster.	Munster.	Ulster.	Connaught.	Counties in which principally found.
*Crosbie (15),	28	20	2	3	3	Dublin.
Cross,	19	5	6	8	–	Dublin, Cork, and Armagh.
*Crossan (15),	17	1	–	16	–	Londonderry.
Crothers,	17	1	–	16	–	10 in Antrim and 5 in Down.
Crotty,	26	2	22	1	1	Clare, Waterford, and Cork.
*Crowe (62),	68	14	27	20	7	Antrim, Tipperary, and Clare.
*Crowley (149),	161	12	142	2	5	116 in Cork.
Crozier,	22	2	–	20	–	Armagh.
*Cruise (7),	8	7	–	–	1	Dublin.
Cryan,	15	–	–	–	15	10 in Roscommon.
Crymble,	6	–	1	5	–	Antrim.
*Cuddihy (5),	6	4	2	–	–	Kilkenny.
Cuddy,	8	3	2	1	2	—
*Cuffe (12),	14	5	2	–	7	Mayo and Wexford.
Culbert,	8	1	–	7	–	Antrim.
Culhane,	16	–	16	..	–	13 in Limerick.
Cull,	10	–	4	4	2	—
*Cullen (196),	203	132	13	34	24	Dublin and Wexford.
*Culleton (10),	12	11	–	–	1	Wexford.
Culligan,	5	–	3	1	1	Clare.
*Cullinane (26)-Cullinan (19),	50	4	37	2	7	" Cullinane," Cork and Waterford — " Cullinan," Clare.
Culloty,	6	–	6	–	–	All in Kerry.
*Cully (15),	22	9	–	11	2	Armagh and Antrim.
*Cumiskey (7),	11	5	–	6	–	Cavan, Longford, and Westmeath.
*Cummings (10),	20	4	2	12	2	Antrim.
Cummins,	77	37	25	11	4	Dublin, Cork, and Tipperary.
*Cunnane (16),	18	1	–	–	17	8 in Mayo and 5 in Roscommon.
*Cunniffe (11),	16	1	–	–	15	Galway, Mayo, and Roscommon.
*Cunningham (202),	215	40	35	89	51	Down, Antrim, Dublin, Galway, Roscommon, and Cork.
Cupples,	7	–	–	7	–	6 in Antrim and 1 in Armagh.
*Curley (28),	36	11	–	3	22	Roscommon, Galway, and Dublin.
*Curran (161),	169	42	37	67	23	Donegal, Dublin, Waterford, and Galway.
Currane,	19	–	19	..	–	All in Kerry.
Currid,	6	1	–	–	5	5 in Sligo and 1 in Wexford.
Corrigan	9	–	–	–	9	7 in Roscommon and 2 in Mayo.
Curry (60)-Currie (15),	75	15	8	48	4	29 in Antrim.
*Curtin (68),	69	1	68	–	–	All except 2 in Cork, Limerick, Clare, and Kerry.
Curtis,	23	20	2	1	–	Dublin.
Cusack,	46	5	23	11	7	Limerick, Cavan, and Clare.
*Cussen (6),	9	1	7	..	1	3 in Cork and 2 in Limerick.
Cuthbert,	7	4	1	2	–	3 in Dublin and 2 in Londonderry.
Dagg,	7	3	4	–	–	—
Dahill,	5	–	5	–	–	All in Tipperary.
Dallas,	6	–	1	5	–	Antrim.
Dalton,	75	38	31	2	4	Dublin, Waterford, Limerick, Kilkenny, and Westmeath.
*Daly (360),	381	109	182	49	41	Cork, Dublin, Kerry, Galway, and King's.
Dalzell,	12	–	–	12	–	Down.
Dansher,	8	2	6	–	–	6 in Limerick and 2 in Dublin.
*Daniel (16),	17	5	10	1	1	Dublin, Tipperary, and Waterford.
*Darby (10),	11	7	–	4	–	—
*Darcy (77),	86	40	24	11	11	Dublin and Tipperary.
Dardis,	6	6	–	–	–	—
*Dargan (11),	13	8	2	2	1	Dublin.
Darling,	5	3	–	1	1	—
Darmody,	12	4	7	–	1	Tipperary.
*Darragh (17),	18	–	–	18	–	Antrim.
*Davern (5),	8	1	6	–	1	4 in Tipperary.
*Davey (18)—Davy (12),	31	7	2	10	12	11 in Sligo and 6 in Antrim.
Davidson,	58	6	–	52	–	Antrim and Down.
*Davin (11),	12	–	5	1	6	Tipperary and Galway.
*Davis (95),	104	41	17	34	12	Dublin and Antrim.
*Davison (44),	45	3	–	42	–	Antrim.
Davitt,	8	2	–	2	4	—
Dawson,	55	14	10	28	3	Antrim.

TABLE showing the SURNAMES IN IRELAND having Five Entries and upwards in the Birth Indexes of 1890, together with the Number in each Registration Province, and the Registration Counties in which these Names are principally found—*continued.*

Names.	IRELAND.	Leinster.	Munster.	Ulster.	Connaught.	Counties in which principally found.
			NUMBER OF ENTRIES IN BIRTH INDEXES FOR 1890.			
Day, ...	13	5	5	3	–	—
Dea, ...	10	1	6	–	3	—
Deacon, ..	5	2	3	–	–	
Deady, ...	8	1	7	–	–	Kerry.
*Deane (35),	45	2	12	10	12	Mayo, Cork, and Donegal.
*Deasy (32), ..	35	–	24	2	9	24 in Cork and 9 in Mayo.
Dee, ...	16	1	14	–	1	Waterford, Cork, and Tipperary.
*Deegan (26), ..	28	23	3	1	1	Dublin, King's, and Queen's.
Deehan, ..	6	..	–	4	2	Londonderry.
*Deely (7),	8	–	2	–	6	Galway.
Deeney (8)—Deeny (7),	15	–	–	15	–	Donegal and Londonderry.
Deering, ...	6	3	–	3	–	Monaghan.
Deery, ...	14	–	..	14	–	Tyrone and Monaghan.
*Deevy (7), ..	9	6	1	2	–	Kilkenny.
Delahunt, ..	6	6	–	–	–	Kildare.
Delahunty, ..	10	4	6	–	–	
Delaney (93)—Delany (65),	158	97	38	10	13	Dublin, Queen's, Tipperary, and Kilkenny.
*Dempsey (108),	117	62	21	22	12	Dublin, Antrim, Cork, Wexford, and King's
*Dempster (12),	13	1	–	12	–	8 in Antrim and 4 in Down.
*Dennehy (30),	36	–	36	–	–	26 in Cork and 9 in Kerry.
*Dennis (7), ..	10	4	4	1	1	Dublin and Cork.
Dennison, ..	6	–	..	6	–	Armagh.
Derby, ...	6	–	1	5	–	Antrim.
Dermody, ..	9	7	1	–	1	
Dermott, ..	6	–	–	3	3	Leitrim.
Desmond, ..	34	1	32	1	–	32 in Cork.
Devane, ...	16	–	11	–	5	Kerry.
*Devany (15)—Devaney (11)—Devenny (8),	44	2	3	13	26	Mayo, Galway, and Leitrim.
*Dever (8)—Devers (6),	15	1	1	2	11	" Dever," all in Mayo—" Devers," 3 in Mayo.
Devereux, ..	16	12	3	1	–	8 in Wexford.
Devery, ..	5	5	–	–	–	4 in King's and 1 in Dublin.
*Devine (70), ..	81	25	9	35	12	Tyrone, Dublin, and Roscommon.
*Devitt (16), ..	17	7	7	1	2	Clare and Dublin.
*Devlin (102), ..	112	19	3	88	2	Antrim, Tyrone, Dublin, Armagh, and Londonderry.
*Diamond (13), ..	16	3	–	11	2	Londonderry and Antrim.
*Dick (12), ..	13	1	1	11	–	8 in Antrim and 2 in Down.
*Dickey (11), ..	13	–	–	13	–	Antrim.
Digan, ...	5	4	–	–	1	King's.
*Diggin (6) ..	8	–	8	–	–	7 in Kerry.
*Dignan (10), ..	11	10	–	1	–	Westmeath.
Dillane, ...	19	–	14	–	5	11 in Limerick, 5 in Galway, and 3 in Kerry.
*Dillon (116), ..	117	52	27	19	19	Dublin, Limerick, Antrim, and Galway.
Dinan, ...	14	1	12	–	1	7 in Cork.
*Dinneen (22)—Dineen (18),	42	–	39	–	3	29 in Cork.
Dinsmore, ..	6	–	–	6	–	Londonderry.
*Dirrane (13), ..	14	1	–	–	13	" Dirrane," all in Galway.
*Diskin (10), ..	14	–	–	–	14	" Diskin," all in Galway.
Diver, ...	29	–	1	27	1	26 in Donegal.
Dixon (51)—Dickson (49),	100	19	2	68	11	" Dixon," Dublin and Mayo—" Dickson," Down and Antrim.
*Dobbin (17), ..	21	5	1	15	–	Antrim.
Dobbs, ...	6	4	–	2	–	—
Dobson, ...	14	1	2	9	2	—
*Dockery (7), ..	9	1	–	–	8	Roscommon.
Dockrell, ..	5	5	–	–	–	Dublin.
*Dodds (18)—Dodd (12),	31	5	3	18	5	Down and Armagh.
*Doherty (414)—Dogherty (27),	457	29	52	318	58	Donegal, Londonderry, and Mayo—160 of the 414 births of persons named " Doherty," are in Donegal.
Dolan, ...	142	37	3	50	52	Fermanagh, Roscommon, Cavan, Galway, Leitrim, and Dublin.
Dollard, ...	5	4	–	1	–	—
*Donaghy (40), ..	49	–	–	48	1	Antrim, Londonderry, and Tyrone.
Donald, ...	6	–	–	6	–	Antrim.
Donaldson, ..	33	2	–	31	–	Antrim and Armagh.
*Donegan (23), ..	31	15	9	5	2	—
*Donnan (10), ..	11	–	–	10	1	9 in Down.

TABLE showing the SURNAMES IN IRELAND having Five Entries and upwards in the Birth Indexes of 1890, together with the Number in each Registration Province, and the Registration Counties in which these Names are principally found—*continued.*

Names.	NUMBER OF ENTRIES IN BIRTH INDEXES FOR 1890.					Counties in which principally found.
	IRELAND.	Leinster.	Munster.	Ulster.	Connaught.	
Donnell, ...	18	–	5	13	–	Londonderry, Tyrone, and Tipperary.
*Donnellan (19)—	76	11	13	4	48	"Donnellan," Clare and Mayo; "Donelan,"
Donelan(16)-Donlon						all in Galway; "Donlon," Longford;
(14)—Donlan (13),						"Donlan," Galway.
*Donnelly (228), ..	240	64	19	135	22	Antrim, Tyrone, Armagh, and Dublin.
*Donoghue (84), ..	97	6	82	2	7	Kerry and Cork.
*Donohoe (137), ..	162	83	26	28	25	Dublin, Longford, Cavan, and Galway.
Donovan, ...	211	14	194	2	1	175 in Cork.
Doody, ...	27	5	22	–	–	Limerick, Cork, and Waterford.
*Doogan (32)—Dougan	53	3	1	41	8	"Doogan," Donegal; "Dougan," Antrim
(13),						and Armagh.
Doohan, ...	11	–	3	7	1	7 in Donegal and 3 in Clare.
*Doolan (35)—Doolin	66	38	21	1	6	Dublin, Louth, Cork, and Tipperary.
(13),						
*Dooley (49), ...	60	33	12	5	10	Dublin and King's.
Doonan, ...	15	2	–	5	8	Leitrim and Roscommon.
Dooney, ...	5	–	–	–	5	Roscommon.
Doran, ...	97	60	13	20	4	Dublin, Wexford, Down, and Armagh
Dore, ...	12	1	11	–	–	9 in Limerick.
Dorgan, ...	13	2	11	–	–	9 in Cork.
Dorman, ...	14	1	2	11	–	7 in Down.
*Dornan (10), ..	11	–	–	11	–	All except 1 in Antrim and Down.
Dorney, ...	7	–	7	–	–	6 in Cork and 1 in Tipperary.
*Dorrian (5), ..	7	–	–	7	–	
*Douglas (47), ..	54	12	–	41	1	Antrim and Londonderry.
*Dowd (64), ...	84	18	15	16	35	Roscommon, Dublin, Kerry, and Galway.
*Dowdall (17), ..	20	19	–	1	–	Dublin and Louth.
Dowling, ...	109	83	15	6	5	Dublin, Kilkenny, and Queen's—half the Leinster entries are in Dublin.
*Downes (35), ...	47	15	21	8	3	Clare, Limerick, and Dublin.
*Downey (90), ...	91	16	42	22	11	Cork, Kerry, Antrim, Galway, and Limerick
Downing, ...	15	4	11	–	–	6 in Kerry and 5 in Cork.
Doyle, ...	514	391	59	37	27	This name is found in nearly every County of Ireland, but three-fourths of them are in Dublin, Wexford, Wicklow, Carlow, Kerry, and Cork.
Drain, ...	5	–	–	5	–	All in Antrim.
Drake, ...	6	1	–	5	–	Down and Monaghan.
Draper, ...	5	2	3	–	–	
*Drennan (19), ..	20	5	4	11	–	Antrim and Tipperary.
Drew, ...	12	7	5	–	–	Louth.
*Driscoll (120), ..	121	1	120	–	–	100 in Cork.
Drohan, ...	10	–	10	–	–	6 in Waterford and 4 in Cork.
Drought, ...	5	3	2	–	–	—
*Drum (12), ...	13	4	1	8	–	Fermanagh
Drummond, ...	6	1	1	4	–	Antrim.
*Drummy (6), ..	9	–	5	–	4	Cork and Sligo.
*Drury (10), ...	11	3	–	2	6	6 in Roscommon.
Duddy, ...	13	–	–	11	2	Londonderry.
Dudgeon, ...	6	1	–	5	–	—
*Dudley (5), ...	6	1	5	–	–	
*Duff (41), ...	45	21	1	21	2	Antrim, Dublin, and Louth.
Duffin, ...	17	3	4	10	–	Antrim and Waterford.
*Duffy (282), ..	305	82	2	126	95	Mayo, Monaghan, Donegal, Dublin, Louth, and Roscommon.
*Dugan (18), ..	20	2	–	16	2	Antrim, Down, and Londonderry.
Duggan, ...	89	22	54	5	8	Cork, Dublin, Tipperary, and Waterford.
Duhig, ...	7	–	7	–	–	5 in Cork and 2 in Kerry.
*Duignan (21), ..	22	8	1	1	12	6 in Leitrim and 6 in Roscommon.
Duke, ...	12	2	1	6	3	Armagh and Roscommon.
Dullaghan, ...	7	6	–	1	–	5 in Louth.
Dullard, ...	6	6	–	–	–	4 in Kilkenny and 2 in Queen's.
Dulles, ...	5	–	5	–	–	All in Cork.
*Dunbar (17), ..	26	11	–	13	2	Wexford, Antrim, Down, and Tyrone.
*Duncan (35), ..	41	8	1	25	7	Antrim and Tyrone.
Dundon, ...	12	3	9	–	–	Clare, Limerick, and Dublin.
Dunlea, ...	11	–	11	–	–	8 in Cork.
*Dunleavy (27), ..	40	6	5	6	23	Mayo and Sligo.
Dunlop, ...	35	2	–	33	–	21 in Antrim.

TABLE showing the SURNAMES IN IRELAND having Five Entries and upwards in the Birth Indexes of 1890, together with the Number in each Registration Province, and the Registration Counties in which these Names are principally found—*continued.*

Names.	NUMBER OF ENTRIES IN BIRTH INDEXES FOR 1890.					Counties in which principally found.
	IRELAND.	Leinster.	Munster.	Ulster.	Connaught.	
Dunne (313)—Dunn (51),	364	248	55	47	14	" Dunne "—Dublin, Queen's, Kildare, King's, Kilkenny, Cork, and Tipperary ; only 13 of the births registered under the name " Dunne " are found in Ulster—half of these being in Cavan. " Dunn "—Ulster contains 34 of the 51, which are chiefly in Antrim, Down, Londonderry, and Tyrone.
Dunphy, ...	34	24	10	–	–	Waterford and Dublin.
Dunwoody, ...	11	–	–	11	–	Antrim.
*Durkan (48), ..	62	3	–	1	58	35 in Mayo and 15 in Sligo.
*Durnin (6), ..	10	5	1	3	1	Louth.
*Dwane (11)—Duane (6),	22	2	13	–	7	" Dwane," Tipperary, Cork, and Kerry— " Duane," Galway.
*Dwyer (152), ...	155	38	107	2	8	80 per cent. are found in Tipperary, Cork, Dublin, Limerick, Kerry, and Kilkenny.
Dyas, ...	5	4	–	–	1	Dublin.
*Dyer (14), ...	16	2	–	2	12	Roscommon and Sligo.
Eagar (4)–Eager (3), ..	7	3	1	3	–	—
*Eakins (6)–Eakin (5),..	14	2	1	10	1	—
*Earl (5)–Earle (5),	16	10	2	3	1	—
*Early (37), ..	42	11	1	10	20	Leitrim.
Eaton, ...	8	2	2	4	–	Londonderry.
Eccles, ...	15	4	–	11	–	Tyrone and Antrim.
Edgar, ...	17	–	–	17	–	Antrim and Down.
*Edmonds (5), ..	10	2	5	3	–	—
Edwards	36	16	4	13	3	Dublin, Wexford, and Antrim.
*Egan (165), ..	171	60	40	2	69	Galway, Dublin, King's, Mayo, and Roscommon. The 40 in Munster are generally distributed.
*Elder (14), ...	16	5	–	11	–	7 in Antrim, and 4 in Londonderry.
*Elliott (71), ...	76	11	2	59	4	Fermanagh, Antrim, Donegal, and Dublin.
Ellis, ...	38	14	3	21	–	Dublin and Antrim.
Ellison, ...	13	1	–	12	–	8 in Antrim and 3 in Down.
*Elwood (10), ..	11	–	1	4	6	Mayo.
Emerson, ...	18	4	1	13	–	7 in Down and 4 in Antrim.
England, ...	5	1	2	2	–	
English, ...	53	14	19	17	3	Tipperary, Antrim, and Dublin contain more than 50 per cent.
Ennis, ...	44	36	2	4	2	Dublin and Kildare.
Enright, ...	49	4	43	–	2	21 in Limerick, 11 in Kerry, 8 in Cork, and 3 in Clare.
Erskine, ...	12	–	1	11	–	Antrim.
*Ervine (14), ...	19	–	1	18	–	10 in Antrim and 7 in Down.
*Erwin (18), ...	19	1	–	18	–	15 in Antrim.
Esler, ...	8	–	–	8	–	All in Antrim.
Eustace, ...	9	6	2	–	1	Dublin.
Evans, ...	55	22	11	19	3	Dublin, Londonderry, and Antrim.
*Evers (5), ...	9	7	–	–	2	4 in Longford and 3 in Dublin.
Ewart, ...	14	–	–	14	–	Antrim.
*Ewing (21), ...	24	1	–	23	–	Londonderry, Tyrone, and Antrim.
*Fagan (47), ...	48	42	2	4	–	50 per cent. of those in Leinster are in Dublin.
Faherty, ...	26	–	–	–	26	All in Galway.
Fahy (72)—Fahey (47),	119	6	31	3	79	Galway, Tipperary, and Mayo. Galway alone contains more than 50 per cent.
Fair, ...	6	2	–	2	2	—
*Fallon (68), ...	70	13	1	1	55	Roscommon and Galway.
*Falloon (9), ...	12	–	–	12	–	Armagh.
Falvey, ...	17	1	16	–	–	All except 1 in Cork, Clare, and Kerry.
*Fanning (22)—Fannin (13),	45	16	12	4	13	Wexford, Tipperary, and Waterford.
Farley, ...	7	2	2	3	–	—
Farmer, ...	6	–	1	3	2	—
Farnau, ...	10	5	–	5	–	—
Farr, ...	5	–	–	5	–	Antrim.
*Farragher (7), ..	9	–	–	–	9	5 in Mayo and 4 in Galway.
*Farist (6), ...	7	7	–	–	–	Wicklow.

TABLE showing the SURNAMES IN IRELAND having Five Entries and upwards in the Birth Indexes of 1890, together with the Number in each Registration Province, and the Registration Counties in which these Names are principally found—*continued.*

Names.	NUMBER OF ENTRIES IN BIRTH INDEXES FOR 1890.					Counties in which principally found.
	IRELAND.	Leinster.	Munster.	Ulster.	Connaught.	
*Farrell (302),	311	205	30	36	40	Found in every County, but chiefly in Dublin, Longford, Louth, Meath, Westmeath, and Roscommon.
Farrelly,	69	32	–	36	1	29 in Cavan, 14 in Meath, and 10 in Dublin.
*Farren (12),	13	2	–	11	–	7 in Donegal and 4 in Londonderry.
Farrington,	5	1	1	–	3	—
Farry,	5	1	1	1	2	—
Faughnan,	8	2	–	1	5	Leitrim.
*Faulkner (18),	35	11	2	21	1	Antrim.
Fay,	27	21	1	5	–	More than 50 per cent. are in Dublin.
Fearon,	21	5	–	16	–	Armagh, Down, and Louth.
*Fee (22),	23	–	–	21	2	Antrim, Cavan, and Fermanagh.
*Feehan (14),	17	7	6	1	3	Louth.
*Feely (28),	41	4	4	16	17	Donegal and Roscommon.
*Feeney (46)—Feeny (26),	73	13	5	11	44	"Feeney," Sligo, Mayo, and Galway "Feeny," Galway and Roscommon.
Feerick,	13	1	–	–	12	9 in Mayo and 3 in Galway.
Fegan,	26	12	–	14	–	Armagh, Dublin, and Louth.
*Fehily (6),	11	2	5	–	4	
*Fenlon (18),	28	28	–	–	–	11 in Carlow, 7 in Dublin, and 7 in Wexford.
*Fennell (28),	29	12	16	1	–	Clare and Dublin.
*Fennelly (14),	15	12	3	–	–	Kilkenny.
Fennessy,	8	–	7	1	–	Waterford.
Fenton,	19	1	11	6	1	Kerry and Antrim.
Fergus,	8	–	–	1	7	7 in Mayo.
*Ferguson (130),	133	11	1	107	14	Antrim, Down, and Londonderry.
*Ferris (32),	33	1	4	26	2	Antrim.
*Ferry (26),	27	1	–	26	–	22 in Donegal.
Fetherston,	6	3	–	..	3	3 in Dublin and 3 in Roscommon.
*Field (18),	29	15	8	6	–	12 in Dublin and 8 in Cork.
*Finan (9),	18	4	2	3	9	"Finan," 6 in Roscommon and 3 in Sligo.
*Finegan (52)-Finnegan (39),	115	37	10	38	30	"Finegan," Monaghan, Galway, and Louth—"Finnegan," Armagh and Cavan.
*Finlay (69),	76	17	1	54	4	Antrim and Down.
*Finn (110),	111	40	34	7	30	Cork, Mayo, Dublin, and Roscommon.
Finneran,	9	1	–	–	8	Galway.
*Finnerty (14)-Finerty (10),	28	2	9	–	17	Galway.
*Finney (7),	8	1	–	5	2	
Finucane,	10	–	10	–	–	
Fisher,	29	9	4	16	–	Antrim and Wicklow.
*Fitzgerald (327),	330	49	257	7	17	Generally distributed throughout Munster, but most numerous in Cork, Limerick, and Kerry. Those in Leinster are for the most part in Dublin.
*Fitzgibbon (31),	34	1	32	–	1	Limerick contains more than 50 per cent.
Fitzmaurice,	21	4	10	–	7	Kerry.
Fitzpatrick,	249	103	62	64	20	Generally distributed throughout the whole of Ireland, but Dublin and Queen's in Leinster—Cork and Tipperary in Munster—Cavan, Antrim, and Down in Ulster, and Mayo and Galway in Connaught, contain the largest numbers.
*Fitzsimons (70),	80	34	6	38	2	Dublin, Down, and Cavan.
Flack,	8	1	–	7	–	
*Flahavan (6),	12	–	12	–	–	Cork and Waterford.
Flaherty,	88	4	30	–	54	47 in Galway, and 16 in Kerry.
*Flanagan (173),	219	61	33	52	73	Roscommon, Dublin, Mayo, Clare, and Galway. The only counties in Ulster containing many entries of this name are Fermanagh, Cavan, and Monaghan.
*Flannery 59),	64	4	26	1	33	About 80 per cent. are in Mayo, Tipperary Galway, and Clare.
Flattery,	6	4	–	–	2	King's.
*Flattley (6),	11	1	–	–	10	10 in Mayo.
Flavell,	5	–	–	5	–	—
*Fleming (157),	170	42	28	63	37	Antrim, Dublin, Galway, Londonderry, Cork, and Mayo.
Fletcher,	22	6	6	10	–	Antrim and Dublin.
Flood,	64	45	1	15	3	20 in Dublin—Remainder generally distributed.

TABLE showing the SURNAMES IN IRELAND having Five Entries and upwards in the Birth Indexes of 1890, together with the Number in each Registration Province, and the Registration Counties in which these Names are principally found—*continued.*

Names.	NUMBER OF ENTRIES IN BIRTH INDEXES FOR 1890.					Counties in which principally found.
	IRELAND.	Leinster.	Munster.	Ulster.	Connaught.	
*Flynn (304), ...	319	71	140	23	85	Cork, Dublin, Waterford, Roscommon, and Leitrim—Cavan is the only Ulster county in which the name is found to any appreciable extent.
*Fogarty (57), ...	61	21	38	–	2	More than half in Tipperary and Dublin.
*Folan (26), ...	28	–	–	–	28	23 in Galway and 5 in Mayo.
*Foley (249), ...	250	57	167	7	19	Kerry, Cork, Waterford, and Dublin.
Folliard, ...	6	–	–	–	6	4 in Mayo and 2 in Roscommon.
*Foran (18), ...	26	8	18	–	–	Dublin, Limerick, and Waterford.
*Forbes (20), ...	22	3	2	14	3	Antrim and Tyrone.
*Forde (114)—Ford (39),	154	26	41	22	65	Galway, Cork, Mayo, and Dublin contain about two-thirds of the entries.
Foreman, ...	5	1	–	4	–	—
*Forkin (7), ...	11	–	–	–	11	All in Mayo.
*Forrest (8), ...	9	1	7	1	–	Cork.
*Forsythe (29), ...	33	1	1	30	1	Antrim and Down.
Fortune, ...	22	20	1	1	–	17 in Wexford.
*Foster (51), ...	57	13	3	37	4	Antrim and Dublin.
Fowler, ...	17	6	1	10	–	—
*Fox (124), ...	125	53	13	34	25	Dublin, Longford, Tyrone, and Leitrim. Representatives of this name are found in every County in Ireland.
Foy, ...	38	8	2	14	14	Mayo, Cavan, and Dublin.
Fraher, ...	5	–	5	–	–	4 in Waterford and 1 in Limerick.
*Frain (16), ...	20	2	1	–	17	" Frain," 10 in Mayo and 6 in Roscommon.
*Francey (8), ...	10	1	–	9	–	7 in Antrim.
Francis, ...	13	1	5	7	–	—
Franklin, ...	12	2	9	1	–	Limerick and Tipperary.
*Frawley (19), ...	20	–	20	–	–	10 in Clare and 6 in Limerick.
Frazer (27)—Fraser (14),	41	8	5	21	7	Dublin, Antrim, and Down.
*Freeburn (7), ...	9	–	–	9	–	Antrim.
Freeman, ...	20	8	3	4	5	—
*French (23), ...	24	7	3	8	6	Antrim.
*Friel (40), ...	43	–	–	38	5	27 in Donegal, 6 in Tyrone, and 5 in Londonderry.
*Frizell (6), ...	12	–	–	11	1	—
Frost, ...	7	1	5	–	1	—
Fry, ...	9	6	–	2	1	Dublin.
*Fulham (5), ...	8	8	–	–	–	7 in Dublin and 1 in King's.
Fuller, ...	6	2	4	–	–	Cork.
Fullerton, ...	25	3	–	22	–	Antrim and Down.
Fulton, ...	32	–	–	32	–	Antrim
Furlong, ...	36	33	3	–	–	26 in Wexford.
Fury (10)—Furey (7),	17	2	–	2	13	Galway.
Gabbey, ...	5	–	–	5	–	3 in Down and 2 in Antrim.
*Gaffey (9), ...	10	–	–	–	10	7 in Roscommon and 3 in Galway.
Gaffney, ...	68	29	2	20	17	Cavan, Dublin, and Roscommon contain 43 entries.
Gahan, ...	11	10	1	–	–	Wexford.
Galbraith, ...	15	2	–	13	–	Antrim.
*Gallagher (471), ...	488	28	21	295	144	Donegal, Mayo, Tyrone, Sligo, Londonderry, and Dublin; Donegal alone furnishing two-thirds of those in Ulster.
*Gallen (10), ...	13	–	–	13	–	7 in Donegal and 4 in Tyrone.
*Galligan (25), ...	26	2	2	21	1	20 in Cavan.
*Gallivan (31), ...	32	–	30	1	1	24 in Kerry.
Galloway, ...	9	–	–	8	1	Antrim.
*Galvin (60), ...	62	10	40	1	11	Cork, Clare, Kerry, and Roscommon.
*Galway (12), ...	13	–	2	11	–	8 in Antrim.
*Gamble (38), ...	40	4	6	29	1	Antrim, Down, and Londonderry.
*Ganley (7), ...	11	2	–	2	7	—
*Gannon (71), ...	73	29	–	1	43	Mayo, Dublin, and Leitrim.
Gara, ...	20	–	–	10	10	9 in Donegal, 6 in Roscommon, 4 in Mayo, and 1 in Down.
*Gardiner (25), ...	26	6	2	14	4	Antrim and Dublin.
Gardner, ...	23	1	1	20	1	Antrim.
Gargan, ...	7	4	–	3	–	—
*Garland (13), ...	24	10	1	12	1	Dublin and Monaghan.

TABLE showing the SURNAMES IN IRELAND having Five Entries and upwards in the Birth Indexes of 1890, together with the Number in each Registration Province, and the Registration Counties in which these Names are principally found—*continued.*

Names.	IRELAND.	Leinster.	Munster.	Ulster.	Connaught.	Counties in which principally found.
Garrett, ...	24	7	3	13	1	Down, Antrim, and Dublin.
Garry, ...	14	8	1	2	3	—
*Garvey (60), ...	64	11	21	10	22	Kerry, Mayo, Galway, and Louth.
Garvin, ...	5	-	-	1	4	—
Gaskin, ...	5	3	-	2	-	Dublin.
Gaston, ...	13	-	-	13	-	All in Antrim.
*Gately (10), ...	11	1	1	-	9	8 in Roscommon.
*Gaughan (25), ..	26	-	-	-	26	25 in Mayo and 1 in Sligo.
Gaughran, ...	5	5	-	-	-	4 in Meath and 1 in Louth.
Gaul (6)—Gaule (5), ..	11	7	4	-	-	4 Wexford, 4 Waterford, 2 Kilkenny, and 1 Kildare.
Gault, ...	16	1	-	15	-	13 in Antrim.
*Gavaghan (13), ..	23	5	-	5	13	"Gavaghan," 10 Mayo, and 3 Sligo.
*Gavin (44)—Gavan (19),	66	11	8	3	44	Of the Connaught entries under this name 30 are in Mayo and 12 in Galway.
Gaw, ...	6	-	-	6	-	4 in Down and 2 in Antrim.
Gawley, ...	6	-	-	3	3	Sligo.
*Gaynard (5), ...	6	-	-	-	6	5 in Mayo.
*Gaynor (21), ...	22	15	2	3	2	Dublin, Westmeath, and Cavan.
Geaney (8)—Geany (7),	15	-	14	-	1	13 in Cork.
*Geary (24), ...	26	3	18	2	3	Cork.
Geddis, ...	13	-	-	13	-	Antrim and Down.
Geelan, ...	6	1	1	-	4	—
*Geoghegan (33), ..	38	19	4	-	15	Dublin and Galway.
George, ...	12	1	2	9	-	—
*Geraghty (54), ..	72	28	2	-	42	Galway, Mayo, and Dublin.
Getty, ...	8	-	-	8	-	6 in Antrim and 2 in Londonderry.
*Gibb (5), ...	8	1	2	4	1	—
*Gibbons (76), ...	78	8	3	10	57	47 in Mayo and 7 in Galway.
*Giblin (29), ...	30	1	-	-	29	19 in Roscommon and 6 in Mayo.
Gibney, ...	26	15	-	11	-	Cavan and Dublin.
Gibson, ...	96	13	2	77	4	Down and Antrim.
*Giffen (8), ...	10	2	-	8	-	Antrim.
Gilbert, ...	16	9	1	5	1	Dublin and Antrim.
*Gilchrist (12), ...	18	4	-	12	2	—
*Gildea (13), ...	18	1	3	7	7	Donegal and Mayo.
Giles, ...	6	3	1	1	1	—
*Gilgan (8), ...	13	1	-	1	11	7 in Sligo.
*Gilhooly (8), ...	9	-	1	1	7	Leitrim.
Gill, ...	62	20	5	10	27	More than half are in Dublin, Galway, Mayo, and Longford.
*Gillan (18)—Gillen (16),	40	7	-	23	10	"Gillan," Antrim and Sligo—"Gillen," Antrim, Donegal, and Tyrone.
*Gilleece (6), ...	14	-	1	13	-	There are six varieties of this name in the Births Index for 1890.
*Gillespie (84), ...	86	3	-	76	7	Antrim, Donegal, Armagh, and Tyrone.
Gillick, ...	9	-	1	8	-	8 in Cavan.
Gilligan, ...	32	14	2	5	11	Dublin.
Gilliland, ...	11	-	-	11	-	Antrim.
Gilmartin, ...	24	-	-	1	23	14 in Sligo and 8 in Leitrim.
*Gilmore (54)—Gilmour (18),	79	5	2	60	12	Antrim.
Gilpin, ...	9	-	-	9	-	7 in Armagh and 2 in Cavan.
Gilroy, ...	16	1	-	7	8	Leitrim and Mayo.
*Gilsenan (6), ...	12	7	-	5	-	—
Ginn, ...	6	1	1	4	-	—
*Ginty (16), ...	19	1	-	-	18	Mayo.
*Girvin (8)—Girvan (6),	15	-	-	15	-	11 in Antrim.
Glancy, ...	5	1	-	1	3	—
Glasgow, ...	7	-	-	7	-	4 in Tyrone, 2 in Antrim, and 1 in Armagh.
Glass, ...	17	-	-	17	-	Antrim and Londonderry.
Glavin, ...	7	-	7	-	-	4 in Cork and 3 in Kerry.
*Gleeson (81), ...	82	18	63	-	1	38 in Tipperary and 13 in Limerick—The remainder are principally in Dublin, Kilkenny, and Cork.
Glenn, ...	12	-	-	12	-	Antrim and Londonderry.
*Glennon (22), ...	28	18	-	3	7	—
Glover, ...	20	3	1	16	-	Antrim.
*Glynn (66), ...	72	15	11	1	45	About 70 per cent. are in Galway Mayo, Dublin, and Clare.

TABLE showing the SURNAMES IN IRELAND having Five Entries and upwards in the Birth Indexes of 1890, together with the Number in each Registration Province, and the Registration Counties in which these Names are principally found—*continued.*

Names.	NUMBER OF ENTRIES IN BIRTH INDEXES FOR 1890.					Counties in which principally found.
	IRELAND.	Leinster.	Munster.	Ulster.	Connaught.	
*Godfrey (17),	18	3	6	4	5	Mayo, Tipperary, and Kerry.
*Godkin (6,)	7	5	1	–	1	Wexford.
Gogarty,	7	5	1	1	–	Meath and Louth.
*Goggin (26),	34	4	26	–	4	The Munster entries are nearly all in Cork and Kerry.
*Golden (22),	24	2	7	–	15	Mayo, Sligo, Kerry, and Cork.
*Good (16),	19	1	12	3	3	11 in Cork.
Goodbody,	5	5	–	–	–	—
Goodman,	9	2	–	7	–	Armagh and Monaghan.
*Goodwin (24),	26	10	2	13	1	Dublin and Monaghan.
Goold,	6	–	5	1	–	Cork.
*Gordon (118),	122	22	3	82	15	Antrim, Down, and Dublin. More than half the Ulster entries are in Antrim.
*Gorham (11),	12	–	–	–	12	All in Galway.
Gorman,	140	57	40	33	10	Antrim, Dublin, and Tipperary—but generally distributed in the counties of Leinster and Munster.
*Gormley (31),	44	5	1	25	13	Antrim and Tyrone.
Gough (17)—Goff (13),	30	15	10	4	1	Dublin and Waterford.
*Gould (10),	12	–	4	8	–	—
*Goulding (15)-Golding (9),	27	9	11	1	6	" Goulding," Dublin and Cork—" Golding," Galway.
*Gourley (20),	23	3	–	20	–	Antrim.
Gowen,	5	1	4	–	–	Cork.
Grace,	36	21	15	–	–	Dublin and Kilkenny.
Gracey,	9	–	1	8	–	Down and Armagh.
Grady	68	11	31	1	25	Mayo, Clare, Kerry, and Roscommon.
*Graham (195),	204	28	5	166	5	Antrim, Down, Dublin, Tyrone, Armagh, and Monaghan.
*Grainger (9),	11	4	3	–	–	—
Grange	6	3	–	3	–	3 in Dublin and 3 in Antrim.
Grant,	77	21	13	42	1	Antrim and Donegal.
*Grattan (3),	5	–	–	5	–	—
*Graves (5),	6	3	2	1	–	—
*Gray (97),	117	33	7	70	7	Antrim, Down, Londonderry, and Dublin.
*Graydon (6),	7	6	–	1	–	—
Gready,	22	5	11	–	6	Tipperary.
*Grealish (6),	7	–	–	–	7	" Grealish," all in Galway.
*Greally (9),	15	1	–	–	14	9 in Galway and 5 in Mayo.
*Greany (19),	30	4	17	–	9	Kerry and Galway.
Greehy,	8	–	5	–	–	3 in Waterford and 2 in Cork.
Green (105)—Greene (47),	152	39	37	54	22	Dublin, Antrim, Galway, Tipperary, and Clare.
Greenan,	8	2	1	5	–	Cavan.
Greenaway,	7	1	–	6	–	Down and Antrim.
Greer,	63	2	2	58	1	Antrim, Armagh, and Down—more than half being in Antrim.
Gregan,	5	4	1	–	–	—
Gregg,	29	6	2	21	–	10 in Antrim and 9 in Down.
Gregory,	14	7	1	5	1	—
*Grehan (22),	23	11	1	–	11	Mayo, Galway, Sligo, and Westmeath.
*Grennan (18),	19	11	–	–	8	Mayo and Dublin.
*Gribben (18),	28	1	–	27	–	All except 3 in Antrim, Armagh, and Down.
*Griffin (206),	216	31	133	16	36	Kerry, Clare, Cork, Limerick, Galway, Mayo, and Dublin—very few in any other County except Tipperary and Waterford.
*Griffith (16),	22	9	3	8	2	—
Grimason,	5	–	–	5	–	Armagh.
Grimes,	39	15	4	13	7	Tyrone and Mayo.
Grimley,	7	1	1	5	–	Armagh.
*Groarke (7),	9	1	–	–	8	Mayo.
*Grogan (39),	44	16	13	5	10	Dublin, Tipperary, Mayo, and Clare.
Groves,	8	–	4	4	–	Kerry and Antrim.
*Gubbins (5),	7	–	5	2	–	Limerick.
*Guerin (11),	12	–	11	1	–	Limerick.
*Guihen (7),	10	–	1	–	9	" Guihen," all in Roscommon.
Gulfoyle,	11	9	–	–	2	Dublin.
*Guinan (13)—Guinane (7),	21	11	7	–	3	"Guinan," 10 in King's Co.—" Guinane," 5 in Tipperary.
*Guiney (16),	17	–	13	4	–	Cork.
Guiry,	8	1	7	–	–	6 in Limerick.

Table showing the Surnames in Ireland having Five Entries and upwards in the Birth Indexes of 1890, together with the Number in each Registration Province, and the Registration Counties in which these Names are principally found—*continued.*

Names.	IRELAND.	Leinster.	Munster.	Ulster.	Connaught.	Counties in which principally found.
Gunn,	9	4	–	5	–	—
Gunning,	12	4	–	7	1	Antrim.
Gurry,	5	3	–	–	2	—
*Guthrie (9),	11	1	5	4	1	Clare.
Guy,	11	3	–	8	–	Armagh and Londonderry.
*Hackett (30),	34	14	8	11	1	Tyrone, Dublin, and Kilkenny.
*Haddock (10),	12	1	1	10	–	Armagh.
Haddon (8)—Hadden (6),	14	2	2	10	–	
Hagan (49)	63	12	–	49	2	Antrim, Tyrone, and Armagh.
*Hale (8),	13	–	6	6	1	Cork and Antrim.
*Halfpenny (8),	12	5	2	5	–	Louth.
Hall,	120	37	13	69	1	Antrim, Dublin, and Armagh.
*Hallahan (4),	8	–	8	–	–	Cork.
*Halliday (18),	19	2	–	16	1	Antrim.
Halligan,	27	10	–	8	9	Roscommon, Dublin, Louth, Armagh, and Mayo.
*Hallinan (9),	10	–	6	–	4	Clare.
*Hallissy (6),	12	–	12	–	–	7 in Cork and 5 in Kerry.
*Halloran (65),	67	2	51	–	14	Clare, Galway, and Cork.
Hally,	13	2	11	–	–	Tipperary.
Halpin,	33	18	12	3	–	Dublin and Clare.
Halton,	9	6	–	3	–	Meath.
*Hamill (68),	77	17	2	56	2	Antrim, Armagh, and Louth.
*Hamilton (166),	167	10	8	143	6	Antrim, Down, Tyrone, and Londonderry.
Hammond,	13	1	3	9	–	Donegal.
Hampton,	5	1	–	4	–	—
Hand,	28	18	4	6	–	Dublin.
*Hanifin (6)—Hanafin (5),	17	–	17	–	–	15 in Kerry.
*Hanlon (93),	95	50	24	20	1	Dublin, Kerry, Louth, and Wexford.
Hanly (60)—Hanley (35),	95	10	39	2	44	"Hanly," Roscommon, Galway, Limerick, and Tipperary—"Hanley," Cork.
*Hanna (81),	86	1	1	84	–	34 in Antrim, 26 in Down, and 10 in Armagh.
*Hannigan (25),	30	7	10	12	1	Dublin, Waterford, and Tyrone.
*Hannon (44)—Hannan (32),	92	14	28	10	40	Galway, Roscommon, Limerick, Cork, and Sligo.
Hanrahan,	54	9	42	1	2	Clare and Limerick.
Hanratty,	30	14	–	16	–	12 in Louth, 9 in Armagh, 7 in Monaghan, and 2 in Dublin.
Hanvey,	5	1	–	4	–	—
Hara,	5	–	–	–	5	All in Galway.
*Haran (16)—Haren (11),	37	1	8	11	17	"Haran," Mayo—"Haren," Clare.
Harbison,	11	–	1	10	–	Antrim.
Hardiman,	7	1	–	–	6	Galway.
Harding,	17	8	7	2	–	Dublin and Tipperary.
Hardy,	19	9	1	8	1	Louth, Dublin, and Tyrone.
*Hare (11)—Haire (10),	22	1	3	13	–	Antrim.
*Harford (16),	17	14	–	2	1	11 in Dublin.
*Hargadon (8),	11	–	–	–	11	9 in Sligo, 1 in Leitrim, and 1 in Roscommon
*Hargan (5),	6	–	1	4	1	
*Harkin (53),	56	3	1	45	7	32 in Donegal and 8 in Londonderry.
Harkness,	13	1	1	10	1	Antrim.
Harley,	7	–	3	3	1	—
*Harmon (7),	12	8	2	2	–	Wicklow.
Harnett,	15	2	13	–	–	10 in Limerick and 3 in Kerry.
Harney,	11	2	4	–	5	3 in Tipperary and 3 in Galway.
Harold (9)—Harrold (6),	15	3	11	1	–	"Harold," Cork—"Harrold," Limerick.
*Harper (32)—Harpur (18),	51	15	2	34	–	"Harper," Antrim—"Harpur," Wexford.
*Harrell (4),	5	4	–	1	–	
Harrington,	119	7	99	1	12	82 in Cork, 11 in Kerry, and 7 in Mayo.
*Harris (58),	59	21	21	15	2	Dublin, Cork, and Antrim.
*Harrison (44),	48	11	4	27	6	Antrim, Dublin, and Down.
Hart (64)—Harte (58),	122	27	16	28	51	"Hart," Antrim, Dublin, and Cork—"Harte," Sligo, Leitrim, and Roscommon.
Hartigan,	16	4	10	–	2	Limerick.
*Hartin (5),	10	5	–	5	–	Antrim and Longford.

TABLE showing the SURNAMES IN IRELAND having Five Entries and upwards in the Birth Indexes of 1890, together with the Number in each Registration Province, and the Registration Counties in which these Names are principally found—*continued.*

Names.	NUMBER OF ENTRIES IN BIRTH INDEXES FOR 1890.					Counties in which principally found.
	IRELAND.	Leinster.	Munster.	Ulster.	Connaught.	
*Hartnett (24),	27	2	25	–	–	10 in Limerick and 13 in Cork.
Hartney,	8	2	5	1	–	3 in Limerick and 2 in Clare.
Harty, ..	17	1	16	–	–	Tipperary, Cork, and Kerry.
*Harvey (53), ..	54	12	5	35	2	Antrim, Dublin, Down, and Donegal.
Haslam, ..	6	5	–	1	–	Dublin.
Hassard,	7	1	–	6	–	—
Hassett, ..	11	1	10	–	–	Clare and Tipperary.
Hastings,	22	4	6	3	9	8 in Mayo and 5 in Clare.
Hatton, ..	7	4	–	3	–	—
Haugh (20)—Hough (7),	27	1	24	2	–	" Haugh," 13 in Clare—" Hough," 4 in Tipperary and 3 in Limerick.
Haughey,	14	–	–	14	–	5 in Armagh, and 5 in Donegal.
Haughton,	9	5	1	2	1	—
*Hawe (7),	10	4	3	3	–	—
Hawes, ..	5	1	3	–	1	—
*Hawkes (6), ..	7	–	5	2	–	Cork.
Hawkins,	18	5	3	6	4	Antrim, Galway, and Cork.
*Hawthorne (15),	27	2	1	23	1	Antrim, Down, and Armagh.
*Hay (5), ..	6	–	1	5	–	Dublin, Carlow, and Tipperary.
*Hayden (43), ..	45	28	9	2	6	Dublin, Carlow, and Tipperary.
*Hayes (271), ..	275	57	181	27	10	Cork, Limerick, Tipperary, Dublin, and Wexford. Antrim is the only County in Ulster, and Galway in Connaught, in which the name is found to any appreciable extent.
Hazlett (10)—Haslett (9).	19	2	–	15	2	Antrim and Londonderry.
*Healy (272), ..	291	50	151	6	84	About two-thirds are found in Cork, Kerry, Dublin, Galway, Roscommon, and Mayo.
*Heaney (39),	56	18	2	32	4	Antrim, Armagh, and Louth.
Heanue, ..	14	–	–	5	9	8 in Galway and 5 in Donegal.
Heaphy, ..	8	2	6	–	–	Cork.
Hearne (6)—Hearn (5),	11	2	8	1	–	8 in Waterford.
Hearty, ..	8	6	–	2	–	6 in Louth and 2 in Monaghan.
*Heavey (6)-Heavy (5),	12	7	2	–	3	—
*Heelan (6),	7	2	5	–	–	Waterford.
Heenan, ..	6	–	3	3	–	Tipperary.
Heffernan,	53	16	36	–	1	Tipperary.
*Heffron (7), ..	20	4	2	–	14	" Heffron," all in Mayo—these 20 entries contain 7 varieties.
Hegan, ..	5	1	–	4	–	Armagh.
*Hegarty (96), ..	100	6	56	27	11	Four-fifths are found in Cork, Donegal, Clare, Londonderry, and Mayo.
*Hehir (24),	28	1	22	–	5	18 in Clare and 4 in Limerick.
Hemphill,	7	–	–	6	1	Londonderry and Tyrone.
Henderson,	72	12	1	57	2	Antrim and Tyrone.
Hendrick,	12	10	1	1	–	7 in Dublin.
*Henehan (14)—Heneghan (11).	49	1	2	–	46	Mayo.
*Henneberry (7),	13	2	11	–	–	Waterford and Tipperary.
*Hennessy (95),	111	31	74	3	3	Cork, Limerick, Tipperary, and Dublin.
*Henry (124), ..	132	17	1	73	41	Antrim, Sligo, and Tyrone.
*Heraghty (12),	16	–	–	6	10	Mayo and Donegal.
Herbert, ..	25	8	12	4	1	Dublin and Limerick.
Herdman,	6	–	–	6	–	Antrim.
*Herlihy (38),	42	1	41	–	–	29 in Cork and 11 in Kerry.
*Hernon (6),	8	2	–	1	5	5 in Galway.
Herron (23)-Heron (22),	45	5	1	38	1	13 in Antrim, and 10 each in Donegal and Down.
Heslin, ..	8	3	–	1	4	Leitrim.
*Hession (17),	21	–	–	2	19	15 in Galway and 4 in Mayo.
Hester, ..	8	1	–	–	7	4 in Mayo and 3 in Roscommon.
*Hetherington (7),	8	1	–	7	–	Tyrone.
*Hewitt (36),	40	4	5	31	–	Antrim and Armagh.
*Hickey (132), ..	139	45	82	7	5	Cork, Tipperary, Dublin, Limerick, and Clare.
Hicks, ..	10	3	2	5	–	—
*Higgins (203),	205	45	32	23	105	Mayo, Galway, Dublin, Roscommon, Cork, and Antrim.
Higginson,	8	–	–	8	–	Antrim.
Hill, ..	118	26	14	71	7	Antrim, Dublin, and Down.
*Hilland (6),	7	–	–	7	–	6 in Antrim and 1 in Down.
Hilliard ..	11	6	2	3	–	Dublin.

Table showing the Surnames in Ireland having Five Entries and upwards in the Birth Indexes of 1890, together with the Number in each Registration Province, and the Registration Counties in which these Names are principally found—*continued.*

Names.	NUMBER OF ENTRIES IN BIRTH INDEXES FOR 1890.					Counties in which principally found.
	IRELAND.	Leinster.	Munster.	Ulster.	Connaught.	
*Hillis (10),	12	5	–	6	1	Antrim.
Hilton,	6	2	3	1	–	—
*Hinchy (7),	14	3	10	1	–	—
Hinds (14)—Hynds (6),	20	2	–	13	5	Down and Roscommon.
*Hoare (18),	30	8	20	–	2	Kerry, Cork, and Dublin.
Hoban,	22	6	4	–	12	10 in Mayo and 6 in Kilkenny.
Hobbs,	5	2	1	2	–	—
Hobson,	11	3	1	7	–	Antrim.
Hodges (6)—Hodge (6),	12	4	3	5	–	—
*Hodgins (11)—Hodgen (5).	19	4	7	8	–	" Hodgins," Tipperary—" Hodgen," Down.
Hodnett,	5	–	5	–	–	4 in Cork and 1 in Tipperary.
Hoey,	33	22	4	6	1	Louth and Dublin.
Hogan,	193	59	115	5	14	Tipperary, Dublin, Limerick, Clare, and Cork.
*Hogg (17),	18	1	2	14	1	Antrim and Londonderry.
Holden,	20	10	4	5	1	Dublin, Waterford, and Antrim.
Holland,	52	10	22	12	8	Cork, Galway, and Dublin.
*Holleran (6),	9	–	–	–	9	6 in Galway and 3 in Mayo.
Holly,	8	1	3	4	–	Londonderry and Cork.
Hollywood,	9	5	–	4	–	Louth.
Holman,	5	–	2	1	2	—
*Holmes (81),	84	24	11	38	11	Antrim and Dublin.
Holt,	8	5	–	2	1	—
Homan,	5	3	2	–	–	—
Hood,	9	2	–	5	2	Antrim.
Hope,	6	2	3	–	1	—
Hopkins,	44	12	2	6	24	Mayo and Dublin—nearly one-half being in the former County.
Hopper,	8	1	–	4	3	Tyrone.
Horan,	63	12	26	2	23	Mayo, Kerry, Tipperary, and Roscommon.
Horgan,	66	–	66	–	–	40 in Cork and 21 in Kerry.
*Horne (4),	6	2	2	2	–	—
Horner,	6	1	–	5	–	Antrim.
Hornibrook,	5	–	5	–	–	All in Cork.
Horrigan,	7	–	7	–	–	Cork.
Hosford,	10	1	9	–	–	9 in Cork.
Hosty,	6	–	–	–	6	5 in Mayo and 1 in Galway.
*Houlihan (38)—Holohan (11).	71	20	49	–	2	" Houlihan," Kerry, Limerick, Cork, and Clare—" Holohan," Kilkenny.
*Hourigan (17),	22	4	17	1	–	Limerick and Tipperary.
*Hourihane (9),	16	–	16	–	–	15 in Cork.
*Houston (49)—Huston (19).	76	4	3	68	1	Antrim, Londonderry, Armagh, and Down.
Howard,	61	20	25	8	8	Dublin, Cork, Clare, and Limerick.
Howe,	16	4	5	6	1	—
Howell,	8	3	4	1	–	Cork.
Howlett,	5	5	–	–	–	3 in Wexford and 2 in Dublin.
Howley,	14	–	4	1	9	Clare, Mayo, and Sligo.
*Howlin (5),	6	6	–	–	–	All in Wexford.
Hoy,	15	1	–	13	1	9 in Antrim and 2 in Down.
*Hoyne (5),	6	6	–	–	–	Kilkenny.
Hudson,	23	15	3	3	2	Dublin.
Huggard,	8	3	2	1	2	—
*Hughes (328),	334	92	7	180	55	Armagh, Antrim, Dublin, Tyrone, Monaghan, Galway, and Mayo.
Hughey,	6	–	–	6	–	Tyrone.
Hull,	10	–	–	9	1	Antrim and Armagh.
*Hume (8),	10	1	–	9	–	Antrim.
*Humphries (15),	32	7	7	18	–	Armagh and Dublin.
Hunt,	76	14	16	4	42	Mayo, Roscommon, Dublin, and Waterford.
Hunter,	95	7	4	80	4	Antrim, Londonderry, and Down.
*Hurley (129),	134	15	113	–	6	86 in Cork, 10 in Waterford, 9 in Dublin, and 6 in Galway.
Hurson,	5	2	–	3	–	Longford and Tyrone.
Hurst,	10	1	–	5	4	—
*Hussey (21),	26	7	9	1	9	Kerry, Galway, and Roscommon.
*Hutchinson (44)—Hutchison (15).	64	13	3	45	3	Londonderry, Antrim, Down, and Dublin.
Hutton,	15	4	–	11	–	Antrim and Londonderry.
*Hyde (11),	15	1	7	7	–	Cork and Antrim.
Hyland,	55	28	9	5	13	Mayo, Dublin, and Queen's.

TABLE showing the SURNAMES IN IRELAND having Five Entries and upwards in the Birth Indexes of 1890, together with the Number in each Registration Province, and the Registration Counties in which these Names are principally found—*continued.*

Names.	IRELAND.	Leinster.	Munster.	Ulster.	Connaught.	Counties in which principally found.
Hyndman,	14	–	–	14	–	8 in Antrim and 5 in Londonderry.
*Hynes (81),	83	20	20	6	37	Galway, Clare, Mayo, and Dublin.
*Igoe (6),	10	3	–	–	7	3 in Longford, 3 in Mayo, and 3 in Roscommon.
*Ingram (12),	13	1	1	11	–	9 in Antrim.
Ireland,	21	3	1	17	–	Antrim and Armagh.
*Irvine (66),	68	3	1	62	2	Antrim and Fermanagh.
Irwin,	118	3	12	96	7	Armagh, Antrim, Tyrone, and Londonderry
*Ivers (8),	11	8	–	2	1	Dublin and Louth.
*Ivory (8),	9	8	–	1	–	Dublin.
Jack,	8	1	2	5	–	—
*Jackson (100),	101	20	12	60	9	Scattered, but chiefly found in Antrim, Armagh, and Dublin. In Munster, Cork contributes the largest number, and in Connaught, Mayo.
*Jacob (9),	11	9	1	1	–	Dublin.
*Jagoe (4),	6	–	5	–	1	5 in Cork.
James,	12	7	2	3	–	—
*Jamison (24)-Jameson (20)—Jamieson (7).	52	10	1	41	–	"Jamison" and "Jamieson," 16 in Antrim and 9 in Down—"Jameson," Dublin.
*Jeffers (12),	16	4	6	3	3	
*Jenkins (25),	29	6	1	19	3	Antrim and Dublin.
Jenkinson,	7	6	–	1	–	Dublin.
*Jennings (61),	63	6	11	12	34	About 75 per cent. in Mayo, Galway, Cork, and Armagh.
Jess,	7	–	–	7	–	All in Down.
Johnson,	58	18	21	16	3	Cork, Dublin, and Antrim. A scattered name.
Johnston (320)—Johnstone (21).	341	43	4	281	13	"Johnston," Antrim, Down, Armagh, Fermanagh, and Dublin, but found in nearly every county in Ireland. "Johnstone," Cavan and Londonderry.
Jolly,	5	4	–	–	1	Dublin.
Jones,	152	60	38	45	9	Though found in nearly every County, considerably more than half are in Dublin, Cork, Antrim, and Armagh.
*Jordan (91),	98	36	10	21	31	Dublin, Mayo, Antrim, and Galway.
*Joy (14),	15	1	10	3	1	Waterford.
Joyce,	164	15	17	1	131	85 in Galway and 46 in Mayo.
Judge,	30	9	1	6	14	Mayo, Dublin, and Tyrone.
*Kane (175),	190	57	10	96	27	Antrim, Londonderry, and Dublin.
*Kavanagh (230),	274	205	27	22	20	Dublin, Wexford, and Wicklow—Dublin alone containing 50 per cent. of the entries in Leinster.
Keady,	16	2	2	–	12	11 in Galway.
*Keane (185),	202	13	113	6	70	Galway, Clare, Kerry, and Mayo.
*Keany (18),	33	1	–	8	24	Leitrim, Galway, and Donegal.
*Kearney (137),	147	50	31	45	21	Found all over Ireland, but chiefly in Dublin, Cork, and Antrim.
*Kearns (71),	87	35	10	16	26	Dublin and Mayo.
Kearon,	7	7	–	–	–	All in Wicklow.
*Keating (121),	130	43	74	10	3	Cork, Kerry, Tipperary, and Dublin.
*Keaveny (15),	33	–	–	1	32	Galway and Sligo.
Kee,	6	–	–	6	–	
*Keeffe (93),	110	29	76	1	4	Cork, Waterford, Kerry, and Kilkenny.
*Keegan (93),	95	61	5	8	21	Dublin, Roscommon, Wicklow, and Leitrim.
Keena,	7	4	–	1	2	
Keenan,	103	34	1	57	11	Antrim, Monaghan, Dublin, and Down.
Keith,	7	–	1	6	–	Antrim and Down.
Kell,	6	–	–	5	1	5 in Antrim.
*Kelleher (92)—Kelliher (24).	148	2	124	5	17	92 in Cork and 23 in Kerry.
*Kellett (7),	8	4	–	4	–	Cavan and Dublin.
Kells,	10	4	–	5	1	—

TABLE showing the SURNAMES IN IRELAND having Five Entries and upwards in the Birth Indexes of 1890, together with the Number in each Registration Province, and the Registration Counties in which these Names are principally found—*continued.*

Names.	IRELAND.	Leinster.	Munster.	Ulster.	Connaught.	Counties in which principally found.
		NUMBER OF ENTRIES IN BIRTH INDEXES FOR 1890.				
*Kelly (1,238), ...	1,242	435	211	267	329	Found in every County in Ireland—chiefly, however, in Dublin, Galway, Mayo, Roscommon, and Cork.
Kelso, ...	7	2	–	5	–	Antrim.
Kemp, ...	6	–	2	4	–	—
Kempton, ...	5	–	–	5	–	Antrim.
Kenna, ...	21	13	7	–	1	Dublin and Tipperary.
*Kenneally (10)—Kennelly (9).	36	1	35	–	–	Cork, Waterford, and Tipperary.
*Kennedy (436), ..	446	123	149	112	62	Found in every County—largest numbers in Tipperary, Dublin, and Antrim.
*Kenny (211), ...	216	95	31	19	71	Dublin, Galway, and Roscommon.
Kenrick, ...	5	1	4	–	–	—
Kent, ...	13	4	9	–	–	Cork.
*Keogh (96)—Kehoe (51).	163	127	25	4	7	"Keogh," Dublin—"Kehoe," Wexford.
*Keohane (21), ...	25	1	23	1	–	"Keohane," all in Cork.
*Keon (8)—Keown (8),	18	–	–	14	4	Donegal, Down, and Fermanagh.
*Kerin (15), ...	17	1	14	2	–	Kerry and Clare.
Kerley, ...	8	6	2	–	–	Louth.
*Kernaghan (11)—Kernohan (8).	26	3	2	20	1	"Kernaghan," Armagh—"Kernohan," all in Antrim.
Kerr, ...	142	12	2	123	5	Antrim, Down, and Tyrone—50 per cent. of those in Ulster being in Antrim.
Kerrane, ...	7	–	–	–	7	5 in Mayo and 2 in Galway.
*Kerrigan (37), ..	41	12	1	11	17	Mayo and Donegal.
Kerrisk, ...	5	–	5	–	–	All in Kerry.
Kerwick, ...	5	3	2	–	–	Kilkenny.
*Kevane (13), ...	19	1	16	1	1	14 in Kerry.
Keys (22)—Keyes (10),	32	9	8	15	..	"Keys," Fermanagh and Antrim—"Keyes," Tipperary and Wexford.
Kidd, ...	28	9	1	18	–	Antrim, Armagh, and Dublin.
Kidney, ...	7	–	7	–	–	All in Cork.
*Kielty (6), ...	9	–	–	2	7	Galway and Roscommon.
*Kiely (36)—Keely (27) —Kealy (18)—Keily (10)—Keeley (9).	110	44	51	3	12	"Kiely" and "Keily," Cork, Limerick, and Waterford—"Keely" and "Keeley," Dublin, Wicklow, and Galway—"Kealy," Kilkenny.
*Kiernan (56), ...	70	45	1	14	10	Almost wholly confined to the Counties of Longford, Cavan, Dublin, and Leitrim.
Kilbane, ...	8	–	–	–	8	All in Mayo.
Kilbride, ...	7	3	–	–	4	—
Kilcoyne, ...	15	–	–	–	15	10 in Mayo and 4 in Sligo.
Kilcullen, ...	6	1	–	–	5	5 in Sligo.
Kilduff, ...	5	3	–	–	2	—
Kilgallon, ...	8	–	–	–	8	All in Mayo.
Kilgannon, ...	8	–	–	–	8	4 in Galway and 4 in Sligo.
*Kilkelly (6), ...	7	–	–	–	7	Galway and Roscommon.
Kilkenny, ...	18	1	–	1	16	Leitrim, Mayo, and Roscommon.
Killeen, ...	40	12	16	..	12	Clare, Mayo, and King's.
*Killelea (6), ...	10	–	–	–	10	7 in Galway and 3 in Roscommon.
Killen, ...	14	3	2	8	1	6 in Antrim.
*Killian (13), ...	18	8	–	..	10	8 in Roscommon and 5 in Westmeath.
Killoran, ...	7	–	–	–	7	Roscommon and Sligo.
Kilmartin, ...	22	8	6	–	8	Roscommon.
Kilpatrick	24	–	–	24	..	16 in Antrim.
Kilroy, ...	15	–	–	1	14	6 in Mayo, 5 in Roscommon, and 3 in Sligo.
*Kinahan (7), ...	15	11	3	–	1	Dublin and Louth.
*Kinane (9)—Kinnane (6),	18	1	16	–	1	Tipperary.
King, ...	203	43	47	51	62	Galway, Dublin, Antrim, Mayo, and Limerick.
Kinghan, ...	5	–	–	4	1	4 in Down and 1 in Mayo.
Kingston, ...	40	3	37	–	–	37 in Cork and 3 in Dublin.
Kinnear, ...	5	1	1	3	–	—
*Kinsella (75), ...	81	73	6	–	2	Dublin, Wexford, Wicklow, and Kildare.
Kirby, ...	33	5	17	3	8	Mayo, Kerry, and Limerick.
*Kirk (28), ...	38	12	4	19	3	Antrim and Louth.
Kirkland, ...	6	–	–	5	1	—
Kirkpatrick, ...	25	–	1	22	2	16 in Antrim.;
Kirkwood, ...	8	–	1	7	–	7 in Antrim and 1 in Limerick.
*Kirrane (6), ...	8	–	–	–	8	"Kirrane," all in Mayo.

Table showing the Surnames in Ireland having Five Entries and upwards in the Birth Indexes of 1890, together with the Number in each Registration Province, and the Registration Counties in which these Names are principally found—*continued.*

Names.	Ireland.	Leinster.	Munster.	Ulster.	Connaught.	Counties in which principally found.
		Number of Entries in Birth Indexes for 1890.				
*Kirwan (42), ...	59	40	13	3	3	Dublin, Wexford, and Tipperary.
Kissane, ...	19	–	18	–	1	16 in Kerry.
*Kitterick (5), ..	6	1	–	–	5	" Kitterick," all in Mayo.
Knight, ...	13	4	4	3	2	
Knowles, ...	13	7	1	5	–	Dublin and Antrim.
Knox, ...	45	5	6	32	2	Antrim.
Kyle, ...	26	1	1	23	1	Antrim and Londonderry.
Kyne, ...	27	–	–	–	27	26 in Galway and 1 in Mayo.
*Lacey (21)—Lacy (19) —Leacy (8).	50	36	9	1	4	Wexford, Dublin, and Galway.
Laffan, ...	8	3	5	–	–	Limerick, Tipperary, and Wexford.
Lafferty, ..	17	–	–	17	–	10 in Donegal, 5 in Londonderry, and 2 in Tyrone.
*Laffey (5), ..	7	–	–	1	6	4 in Galway and 1 in Mayo.
Lagan, ...	8	–	1	7	–	Londonderry.
*Lahey (4), ..	7	1	3	–	3	—
Lahiff, ...	8	3	5	–	–	Dublin and Clare.
Laird, ...	17	–	–	16	1	Antrim.
*Lally (33), ..	34	1	1	2	30	17 in Mayo and 11 in Galway.
Lamb (37)—Lambe (13),	50	26	6	13	5	Dublin.
Lambert, ..	22	13	1	4	4	Wexford and Dublin.
*Lamont (16), ..	18	2	–	16	–	11 in Antrim.
*Landers (18), :.	19	1	16	–	2	Waterford and Kerry.
Landy, ...	9	1	4	–	4	Tipperary and Galway.
Lane, ...	69	10	49	3	7	38 in Cork and 10 in Limerick.
Lang, ...	15	–	–	10	5	Cavan.
Langan, ..	19	6	1	2	10	Mayo.
Langton, ..	6	4	1	–	1	—
*Lanigan (18), ..	21	14	5	1	1	Kilkenny.
*Lannon (7), ..	11	8	1	–	2	Kilkenny.
Lappin, ...	26	2	–	24	–	Armagh, Tyrone, and Antrim.
Larkin, ...	85	34	19	20	12	Dublin, Armagh, Galway, and Tipperary.
*Larmour (15), ..	17	–	–	17	–	9 in Antrim and 6 in Down.
Latimer, ..	8	4	–	4	–	Dublin.
*Lavelle (33), ..	38	–	–	4	34	28 in Mayo and 5 in Galway.
Laverty, ..	26	–	–	26	–	Antrim.
Lavery, ...	51	–	–	51	–	Armagh, Antrim, and Down.
Lavin (28), Lavan (14),	42	1	–	–	41	22 in Mayo and 13 in Roscommon.
*Law (18), ...	19	1	2	16	–	Antrim.
Lawder (3), Lauder (3),	6	4	1	1	–	
Lawless, ...	42	21	3	4	14	13 in Dublin and 12 in Galway, the remaining 17 being scattered over 14 counties.
Lawlor (59)—Lalor (42) —Lawler (41),	142	115	25	2	–	Dublin, Queen's, Wicklow, and Wexford.
*Lawn (6), ..	7	–	–	7	–	5 in Donegal and 2 in Tyrone.
*Lawrence (1 2),— Laurence (7).	19	12	3	3	1	Dublin and Tipperary.
Lawson, ..	15	3	1	10	1	Dublin, Armagh, and Down.
Lawton, ..	10	1	7	2	–	7 in Cork.
*Leahy (99), ..	105	13	82	7	3	Cork, Kerry, Limerick, and Tipperary.
*Leane (9), ..	11	–	11	–	–	9 in Kerry and 2 in Limerick.
*Leary (185), ..	186	38	142	3	3	93 in Cork, 38 in Kerry, and 21 in Wexford.
*Leathem (8), ..	11	–	2	9	–	Armagh.
*Leavy (22), ..	31	22	6	2	1	Longford and Westmeath.
*Leckey (6), ..	10	–	1	9	–	—
Leddy, ...	15	3	2	9	1	9 in Cavan.
*Ledwith (5), ..	10	9	–	–	1	Dublin.
*Lee (118), ..	120	33	21	43	23	A very scattered name, but 50 per cent. are found in Antrim, Dublin, Galway, and Limerick.
*Leech (28), ..	35	14	4	9	8	Dublin.
Lees, ...	6	2	2	2	–	
Leeson, ...	6	3	1	2	–	Dublin.
*Legge (6), ..	8	1	2	5	–	—
*Lehane (23), ..	30	–	30	–	–	29 in Cork and 1 in Kerry.
Leigh, ...	8	8	–	–	–	—
*Lemon (13), ..	15	1	–	12	1	Antrim.
*Lennon (102), ..	103	49	6	36	12	Dublin and Armagh.

TABLE showing the SURNAMES IN IRELAND having Five Entries and upwards in the Birth Indexes of 1890, together with the Number in each Registration Province, and the Registration Counties in which these Names are principally found—*continued.*

Names.	IRELAND.	Leinster.	Munster.	Ulster.	Connaught.	Counties in which principally found.
		NUMBER OF ENTRIES IN BIRTH INDEXES FOR 1890.				
Lennox, ..	18	3	1	13	1	Antrim and Londonderry.
Leo, ..	5	–	5	–	–	All in Limerick.
Leonard, ..	99	31	15	18	35	Dublin, Sligo, and Cork.
Leslie, ..	15	3	3	9	–	Londonderry.
Lester, ..	5	1	2	2	–	—
L'Estrange,	8	8	–	–	–	—
*Levins (6),	7	7	–	–	–	—
Lewis, ..	51	16	16	18	1	About 70 per cent. in Dublin, Antrim, Cork, and Tipperary.
*Leyden (10), ..	11	1	4	1	5	Sligo and Clare.
*Liddane (6), ..	7	1	5	–	1	Clare.
*Liddy (8), ..	9	–	6	3	–	6 in Clare and 3 in Antrim.
Liggett, ..	6	1	–	5	–	3 in Armagh and 2 in Antrim.
Lightbody, ..	6	–	–	6	–	All in Down.
Lillis, ..	5	–	4	–	1	—
Lilly (8)—Lilley (6), ..	14	–	–	13	1	Antrim and Down.
Linane (10)-Linnane (5),	15	–	13	–	2	Limerick, Kerry, and Clare.
*Lindsay (36), ..	38	5	1	31	1	50 per cent. in Antrim.
*Linehan (50)-Lenaghan (18)-Lenihan (14),	104	7	63	7	27	"Linehan," 41 in Cork—"Lenaghan," Antrim—"Lenihan," Limerick.
Linton, ..	13	1	1	11	–	Antrim.
*Lipsett (6), ..	7	–	2	4	1	—
Liston, ..	12	–	11	–	1	10 in Limerick.
*Little (43)-Lyttle (14),	59	15	1	42	1	Antrim, Dublin, and Fermanagh.
Livingston (19)—Livingstone (14)—Levingston (10),	43	1	4	37	1	Armagh, Antrim, and Down.
*Lloyd (19), ..	20	4	8	3	5	Tipperary.
*Locke (5), ..	8	4	2	1	1	—
Lockhart, ..	21	2	–	17	2	Armagh and Antrim.
Loftus, ..	34	3	2	–	29	23 in Mayo.
Logan, ..	55	9	3	39	4	Antrim.
Logue, ..	31	–	–	31	–	17 in Londonderry and 9 in Donegal.
*Lohan (12), ..	14	–	1	–	13	11 in Galway.
Lombard, ..	6	–	6	–	–	All in Cork.
*Lonergan (49)—Londrigan (5),	56	10	46	–	–	Tipperary, Waterford, Kilkenny, and Cork.
Long, ..	91	19	46	21	5	Cork, Dublin, Limerick, Kerry, and Donegal.
Looby (11)—Luby (5),	16	4	9	–	3	Tipperary.
*Looney (22), ..	23	–	23	–	–	Cork and Clare.
Lord, ..	5	2	1	2	–	—
*Lordan (12), ..	13	–	13	–	–	All in Cork.
*Lorimer (7), ..	8	–	1	7	–	6 in Antrim.
*Lougheed (5), ..	7	2	1	3	1	—
*Loughlin (39)-Laughlin (14),	57	18	7	22	10	"Loughlin," Leitrim, Dublin, and Kilkenny "Laughlin," Tyrone and Antrim.
*Loughman (9), ..	10	4	5	–	1	—
*Loughnane (10), ..	13	1	6	–	6	—
*Loughran (37), ..	41	6	–	35	–	Tyrone, Antrim, and Armagh.
*Loughrey (12), ..	13	2	1	8	2	—
Love, ..	22	5	2	15	–	Londonderry.
Lovett, ..	9	2	6	1	–	6 in Kerry.
*Lowe (18), ..	21	10	1	9	1	Dublin.
Lowney, ..	6	–	6	–	–	All in Cork.
*Lowry (53), ..	71	21	4	37	9	Dublin, Antrim, and Down.
Loy, ..	5	1	–	4	–	—
Lucas, ..	22	5	5	12	–	Tyrone and Cavan.
*Lucey (29), ..	42	1	41	–	–	35 in Cork and 4 in Kerry.
Luke, ..	9	3	–	6	–	6 in Antrim.
Lundy, ..	12	1	–	7	4	—
Lunn, ..	9	2	–	6	1	Armagh.
*Lunney (11)-Lunny (9),	24	1	–	20	3	Fermanagh.
*Lydon (49), ..	57	1	–	–	56	33 in Galway and 22 in Mayo.
Lyle, ..	5	–	–	5	–	4 in Antrim.
Lynagh, ..	6	1	1	3	1	—
Lynam, ..	22	19	1	–	2	Dublin and King's.
*Lynas (10)-Lyness (9),	23	–	–	23	–	Antrim and Down.
Lynch, ..	444	125	184	94	39	Found in nearly every county, but chiefly in Cork, Cavan, Dublin, Kerry, Limerick, Clare, Meath, and Londonderry.
Lyne, ..	17	–	17	–	–	16 in Kerry.

TABLE showing the SURNAMES IN IRELAND having Five Entries and upwards in the Birth Indexes of 1890, together with the Number in each Registration Province, and the Registration Counties in which these Names are principally found—*continued*.

Names.	NUMBER OF ENTRIES IN BIRTH INDEXES FOR 1890.					Counties in which principally found.
	IRELAND.	Leinster.	Munster.	Ulster.	Connaught.	
Lynn,	24	6	–	15	3	Antrim.
*Lynskey (9),	11	–	–	–	11	6 in Galway and 5 in Mayo.
Lyons,	210	34	85	20	71	Mayo, Cork, Galway, Dublin, Kerry, and Limerick. Of the 34 in Leinster, 22 are in Dublin.
*Lysaght (12),	13	–	12	–	1	Limerick.
Mack,	20	2	11	7	–	Limerick, Tipperary, and Antrim.
Macken (29)—Mackin (9),	38	15	2	8	13	" Macken," Mayo, Louth, and Dublin—" Mackin," Monaghan.
*Mackey (33),	38	11	15	10	2	Dublin, Cork, Tipperary, and Antrim.
Mackle,	8	–	–	8	–	Armagh.
*Madden (106),	107	21	33	16	37	Galway, Cork, Dublin, and Antrim.
*Maddock (7),	10	6	2	1	1	Wexford.
*Madigan (26),	27	1	26	–	–	16 in Limerick and 7 in Clare.
Madill,	5	1	–	4	–	—
*Magauran (9),	10	–	–	10	–	8 in Cavan.
Magee (138)—McGee (55),	193	28	4	150	11	" Magee," Antrim, Armagh, and Down—" McGee," Donegal and Tyrone.
Magill (65)—McGill (19),	84	10	4	69	1	" Magill," Antrim, Armagh, and Down—" McGill," Donegal and Tyrone.
*Magner (12),	17	–	17	–	–	15 in Cork and 2 in Limerick.
*Magrane (12)-McGrane (8),	22	20	–	2	–	16 in Dublin.
Maguire (248)-McGuire (74),	322	85	27	156	54	" Maguire," Fermanagh, Dublin, Cavan, and Donegal—" McGuire," Roscommon and Mayo.—This name, however, is generally distributed.
Maher (170)—Meagher (27),	203	91	107	3	2	Tipperary, Dublin, and Kilkenny contain nearly 50 per cent.
*Mahon (85),	87	40	3	16	28	Dublin and Galway.
*Mahony (243),	276	17	256	–	3	182 in Cork, 37 in Kerry, and 13 in Limerick.
Mahood,	8	–	–	8	–	Antrim and Down.
Mailey,	6	–	–	6	–	Antrim.
*Mairs (8),	12	1	–	10	1	Antrim.
Maitland,	7	–	–	7	–	—
Major,	12	–	–	12	–	Antrim and Down.
Malcolm,	10	2	–	8	–	Antrim.
Malcomson (11)—Malcolmson (3),	14	2	1	11	–	Armagh.
*Malley (65),	85	4	2	3	76	62 in Mayo and 14 in Galway.
*Mallon (44),	48	7	1	38	2	Armagh, Antrim, and Tyrone.
Malone,	100	63	17	11	9	Dublin, Wexford, and Clare.
Malseed,	5	–	–	5	–	3 in Donegal and 2 in Londonderry.
*Mangan (50),	52	18	22	2	10	Dublin, Limerick, Kerry, and Mayo.
*Manley (15),	21	9	7	2	3	Cork and Wicklow.
Mann,	19	1	2	16	–	12 in Antrim.
Manning,	54	22	27	2	3	Cork and Dublin.
*Mannion (73),	91	7	1	5	78	Galway and Roscommon.
Mannix,	6	–	6	–	–	3 in Cork and 3 in Kerry.
Mansfield,	13	2	11	–	–	Cork and Kerry.
Markey,	16	7	–	9	–	Dublin and Monaghan.
Markham,	5	–	4	–	1	Clare.
*Marks (13),	19	–	2	17	–	12 in Antrim.
*Marley (12),	14	–	–	9	5	Donegal and Mayo.
Marlow,	7	3	–	4	–	Dublin and Tyrone.
*Marron (23)—Marren (6),	31	3	–	21	7	" Marron," Monaghan—" Marren," Sligo.
Marsh,	5	4	–	1	–	—
*Marshall (58),	59	11	4	42	2	Antrim, Londonderry, Down, and Dublin.
*Martin (325),	326	74	34	186	32	Found all over Ireland—principally in Antrim. Down, Dublin, and Monaghan.
Mason,	32	10	11	10	1	Dublin.
*Massey (10),	11	3	2	6	–	Down.
Masterson,	47	31	–	12	4	Dublin, Longford, and Cavan.
*Matchett (12),	14	–	–	14	–	Armagh, Antrim, and Down.
Mateer,	9	–	–	8	1	7 in Antrim.
Mathers,	9	1	1	7	–	Armagh.
*Mathews (51)—Matthews (26),	78	38	5	32	3	Louth, Dublin, Antrim, and Down.

Table showing the Surnames in Ireland having Five Entries and upwards in the Birth Indexes of 1890, together with the Number in each Registration Province, and the Registration Counties in which these Names are principally found—*continued*.

Names.	NUMBER OF ENTRIES IN BIRTH INDEXES FOR 1890.					Counties in which principally found.
	IRELAND.	Leinster.	Munster.	Ulster.	Connaught.	
Maughan, ...	9	2	–	–	7	Mayo.
Mawhinney (10)— Mawhinny (8),	18	–	–	18	–	Antrim.
Maxwell, ...	68	16	3	46	3	Antrim, Down, and Dublin.
*May (25), ...	28	7	4	6	11	Sligo.
Mayberry (9)-Maybury (3),	12	3	3	4	2	"Mayberry," Antrim—"Maybury," 2 in Kerry and 1 in Limerick.
*Mayes (6), ..	7	–	–	7	–	Antrim and Armagh.
*Mayne (13), ..	16	1	1	14	–	Antrim.
*McAdam (21),	25	2	–	23	–	Monaghan.
*McAfee (8), ..	11	–	–	11	–	Antrim.
*McAleavey (5),	10	–	–	10	–	Down and Armagh.
McAleer, ..	17	1	–	16	–	13 in Tyrone.
*McAleese (10), ..	12	–	–	12	–	Antrim and Londonderry.
*McAlinden (19),	24	–	–	24	–	17 in Armagh.
*McAllen (6)—McCallan (5),	13	–	2	10	1	Antrim.
*McAllister (40)— McAlister (34),	87	7	2	78	–	Antrim.
McAloney, ..	5	–	–	5	–	4 in Antrim and 1 in Down.
McAndrew, ..	16	–	–	–	16	All in Mayo.
*McAneny (9)— McEneaney (8)— McEneany (5),	32	7	–	25	–	"McAneny," all in Tyrone.—"McEneaney" Louth—"McEneany," Monaghan.
*McArdle (45), ..	55	24	–	31	–	Nearly all in Louth Monaghan, and Armagh.
McAree, ...	6	–	–	6	–	3 in Antrim and 3 in Monaghan.
McAtamney, ..	6	–	–	6	–	Londonderry.
McAteer, ..	36	–	–	34	2	Armagh, Antrim, and Donegal.
*McAuley (49)-McCauley (30),	107	6	–	90	11	Antrim and Donegal.
*McAuliffe (39),	40	–	40	–	–	29 in Cork.
McBarron, ..	5	–	–	5	–	4 in Fermanagh and 1 in Donegal.
McBratney, ..	5	–	–	5	–	3 in Antrim and 2 in Down.
McBrearty, ..	8	–	–	8	–	Tyrone and Donegal.
McBride, ..	118	10	2	105	1	Antrim, Donegal, and Down.
*McBrien (13), ..	16	1	1	12	2	Fermanagh and Cavan.
*McBurney (11)—Mc-Birney (6).	19	–	1	18	–	Down and Antrim.
McCabe, ...	145	44	8	84	9	Cavan, Monaghan, and Dublin.
*McCafferty (24),	25	–	–	25	–	14 in Donegal 7 in Londonderry, and 4 in Antrim.
*McCaffrey (31),	61	5	–	56	–	Fermanagh and Tyrone.
McCahon, ..	6	–	–	6	–	Antrim.
McCallion, ..	24	–	–	24	–	Londonderry and Donegal.
McCambridge, ..	9	–	–	9	–	8 in Antrim and 1 in Donegal.
McCamley, ..	5	1	–	4	–	—
*McCandless (5), ..	7	–	–	7	–	Antrim.
*McCann (175)	177	47	3	105	22	Antrim, Armagh, Dublin, and Tyrone.
*McCarroll (9), ..	13	–	–	13	–	Londonderry.
McCarron, ..	33	–	–	32	1	Donegal and Londonderry.
McCarry, ..	5	–	–	5	–	Donegal.
*McCart (5), ..	6	–	–	6	–	Antrim.
*McCartan (21), ..	35	2	–	29	4	Down and Armagh.
McCarter, ..	9	–	–	9	–	Antrim and Londonderry.
*McCarthy (481), ..	498	35	438	19	6	Cork—in which more than one-half are found —Kerry, and Limerick. Dublin and Antrim are the only Counties outside Munster in which an appreciable number is found.
*McCartney (44), ..	53	7	–	46	–	29 in Antrim.
*McCaughan (7), ..	10	–	–	10	–	Antrim.
*McCaughey (23), ..	24	–	1	23	–	Antrim and Tyrone.
*McCaul (12)-McCall (11)	24	2	2	20	–	Armagh and Cavan.
McCausland, ..	16	3	–	13	–	Antrim.
McCaw, ...	9	–	1	7	1	Antrim.
McClafferty, ..	11	–	–	11	–	10 in Donegal and 1 in Tyrone.
*McClatchey (7), ..	8	1	–	7	–	Antrim and Armagh.
*McClay (5), ..	7	–	–	7	–	Londonderry and Donegal.
*McClean (54)—McLean (43).	106	15	5	81	5	Antrim and Derry.
*McCleary (14), ..	19	–	–	19	–	Antrim and Londonderry.

TABLE showing the SURNAMES IN IRELAND having Five Entries and upwards in the Birth Indexes of 1890, together with the Number in each Registration Province, and the Registration Counties in which these Names are principally found—*continued.*

Names.	NUMBER OF ENTRIES IN BIRTH INDEXES FOR 1890.					Counties in which principally found
	IRELAND.	Leinster.	Munster.	Ulster.	Connaught.	
*McClelland (57),	66	7	2	57	–	Antrim, Down, Armagh, Londonderry, and Monaghan.
*McClenaghan (8)— McLenaghan (5).	19	–	1	18	–	Antrim.
McClintock,	25	2	–	23	–	Antrim and Londonderry.
*McClory (10),	11	1	–	10	–	Down.
*McCloskey (47)— McCluskey (24).	79	10	1	67	1	" McCloskey," 35 in Londonderry— " McCluskey," Antrim and Dublin.
McCloy,	14	–	–	14	–	Antrim.
McClughan,	5	–	–	5	–	3 in Antrim and 2 in Down.
McClung,	7	–	–	7	–	—
McClure,	35	2	2	31	–	Antrim and Down.
McClurg,	10	–	–	10	–	5 in Antrim and 5 in Down.
*McCole (9),	12	1	–	11	–	11 in Donegal.
McColgan,	16	–	–	16	–	Donegal and Londonderry.
*McCollum (10),	19	–	–	19	–	Antrim, Tyrone, and Donegal.
*McComb (23),	26	4	–	22	–	Antrim, Down, and Londonderry.
*McConaghy (14),	16	–	–	16	–	Antrim.
McConkey,	17	3	1	13	–	Antrim.
*McConnell (98),	101	8	2	89	2	Antrim, Down, and Tyrone.
McConnon,	9	6	–	3	–	Louth.
*McConville (24),	29	1	–	26	2	Armagh and Antrim.
McCoo,	10	–	–	10	–	7 in Armagh and 3 in Antrim.
McCool,	22	–	–	22	–	Donegal and Tyrone.
McCord,	15	3	–	12	–	Antrim.
*McCormack (111),	118	48	22	20	28	Found in nearly every county — chiefly Dublin, Mayo, Roscommon, and Limerick.
*McCormick (164),	165	40	2	107	16	Antrim, Dublin, and Down.
McCorry,	16	–	–	16	–	Armagh and Down.
*McCoubrey (5),	11	–	–	11	–	7 in Down and 4 in Antrim.
McCourt,	44	13	–	29	2	Louth, Armagh, and Antrim.—12 of the 13 Leinster entries are in Louth.
McCoy,	41	7	2	30	2	Antrim, Armagh, and Monaghan.
McCracken,	33	1	1	31	–	15 in Antrim and 8 in Down.
*McCrea (28),	33	2	1	30	–	Antrim and Tyrone.
*McCready (27),	39	6	1	32	–	Down, Antrim, and Londonderry.
McCrery,	5	2	–	3	–	—
McCreesh,	6	–	–	6	–	Monaghan.
McCrohan,	5	–	5	–	–	All in Kerry.
*McCrory (32),	34	–	–	33	1	17 in Tyrone and 10 in Antrim.
*McCrossan (13),	14	–	–	14	–	11 in Tyrone.
McCrudden,	8	1	–	7	–	Antrim.
McCrum,	8	2	–	6	–	—
*McCullough (69)— McCullagh (40).	130	16	2	106	6	Antrim, Tyrone, and Down.—The form " McCullough " appears to be peculiar to Antrim and Down.
McCully,	5	1	–	4	–	—
McCune,	8	–	–	8	–	6 in Antrim and 2 in Armagh.
*McCurdy (15),	19	–	–	19	–	17 in Antrim and 2 in Londonderry.
*McCurry (11),	12	–	–	12	–	Antrim.
McCusker,	19	2	–	17	–	Tyrone.
*McCutcheon (25),	27	1	2	24	–	Tyrone, Antrim, and Down. [Tyrone.
*McDaid (35),	48	3	–	45	–	26 in Donegal, 8 in Londonderry, and 7 in
*McDaniel (8),	9	1	2	5	1	—
*McDermott (176),	189	42	5	55	87	Roscommon, Dublin, Donegal, Galway, and Tyrone.—Half of those in Connaught are in Roscommon.
*McDevitt (13),	15	–	–	14	1	Donegal, Londonderry, and Tyrone.
*McDonagh (100),	174	13	11	9	141	Galway, Roscommon, and Mayo.
*McDonald (173),	191	89	10	88	4	Dublin, Antrim, Cavan, Wexford, and Carlow.
*McDonnell (237),	247	71	49	58	69	Dublin, Mayo, Antrim, Galway, and Cork.— Very generally distributed throughout the entire country.
*McDowell (89),	91	9	–	80	2	Antrim and Down—very few found elsewhere.
McEldowney,	6	–	–	6	–	All in Londonderry.
*McElhinney (17),	26	–	1	24	1	Donegal, Tyrone, and Londonderry.
McElligott,	24	1	23	–	–	10 in Kerry.
McElmeel,	6	–	–	6	–	Monaghan.
McElwee,	7	–	–	7	–	5 in Donegal and 2 in Londonderry.
McEnroe,	9	3	–	6	–	6 in Cavan.
McEntee,	13	2	–	11	–	Monaghan and Cavan.

TABLE showing the SURNAMES IN IRELAND having Five Entries and upwards in the Birth Indexes of 1890, together with the Number in each Registration Province, and the Registration Counties in which these Names are principally found—*continued*.

Names.	NUMBER OF ENTRIES IN BIRTH INDEXES FOR 1890.					Counties in which principally found
	IRELAND.	Leinster.	Munster.	Ulster.	Connaught.	
*McErlain (11)—McErlean (8).	21	–	–	21	–	13 in Antrim and 8 in Derry.
*McEvoy (85), ..	99	54	6	36	3	Dublin, Louth, Armagh, and Queen's.
*McFadden (72),	79	2	1	73	3	Donegal, Antrim, and Londonderry.
*McFall (20), ..	24	1	–	23	–	16 in Antrim and 7 in Londonderry.
McFarland,	46	2	–	44	–	Tyrone and Armagh.
*McFarlane (7),	12	4	–	8	–	—
*McFeeters (6),	7	–	–	7	–	Londonderry.
McFerran, ..	7	1	–	6	–	6 in Antrim.
*McFetridge (8),	9	–	–	9	–	6 in Antrim and 3 in Londonderry.
McGahan, ..	13	7	–	6	–	7 in Louth.
*McGahey (12),	13	–	–	13	–	Antrim and Monaghan.
*McGann (18), ..	21	9	3	3	6	—
*McGarry (64),	79	21	–	29	29	Antrim, Dublin, Roscommon, and Leitrim—very few elsewhere.
*McGarvey (28), ..	30	1	–	29	–	18 in Donegal and 5 in Londonderry.
McGaughey, ..	7	–	–	7	–	3 in Antrim and 3 in Armagh.
McGeady, ..	5	–	–	5	–	All in Donegal.
McGeary, ..	8	1	–	7	–	Tyrone.
*McGeehan (7), ..	11	–	–	11	–	9 in Donegal.
McGeough, ..	11	3	–	8	–	Monaghan and Louth.
McGeown, ..	19	2	–	17	–	12 in Armagh.
McGettigan, ..	10	–	–	10	–	All in Donegal.
McGillicuddy, ..	6	–	6	–	–	All in Kerry.
*McGilloway (8),	10	–	–	10	–	5 in Londonderry and 5 in Donegal.
McGimpsey, ..	8	–	–	8	–	7 in Down and 1 in Antrim.
McGing, ...	10	–	–	–	10	7 in Mayo and 2 in Leitrim.
*McGinley (45), ..	47	–	–	46	1	37 in Donegal.
*McGinn (17)—Maginn (13),	31	4	–	25	2	Generally distributed in Ulster.
*McGinty (10), ..	12	–	1	9	2	Donegal.
McGirr, ...	12	1	–	9	2	Tyrone.
*McGivern (17), ..	18	–	–	18	–	7 in Armagh, 7 in Down, and 4 in Antrim.
McGivney, ..	6	–	–	6	–	All in Cavan.
McGlade, ..	8	1	–	7	–	Antrim and Londonderry.
*McGlinchey (17),	22	–	–	22	–	Tyrone and Donegal.
*McGloin (14), ..	16	1	–	7	8	Donegal and Sligo.
McGlone, ..	12	–	–	11	1	Tyrone.
*McGlynn (26),	39	9	3	16	11	—
McGoey, ..	5	2	–	1	2	—
*McGoldrick (34),	41	3	1	26	11	Tyrone, Fermanagh, and Sligo.
*McGonigle (24),	38	–	–	38	–	Donegal and Londonderry.
McGookin, ..	7	–	–	7	–	5 in Antrim and 2 in Armagh.
*McGough (8), ..	11	2	–	1	8	Mayo.
McGourty, ..	5	–	–	2	3	Leitrim.
*McGovern (92), ..	102	13	1	65	23	Fermanagh, Cavan, and Leitrim.
*McGowan (112)—Magowan (28),	152	5	2	91	54	Donegal, Leitrim, and Sligo.
McGrady, ..	6	–	–	6	–	3 in Antrim and 3 in Down.
*McGrath (233)—Magrath (31),	266	49	131	60	26	This name is found in every county, but more than 50 per cent. are in Tipperary, Cork, Waterford, Antrim, and Tyrone.
McGraw, ..	5	–	–	5	–	—
*McGreal (21), ..	22	–	2	1	19	11 in Mayo and 6 in Leitrim.
*McGreevy (16),	18	–	2	11	5	Down and Antrim.
*McGregor (14),	16	2	2	11	1	Londonderry.
McGrory, ..	12	1	–	11	–	Donegal and Londonderry.
McGuane, ..	6	–	6	–	–	All in Clare.
*McGuckin (8), ..	11	1	–	10	–	Londonderry.
*McGuigan (36),	43	–	–	40	3	Antrim and Tyrone.
McGuinn, ..	5	–	–	1	4	Sligo.
*McGuinness (47),	128	42	3	69	14	Dublin, Monaghan, and Louth. There are no fewer than 16 varieties in the spelling of this name in the Birth Indexes for 1890.
*McGurk (32)—McGuirk (17),	51	19	–	30	2	"McGurk," Tyrone and Antrim—"McGuirk," Dublin.
McHale, ...	51	–	1	–	50	50 in Mayo.
*McHenry (14)—McEniry (5),	27	2	11	13	1	"McHenry," Antrim and Londonderry—"McEniry," and other forms in Limerick.
*McHugh (165), ..	176	18	4	73	81	Mayo, Donegal, Fermanagh, Galway, and Leitrim.

TABLE showing the SURNAMES IN IRELAND having Five Entries and upwards in the Birth Indexes of 1890, together with the Number in each Registration Province, and the Registration Counties in which these Names are principally found—*continued.*

Names.	IRELAND.	Leinster.	Munster	Ulster.	Connaught.	Counties in which principally found.
McIlroy (40)—McElroy (39),	79	6	3	69	1	Antrim, Down, Fermanagh, and Londonderry.
*McIlveen (15),	16	1	–	15	–	9 in Antrim and 5 in Down.
*McIlwaine (20),	29	–	–	29	–	Antrim, Down and Armagh.
*McInerney (40),	64	8	53	1	2	Clare and Limerick.
McIntosh,	7	–	–	6	1	Antrim.
*McIntyre (42),	58	8	1	34	15	Londonderry, Antrim, and Sligo.
*McIvor (19),	24	1	–	23	–	Tyrone and Londonderry.
McKane,	8	2	–	5	1	—
*McKay (53),	64	3	1	56	4	Antrim.
*McKeag (11),	16	–	–	16	–	
McKee,	96	1	2	93	–	
*McKeever (30),	34	7	1	26	–	Antrim, Down, and Armagh.
*McKelvey (21),	24	1	–	23	–	Londonderry and Antrim.
McKendry,	19	–	–	19	–	17 in Antrim.
McKenna,	201	37	22	134	8	Antrim, Monaghan, Tyrone, Kerry, Armagh, Dublin, and Louth.
*McKenzie (21),	22	7	–	13	2	Antrim and Dublin.
*McKeogh (12),	13	8	4	1	–	Westmeath.
*McKeown (119)—McKeon (40)—McKeone (12).	175	33	2	115	25	"McKeown," Antrim, Down, Armagh, Londonderry, and Louth—"McKeon" and "McKeone," Leitrim and Louth.
*McKernan (12),	18	–	–	17	1	
McKevitt,	9	6	–	3	–	6 in Louth.
*McKibbin (14),	20	–	–	20	–	13 in Down and 7 in Antrim.
McKiernan,	9	1	–	6	2	
*McKillen (8),	9	–	–	9	–	"McKillen," all in Antrim.
*McKinley (23),	35	1	2	32	–	Antrim and Donegal.
*McKinney (37),	42	–	–	42	–	Antrim and Tyrone.
McKinstry	11	–	–	11	–	9 in Antrim and 2 in Down.
*McKitterick (5),	9	1	1	7	–	
McKnight (38),	39	5	3	31	–	Antrim and Down.
McLarnon (8)—McClarnon (5).	13	–	–	13	–	9 in Antrim.
*McLaughlin (191)—McLoughlin (170).	391	62	7	228	94	"McLaughlin," about 75 per cent. in Antrim, Donegal, and Londonderry—a few in Tyrone, but very few elsewhere. "McLoughlin," chiefly in Dublin and the Counties of Connaught, but found scattered throughout Ireland generally.
McLernon,	8	–	–	8	–	
*McLoone (9),	10	–	–	10	–	8 in Donegal.
*McMahon (236),	241	34	118	86	3	Clare, Monaghan, Limerick, and Dublin.
McManamon,	6	–	–	–	6	All in Mayo.
*McManus (129),	138	19	2	89	28	Fermanagh.
McMaster,	38	–	–	37	1	Antrim and Down.
McMeekin,	7	–	–	6	1	Antrim.
*McMenamin (34),	36	1	–	34	1	22 in Donegal and 10 in Tyrone.
McMichael,	5	–	–	5	–	
*McMillen (12)—McMillan (11).	25	–	–	25	–	Antrim and Down.
*McMinn (12),	13	–	–	13	–	8 in Antrim.
*McMonagle (10),	12	–	–	12	–	Donegal.
McMorrow,	21	–	1	1	19	17 in Leitrim.
*McMullan (80),	108	4	4	99	1	Antrim and Down.
*McMurray (16),	19	–	–	18	1	Antrim and Armagh.
*McMurtry (6),	7	–	–	7	–	All in Antrim.
*McNabb (8),	10	1	–	7	2	
McNair,	5	–	–	4	1	Antrim.
*McNally (72)—McAnally (23).	101	27	3	59	12	Antrim, Armagh, Monaghan, and Dublin.
*McNamara (175),	192	28	118	12	34	Clare, Limerick, Mayo, Dublin, and Cork.
McNamee,	40	14	–	26	–	Londonderry.
McNeice (8)—McNiece (8).	16	–	–	15	1	Antrim.
*McNeill (53),	58	5	2	46	5	Antrim and Londonderry.
*McNeilly,	7	–	–	7	–	6 in Antrim and 1 in Down.
McNelis,	8	–	–	8	–	All in Donegal.
McNicholas,	32	–	–	–	32	All in Mayo.
*McNickle (10),	13	–	–	11	2	Tyrone.

TABLE showing the SURNAMES IN IRELAND having Five Entries and upwards in the Birth Indexes of 1890, together with the Number in each Registration Province, and the Registration Counties in which these Names are principally found—*continued*.

Names.	IRELAND.	Leinster.	Munster.	Ulster.	Connaught.	Counties in which principally found.
*McNiff (13), ...	14	–	–	3	11	9 in Leitrim.
McNinch, ..	5	–	–	5	–	All in Antrim.
*McNulty (59),	69	4	1	43	21	Donegal and Mayo.
*McPaden (6), ...	8	–	–	–	8	Mayo.
*McParland (24)— McPartlan (12)— McPartlin (11),	55	3	–	36	16	" McParland," Armagh—" McPartlan " and " McPartlin," Leitrim.
*McPhillips (13), ..	17	3	–	14	–	Cavan and Monaghan.
McPolin, ..	5	–	–	5	–	All in Armagh.
* M c Q u a i d (2 8)— McQuade (25),	55	4	–	49	2	"McQuaid," Monaghan and Fermanagh— "McQuade," Antrim.
*McQuillan (30), ..	33	6	–	25	2	Antrim and Monaghan.
*McQuinn (5), ...	7	1	4	2	–	Kerry.
McQuiston, ..	5	–	–	5	–	Antrim.
McRedmond, ..	5	5	–	–	–	King's.
McReynolds, ..	9	–	1	8	–	Antrim.
McRoberts, ..	9	–	–	9	–	Down and Antrim.
McShane, ..	34	9	–	25	–	Donegal and Louth.
McSharry, ..	29	–	–	9	20	13 in Leitrim, 9 in Donegal, and 7 in Sligo.
McSherry, ..	10	1	1	8	–	Armagh.
McSorley, ..	15	1	–	14	–	Tyrone and Fermanagh.
*M'Stay (9), ..	10	–	–	10	–	Armagh.
McStravick, ..	6	–	–	6	–	4 in Armagh and 2 in Antrim.
*McSweeney (13), ..	29	2	27	–	–	Cork.
*McTernan (16), ..	20	–	–	1	19	17 in Leitrim.
McTigue (12)—McTague (4)—McTeague (3),	19	–	1	7	11	"McTigue," Mayo—"McTague," Cavan— "McTeague," all in Donegal.
*McVeigh (47), ..	68	9	–	57	2	Antrim and Down.
*McVicker (10),	13	1	–	12	–	9 in Antrim and 3 in Londonderry.
McWatters, ..	6	–	–	6	–	Antrim.
*McWeeney (6),	8	1	–	–	7	7 in Leitrim.
*McWhinney (6), ..	7	–	–	7	–	Down and Antrim.
McWhirter, ..	5	–	–	5	–	3 in Antrim, and 2 in Armagh.
*McWilliams (40), ..	43	2	1	38	2	Antrim and Londonderry.
*Meade (24), ..	25	8	17	–	–	Cork.
*Meany (25), ..	34	12	20	2	–	Kilkenny and Clare.
Meara (33)—Mara (21),	54	12	36	–	–	Tipperary.
Mee (10)—Mea (5), ..	15	1	–	4	10	" Mee," Roscommon—" Mea," all in Mayo.
*Meegan (11), ...	12	3	1	6	2	Monaghan.
*Meehan (112),	121	34	25	32	30	Galway, Sligo, Donegal, Dublin, and Clare. Found in nearly every County—10 entries (in Galway) being the largest number.
Meek, ...	7	1	1	5	–	Antrim.
*Meenan (9), ..	14	1	–	9	4	Donegal and Tyrone.
Meharg, ..	5	–	–	5	–	All in Antrim.
Melia, ...	11	4	–	–	7	Galway.
*Mellon (11), ..	12	3	–	9	–	Tyrone.
Melody, ..	5	–	2	–	3	—
Melville, ..	6	1	–	5	–	Antrim and Down.
Melvin, ..	11	–	–	2	9	Mayo.
Mercer, ..	22	2	–	20	–	9 in Antrim and 7 in Down.
*Meredith (5), ..	7	3	2	2	–	—
*Merrick (6), ..	7	2	3	1	1	—
Merrigan, ..	7	5	2	–	–	Dublin.
*Metcalf (7), ..	9	4	–	5	–	5 in Armagh.
Meyler, ..	9	8	1	–	–	7 in Wexford.
*Middleton (5), ..	6	2	1	3	–	—
Millar (87)—Miller (79),	166	22	7	133	4	Antrim, Londonderry, and Dublin—50 per cent. being found in Antrim alone.
Millen, ...	10	–	1	9	–	7 in Antrim.
*Milligan (22)-Milliken (17),	40	–	1	37	2	Half are in Antrim—remainder chiefly in Down and Londonderry.
Mills, ...	59	16	2	34	7	Antrim.
*Minihane (12), ..	28	1	27	–	–	19 in Cork. Seven varieties of this name are found in the Birth Indexes for 1890.
Minnis, ...	6	–	–	6	–	Antrim.
Minnock, ...	5	5	–	–	–	4 in King's.
*Minogue (16), ..	17	–	15	–	2	11 in Clare.
Miskelly, ..	5	–	–	5	–	All in Antrim.

TABLE showing the SURNAMES IN IRELAND having Five Entries and upwards in the Birth Indexes of 1890, together with the Number in each Registration Province, and the Registration Counties in which these Names are principally found—*continued.*

Names.	NUMBER OF ENTRIES IN BIRTH INDEXES FOR 1890.					Counties in which principally found.
	IRELAND.	Leinster.	Munster.	Ulster.	Connaught.	
*Mitchell (120),	128	26	9	63	30	Antrim, Galway, and Dublin. They are found in nearly every county in Ireland.
Mitten,	7	5	–	–	2	—
*Mockler (7),	9	2	5	–	2	Tipperary.
Moffatt (17)—Moffat (11)—Moffett (12)—Moffet (10)—Moffitt (11)—Moffit (7),	68	7	–	45	16	Antrim, Sligo, and Tyrone.
*Mohan (11)—Moan (9),	25	1	–	21	3	Monaghan.
*Molloy (127),	153	63	8	37	45	Dublin, Galway, Mayo, King's, and Donegal
*Moloney (119)—Molony (34),	187	26	133	3	25	Limerick, Clare, Tipperary, and Waterford.
*Molyneaux (6),	10	2	6	2	–	—
*Monaghan (96)—Monahan (42),	140	36	11	44	49	Galway, Mayo, Dublin, and Fermanagh.
Mongan,	6	–	1	–	5	—
Monks,	12	12	–	–	–	11 in Dublin.
Monnelly (9)—Munnelly (6),	15	1	–	–	14	14 in Mayo.
*Montague (8),	9	1	–	8	–	Tyrone.
*Montgomery (110),	111	12	–	97	2	More than half are in Antrim and Down.
*Moody (12),	13	3	1	9	–	Antrim and Down.
*Moon (6),	8	2	1	4	1	—
Mooney,	136	77	9	38	12	Dublin, Antrim, and King's.
*Moore (395),	396	135	52	185	24	Antrim, Dublin, Londonderry, Cork, Kildare, and Tyrone—Every county in Ireland has representatives of this name—from 1 entry in Westmeath to 93 in Antrim.
*Moorhead (17),	25	3	2	18	2	Antrim.
*Morahan (7),	10	–	2	–	8	Leitrim.
Moran,	265	82	36	15	132	Mayo, Dublin, Galway, Roscommon, Leitrim, and Kerry—This name, however, is found in nearly every county.
Moreland,	11	–	–	11	–	Antrim and Down.
Morey,	7	–	7	–	–	—
Morgan,	132	37	16	67	12	Antrim, Armagh, Down, Dublin, and Louth
Moriarty,	83	4	79	–	–	74 in Kerry.
Morley,	23	2	–	–	21	20 in Mayo.
*Moroney (35),	44	3	41	–	–	Clare, Limerick, and Tipperary.
*Morrin (6),	8	1	3	4	–	—
*Morris (102),	115	49	6	32	28	Dublin, Mayo, Tyrone, and Monaghan—A very scattered name.
*Morrison (93),	111	12	18	66	15	Antrim, Down, and Dublin.
Morrisroe,	7	–	–	–	7	Roscommon.
*Morrissey (62),	90	20	67	–	3	Waterford, Limerick, and Cork.
*Morrow (90),	91	3	1	83	4	Antrim, Donegal, Armagh, and Down.
*Morton (30),	32	6	1	24	1	One half in Antrim.
Moss,	6	1	1	4	–	Tyrone.
Motherway,	5	–	5	–	–	All in Cork.
Moylan,	23	7	12	1	3	Clare, Cork, and Tipperary.
*Moynihan (50),	66	1	64	–	1	36 in Kerry and 24 in Cork.
Muir,	5	–	2	3	–	—
Mulcahy,	76	3	72	1	–	All except 6 in Cork, Limerick, Waterford, and Tipperary.
Muldoon,	26	3	–	14	9	Fermanagh and Galway.
*Muldowney (5),	7	2	–	–	5	—
Mulgrew,	7	–	–	6	1	5 in Tyrone.
Mulhall,	33	32	1	–	–	Dublin, Kilkenny, Carlow, and Queen's.
*Mulherin (8)—Mulherin (7),	21	–	2	13	6	—
*Mulholland (71),	73	3	1	65	4	Antrim, Down, and Londonderry.
Mulkeen,	7	–	–	–	7	6 in Mayo and 1 in Roscommon.
*Mulkerrin (5),	10	–	–	1	9	9 in Galway.
*Mullally (8),	14	7	5	1	1	—
*Mullan (92)—Mullen (72)—Mullin (53),	218	39	2	128	49	Tyrone, Londonderry, Galway, and Antrim.
Mullane,	31	–	29	–	2	16 in Cork and 8 in Limerick.
*Mullany (27),	32	1	7	2	22	Roscommon, Mayo, and Sligo.
Mullarkey,	21	–	–	1	20	Mayo, Galway, and Sligo.
Mulligan,	105	32	1	34	38	Dublin, Mayo, and Monaghan.
Mullins,	47	8	35	–	4	Cork and Clare.

TABLE showing the SURNAMES IN IRELAND having Five Entries and upwards in the Birth Indexes of 1890, together with the Number in each Registration Province, and the Registration Counties in which these Names are principally found—*continued.*

Names.	NUMBER OF ENTRIES IN BIRTH INDEXES FOR 1890.					Counties in which principally found.
	IRELAND.	Leinster.	Munster.	Ulster.	Connaught.	
Mulqueen, ...	6	–	6	–	–	4 in Limerick and 2 in Clare.
Mulrennan, ...	5	1	–	–	4	—
Mulroe, ...	5	–	–	–	5	3 in Mayo and 2 in Galway.
*Mulrooney (9), ..	12	4	1	–	7	—
Mulroy, ...	12	2	–	–	10	10 in Mayo.
Mulry, ...	5	–	–	1	4	Galway.
*Mulvany (4)-Mulvanny (4),	15	12	–	2	1	—
Mulvenna, ..	5	–	–	5	–	All in Antrim.
*Mulvey (21), ..	27	3	4	1	19	13 in Leitrim.
*Mulvihill (18), ..	21	4	12	1	4	Kerry and Limerick.
M u r d o c k (1 8)— Murdoch (12),	30	2	1	27	–	Antrim.
*Murnane (13), ..	14	4	10	–	–	Limerick and Cork.
*Murphy (1385), ..	1386	476	611	189	110	Generally distributed, but the largest numbers are found in Cork, Dublin, and Wexford. They vary from 5 in each of the counties of Westmeath, Tyrone, and Sligo, to close on 500 in Cork.
*Murray (405), ..	438	120	65	161	92	Dublin, Antrim, Cork, Down, Galway, and Mayo. There is no county, however, without representatives of this name.
*Murrin (6), ...	8	5	–	1	2	
*Murtagh (58), ...	66	30	1	17	18	Dublin and Sligo.
*Myers (10), ...	11	4	4	3	–	Wexford and Antrim.
Myles (7)—Miles (5), ..	12	7	3	2	–	
*Nagle (32), ...	39	3	32	3	1	Cork.
Nally, ...	20	4	–	–	16	Mayo and Roscommon.
Napier, ...	8	–	–	8	–	Antrim and Down.
*Nash (20), ...	21	5	15	–	1	Kerry and Limerick.
*Naughton (52), ..	71	1	19	1	50	Galway, Mayo, Roscommon, and Clare.
Navin, ...	6	1	–	–	5	Mayo.
*Naylor (5), ...	6	4	–	2	–	Dublin.
Neal (6)—Neale (4), ..	10	7	1	2	–	
*Neary (34), ...	43	12	2	2	27	Mayo, Roscommon, Dublin, and Louth.
Nee, ...	17	1	1	–	15	15 in Galway.
Needham, ...	7	–	1	1	5	5 in Mayo.
*Neely (9), ...	12	–	–	11	1	—
Neenan, ...	7	1	6	–	–	Clare.
Neeson, ...	17	–	–	17	–	Antrim.
*Neilan (12)—Nilan (7),	36	3	9	–	24	Galway, Roscommon, and Sligo.
*Neill (215), ...	244	97	78	63	6	Antrim, Cork, Kerry, Carlow, Dublin, and Wexford.
Nelis, ...	5	–	–	3	2	Londonderry and Mayo.
Nelson, ...	72	8	2	59	3	Antrim, Down, Londonderry, and Tyrone.
*Nesbitt (25), ...	30	5	1	23	1	Antrim, Armagh, and Dublin.
*Nestor (13), ...	15	2	5	–	8	Galway and Clare.
*Neville (36), ...	39	8	27	4	–	Limerick and Cork.
*Nevin (22), ...	23	8	2	5	8	—
*Newell (31), ...	34	2	1	27	4	Down and Antrim.
Newman, ...	36	13	20	3	–	Cork, Meath, and Dublin—15 in Cork.
*Neylon (10), ...	13	1	11	–	1	11 in Clare.
Niblock, ...	6	–	–	6	–	Antrim.
*Nicholl (25), ...	49	2	5	40	2	Antrim and Londonderry.
*Nicholson (43), ..	44	10	2	16	16	Antrim, Sligo, and Dublin.
*Nixon (46), ...	47	7	–	37	3	Antrim, Cavan, and Fermanagh.
Noble, ...	25	7	1	15	2	Antrim and Dublin.
*Nolan (313), ...	321	220	57	13	31	Dublin, Wexford, Carlow, Wicklow, Kildare, Kerry, Tipperary, Mayo, and Galway.
*Noonan (69), ...	83	8	66	1	8	Cork, Clare, Limerick, and Tipperary.
*Noone (29), ...	48	7	–	1	40	Galway, Roscommon, and Mayo.
*Normile (5), ...	9	–	9	–	–	Limerick and Clare.
*Norris (21), ...	22	7	8	7	–	—
*North (8), ...	9	5	–	4	–	—
Northridge, ...	5	–	5	–	–	All in Cork.
Norton, ...	11	8	1	–	·2	Dublin.
Nugent, ...	75	19	25	30	1	Armagh, Dublin, Cork, Tipperary, and Tyrone.
Nulty, ...	16	8	1	2	5	Meath.

TABLE showing the SURNAMES IN IRELAND having Five Entries and upwards in the Birth Indexes of 1890, together with the Number in each Registration Province, and the Registration Counties in which these Names are principally found—*continued.*

Names.	NUMBER OF ENTRIES IN BIRTH INDEXES FOR 1890.					Counties in which principally found.
	IRELAND.	Leinster.	Munster.	Ulster.	Connaught.	
Oakley, ...	5	–	2	1	2	—
*O'Beirne (9), ..	10	4	–	2	4	—
O'Boyle, ...	20	–	–	5	15	14 in Mayo and 5 in Antrim.
*O'Brien (488),	502	105	291	56	50	Dublin is the only county in Leinster in which found to an appreciable extent. Each county in Munster is largely represented; Cavan takes the lead in Ulster, and Galway in Connaught.
O'Byrne, ...	8	6	2	–	–	6 in Dublin.
*O'Callaghan (63),	64	8	51	5	–	Cork.
O'Carroll, ..	5	1	4	–	–	—
*O'Connell (128),	130	14	100	6	10	Cork, Limerick, Kerry, and Dublin contain about 80 per cent.
*O'Connor (259).	266	50	174	13	29	Kerry, Cork, Limerick, Dublin, Clare, and Galway contain about 80 per cent.
*O'Dea (34), ..	35	5	25	–	5	17 in Clare and 6 in Limerick.
*O'Doherty (7), ..	8	4	1	3	–	
*O'Donnell (292),	294	9	102	132	51	Donegal, Mayo, and Galway. Generally distributed in Munster.
*O'Donoghue (28),	39	5	34	–	–	Kerry and Cork.
O'Donovan, ..	11	1	9	–	1	7 in Cork and 2 in Limerick.
O'Dowd, ...	15	5	1	–	9	Sligo.
O'Driscoll, ..	13	2	11	–	–	10 in Cork.
O'Dwyer, ...	25	3	21	–	1	Tipperary, Limerick, and Clare.
O'Farrell, ..	19	5	10	2	2	—
O'Flaherty, ..	16	2	10	3	1	—
O'Flynn, ..	5	–	–	3	2	—
*O'Gara (6), ..	7	–	–	–	7	4 in Roscommon and 3 in Mayo.
Ogle, ...	6	–	–	6	–	—
*O'Gorman (22),	24	3	21	–	–	Clare.
*O'Grady (46), ..	47	8	29	2	8	Clare, Limerick, Dublin, and Roscommon.
*O'Hagan (32),	33	7	–	26	–	Armagh, Louth, and Down.
*O'Halloran (17),	25	2	21	1	1	Limerick.
O'Hanlon, ..	22	9	1	12	–	Dublin and Armagh.
*O'Hara (104), ..	105	31	5	31	38	Dublin, Antrim, and Sligo.
*O'Hare (57), ..	59	12	1	45	1	31 in Armagh, 11 in Louth, and 9 in Down.
*O'Hora (6), ..	8	–	–	–	8	All in Mayo.
*O'Kane (27), ..	29	–	1	27	1	Londonderry and Antrim.
*O'Keeffe (76), ..	83	10	68	2	3	Cork, Limerick, and Dublin, more than one-half being in Cork.
O'Kelly, ...	9	3	4	–	2	—
O'Leary, ...	64	5	57	1	1	41 in Cork, 9 in Kerry, and 5 in Limerick.
*Oliver (15), ..	16	3	1	10	2	—
*O'Loughlin (30),	40	12	21	3	4	Clare and Dublin.
*O'Mahony (18),	25	5	20	–	–	Cork.
*O'Malley (25),	30	3	4	3	20	16 in Mayo.
*O'Meara (20), ..	31	11	19	–	1	Dublin, Limerick, and Tipperary.
*O'Neill (359), ..	407	124	110	145	28	Dublin, Antrim, Cork, and Tyrone contain 50 per cent. Found, however, in nearly every county in Ireland.
*O'Rawe (7), ..	10	–	–	10	–	All in Antrim.
O'Regan, ..	16	1	15	–	–	Cork and Limerick.
*O'Reilly (58), ..	62	37	14	9	2	Dublin.
O'Riordan, ..	11	–	11	–	–	Cork.
*Ormond (6), ..	8	3	5	–	–	—
Ormsby, ...	10	3	1	3	3	—
*O'Rourke (31),	49	10	12	11	16	—
Orr, ...	73	5	2	65	1	Antrim, Down, Londonderry, and Tyrone.
Osborne, ..	23	5	5	12	1	—
O'Shaughnessy, ..	30	8	18	1	3	Limerick.
O'Shea, ...	46	5	36	2	3	Cork, Kerry, and Limerick.
O'Sullivan, ..	136	8	122	–	6	54 in Kerry, 45 in Cork, and 19 in Limerick.
Oswald, ...	5	–	–	5	–	—
*O'Toole (36), ..	39	26	7	6	–	Dublin, Wicklow, and Limerick.
*Owens (84), ..	89	26	9	33	21	Dublin, Roscommon, and Cork. This name has representatives in 23 counties in the Birth Indexes for 1890.
*Padden (5), ...	10	–	–	1	9	Mayo.
Page, ...	15	4	1	7	3	Antrim and Dublin.

Table showing the Surnames in Ireland having Five Entries and upwards in the Birth Indexes of 1890, together with the Number in each Registration Province, and the Registration Counties in ' which these Names are principally found—*continued.*

Names.	IRELAND.	Leinster.	Munster.	Ulster.	Connaught.	Counties in which principally found.
		NUMBER OF ENTRIES IN BIRTH INDEXES FOR 1890.				
Paisley, ...	12	8	–	4	–	Dublin and Antrim.
Palmer, ...	32	5	9	18	–	Antrim.
*Park (15), ..	21	–	–	18	3	Antrim and Tyrone.
Parker, ...	40	6	8	24	2	Antrim and Cork.
Parkhill, ..	8	–	1	7	–	Londonderry.
Parkinson, ..	14	4	3	7	–	Dublin, Antrim, and Down.
*Parks (16), ..	23	5	1	16	1	Antrim and Armagh.
Parle, ...	5	5	–	–	–	All in Wexford.
Parr, ...	5	1	1	2	1	—
Parsons, ...	12	3	1	1	7	—
*Patterson (137),	153	14	6	130	3	Down, Antrim, Armagh, Londonderry, and Tyrone.
*Patton (49)—Patten (10),	60	2	1	48	9	"Patton," Antrim and Down—"Patten," Mayo.
*Paul (13), ..	14	2	2	10	–	Londonderry and Antrim.
*Payne (25), ..	26	12	2	9	3	Dublin and Antrim.
*Peacock (7), ..	9	2	2	4	1	—
*Pearson (26), ..	31	11	4	16	–	Antrim and Dublin.
*Peel (11), ..	12	3	1	8	–	Antrim.
Pender, ...	25	14	9	1	1	Wexford.
Penny, ...	5	1	–	4	–	4 in Antrim and 1 in Dublin.
Pentland, ..	7	1	–	6	–	Down and Armagh.
*Peoples (9), ..	10	–	–	10	–	Donegal.
Pepper, ...	10	4	1	5	–	Dublin and Antrim.
*Perrott (5), ..	6	1	4	1	–	Cork.
Perry, ...	23	6	5	10	2	Dublin and Down.
Peters, ...	12	1	5	4	2	Tipperary.
Petticrew (7)—Pettigrew (5),	12	1	1	9	1	Antrim.
Peyton, ...	11	1	1	1	8	Mayo.
*Phelan (91), ..	92	46	43	2	1	Waterford, Kilkenny, Queen's, and Tipperary contain nearly 80 per cent.
Phibbs, ...	6	1	1	–	4	Sligo.
*Philbin (9), ..	10	–	–	–	10	9 in Mayo and 1 in Galway.
*Phillips (64), ..	77	27	8	21	21	Mayo, Antrim, and Dublin.
*Picken (5), ..	6	–	–	6	–	" Picken," all in Antrim.
*Pidgeon (5), ..	6	6	–	–	–	—
*Pierce (22), ..	38	21	9	6	2	Dublin and Wexford.
*Pigott (15), ..	20	7	11	1	1	Cork and Dublin.
Pilkington, ..	8	3	1	1	3	—
Pinkerton, ..	7	1	–	6	–	Antrim.
Platt, ...	8	1	–	7	–	Londonderry.
*Plunkett (21), ..	28	20	–	6	2	Dublin.
Poland, ...	5	2	–	3	–	—
Pollard, ...	15	12	3	–	–	Dublin and Kilkenny.
*Pollock (39), ..	41	4	–	36	1	Antrim and Tyrone.
Poots, ...	5	–	–	5	–	3 in Down and 2 in Antrim.
Pope, ...	6	4	2	–	–	—
Porter, ...	73	9	–	64	–	Antrim, Down, Londonderry, and Armagh.
Potter, ...	14	4	1	5	4	—
Powell, ...	23	4	7	7	5	—
*Power (271), ..	272	68	196	6	2	All except 17 in Waterford, Cork, Dublin, Tipperary, Wexford, Kilkenny, and Limerick.
Pratt, ...	10	4	2	4	–	—
*Prendergast (46),	52	15	16	1	20	Mayo, Dublin, and Waterford—18 in Mayo.
Prentice, ..	8	1	–	7	–	—
*Prescott (5), ..	6	3	–	3	–	—
Preston, ...	17	5	2	10	–	—
*Price (45), ..	47	22	7	12	6	Dublin and Antrim.
Prior, ...	15	1	–	10	4	10 in Cavan.
Pritchard, ..	11	1	1	9	–	Antrim.
Proctor, ...	15	3	–	12	–	Antrim.
Prunty, ...	10	7	–	3	–	6 in Longford.
Punch, ...	6	–	6	–	–	4 in Cork and 2 in Limerick.
*Purcell (76), ..	79	41	28	3	7	Kilkenny and Dublin contain nearly all the entries in Leinster ; Tipperary, most of those in Munster.
*Purdy (15), ..	16	1	–	15	–	Antrim.
*Purtill (6), ..	9	–	9	–	–	Limerick.
Purvis, ...	8	1	–	4	3	—
Pyne, ...	11	–	10	1	–	7 in Cork and 3 in Clare.

TABLE showing the SURNAMES IN IRELAND having Five Entries and upwards in the Birth Indexes of 1890, together with the Number in each Registration Province, and the Registration Counties in which these Names are principally found—*continued.*

Names.	NUMBER OF ENTRIES IN BIRTH INDEXES FOR 1890.					Counties in which principally found.
	IRELAND.	Leinster.	Munster.	Ulster.	Connaught.	
*Quail (10),	14	5	–	9	–	Antrim and Down.
Quee,	5	–	–	5	–	All in Antrim.
Quigg,	6	–	–	6	–	—
*Quigley (82),	89	23	10	39	17	Londonderry, Dublin, Donegal, Galway Louth, and Sligo.
Quill,	10	–	9	–	1	Cork.
Quilligan,	7	–	7	–	–	5 in Limerick and 2 in Cork.
Quillinan,	5	–	4	1	–	Tipperary.
Quilty,	9	–	8	–	1	5 in Limerick and 3 in Waterford.
*Quinlan (52),	54	10	44	–	–	Tipperary and Kerry.
*Quinlivan (12),	13	2	–	11	–	Clare.
*Quinn (349)—Quin (58),	408	114	63	155	76	Dublin, Tyrone, Antrim, Roscommon, and Galway—Found in every County in Ireland, from 1 entry in Cavan to 44 in Dublin.
*Quirke (27),	40	10	28	–	2	Tipperary and Kerry.
*Rabbit (10),	13	4	1	–	8	—
Ractigan,	5	–	–	–	5	All in Mayo.
Radford,	7	5	2	–	–	—
*Rafferty (54),	55	17	–	34	4	Antrim, Tyrone, and Louth.
*Rafter (17),	20	12	–	2	6	Dublin, Queen's, and Mayo.
*Raftery (25),	26	–	–	–	26	20 in Galway and 6 in Roscommon.
Rahilly,	11	–	11	–	–	8 in Kerry and 3 in Cork.
Rainey,	39	1	–	36	2	22 in Antrim and 10 in Down.
Raleigh,	11	2	9	–	–	Limerick and Tipperary.
*Ralph (12),	14	7	2	1	4	Antrim.
Ramsay (16)—Ramsey (12),	28	5	–	22	1	Antrim.
Rankin,	36	6	–	29	1	Londonderry and Donegal.
Ratigan (4)—Rattigan (4),	8	1	–	–	7	Mayo and Roscommon.
Ray,	7	2	2	3	–	—
Raymond,	6	2	4	–	–	—
Rea,	49	3	4	42	–	31 in Antrim and 7 in Down.
*Reaney (5),	9	–	–	3	6	—
*Reddan (7)—Reddin (6),	15	6	8	–	1	—
Reddington (7)—Redington (7),	14	1	1	–	12	7 in Mayo and 5 in Galway.
*Reddy (25),	32	21	7	1	3	Dublin and Kilkenny.
Redfern,	5	1	1	2	1	—
Redmond,	79	74	–	5	–	30 in Wexford, 29 in Dublin, and 10 in Wicklow.
Redpath,	9	–	–	9	–	Antrim.
Reel,	5	2	–	3	–	—
Reen,	10	–	10	–	–	7 in Cork and 3 in Kerry.
Regan,	219	20	110	9	80	Cork, Roscommon, and Mayo.
*Reid (181),	206	50	13	137	6	Antrim, Dublin, Down, Tyrone, and Armagh.
Reidy,	49	2	45	–	2	Kerry and Clare.
*Reilly (503)—Rielly (58),	586	254	50	199	83	Cavan, Longford, Dublin, Meath, Mayo, and Cork contain about 65 per cent., but found in every county.
Relihan,	7	–	7	–	–	Cork and Kerry.
*Reville (5),	6	5	1	–	–	Wexford.
*Reynolds (112),	113	30	15	22	46	Leitrim, Dublin, Antrim, and Louth.
Rice,	99	33	18	48	–	Antrim, Armagh, Louth, and Dublin.
Richards,	9	4	2	3	–	—
*Richardson (53),	54	14	8	32	–	Dublin and Antrim.
Richmond,	9	–	–	9	–	All in Antrim.
*Rickard (6),	7	6	1	–	–	—
*Riddell (8),	12	1	–	11	–	Antrim.
Ridge,	10	–	–	1	9	9 in Galway.
Rigney,	9	7	1	1	–	King's.
Ring,	18	1	14	1	2	12 in Cork.
Ringland,	7	–	–	7	–	6 in Down and 1 in Antrim.
*Riordan (134),	159	4	154	1	–	89 in Cork, 30 in Kerry, and 24 in Limerick.
*Ritchie (23),	24	2	–	22	–	Antrim.
Roarty,	5	–	–	5	–	4 in Donegal and 1 in Tyrone.
Robb,	21	–	2	19	–	Antrim.

TABLE showing the SURNAMES IN IRELAND having Five Entries and upwards in the Birth Indexes of 1890, together with the Number in each Registration Province, and the Registration Counties in which these Names are principally found—*continued.*

Names.	IRELAND.	Leinster.	Munster.	Ulster.	Connaught.	Counties in which principally found.
						NUMBER OF ENTRIES IN BIRTH INDEXES FOR 1890.
Roberts, ..	40	14	10	15	1	—
Robertson,	18	5	3	9	1	—
Robinson,	217	29	9	168	11	Antrim, Down, Dublin, Armagh, and Tyrone.
Robson,	5	–	–	5	–	Down.
*Roche (141), ..	183	69	89	3	22	Cork, Wexford, Dublin, Limerick, and Mayo.
*Rochford (16),	18	12	2	–	4	Dublin.
*Rock (17), ..	23	9	–	8	6	Dublin.
*Rodden (9), ..	11	1	–	9	1	Donegal.
*Roddy (15), ..	17	1	1	6	9	Mayo and Roscommon.
Roe, ...	21	14	4	3	–	—
Rogan, ..	24	6	1	13	4	Antrim, Down, and Leitrim.
*Rogers (100)—Rodgers (68),	170	40	12	98	20	Antrim, Down, Dublin, and Roscommon—Very generally distributed.
Rohan, ...	8	1	7	–	–	7 in Kerry and 1 in Queen's.
Rollins, ..	7	1	–	6	–	4 in Antrim and 2 in Down.
Ronayne (13)—Ronan (12),	25	9	15	–	1	13 in Cork.
Rooney, ..	119	36	3	43	37	Dublin, Leitrim, Down, Antrim, and Mayo.
Rose, ...	10	5	5	–	–	—
Ross, ..	73	8	10	54	1	Antrim, Londonderry, Cork, and Down.
*Rossiter (12), ..	14	14	–	–	–	13 in Wexford and 1 in Wicklow.
Rothwell,	10	9	–	1	–	Wexford and Dublin.
*Roulston (8)—Rolston (7),	25	1	3	20	1	Tyrone and Antrim.
*Rountree (5), ..	9	2	–	7	–	Armagh.
*Rourke (90), ..	136	77	17	15	27	Dublin, Leitrim, Roscommon, and Wexford.
*Rowan (15)—Roughan (5),	27	7	4	11	5	—
*Rowland (11),	12	–	1	4	7	Mayo and Galway.
Rowe, ...	21	13	3	4	1	7 in Wexford.
Rowley, ..	11	2	–	4	5	Mayo.
Roy, ..	16	2	–	14	–	Antrim and Down.
*Roycroft (5), ..	7	–	6	–	1	6 in Cork.
*Ruane (35), ..	37	–	–	–	37	29 in Mayo and 6 in Galway.
Rudden, ..	9	1	–	8	–	Cavan.
Ruddle (5)-Ruddell (4),	9	–	4	5	–	4 in Limerick and 4 in Armagh.
Ruddock, ..	6	1	–	5	–	Down and Armagh.
*Ruddy (22), ..	23	1	–	9	13	13 in Mayo, 5 in Donegal, and 4 in Armagh.
Rush, ...	22	1	–	8	13	Mayo.
*Russell (99), ..	101	26	16	57	2	Antrim, Dublin, and Down.
Ruth, ..	6	5	1	–	–	—
*Rutherford (25), ..	26	1	2	21	2	Antrim, Londonderry, and Down.
*Rutledge (19), ..	23	3	–	15	5	Tyrone.
Ruttle, ..	6	5	1	–	–	—
Ryan, ...	715	180	473	13	49	Tipperary (which has by far the largest number), Limerick, Dublin, Cork, Waterford, Kilkenny, Wexford, Clare, and Galway.
Ryder, ...	9	2	–	–	7	Mayo.
*Ryle (6), ..	9	–	8	1	–	6 in Kerry.
*Sadlier (6), ..	12	2	5	2	3	—
*Salmon (21), ..	24	7	2	6	9	—
*Sands (17), ..	18	2	1	15	–	6 in Antrim and 6 in Armagh.
Santry, ..	7	–	7	–	–	All in Cork.
*Sargent (7), ..	11	5	1	5	–	—
*Sarsfield (10), ..	11	2	4	–	5	—
*Saunders (22), ..	29	11	8	8	2	Dublin and Antrim.
Savage, ...	61	13	7	38	3	Antrim, Down, Dublin, and Cork.
Sayers, ..	8	1	3	4	–	—
Scallan, ..	10	6	–	–	4	5 in Wexford.
*Scally (24), ..	25	15	2	1	–	Roscommon, Westmeath, and Dublin.
*Scanlon (54)—Scanlan (42),	97	6	60	3	28	Kerry, Clare, Sligo, Limerick, and Cork.
*Scannell (40), ..	42	–	42	–	–	24 in Cork and 15 in Kerry.
Scott, ...	196	27	4	147	18	Antrim, Down, Londonderry, and Dublin.
Scullion, ..	17	–	–	17	–	10 in Antrim and 5 in Londonderry.
Scully, ..	65	32	28	1	4	Cork, Dublin, Carlow, and King's.
Seaton, ..	6	–	1	5	–	—
*Seeds (6), ..	7	–	–	7	–	4 in Antrim and 3 in Down.

TABLE showing the SURNAMES IN IRELAND having Five Entries and upwards in the Birth Indexes of 1890, together with the Number in each Registration Province, and the Registration Counties in which these Names are principally found—*continued.*

Names.	NUMBER OF ENTRIES IN BIRTH INDEXES FOR 1890.					Counties in which principally found.
	IRELAND.	Leinster.	Munster.	Ulster.	Connaught.	
*Seery (20),	22	18	1	–	3	Westmeath and Dublin.
Semple,	19	1	–	18	–	Antrim.
Sewell,	6	1	2	3	–	—
Sexton,	43	4	31	6	2	30 of the Munster entries are in Cork, Clare, and Limerick. Cavan has 5 out of the 6 in Ulster.
Seymour,	15	5	6	4	–	—
*Shally (6),	7	2	–	–	5	Galway.
*Shanahan (53),	65	4	58	3	–	Cork, Kerry, Tipperary, Limerick, and Waterford.
Shanks,	21	–	–	21	–	10 in Antrim and 7 in Down.
*Shanley (14),	22	8	2	–	12	Leitrim.
Shannon,	72	10	19	29	14	Antrim, Clare, and Roscommon.
*Sharkey (57),	58	12	3	26	17	Roscommon, Donegal, Tyrone, Dublin, and Louth contain 49 out of the 58.
*Sharpe (10),	17	3	1	12	1	Antrim.
*Shaughnessy (40),	41	6	9	–	26	Nearly 50 per cent. in Galway.
Shaw,	80	17	8	51	4	Antrim, Down, and Dublin.
Shea,	246	24	217	2	3	Kerry, Cork, Kilkenny, Tipperary, and Waterford—Very few found outside these counties—More than one half of the Munster entries are in Kerry.
Shearer,	5	1	–	4	–	—
Sheedy,	13	1	12	–	–	Clare.
*Sheehan (171)-Sheahan (43),	215	22	190	–	3	Cork, Kerry, and Limerick, more than one half of the Munster entries being in Cork.
*Sheehy (54),	55	3	51	1	–	22 in Kerry, 15 in Limerick, and 9 in Cork.
*Sheeran (18),	30	18	2	2	8	—
*Shelly (16),	17	9	5	1	2	Dublin and Tipperary.
*Sheppard (12),	22	9	4	9	–	—
*Sheridan (135),	145	52	11	45	37	Cavan, Dublin, and Mayo—very generally distributed, however, throughout Ireland.
Sherlock,	23	11	4	5	3	Dublin.
Sherman,	5	2	–	3	–	—
Sherrard,	7	–	–	7	–	4 in Londonderry and 3 in Antrim.
Sherry,	25	10	–	15	–	9 in Monaghan, 5 in Dublin, and 3 in Meath.
Sherwood,	8	2	2	4	–	—
*Shevlin (8),	11	2	–	7	2	—
Shields (36)—Shields (19),	55	6	4	45	–	Antrim and Down.
*Shiels (28)—Sheils (28),	88	31	2	45	10	Dublin, Donegal, and Londonderry.
*Shilliday (5),	6	–	–	6	–	4 in Antrim and 2 in Down.
Shine,	26	2	21	–	3	12 in Cork.
Shirley,	7	5	–	2	–	—
*Short (21)—Shortt (8),	30	13	4	12	1	—
*Shortall (10),	11	9	1	–	1	Dublin and Kilkenny.
Shorten,	7	1	6	–	–	5 in Cork.
*Silk (7),	8	1	–	–	7	7 in Galway.
Silver,	5	–	1	–	4	4 in Galway.
*Simmons (6),	11	6	–	5	–	—
*Simms (11),	24	6	1	16	1	Antrim.
Simpson,	75	8	2	59	6	Antrim.
Sinclair,	18	3	–	15	–	Armagh and Londonderry.
Singleton,	17	3	6	8	–	Cork and Down.
*Sinnott (22)—Synnott (12),	37	33	2	1	1	" Sinnott," Wexford—" Synnott," Dublin.
*Skeffington (6),	8	–	–	4	4	—
*Skehan (7),	8	4	4	–	–	—
Skelly,	18	11	–	6	1	Dublin and Down.
Skelton,	8	4	–	4	–	—
Skillen,	6	–	–	6	–	3 in Down and 2 in Antrim.
*Slator (5),	10	6	1	1	2	Dublin.
Slattery,	69	9	55	–	5	53 of the 55 in Munster are in Tipperary, Kerry, Cork, Clare, and Limerick, each county having about the same number.
*Slavin (11),	14	3	–	11	–	—
Slevin,	13	7	–	4	2	—
*Sloan (44)—Sloane (16),	61	4	1	55	1	34 in Antrim.
Small,	30	4	4	19	3	Antrim, Armagh, and Down.
*Smiley (5)—Smylie (5),	13	2	–	11	–	Antrim.

TABLE showing the SURNAMES IN IRELAND having Five Entries and upwards in the Birth Indexes of 1890, together with the Number in each Registration Province, and the Registration Counties in which these Names are principally found—*continued.*

Names.	IRELAND.	Leinster.	Munster.	Ulster.	Connaught.	Counties in which principally found.
	NUMBER OF ENTRIES IN BIRTH INDEXES FOR 1890.					
*Smith (471)—Smyth (277),	753	232	62	412	47	Antrim, Cavan, and Dublin have the largest numbers, but they are found in every county, from 1 entry in Kerry to 134 in Antrim.
Smullen,	8	8	–	–	–	Dublin.
Snee, ..	7	–	–	–	7	Mayo.
Snoddy, ..	7	–	–	7	–	All in Antrim.
*Somers (29),	38	21	6	7	4	Wexford and Dublin.
*Somerville (18),	24	4	1	17	2	—
*Spain (7),	8	2	3	–	3	—
Sparks, ..	6	4	–	2	–	—
*Speers (17),	38	5	–	32	1	Antrim.
*Spelman (24), ..	30	–	1	1	28	Galway, Roscommon, and Mayo.
*Spence (57),	58	3	3	52	–	33 in Antrim and 11 in Down.
Spencer, ..	19	10	7	2	–	Dublin and Cork.
Spillane, ..	44	1	42	1	–	23 in Cork and 11 in Kerry.
Spratt, ..	14	–	1	13	–	Antrim.
Spring, ..	6	2	2	–	2	
Sproule, ..	17	3	–	11	3	10 in Tyrone.
Stacey, ..	5	4	1	–	–	—
Stack, ..	54	–	53	–	1	29 in Kerry, 10 in Cork, and 10 in Limerick.
Stafford, ..	33	22	2	9	–	Wexford and Dublin.
*Stanley (20), ..	21	9	8	4	–	Dublin.
Stanton (39)—Staunton (28),	67	6	16	2	43	"Stanton," 17 in Mayo and 14 in Cork—"Staunton," 11 in Mayo and 8 in Galway.
Stapleton, ..	28	18	10	–	–	Tipperary and Kilkenny.
*Starrett (7), ..	10	–	–	10	–	6 in Antrim and 3 in Londonderry.
Steele (37)—Steel (17),	54	3	–	47	4	33 in Antrim and 8 in Londonderry.
Steen, ..	6	–	–	6	–	—
Steenson, ..	19	–	–	19	–	Antrim and Armagh.
Stenson, ..	15	–	–	3	12	11 in Sligo.
*Stephens (32),	36	12	5	8	11	Mayo.
*Stevenson (81)—Stephenson (20),	106	8	2	92	4	Antrim, Armagh, and Down. [Tyrone.
*Stewart (236), ..	255	11	10	228	6	Antrim, Down, Londonderry, Donegal, and
Stinson, ..	12	–	–	11	1	—
Stirling (9)-Sterling (7),	16	1	–	15	–	14 in Antrim.
Stitt, ..	12	1	–	11	–	9 in Antrim.
St. John, ..	10	1	9	–	–	Tipperary.
*St. Leger (5), ..	7	4	3	–	–	—
Stockman, ..	7	1	–	6	–	—
Stokes, ..	28	10	13	3	2	—
*Stone (7), ..	12	7	1	1	3	—
*Storey (9), ..	13	3	–	10	–	8 in Antrim.
*Strahan (9), ..	11	5	–	6	–	—
Strain, ..	14	–	–	14	–	Down.
Strange, ..	6	1	–	5	–	5 in Antrim.
Stringer, ..	9	4	5	–	–	—
*Strong (12), ..	15	6	2	6	1	—
Studdert, ..	6	–	6	–	–	5 in Clare and 1 in Kerry.
Sturgeon, ..	8	–	–	8	–	22 in Kerry and 1 in Cork.
*Sugrue (21), ..	23	–	23	–	–	In every county of Munster, 373 of the entries being in Cork and 295 in Kerry.—In Leinster, Dublin has the largest number; in Ulster, Antrim; and in Connaught, Galway.
*Sullivan (838), ..	839	53	753	15	18	
Sunderland, ..	7	7	–	–	–	Wexford.
*Supple (5), ..	6	1	5	–	–	
*Surgeoner (5)—Surgenor (4).	10	–	–	9	1	9 in Antrim.
Sutherland, ..	6	2	2	2	–	—
Sutton, ..	27	19	7	1	–	Dublin, Wexford, and Cork.
*Swan (19), ..	23	9	–	14	–	Dublin and Antrim.
Swanton, ..	7	2	5	–	–	5 in Cork and 2 in Dublin.
*Sweeney (166)—Sweeny (82),	254	29	82	70	73	Cork, Donegal, Mayo, and Kerry.
*Sweetman (6), ..	8	4	4	–	–	Cork and Dublin.
Swift, ..	12	4	1	1	6	Mayo.
Switzer, ..	7	4	3	–	–	—
Swords, ..	8	8	–	–	–	Dublin.

TABLE showing the SURNAMES IN IRELAND having Five Entries and upwards in the Birth Indexes of 1890, together with the Number in each Registration Province, and the Registration Counties in which these Names are principally found— *continued.*

Names.	IRELAND.	Leinster.	Munster.	Ulster.	Connaught.	Counties in which principally found.
*Taaffe (11),	15	7	4	–	4	—
*Taggart (27),	42	1	1	39	1	Antrim.
*Talbot (17),	18	6	8	–	4	—
Tallon,	15	14	–	1	–	Dublin.
Talty,	12	–	10	–	2	10 in Clare.
Tangney,	8	–	8	–	–	7 in Kerry and 1 in Cork.
Tanner,	7	1	2	4	–	—
*Tansey (10),	13	–	–	–	13	
*Tarpey (10),	12	–	–	–	12	8 in Mayo, 3 in Roscommon, and 1 in Galway.
*Tarrant (10),	7	2	5	–	–	Cork.
*Tate (25)—Tait (10),	36	8	2	26	–	" Tate," Antrim and Down—" Tait," Londonderry.
*Taylor (150),	151	21	21	97	12	Antrim, Down, Londonderry, and Dublin.]
*Teague (5),	6	–	–	6	–	—
*Teahan (10),	11	1	10	–	–	9 in Kerry.
Teeling,	6	6	–	–	–	4 in Dublin.
Telford,	14	2	–	12	–	10 in Antrim.
Temple,	6	3	–	1	2	
Templeton,	18	2	–	15	1	13 in Antrim.
Tennant,	5	1	–	2	2	
Terry,	9	2	7	–	–	5 in Cork.
Thomas,	28	9	4	14	1	Antrim.
*Thompson (304),	317	44	23	239	11	Antrim, Down, Armagh, Londonderry, Dublin, Fermanagh, and Longford. Not many in any other county.
Thornton,	54	21	3	6	24	Galway, Dublin, and Mayo.
*Thorpe (5),	6	4	–	2	–	—
Thunder,	5	5	–	–	–	All in Dublin.
*Tiernan (26),	27	13	1	1	12	Louth.
*Tierney (74),	78	27	26	11	14	Dublin, Tipperary, and Galway—A very scattered name.
Tighe,	33	6	–	5	22	Mayo.
Timlin,	13	–	–	–	13	12 in Mayo and 1 in Sligo.
*Timmins (16),	25	21	2	2	–	Dublin, Kildare, and Wicklow.
*Timony (9),	14	1	1	4	8	—
Tinsley,	5	2	–	3	–	
Tisdall,	6	5	–	1	–	Dublin.
*Toal (19),	20	3	–	17	–	8 in Armagh and 6 in Antrim.
*Tobin (97),	98	27	69	1	1	Waterford, Cork, Tipperary, Limerick, Dublin, and Kilkenny.
Todd,	38	3	1	34	–	20 in Antrim and 8 in Down.
Tolan,	19	1	–	6	12	11 in Mayo.
Toland,	9	–	–	9	–	Antrim.
Toman,	5	–	–	5	–	3 in Down and 2 in Antrim.
*Tomkins (7),	9	8	1	–	–	—
Tomlinson,	5	2	2	1	–	
*Toner (39),	42	6	–	35	1	Armagh, Londonderry, and Antrim.
Tooher,	5	3	2	–	–	
Toolan,	10	2	1	–	7	Roscommon.
*Toole (98),	100	61	4	1	34	Dublin, Galway, Mayo, Wicklow, and Kildare contain 75 per cent.
*Topping (8),	10	–	1	9	–	Antrim and Armagh.
*Tormey (9),	11	8	–	2	1	—
*Torrens (8),	9	–	–	9	–	Antrim.
Totten (9)—Totton (8),	17	–	–	17	–	" Totten," 6 in Antrim ; " Totton," 5 in Armagh.
Tougher,	5	–	–	–	5	All in Mayo.
*Towey (28),	30	–	–	1	29	22 in Roscommon and 7 in Mayo.
*Townsend (9),	11	7	–	4	–	—
Trant,	6	–	6	–	–	Kerry.
Travers,	38	14	1	14	9	Donegal, Dublin, and Leitrim.
*Traynor (35)—Treanor (28)—Trainor (12),	77	24	1	48	4	" Traynor," Dublin—" Treanor " and " Trainor," Antrim, Armagh, Monaghan, and Tyrone.
Treacy (37)—Tracey (31)—Tracy (16),	84	30	29	10	15	" Treacy," Tipperary and Galway—" Tracey " and " Tracy," Dublin.
Trimble (12),	13	2	–	10	1	
Trotter,	12	–	–	11	1	
Troy,	31	15	16	–	–	King's, Cork, and Tipperary.

TABLE showing the SURNAMES IN IRELAND having Five Entries and upwards in the Birth Indexes of 1890, together with the Number in each Registration Province, and the Registration Counties in which these Names are principally found—*continued*.

Names.	IRELAND.	Leinster.	Munster.	Ulster.	Connaught.	Counties in which principally found.
	NUMBER OF ENTRIES IN BIRTH INDEXES FOR 1890.					
Trueman,	5	1	–	4	–	—
Tucker,	10	4	3	–	3	—
Tuite,	14	10	1	3	–	—
Tully,	45	8	4	14	19	Galway, Dublin, and Cavan.
*Tumelty (5),	10	3	–	7	–	—
*Tuohy (22),	40	8	23	–	9	Clare and Galway.—There are 9 varieties of this name in the Birth Indexes for 1890. 9 in Armagh.
Turkington,	12	–	–	12	–	—
*Turley (7),	9	2	–	4	3	—
Turnbull,	5	3	–	2	–	—
Turner,	67	22	13	30	2	Dublin, Antrim, and Cork.
Turtle,	9	–	–	9	–	7 in Antrim and 2 in Armagh.
Tutty,	5	3	2	–	–	—
Twamley,	6	2	4	–	–	—
*Tweedie (10),	15	1	–	14	–	—
Twohig,	15	–	15	–	–	All in Cork.
*Twomey (63)—Toomey (15),	80	8	72	–	–	"Twomey," 59 in Cork and 4 in Kerry; "Toomey," Dublin and Limerick.
Tynan,	20	14	5	1	–	Queen's.
Tyner,	6	4	2	–	–	—
*Tyrrell (27),	30	25	1	3	1	Dublin, Kildare, and Wicklow.
*Uprichard (9),	10	–	–	10	–	6 in Armagh and 4 in Antrim.
Upton,	6	3	2	1	–	—
*Usher (6),	8	5	–	3	–	—
*Valentine (8),	9	8	–	1	–	Dublin.
*Vallely (7),	9	1	–	8	–	Armagh.
Vance,	19	1	1	17	–	Antrim.
Vaughan,	35	5	18	9	3	Cork, Clare, Limerick, Antrim, and Down.
Veale,	12	1	11	–	–	Waterford.
Vickers,	5	2	3	–	–	—
Vincent,	8	2	3	3	–	—
Vogan,	5	–	–	5	–	—
Waddell,	12	–	–	12	–	—
Wade,	30	17	6	7	–	Dublin.
Waldron,	43	9	–	–	34	Mayo, Roscommon, and Dublin.
Walker,	123	28	7	84	4	Antrim, Dublin, Down, and Derry.
Wall,	58	31	26	–	1	Dublin, Waterford, Cork, Kilkenny, Limerick, and Tipperary.
*Wallace (140),	144	17	26	80	21	Antrim, Galway, Cork, Limerick, Dublin, Down, and Londonderry.
Waller,	6	3	1	1	1	—
Walls,	11	3	–	7	1	—
Walsh (877)—Walshe (55),	932	237	388	58	249	Cork, Mayo, Waterford, Galway, Dublin, and Wexford. Found in large numbers in nearly every county.
*Walters (5),	7	1	2	4	–	—
Walton,	8	4	2	2	–	—
*Ward (211),	213	57	22	87	47	Found in every county in Ireland, but chiefly in Donegal, Dublin, and Galway.
Wardlow,	5	–	–	5	–	4 in Antrim and 1 in Armagh.
Waring,	7	1	–	6	–	—
Warner,	6	1	5	–	–	4 in Cork.
Warnock,	15	–	–	15	–	Tyrone and Down.
*Warren (31),	35	13	16	2	4	Kerry, Dublin, and Cork.
*Warwick (6),	7	–	–	7	–	All in Antrim.
*Wasson (5),	8	–	–	8	–	—
Waters,	47	16	10	8	13	Sligo, Wexford, and Monaghan.
Watkins,	7	3	1	1	2	—
Watson,	120	11	2	104	3	Antrim, Armagh, and Down.
Watt,	33	1	1	31	–	Antrim.
Watters,	22	5	–	17	–	Tyrone, Antrim, and Louth.
Watterson,	14	1	1	12	–	Antrim.
Waugh,	5	–	–	5	–	—
Westterup,	6	–	–	6	–	All in Antrim.
Webb,	33	12	5	13	3	Dublin and Antrim.

TABLE showing the SURNAMES IN IRELAND having Five Entries and upwards in the Birth Indexes of 1890, together with the Number in each Registration Province, and the Registration Counties in which these Names are principally found—*continued.*

Names.	NUMBER OF ENTRIES IN BIRTH INDEXES FOR 1890.					Counties in which principally found.
	IRELAND.	Leinster.	Munster.	Ulster.	Connaught.	
Webster, ⋯ ⋯	21	12	2	7	–	Antrim and Dublin.
Weir, ⋯ ⋯ ⋯	56	2	1	50	3	31 in Antrim and 10 in Armagh.
Welby, ⋯ ⋯	5	–	–	–	5	All in Galway.
Weldon, ⋯ ⋯	14	10	3	1	–	—
Wells, ⋯ ⋯	9	2	1	6	–	Armagh.
*Welsh (27), ⋯	32	3	2	25	2	Antrim.
West, ⋯ ⋯	26	7	8	9	2	—
Weston, ⋯ ⋯	7	4	–	3	–	—
Wharry, ⋯ ⋯	5	–	–	5	–	All in Antrim.*
Wharton, ⋯ ⋯	5	2	3	–	–	—
Wheeler, ⋯ ⋯	14	8	3	3	–	Dublin.
*Whelan (213), ⋯	214	135	63	3	13	Dublin, Wexford, Waterford, Tipperary, Carlow, and Queen's.
*Wheiehan (5), ⋯	8	8	–	–	–	—
Whelton, ⋯ ⋯	11	–	11	–	–	10 in Cork and 1 in Kerry.
White (269)—Whyte (22),	291	82	91	94	24	Found in every county in Ireland—chiefly in Antrim, Cork, Dublin, and Wexford.
Whiteside, ⋯ ⋯	18	1	1	16	–	Antrim and Armagh.
Whitney, ⋯ ⋯	5	5	–	–	–	3 in Longford and 2 in Wexford.
Whittle, ⋯ ⋯	6	1	2	3	–	—
*Whitton (5), ⋯	8	4	1	3	–	—
Whitty, ⋯ ⋯	19	17	2	–	–	11 in Wexford.
Wickham, ⋯ ⋯	6	5	–	1	–	Wexford.
Wiggins, ⋯ ⋯	6	2	1	3	–	—
Wightman, ⋯ ⋯	6	–	–	6	–	Down.
Wilkinson, ⋯ ⋯	33	8	1	21	3	Antrim and Armagh.
Williams, ⋯ ⋯	90	40	25	14	11	A scattered name—principally found in Dublin, Cork, Limerick, and Antrim.
*Williamson (56), ⋯	57	3	–	54	–	Antrim, Armagh, Londonderry, and Tyrone.
Willis, ⋯ ⋯	33	6	5	22	–	Antrim and Down.
Wills, ⋯ ⋯	9	2	2	4	1	—
*Wilson (365), ⋯	366	49	22	287	8	Antrim, Armagh, Down, Tyrone, Dublin, Londonderry, and Fermanagh.
*Winters (15), ⋯	18	6	5	5	2	—
Wise (5)—Wyse (3), ⋯	8	2	6	–	–	—
Wiseman, ⋯ ⋯	5	1	3	1	–	—
Withers, ⋯ ⋯	5	1	–	4	–	—
Wood, ⋯ ⋯	14	7	3	4	–	—
Woodhouse, ⋯ ⋯	6	2	–	4	–	—
Woods, ⋯ ⋯	137	27	18	84	8	Antrim, Armagh, Down, Monaghan, Tyrone, Dublin, Louth, and Cork—A scattered name.
Woodside, ⋯ ⋯	9	1	–	8	–	8 in Antrim and 1 in Dublin.
Workman, ⋯ ⋯	5	–	–	5	–	4 in Antrim.
*Woulfe (12), ⋯	22	4	13	1	4	Limerick.
Wray, ⋯ ⋯	15	1	–	14	–	6 in Donegal and 5 in Londonderry.
Wren, ⋯ ⋯	12	1	10	–	1	—
Wright, ⋯ ⋯	103	20	8	72	3	Antrim, Down, Dublin, and Armagh.
*Wylie (32), ⋯	51	–	2	49	–	Antrim.
*Wynne (46), ⋯	47	18	9	3	17	Dublin and Sligo.
Yeates (14)—Yates (4),	18	6	3	9	–	"Yeates," 8 in Antrim and 5 in Dublin— "Yates," 3 in Cork.
*Young (131), ⋯ ⋯	132	25	20	87	–	Antrim, Tyrone, Dublin, Cork, Down, and Londonderry.

ADDENDUM.

List of Names of Irish Septs as given in the Book of Arms, compiled by Sir James Terry, Athlone Herald (1690), now preserved in the British Museum. [Harleian MSS. Nos. 4039 & 4040.]*

MA CARTY.
O BRIEN
O CARROLL.
MA GENNIS.
O NEILL.
O DONEL.
MAC DONEL.
O CONOR, KERRY.
O SEAGNASEY.
MA GUIRE.
MAC MURCHA.
O DRISCOL.
O DEMPSY.
MAC MAHON.
MA CANN.
O DWYER.
O DONEL, RAMALTAN.
MAC GULA PADRIGE.
O CONNOR ROE.
O RONAN.
MAC DERMOT.
MAC SWINY DUAG.
O CONOR, CORCMROE.
O FALLAN.
MAC SWINY FANID.
MAC SIHY.
O CONOR DON.
O DOGHERTY.
MAC KANNA.
MAC DONOUGH.
O MEARA.
O MADDEN.
MAC SWINY, BADUINE.
MAC GILL.
O MAHER.
O MULRIAN.
MAC CARTAN.
MAC AILIN.
O SHANLYS.
O ROURKE.
O SUILLUAN MORE.
MAC ELLIGOT.
MAC GILLYCUDY.
O CALAGHAN.
O DOUDE.
MAC SURDAINE.
MAC BRIN NA COMORA.
O FLAHERTY.
O GARA.
MAC AULY.
MAC QUYLIN.

O HARA.
O MALOY.
MAC AULIFFE.
MAC LAUGLIN.
O HANLON.
O LEARY.
MAC MANUS.
MAC GEES.
O DOULEE.
O MORIARTY.
MAC EGANE.
MAC DONOUGH.
O DONOGHOUE.
O DOUGAN.
MAC ENNERY.
MAC BROUDER.
O MAHONY.
O GARUAN.
MAC COGHLAN.
MAC HUGH.
O CULLEN.
O HOGAN.
MAC DUGOILE.
MAC GUILLIFOYLE.
O CALLENANE.
O CROWLY.
MAC BRIEN CARIGOGINEL.
MAC GRAGH.
O KEEFE.
O MULLANE.
MAC GRANELL.
MAC ROURRY.
O DONNAUANE.
O FINAGHTY.
MAC NAMIEE OFLORGON.
MAC HENRI.
O KEARNA.
O DRAUGHIE siue DORSY.
MAC CRUHIN siue KRUHIN.
MAC MURCHOE COLE-
    KNOCK.
O DULIN.
O GAWAN.
MAC GIARRE.
MAC VADAGH.
O DUIN.
O HALY.
MAC CABE.
MAC QUYLIN.
O TUAHOIL.
O BRINE CARLAUGH.

* Note —The names are given exactly as they appear in the List

MAC BRINE FIN IN
LINSTER.
MAC MILE.
O DALY, CONAUGHT.
O BRENAN.
MAC TIGERNAN.
MAC KEOU.
O KEARNA, KILMALOK.
O HAUGHIERN.
MAC MOYLIN.
MAC GIOLLA FINEN.
O DONOGANE.
O FOIN.
MAC FININ CARTY.
MAC BRINE O KUONAGH.
O CULLENAN.
O HART.
MAC KEAGHA.
MAC CAFFRY.
O FLOIN ARDA.
O BRINE ARRA.
MAC MORISCH.
MAC KINERINY.
O CONOR FAILGE.
O CONOR, SLIGO.
MAC NAMARA.
MAC MAHON.
O DINE siue DUNNE.
O KENNEDY.
MAC ODA.
MAC DABHY, BOURK.
O KELLY.
O CAHAN.
O HAGAN.
MAC SHANE.
MAC KALLIN.
O MALLY.
O FEOLANE.
MAC COLGAN.
MAC GRODDY.
O HINE.
O MULRONEY siue MEAL-
RONEY.
O LOCLAIN BORNIE.
O FARALL.
MAC ADIRE siue STAPL-
TON.
MAC TIBBOT siue THIBBOT.
BOURK.
MAC SEONIN. BOURK.
MAC PHILIBIN. BOURK.
O BOILL.
O GORMELY
O QUIN.
O NAUGHTEN.
MAC VATER. BOURK.
MAC REMON. BOURK.

MAC RICHARD BOURK.
MAC HUBERT. BOURK.
O CONOR.
O LONOGHER.
O HOGERTA.
O CRELLY.
MA CONDON.
MAC PADIN. BOURK.
MAC EUELLIN.
MAC MAOILRE. BOURK.
MAC VGHAK. BOURK.
O GORMAN.
OCLEIRIG.
O CREGAN.
O REYLEY.
O MALUNE.
O BRIN siue BRRIN.
O BRUIN.
O HAULLARAN.
O MORA.
O CREAN.
O BERNES.
O CALLINS siue O CALANE.
O CAUANAGH.
CINSIOLAGH. KENSIL-
LAGH.
O CLANCY.
O SEHIGHANE.
O FLANAGAIN.
O SUILLIUAN BEAR.
O CREGAN.
O GALUAN.
O CREHALL.
O DENEEN.
O LAUREY.
O LAWLOR.
O HYRE.
O TUOHIL.
O REGAN.
O HURLY.
O SESNAN.
O COGLAN.
O GRADY.
O CASSEY.
O DEA.
O LOINSIG.
O BEALLAN.
O NELAN.
O DEORANE.
O MOYLAN.
O LININ.
O CONALY.
O HALPIN.
O SCANLAN.
O MULLONY.
O LOUNDERS.
O BOUGHELLY.

O CORMCANE.
O KENELLY.
O HIGGIN.
O MEHEGAN.
MAC GEOHEGAINE.
MAC GUILLEGAN.
MAC CAUHIL. IRIGHTS.
MAC QUARD. item.
MAC NIELUS. item.
MAC DONNELLS GALOG-
  LAGH.
MAC CLOSKY. item.
MAC GORK. TERMANAGH.
MAC GABFRAIGH. item.
MAC GENNIS. KILUUAR-
  LIN.
MAC DEUETT.
MAC WARD.
MAC ERIGE.
MAC MACHON.
MAC FLANNCHA.
O MELAGHLEN, siue
  MLACHLEIN.
O MALAGHLIN.
O DOUGAN.
O NUOLAN.
O DUIGENAN.
O DELANY.
O GALCHOR.
O SUNIGAN.
O DONNOLAN.
O FEINIELA.
O FOGERTY.
O BRUODIN.
O CONRY.
O CONSIDIN.
O ENOS.
O BRADY.
O HEHER.
O HERNAN.
O HEGERTY.
O CORMACAN.
O GRIPHA.
O SINAN.
O KRIHONE.
O HENRAUGHTY.
O CONNELL.
O SCHANLA.
O HUOLOGHAN.
O HAININ.
O HORAIN.
O CONCEANAIN.
O MORAN.

O MALRY.
O MOGAIR.
O SINNAGII siue FOX.
O MORRIJ.
O CULLINAN.
O CORUIN.
O UILCUTH.
O MULTULLE.
O CULIN.
O CAISHIN.
O FLINN.
O SURIDIN siue SHERI-
  DAN.
O CASTULY.
O FOREHANE.
O CUSSIN.
O COULTAN.
O MEOILBRAENOIN.
O TOMA.
O FALUEY.
O SHIELS.
O HEFERNAN.
O FERENAN.
O HEDERIMAN.
O HOURAGNE.
O GORAN.
O CULLINAN.
O BOUGHAULA.
O SPILAN.
O BRISANE.
O RERDANE.
O HANNAN.
O LINE.
O CONSIDIN.
O SHEA.
O FREEL. TERMANAGH.
O NAHAN, supr. T.
O DIRY, supr. T.
O DUFFY.
O MALLAN. T.
O MUNGAN. T.
O DUUIN. T.
O ONNELLY. T.
O GILRIAGH.
DUIGENAN.
O TYERNAN.
O COWHY.
O DUILCUTH.
NOGOLOUGH.
BEATHEACH.
MAC BRINE FIN IN
  LINSTER.
MAC IAMES.

(27037.) Wt. P. 279—50/137. 1,000. 10/09. G. III.—A. T. & Co., Ltd.

VARIETIES AND SYNONYMES

OF

SURNAMES AND CHRISTIAN NAMES

IN IRELAND.

FOR

THE GUIDANCE OF REGISTRATION OFFICERS AND
THE PUBLIC IN SEARCHING THE INDEXES OF
BIRTHS, DEATHS, AND MARRIAGES.

BY

ROBERT E. MATHESON

BARRISTER-AT-LAW,

REGISTRAR-GENERAL.

DUBLIN:

PRINTED FOR HIS MAJESTY'S STATIONERY OFFICE,
BY ALEX. THOM & CO. (LIMITED), 87, 88, & 89, ABBEY-STREET.

And to be purchased, either directly or through any Bookseller, from
E. PONSONBY, 116, GRAFTON-STREET, DUBLIN ; or
EYRE & SPOTTISWOODE, EAST HARDING-STREET, FLEET-STREET, E.C.; or
OLIVER & BOYD, EDINBURGH.

1901.

PREFACE.

THE First Edition of this book was issued in the year 1890 with the object of assisting Registration Officers and the Public searching the Indexes of Births, Deaths, and Marriages by collating the varieties in the form and spelling of names usually met with, and also those names differing altogether in form, which had been ascertained to be used interchangeably.

A careful note has been made during the decade of cases where additional varieties or peculiarities in Surnames and Christian names have come under notice in this Office, or have been reported by local Officers.

In view of the revision of the Work, I addressed a special circular to the Superintendent Registrars and Registrars asking for information as to the nomenclature in their respective Districts, and I now beg to thank those Officers who have so kindly responded to my request, and in many cases furnished additional information of interest and value.

In the preparation of this Edition I have been cordially assisted by Mr. William A. Squires, Superintendent of Records, to whom my best thanks are due.

ROBERT E. MATHESON,
Registrar-General.

GENERAL REGISTER OFFICE,
CHARLEMONT HOUSE, DUBLIN,
March, 1901.

TABLE OF CONTENTS.

CHAPTER I.

INTRODUCTORY REMARKS.

THE subject of names presents an attractive field for investigation, but some of its most interesting aspects are beyond the scope of the present treatise, which is necessarily confined to those variations and peculiarities affecting our national records of Births, Deaths, and Marriages.

In January, 1894, I prepared for the late Registrar-General a Special Report on Surnames in Ireland, with notes as to numerical strength, derivation, ethnology, and distribution, based on information extracted from the Births Indexes of the General Register Office for the year 1890. This treatise was published as an Appendix to the Twenty-ninth Annual Report of the Registrar-General, and presented to Parliament.

There is, unfortunately, no complete record of the surnames in this country. An attempt was made by the Census Commissioners of 1851 to compile such a work, but when only partially done it was given up.

Our national Indexes of Births, Deaths, and Marriages for the last thirty-six years probably contain almost all the surnames in use in this country, but the information is necessarily scattered over many volumes, and the task of presenting in a complete and readable form the surnames of the population yet remains to be accomplished.

Apart from the official purpose for which they have been prepared, the Indexes form a most interesting study. Like the figures in the kaleidoscope, names are continually changing, old names dropping out and new ones appearing.

In addition to our Celtic, Anglo-Saxon and Norman surnames, we find Highland Gaelic names, represented by "MacDougal," "MacGregor," "MacIntosh." Welsh names are found, such as "Morgan," "Richards," "Apjohn." Danish names appear as "Dowdall," "Dromgoole," "Gould," "Coppinger." There are many Huguenot names, as "La Touche," "Du Bedat," "Lefroy," "Dubourdieu," "Le Fanu," "Drelincourt," "Dombrain," "Crommelin," "Boileau," "De Blacquiere." Italian names are represented, as "Bassi," "Ceppi," "Casciani." We have various German Palatinate names, as "Bovenizor," "Delmege," "Switzer," "Doupe," "Teskey," "Shire," and "Moddler." Jewish names are found, such as "Cohen," "Levi," "Aaron," and the Indexes are now showing the result of the recent migration to this country of Jews from Russia in such names as "Rabinovitch," "Weiner," "Matufsky," "Hesselberg," "Stuppel," "Rossin," "Winstock," "Greenberg," "Maisell," "Statzumsky," "Coplau," "Wachman," "Wedeclefsky," and "Fridberg."

None but those actually engaged in registration work can have any idea of the practical difficulties which are encountered by persons searching the Indexes, owing to the great variations in names in Ireland.

These variations are not only in spelling and form, but entirely different names are used synonymously by the same person or by members of the same family.

Many of these cases are direct translations of Irish names into English, or *vice versa*, while in others they are equivalents, modifications, or corruptions of them.

In a country where two different languages are spoken, it might be expected some such cases would occur, but in Ireland the practice is much more widespread than is commonly supposed.

In addition to the changes attributable to the difference of language, time has a powerful effect in altering names, which have also a tendency to assume various forms in different districts.

Illiteracy also operates in corrupting names, while they are also frequently varied in spelling and form at pleasure.

It is proposed in this treatise first to analyse the orthographical changes usually met with, and then to consider the use of different surnames interchangeably.

As some peculiarities have been met with in Christian names which affect the Indexes, it has been deemed advisable to insert a notice of them.

To the alphabetical list of surnames, with their varieties and synonymes, is prefixed a short explanation of the principles on which it has been prepared. The list is followed by an Index, enabling the reader to trace without difficulty each variety to the principal name or names with which it has been found to be used interchangeably.

CHAPTER II.

Orthographical Changes in Surnames.

It would be impossible to codify all the varieties in the spelling of surnames, but the following will illustrate the character of those changes most frequently met with, and indicate the direction in which the variety may be looked for.

Prefixes.

The most common prefixes in Ireland are the Celtic prefixes O and Mac.

I have received tne following reports as to the resumption of the prefix O by Celtic families :—

Armagh District—"A very large number have added 'O' as a prefix. Those who were formerly known as Neill are now O'Neill; Reilly, now O'Reilly; Hagan, now O'Hagan, &c. Indeed I think every one in my district who by any possibility could prefix the O has done so, and this was only commenced a few years ago. I have known earlier births registered without the O, but later ones of same family must have the O prefixed."

Mountshannon District—"It is becoming customary with the people of this district to add an O to such names as Callaghan, Kelly, Flanagan, Grady, Farrell, and call themselves O'Callaghan, O'Kelly, O'Flanagan, &c." On the other hand, the Registrar of Broughshane District, Ballymena Union, reports—"Some families have dropped the O, as O'Hamill, Hamill; O'Kane, Kane; O'Mellan, Mellan; O'Donnell, Donnell; O'Dornan, Dornan."

Prefixes may affect the Index in several ways. The name may be given without the prefix, or the prefix may be added to the name so as to form one word, or it may be incorporated in a modified form, producing a fresh variety of the name.

The following are instances :—

Prefix Fitz.	Name	Harris.
	With Prefix	FitzHarris.
	Prefix incorporated	Feeharry.
Prefix M^c or Mac.	Name	Guinness.
	With Prefix	McGuinness.
	Prefix incorporated	Maginnis.

The prefix Mac with surnames beginning with "Il" is sometimes incorporated as "Mackle," thus :—" MacIlhatton "—" Macklehattan "; " MacIlmoyle "—" Macklemoyle."

Prefix O.	Name	Reilly.
	With Prefix	O'Reilly.
Prefix D', De and DeLa.	Name	Courcy.
	With Prefix	D'Courcy, De Courcy.
	Name	Hunt.
	With Prefix	De La Hunt.
	Prefix incorporated	Delahunt.
Prefix Le.	Name	Fevre.
	With Prefix	Le Fevre.
	Prefix incorporated	Lefevre.

In some instances the name with the prefix has become obsolete. Thus for example the Registrar of Keady District (Armagh Union) reports:—

" I may mention that my own family name Dorman has been abbreviated from De Dormans."

Other prefixes have been reported from various districts.

The prefix " St." (abbreviation of Saint), is found incorporated in several names in a modified form, thus :—"St. Clair"—"Sinclair"; " St. John "—" Singen " or " Cingen "; " St. Leger "—" Sellinger."

The Registrar of Moira District has supplied an interesting note regarding various prefixes to the name Lavery. He states :— " Of Laverys there are several races in this vicinity, all having prefixes, and all rigidly denying relationship or common descent. They are Baun-Lavery (Bawn—White) ; Roe-Lavery (Rue—Red); Trin-Lavery, and Hard-Lavery. Of these Baun is the most usually or persistently adhered to, so much so that several people about here are known only by their prefix, as Charley, Ned, or Dan Baun. Many people would not know where any of these people lived were you to call them by the name Lavery without the prefix; indeed the last-named man in the above samples denies the Lavery altogether.

" Of Roe-Laverys, none now use the prefix that I am aware of. One man (who died recently at a very advanced age), used to be called Hugh Roe simply. . . His sons are simple Laverys, and never have I heard them referred to as Roes.

" The Trin-Laverys call themselves Armstrong. I can't see the connection, but it is worth noting.* I am not aware of any Trin-Laverys in this immediate neighbourhood, but there are a good many Armstrongs about four or five miles off, who I suspect are Trin-Laverys.

" Hard-Laverys are few. I only know one race. They have been occasionally called Hardy, but this name attends only two branches, and is not likely to be entered as a surname, having lapsed into a mere colloquial distinction."

It may be mentioned that the use of a prefix in connection with the name Lavery, has been reported to exist in other districts. Thus in Crumlin District (Antrim Union), the name appears as " Trim-Lavery," in Aghalee District (Lurgan Union), as " Tryn-Lavery," while in Glenavy District (Lisburn Union), the prefix is incorporated with the name forming " Trin-lavery."

The Registrar of Aghalee District also reports that the prefix Baun is used in his district with the name Lavery, and that Trin-lavery and Armstrong are used interchangeably.

---

* The prefix " Trin " or " Tryn " is probably the anglicised form of the Irish ᴄᴘéun '—" strong," and the synonymous use of the name " Trin–Lavery " with " Armstrong " may, perhaps, be explained by the fact that " Strong-handed " is in Irish " ᴄᴘéanᴌaṁaċ " [treanlamhach], from ᴄᴘéun, strong, and ᴌáṁ (lamh) a hand.

The tendency of a prefix to take the place of the entire name has been observed in several names such as "Mack" for Mackaleary, McDermott, McDonald, McEvoy, McInerney, McNamara, and McNamee, &c., and "Fitz" for "Fitzgerald," "Fitzsimons," "Fitzpatrick," &c. With regard to this last name a Registrar reports with respect to a Birth Entry where this peculiarity was observed,—"The name originally appears to have been 'Fitzpatrick,' but the name 'Fitz' has been used by this family for a generation, and it was the name which they have entered in the local Church Marriage Register."

The Assistant Registrar of Garvagh District (Coleraine Union) reports that "Fitz" is a familiar contraction *almost everywhere* of *all* names so beginning, just as "Mac" is similarly used for *all* names beginning with it.

Affixes.

Affixes are found either separately or in combination with the surname.

The following instances of affixes commonly in use may be given :—

Haugh	. .	Fetherston.
		Fetherston Haugh.
		Fetherston H.
		Fetherstonhaugh.
Roe	. . .	McDermott.
		McDermott Roe.
		McDermott-roe.
		Morris.
		Morrisroe.

Sometimes names are altered both by prefixes and affixes. The name Johnston, Johnson or Jonson, affords a good illustration of this. "Johnson," *i.e.*, the son of John, is in use interchangeably with "McShane," *i.e.*, the son of Shane or Shawn (Irish for John), and with "Mac-eown," the son of Eoin, another Irish form of John. "McHugh," *i.e.*, the son of Hugh, is synonymous with "Hewson." "McAimon," *i.e.*, the son of Aimon (an Irish form of Edmond), is found to be interchangeably used with "Edmundson."

In some districts, where there are many families of the same name, additional names are given for purposes of distinction, and these names frequently appear in the Index—thus :—

| Ryan | . . | Ryan (Slater). |
| Sullivan | . . | Sullivan (Magrath). |

The Registrar of Murroe District (Limerick Union) reports—"There are dozens of distinctions for 'Ryan' in this district, all well known locally."

The Registrar of Murragh District (Bandon Union) gives the

following affixes as in use in his district:—To the name Leary—Bue, Reagh, Dreedar, Rue; to the name McCarthy—Cahereen, More, and Reagh, and to the name Sullivan—Beara and Bogue.

Frequently the affix is the father's or mother's Christian name, the mother's maiden surname, or the grandfather's Christian name. A Registrar of Marriages reports:—" I know a ' Quinlan ' whose father was ' Cleary,' a ' Ryan English' whose father was ' Ryan.' "

The entry of the birth of a "John John Murphy " was met with in Millstreet District. On inquiry the Registrar stated:— " It is the habit in this part of the country to take the father's name to distinguish them from others of same name ; for example, ' John Daniel Murphy,' ' John Jeremiah Murphy,' and as in this case, ' John John Murphy,' there being so many families of the same surname."

The Registrar of Castlebar No. 1 District reports :—" Joyce, a very common name, is distinguished by affixing father's name, e.g., Tom Joyce (Tom), Tom Joyce (Martin), and in many cases further distinguished by any peculiarity of complexion, colour of hair, or special dress, or if exceptionally tall, and those are transmitted in the Irish language."

The Registrar of Tuosist District (Kenmare Union) furnishes the following note:—" The name Sullivan being exceedingly common, it is often omitted, and the Christian name of father (or mother) substituted, e.g., ' Johnny O'John,' ' John Williams,' or name of farm, as ' Dan Rusheen,' &c."

Occasionally the complexion of the members gives a surname to the family, e.g., Mike Bawn, or a distinction is made as " Shawn Og "—" Young John."

The Registrar of Kilkeel No. 2 District, remarks :—Often the grandfather's Christian name is used as an affix, as " Charles Cunningham Dick."

The Registrar of Sneem District, in Kenmare Union, reports —" ' Dorohy ' is applied to Sullivan, such as Sullivan Dorohy, also ' Mountain,' as Sullivan Mountain, and the other Sullivans are called after the locality they live in, &c., as ' Sullivan Glanac,' ' Sullivan Brachae,' ' Sullivan Dillough,' ' Sullivan Budoch.' "

The Registrar of Rathmullan District (Milford Union), states that—" The trade or occupation is often added *in Irish* after a surname, such as ' Mulrine (saorcloch ');—saorcloch, ꝛaoꞃcloċ, signifies a Mason.

Sometimes the affix entirely displaces the surname. A certificate of a marriage came under examination¯in the General Register Office, in which the bridegroom's name was given as " Patrick Sullivan," and his father's name as " Patrick Cooper." On inquiry it was ascertained that the father's real name was Patrick Sullivan (Cooper).

Initial Letters following Prefixes.

Initial letters following prefixes are sometimes dropped thus :—

| MᶜCusker | . | . | MᶜUsker. |
| MᶜClure | | | MᶜLure. |

One initial letter is substituted for another, as—

| MᶜIlmoyle | . | . | MᶜElmoyle. |

Or the letters following the prefix transposed,

| MᶜElroy, | . | . | MᶜLeroy. |

The letter " C " is sometimes repeated after " Mᶜ," as—

| MᶜAdam | . | . | MᶜCadam. |
| MᶜArdle . | . | . | MᶜCardle. |

Initial Letters.

Cases of substitution of one letter for another are very common, thus :—

A and E	.	.	Allison	.	.	Ellison.
C and G	.	.	Cannon	.	.	Gannon.
C and K	.	.	Carr	.	.	Kerr.
C and Q	.	.	Cuddihy	.	.	Quiddihy.
F and Ph	.	.	Fair	.	.	Phair.
F and V	.	.	Farrelly	.	.	Varrelly.
G and J	.	.	Gervis	.	.	Jervis.
G and K	.	.	Gilfoyle	.	.	Kilfoyle.
P and W	.	.	Phelan	.	.	Whelan.
Q and T	.	.	Quigg	.	.	Twigg.
Q and W	.	.	Quinton	.	.	Winton.

Initial consonants are sometimes doubled, as—

| French | . | . | Ffrench. |
| Folliott | . | . | Ffolliott. |

Initial letters are sometimes dropped or added, as—

| Ahearn | . | . | Hearn. |
| Hammond . | . | . | Whammond. |

Second Letters.

The following are some of the changes in second letters most commonly met with :—

Changes from one vowel to another—

a changed into e	as Bagley	.	Begley.
a	„	o	„ Laughlin	.	Loughlin.
e	„	i	„ Nesbitt	.	Nisbett.
e	„	o	„ Delahunty	.	Dolohunty.
o	„	u	„ Molloy	.	Mulloy.
u	„	i	„ Mulligan	.	Milligan.

Second letter, where a vowel, is dropped, as—

a	.	.	Eagan	.	.	Egan.
i	.	.	Aiken	.	.	Aken.

Second and Third Letters.

The following changes in these letters may be noted :—

Change of vowels—

a	changed into	ea	as Daly	.	.	Dealy.
ai	,,	ea	,, Kain	.	.	Kean.
au	.,	a	,, Maunsell	.	.	Mansell
ei	,,	ea	,, Reid	.	.	Read.
eo	,,	ou	,, Keogh	.	.	Kough.
i	,,	ui	,, Gilmartin	.	.	Guilmartin
o	,,	oo	,, Gogarty	.	.	Googarty.
o	,,	ou	,, Rorke	.	.	Rourke.
u	,,	ou	,, Burke	.	.	Bourke.

Transposition of vowels—

e and i	.	.	as Reilly,	.	.	Rielly.
,,	.	.	,, Neill,	.	.	Niell.

Intermediate Letters.

There are many changes observable in intermediate letters.
The following may be mentioned :—

Consonants dropped—

c before k	as Shackleton	.	.	Shakleton.
p after m	as Thompson	.	.	Thomson.

Consonants repeated—

	Mathews	.	.	Matthews.

Consonants interchangeable—

ff and v .	as Rafferty	.	.	Raverty.
s and z .	as Fraser	.	.	Frazer.

Syllables interchangeable—

ok, ogh, and ough, as Doherty	.	Dougherty.
Dogheny	.	Dougheny.

Syllables omitted or contracted—

Omitted,	as Donnellan	.	.	Donlan.
	Farrelly	.	.	Farley.

Contracted, as Corcoran	.	.	Cochrane.
Fennelly	.	.	Finlay.

Terminals.

The alterations in Terminals are numerous, both as regards single letters and syllables. The following examples may be given :—

Terminations interchangeable—

ie for *y*	. .	as Beattie	.	Beatty.
ies for *is*	. .	as Davies	.˙	Davis.
ce for *se*	. .	as Boyce	.	Boyse.
x for *cks*	. .	as Rennix	.	Rennicks.
y for *ey*	. .	as Mahony	.	Mahoney.

Dropping Consonants, Vowels.

Consonants—*d*	. .	as Boland	.	Bolan.
s (where double),	as Burgess	.	Burges.
t . .	as Lamont	.	Lamon.
gh (where silent),	as McWhaugh	.	McWha.
Vowels— *e*	. .	as Sloane	.	Sloan.

Adding *final s*

as	.	Askin	. Askins.
		Connor	. Connors.

Contraction or Abbreviation of Names.

There are many cases where a Contraction is substituted for the full name. The following will serve as examples :—

Free for Freeman.
Neazor for Bovenizor.
Pender for Prendergast.
Pendy for Prendeville.
Roy for M'Elroy and Royston.
Turk for Turkington.

Spelling according to usual Pronunciation.

All names are more or less liable to be spelled according to their pronunciation, but there are several instances where the name is pronounced quite differently from the spelling, and in these names almost invariably the spelling according to pronunciation is also found.

Thus—	Chism	for Chisholm.
	Chumley	,, Cholmondeley.
	Coburn	,, Cockburne.
	Cohoun	,, Colquhoun.
	Coakley	,, Colclough.
	Beecham	,, Beauchamp.
	Lester	,, Leicester.

Older Forms of Names.

In many cases the original form of a name has become lost or obsolete. In some instances, however, the alphabetical list still shows the original form of the name and the one now more commonly used, with indications of the various stages through which, in course of time, the name has passed into its present more usual form.

The name "Whittaker" appears to have come from White-acre, with which form it has been found to be used interchangeably. Thus—

> Whiteacre.
> Whiteaker.
> Whitegar.
> Whittegar.
> Whittacre.
> Whitaker.
> Whittaker.

Again, "Lammy" is traceable to the French "L'Ami," both forms being still in use. Thus—

> L'Ami.
> Lamie.
> Lammie.
> Lammy.

Another instance is the name Loughran, from the Irish O'Luchairen—

> O'Luchairen.
> Lucairen.
> O'Loughraine.
> Lochrane.
> Loughren.
> Loughran.

The Registrar of Cappoquin District (Lismore Union) reports:—"De Laundres or De Londres, an old Norman name, is found in this district in the forms of 'Landers' and 'Glanders'".

The French Huguenot name "Blanc," and its modern form "Blong," both appear in the Register Books of Cloneygowan District (Mountmellick Union). These names also occur in Rathangan District (Edenderry Union), the Registrar of which remarks —"The French spelling, 'Blanc,' is disliked owing to the literal pronunciation 'blank.'"

The name "Nestor" has been observed in the Records almost exclusively in the counties of Galway, Limerick, and Clare. In reply to a query regarding the origin or transformation of this name the Superintendent Registrar of Rathkeale Union states:—

"A.D. 1396. Iriel O'Loughlen was killed by Mac Girr-an-Adhastair (now Nestor), one of his own tribe.—(See History of Co. Clare, by James Frost). Adhastair (aóaſcaiſ) signifies a halter. There are two families named 'Nestor' living in the Rathkeale Dispensary District, Townland of Kilquain, and other families of that name reside in the Manor."

It may be added that this name has also been found in the Indexes in the form "Nester."

Local Variations in Spelling and Form.

The fact that names have a tendency to assume different forms in different localities is well known. The following may be cited as examples:—

The name MacAlshinder [synonyme for Alexander], which is the form used in Larne District, is found in the following forms in other districts:—

Elchinder,	in	Ballymoney District.
Elshander,	„	Ballylesson „ [Lisburn Union].
Elshinder,	„	Lisburn Union.
Kalshander,	„	Dromore District [Banbridge Union].
M'Calshender,	„	Ballymena Union.
M'Calshinder,	„	Banbridge „
M'Elshender,	„	Doagh [Antrim Union].
M'Elshunder,	„	Ballymoney Union.
M'Kelshenter,	„	Tanderagee District [Banbridge Union].

The names Archibald (or Archbold) and Aspel are found to be used synonymously in Rathcoole District (Celbridge Union). The following varieties have also been met with:—

Aspill,	in	Balrothery Union.
Esbal,	„	Portrush District.
Esbald,	„	Eglinton „ [Londonderry Union].
Esbel,	„	Limavady „
Esbil,	„	Coleraine „
Esble,	„	Ballymoney „

Again, the name "Ferguson," in addition to several variations in spelling, is found under the following forms:—

Faraday,	in	Lusk District.
Fargy,	„	do. do.
Fergie,		
Forgie,	„	Greyabbey District [N.T. Ards Union].
Forgay,	„	Ballymoney Union.
Forgey,	„	Portrush and Warrenpoint Districts.
Hergusson,	„	Lusk District.
Vargis	„	Bannow District [Wexford Union].
Vargus,	„	Broadway „ „

The name "Quigley" in Ferns District (Enniscorthy Union) and in Fethard No. 2 District (New Ross Union) has become "Cogley." In Monaghan Union it has assumed the form "Kegley," and in Belfast No. 6 District it has been found as "Twigley." It is worthy of note in connection with the last variety that "Quigg" and "Twigg" are reported by the Registrar of Belfast No. 7 District to be different forms of the same name.

Local pronunciation often affects the spelling of names. The Registrar of Clonavaddy District (Dungannon Union) has drawn attention to the fact that a number of people in his District spell their name "Hoins," and not "Hynes," the more usual form.

C

Variations in Spelling at Pleasure.

The following cases will illustrate the variation in spelling of names at pleasure :—

Some years ago the marriages of a brother and of a sister in the same family were solemnized in a Registrar's office. The son gave his surname as " Faulkner," and his father's surname as "Faulkner." The daughter gave her surname as " Falconer," and her father's surname as " Falconer." Both marriages were subsequently re-solemnized in a place of worship, and the same orthographical differences were found to exist in the records kept by the officiating minister.

A young man called at the General Register Office to obtain a certificate of his sister's birth, giving his surname and hers as " Milligan." When search for the entry proved unsuccessful, he suggested a search under the name " Mulligan," when the required entry was found. The entry was signed by the father, who, as occupier of a public institution, had signed a large number of entries, from which it appeared without doubt that the proper name was " Mulligan."

A record came under examination in which the informant, when registering the death of his brother, gave the name of deceased as " Fawcett," and signed his own name as " Fossitt." On inquiry into the case it was ascertained that the parties were in the habit of writing their names respectively as given in the entry.

A birth entry was found in Mountmellick District, where the informant signed his surname as " Headen." In a previous entry he had signed his name as " Hayden." In explanation the Registrar reported that the man wrote his name in both ways.

In another case the same informant wrote her name in different entries as "Kinnealy," "Kinneally," " Kenneally," and "Kenelly."

The Registrar of Drimoleague District, in Skibbereen Union, observes with reference to two death entries :—" In the same family, the father was known as ' Cue,' the son signs himself ' Hue,' and the two deceased children used to sign themselves ' MacCue.' "

The Registrar of Street District (Granard Union) reports :— "There is one family in this district, one member of which uses the name ' Murphy,' whilst another employs the designation ' Molphy' they being brother and sister."

Changes owing to Illiteracy and other Causes.

The differences caused by illiteracy are too numerous and well known to require much comment. To such a cause may be referred " Lannan " and " Linnen" for " Lennon," " Nail" for " Neill." " Dulinty " and " Dulanty" have been found written by uneducated persons for " Delahunty."

Religious and social differences sometimes cause varieties in surnames.

Two local officers have reported that, in the case of the name Wallace or Wallis, it is spelled "Wallis" by the members of one religious communion, and "Wallace" by those of another.

Similar reports have been received regarding the use of the names "Neill" and "O'Neill," "Coole" and "Coyle," and of the names "M'Cusker" and its equivalent "Cosgrove."

In one district the name "Connellan" is said to be so spelled by persons of good social position, while the peasantry use the form "Conlan."

Another Registrar, in County Kildare says :—"A man who would get a little money would change from 'Doolin' to 'Dowling.'"

Variations are also produced by other causes, such as the tendency to assimilate names to those of distinguished persons. One Registrar reports "Nielson" has become "Nelson," while another states "Parlon" has become "Parnell," so that all the families in his district of the former name now use the latter.

CHAPTER III.

USE OF DIFFERENT SURNAMES INTERCHANGEABLY.

THE use of entirely different names interchangeably by the same person prevails in Ireland to a much greater extent than is commonly supposed. This is principally owing to the differences in language—many of these being cases of translation of Irish names into English, or *vice versa*, or equivalents, modifications, or corruptions of them. There are, however, other cases which cannot apparently be accounted for in this way.

Registration officers are sometimes placed in considerable doubt which name to record. A Registrar recently reported that some families are invariably called by other than their real names, and that it is often a matter of some difficulty to ascertain the correct name.

A Superintendent Registrar writes :—"If any local person called at the office to know if Christopher Sherwin had registered the death of a friend, he would ask, was the information given by 'Kitty Sharvin.' A man living within a hundred yards of James Fitzpatrick or Christopher O'Malley, would never know who was meant unless they were called 'Jem Parrican' or 'Kit Melia'; there are many such cases, and yet those are not what are called nicknames."

It is proposed to refer first to the cases of English and Irish names used synonymously, and then to other cases not falling within that category.

English and Irish Names.

The practice which prevails in Ireland of using two names appears to be largely traceable to the influence of ancient legislative action.

By a Statute of 1366, it was provided, *inter alia*, that " every Englishman do use the English language and be named by an English name, leaving off entirely the manner of naming used by the Irish"; and in 1465 [5 Ed. IV., cap. 3] a law was passed enacting "that every Irishman that dwells betwixt or amongst Englishmen in the County of Dublin, Myeth, Vriell, and Kildare . . . shall take to him an English surname of one town, as Sutton, Chester, Trym, Skryne, Corke, Kinsale; or colour, as white, blacke, browne; or arte or science, as smith or carpenter; or office, as cooke, butler . . ."

In many cases, where English and Irish names are used interchangeably, they are translations from one language into the other or translations of words similar in sound.

The following may be cited as examples:—

English Form.	Anglicised Irish Form.	Irish Words.
Bird, .	Heany, Henehan, Henekan, McEneany.	ean (ean)—a bird.
Bishop, .	Easping, Aspig,	eaṛboṡ (easbog)—a bishop.
Black, .	Duff, . .	ᴅuḃ (dubh)—black.
Boar, .	McCullagh, . .	collaċ (collach)—a boar.
Bywater, .	Sruffaun, .	ṛṛuṫán (sruthan)—a streamlet.
Church, .	Aglish, . .	eaᵹlaiṛ (eaglais)—a church.
Crozier, .	Bachal, . .	baċal (bachal)—a crozier.
Farmer, .	McScollog, . .	ṛcolóᵹ (scolog)—a petty farmer.
Fox, .	Shanaghy, Shanahan, . Shinnagh, Shinnock, . Shonogh, Shunagh, &c.	ṛionnaċ (sionnach)—a fox.
Freeman, .	Seerey, Seery, . .	ṛaoṛ (saor)—free.
Godwin, .	O'Dea, . .	ua(ua)—a descendant, ᴅia(Dia) —God.
Gray, .	Colreavy, Culreavy, .	ṛiaḃaċ (riabhach)—gray.
Green, .	Houneen, Huneen, Oonin.	uaine (uaine)—green.
Hand, .	McClave, . .	láṁ (lamh)—a hand.
Holly, .	Quillan, . .	cuileann (cuileann)—holly.
Hunt, .	Feighery, Feighney, Feighry, Fehoney, Feghany.	ṛiaḋaiᵹe (fiadhaighe)—a huntsman.
Hurley, .	Commane, . .	comán (coman)—a hurling stick.
Judge, .	Breheny, Brehony, .	bṛeaṫaṁ (breathamh)—a judge.
King, .	Mac-an-Ree, McAree, Muckaree, &c.	ṛíᵹ (righ)—a king.
Kingston, .	Cloughry, .	cloċ (cloch) — a stone; ṛíᵹ (righ)—a king.
Little, .	Begg, Beggan, . .	beaᵹ (beag)—little.
Long, .	Fodha, . .	ṛaᴅa (fada)—long.
Oaks, .	Darragh, McDara, &c.	ᴅaiṛ (dair)—an oak.
Oats, .	Quirk, . .	coiṛce (coirce)—oats.
Rabbit, .	Conheeny, Cuneen, Cunneen, Cuuneeny, Kinneen, &c.	coinín (coinin)—a rabbit.
Roche, .	Rostig, . .	ṛóiṛteaċ (roisteach)—a roach.
Rock, .	Carrick, . .	caṛṛaicc (carraicc)—a rock.
Sharpe, .	Gearn, Gearns, .	ᵹéaṛ (gear)—sharp.
Short, .	McGirr, . .	ᵹoṛ (gor)—short.
Silk, .	Sheedy, . .	ṛíoᴅa (sioda)—silk.
Smith, .	Goan, Gow, Gowan, McGowan, O'Gowan.	ᵹoḃa (gobha)—a smith.
Thornton, .	Drinan, . .	ᴅṛoiᵹeann (droigheann)—blackthorn.
Walsh, .	Brannagh, Brannach, .	bṛeaṫnaċ, (breathnach) — a Welshman.
Waters, .	Toorish, Tourisk, Turish, Uiske.	uiṛᵹe (uisge)—water.
Weir, .	Corra, . .	cóṛa (cora)—a weir.
White, .	Banane, Baun, Bawn,	bán (ban)—white.
Whitehead, .	Canavan, . .	ceann (ceann)—a head; bán (ban)—white.

The Registrar of Cappoquin District reports that a man named Bywater came into his office in order to register the death of his brother. He gave his brother's name as Michael Sruffaun. On being interrogated as to the difference in the surnames, he said that he was always known by the name of Bywater, but his brother by the name Sruffaun. *Sruffaun* is a local form of *sruthan*, an Irish word for a little stream.

In Rynn District (Mohill Union) an entry came under observation where the surname " Colreavy " was altered to " Gray." The Registrar reported in explanation that the family signed their names both as " Colreavy " and " Gray." The deceased had been in America where he signed his name as " Gray."

The Registrar of Murragh District (Bandon Union) notes the synonymous use of " Hurley " and " Commane " in his District, and remarks " Comman " is the Gaelic for " Hurley," and is a " stick with a curved boss to play goal with."

The Registrar for Riverstown District (Sligo Union) reports, regarding the names " Breheny " or " Brehony " and " Judge," above mentioned, that they were almost all " Brehenys " some time ago, but now they are becoming " Judge."

A person applied recently to one of the Registrars for the certificates of the births of his two daughters, registered as Anne and Margaret M'Girr. He stated they were christened by the name of " Short," and that he was married as " Short," but always received the name of " M'Girr"—" Short " and " M'Girr " being synonymous names.

In a death entry in Dundrum District (Union of Rathdown), the surname of deceased appeared as " Smith," while the entry was signed by his son, who gave his surname as " O'Gowan."

A marriage certificate from Enniskillen District came recently under my observation in which the bridegroom and one of the witnesses signed their surnames " Going or Smyth," the other witness signing " Going or Smith."

The Registrar of Termonfeckin District reports :—" The surnames ' Markey ' and ' Rhyder ' are used synonymously in my district. The more usual surname ' Markey ' is most frequently used, but in the case of some families ' Rhyder ' is used interchangeably for ' Markey,' one branch of a family being known by the surname ' Markey,' another by that of ' Rhyder,' and in some instances the father taking the surname ' Rhyder ' and the son that of ' Markey.' I may add, that this use of the name ' Rhyder ' for ' Markey ' is not peculiar to my district, many of the neighbouring districts having for residents persons who are known by the synonymes ' Rhyder '—' Markey.' " " Markey " is the anglicised form of the Irish mapcac (marcach), a horseman, hence the equivalent " Ryder," or " Rhyder."

There are many cases, shown in the Alphabetical List, which are not direct translations, in which equivalents, modifications, or corruptions are used interchangeably.

A Registrar reports :—" There are two brothers—one Berming-ham, and the other M'Gorisk." In other Districts the name " Bermingham " has been found to be used interchangeably with " Magorisk " and " Korish."

The names " Blessing " and " Mulvanerty " are reported to be sed synonymously in two Districts in the Union of Mohill Mohill and Rowan) and in Ballinamore District (Bawnboy nion).

The Registrar of Birr District reports :—" A family here named ' Renehan ' is sometimes called ' Renehan ' and sometimes ' Ferns.' They are both the same. ' Renehan,' I believe, is the Irish and ' Ferns ' the English synonyme."

The Registrar of Carrigallen District (Mohill Union) reports :— " ' Minagh ' or ' Muinagh ' is a synonyme for Kennedy. In two cases of these names the fathers of the families are called ' Pat Muinagh ' and ' Francis Muinagh,' respectively, and would scarcely be known by ' Kennedy.' The children are generally called ' Kennedy."

The Superintendent Registrar at Cavan states :—" The name ' M'Grory ' is used as the Irish substitute for ' Rogers,' and there is an instance in the townland of Mullaghboy, in the Electoral Division of Drumlane, in which a person has been rated both as ' M'Grory ' and ' Rogers.' "

The Registrar of Draperstown District (Magherafelt Union) reports :—" ' Rogers ' now prevails here, but up to recently they were all ' M'Rory.' "

The names " Loughnane " and " Loftus " are found to be used interchangeably. These are probably anglicised forms of the Irish name " O'Lachtnain."

The effect of the difference in language on surnames is further evident in many cases given in the alphabetical list in modifying the forms of names. Thus the name " Hyland " has been found in the following forms :—" Heelan," " Heyland," " Highland," " Hiland," and also used synonymously with " Whelan." The Registrar of Ballinrobe District has furnished an interesting note regarding this name, which accounts for these variations, and also for the fact that the names " Whelan " and " Phelan " have been found to be used interchangeably in numerous districts. The Registrar remarks :—" ' Hyland ' is used interchangeably for ' Whelan ' by a family who live near Kilmilkin, in the Cloonbur No. 2 District ; and though the name in this District of Ballinrobe is spelled ' Hyland,' still the Irish pronunciation of it is ' Ui-Holan ' or ' Ui-Hilan,' which would also be the exact Irish pronunciation of the names ' Whélan,' ' Faelan,' ' Félan,' ' Phélan '—in fact, the spelling in Irish of each of the names is ' Ui-Faolain.' The ' F ' is aspirated, and then sounds like ' H,' so that the Irish *sound* of the name is ' O'Helan.' "

The late Registrar of Murragh District (Bandon Union), stated :—" The name ' Keohane ' is changed to ' Cowen ' in this district, and several parts of the County Cork, and the euphony which favours this change is the same as that which occurs in the word 'Bohane,' changed into 'Bowen.'"

The Irish form of "Conway" is "Conmee." The Registrar of Draperstown District (Magherafelt Union) observes that "Conway" is the nearest approach to the full sound of the Irish word in English. The Irish "m," being aspirated, is pronounced as "w."

The following interesting note has been furnished by the late Registrar of Lettermore District:—

"The principal facts with regard to personal nomenclature in this locality are:—

"(1.) The English names or surnames are never used by the peasantry in speaking to or of one another, or even when acting as informants at registration, except where the name is so strange that it cannot be easily hibernicized, and in the latter case it is often contracted or corrupted as 'Anderson,' 'Landy'; 'Wyndham,' 'Wind,' &c.

"(2.) In many cases the English form is traceable (though often faintly) in the Irish form, which consists in the prefix 'O,' and a softening of the sound of the name to suit the Irish tongue.

"(3.) In other cases, no trace, or very little, of the English form remains, as 'M'Donogh,'—'O'Cunnacha;' 'Walsh,'— 'Brannach' (without 'the O').

"(4.) In still other cases, if the English name happens also to be a common noun or adjective, as Black, Green, Ridge, &c., the Irish form of the common noun is used, such as 'Ridge'—'Canimurra.' Canimurra means 'head of a ridge,' (as of potatoes, &c.)."

Other Names used Interchangeably.

Many cases of the synonymous use of different surnames other than the foregoing have come under the notice of this office.

A widow named "M'Dermott" applied to this Department for proof of her marriage and of the births of her children, with the view of obtaining a Government pension. Search was made in the Indexes in the usual way, with the result that the records of the marriage and of the births of all the children were found, except one. In this case the applicant was informed that the name did not appear in the Index. As, however, the locality in which the birth occurred was stated, a special examination was made of the records themselves, with the view of ascertaining whether there was any entry at all corresponding with the particulars furnished, and then it was discovered that the child had been registered under the surname "Dermody," which is known to be a synonyme for the name "M'Dermott."

The Registrar of Killeen District (Dunshaughlin Union) reports that "Tiger" is used in his district for "McEntegart."

A Registrar writes :—"'Hayes' and 'Hoy' are used indifferently by one family connection. In the Registers, at their selection, 'Hoy' is entered. I requested them to select."

In another District a Registrar reports :—"McIneely, Conneely, and Connolly are written indiscriminately by the same family."

The names "Halfpenny" and "Halpin" are reported to be interchangeably used in several Districts. A search was recently made for the entry of the birth in Drumconrath District (Ardee Union) of a "Joseph Halpin," and he was found to be registered as "Joseph Halpenny."

The Norman name "Petit" or "Pettit" is, in one District, stated to be used synonymously with its English translation, " Little."

The Alphabetical List contains a record of numerous other cases falling within this category.

Irregular Use of Maiden Surnames.

It is a common practice for mothers of children, when registering births, to sign the entry with their maiden surname.

Cases have also frequently come under notice where in death entries deceased widows are registered under their maiden name, instead of their married name, the maiden name having been resumed on the death of the husband.

The Registrar of Tuam No. 2 further reports that in some cases in his District the mother's maiden surname is used by the children, instead of the father's, as—"John Keane," real name—" John Dunne."

CHAPTER IV.

CHRISTIAN NAMES.

ALTHOUGH variations in Christian names are not so likely to mislead as variations in surnames, yet in many cases the difference is of such a nature that names of common occurrence would be thrown out of their proper place in the Index and escape notice altogether, or, if seen, might be taken to refer to other persons.

The peculiarities in Christian names which may affect the Index may be divided into *six* classes.

Names applied to both Sexes.

The following may be mentioned as commonly in use :—

Florence.
Sydney or Sidney.
Evelyn.

" Cecil " may now be placed in the same category, reports having been received from Registrars in various parts of the country of its use for females as well as males.

In certain parts of County Donegal " Giles " is applied to both males and females. It occurs also as " Giley " and " Jiley." A marriage record from Milford Union, in that county, came under my observation, in which the bride, and one of the witnesses (a female) were named " Giles."

Sometimes ordinary Christian names distinctively belonging to one sex are given to the other. Thus a child named " Winifred " was recently registered in Cork as a male. On inquiry it was ascertained that the name and sex were both correctly entered. This name contracted to " Winfred " has also been found applied to a male. " Jane " has also been notified as applied to a male, and " Augustus " to a female.

" Nicholas " has been reported from two districts as applied to females, and " Valentine " from another district. In Belfast a female child was lately registered from the Maternity Hospital as " Irene," but the name was subsequently corrected by the father, on statutory declaration before a magistrate, to " Robert." In reply to a query on the subject, the Registrar stated the name given to the female child being a male name (Robert), he called the attention of the father to the fact at the time, and the father replied it was his wish to have the child called " Robert."

The names of saints are frequently given to male and female children as Christian names without reference to the sex, for instance, " Joseph Mary," or " Mary Joseph," for a male ; " Mary Joseph," or " Johanna Mary Aloysius," for a female.

There are some names similar in sound, where the sex is indicated only by a slight difference in spelling, which, when badly written are liable to be mistaken, such as Francis—Frances, Olave —Olive, Jesse — Jessie.

Occasionally surnames are used as Christian names, and applied to either sex.

Abbreviations applicable to both Sexes.

The following abbreviations are applicable to both sexes :—
" Joe " for " Joseph," " Josephine," and " Johanna"; " Phil " for
" Philip " and " Philomena "; " Fred " for " Frederick " and
" Frederica "; " Matty " for Matthew " and " Matilda "; " Jemmie "
for " James " and " Jemima"; " Harry " for " Henry " and
" Harriett"; " Ally " for " Aloysius " and " Alice."

In some cases contractions usually applied to one sex are
applied to the other, such as—
" Edie " (usual contraction for " Edith " female name) for
" Adam," male.
" Elly " (usual contraction for " Ellen " or " Ella," female
name) for " Oliver," male.
" Kitty " (usual contraction for " Catherine," female name) for
" Christopher," male.
" Amy " (usual contraction for " Amelia," female name) for
" Ambrose," male.
" Jerry " (usual contraction for " Jeremiah," male name) for
' Gertrude," female.
" Lotty " (usual contraction for " Charlotte," female name) for
" Laughlin," male.

Abbreviations materially differing from the Original Name.

The following may be mentioned in illustration :—

Males—	
Bartly, Bartel, Bat	for Bartholomew.
—— Tatty	for Clotworthy.
—— Criddy	for Christian.
—— Larry	for Laurence.
—— Rody, Rory	for Roderick.
—— Lack, Lacky	for Laughlin.
—— Moss	for Maurice.
—— Mundy	for Redmond.
Females—	
Nancy, Nanny	for Anne.
—— Bessie, Lizzie	for Elizabeth.
—— Cassie	for Catherine.
—— Honor, Norah, Noey, Onny	for Hanorah.
—— Polly, Molly	for Mary.
—— Jugge	for Judith.
—— Nappy	for Penelope.
—— Shibby	for Isabella.
—— Sia	for Cecilia.
—— Louie	for Lucinda.
—— Peggy	for Margaret.

The Registrar of Toome District (Ballymena Union) reports :—
" As a Christian name ' Clotworthy' becomes ' Tatty.' Two men
called ' Clotworthy'—Livingstone, are known respectively as
' Black Tatty' and ' Red Tatty' Levesen."

The Registrar of Westport No. 2 District observes—"'Nappy' is a very common name in the Leenane District, and the people generally are unaware that it is 'Penelope'; the latter is obsolete."

Different names used interchangeably.

The following may be instanced :—

Males—Alexander . . Alaster, Sandy.
—— Edward . . Edmond.
—— Florence . . Finian.
—— Gerald . . Garrett, Garret, Gerard.
—— Owen . . Eugene.
—— Hugh . . Hubert.
—— Moses . . Aidan.
—— Peter . . Pierce.
—— Ulysses . . Ulick.
—— Connor . . Cornelius.

Females—Bridget . . Bedelia, Delia, Beesy.
—— Gobinet . . Abigail, Deborah.
—— Johanna, Joanna . Jane.
—— Julia . . Judith.
—— Julia . . Johanna.
—— Winifred . . Unity, Una, Uny.

An application was recently made to me for the correction of the age of an "Aidan Dillon" in a death entry. On investigation it transpired that his birth, which occurred in Camolin District (Gorey Union), was registered under the name "Moses Dillon."

Not only are the names "Gobinet" and "Abigail" used interchangeably, but their contractions, "Gubbie" and "Abbie" or "Abby," are similarly used.

In the certificate of a marriage in Darrynane District (Caherciveen Union), the bride's name was given as "Gubbie" in the body of the record, while her signature appeared as "Abbie." The Registrar reported—"I find that 'Gubbie' is really a contraction of 'Gobinet,' and 'Abbie' a name in itself; but the custom among the people here appears to be to use the names 'Gubbie,' 'Abbie,' and 'Webbie' as if they were different forms of the same name." In Emlagh District, in the same Union, the forms "Gubby" and "Deborah" or "Debbie" have been found to be used interchangeably.

The Superintendent Registrar of Castlecomer Union reports— "the people of the County Kilkenny and some other places consider the names 'Johanna,' 'Judith,' and 'Julia' to be the same."

Irish Equivalents for English Names.

Several such cases have been found. The following may be mentioned :—

English Names.		Anglicised Irish Forms.
Males—Bernard	. .	Bryan.
—— Daniel	. .	Dhonal.
—— Edmond	. .	Aimon, Eamon, Mon.
—— Jeremiah	. .	Darby, Dermot, Diarmid, Diarmud.

English Names.		Anglicised Irish Forms.
Males—John	. .	Shane.
—— Moses	. .	Magsheesh, Mogue.
—— James	. .	Shemus, Shamus.
—— Timothy	. .	Teigue, Thiag, Thigue, Theigue.
—— Michael	. .	Meehal, Meehall.
—— Patrick	. .	Paudrick, Phadrig.
—— Cornelius	. .	Nahor.
—— Philip	. .	Phelim.
—— William	. .	Laymeen, Leam.
—— Dudley	. .	Dualtagh.
—— Francis	. .	Phrinchas.
—— Denis	. .	Dinogha.
Females—Susan }		
—— Johanna }	. .	Shovaun.
—— Bridget	. .	Brideen, Breeda.
—— Mary	. .	Maura, Maureen, Moira, Moya.
—— Maud	. .	Meav.
—— Mabel	.	Nabla.
—— Celia, Cecily or }		
—— Cicely }	.	Sheela, Sheelah.
—— Sophia	. .	Sawa.
—— Julia	. .	Sheela.

The Registrar of Stewartstown District, Cookstown Union, reports:—"*Darby* Martin lived in Brookend and his son is called *Jeremiah* Martin, after his father."

The name "Mago" has been observed in Kiltegan District (Baltinglass Union), in Kilrush District, and in Annascaul and Dingle Districts, in Dingle Union. To a query addressed to the Registrar of the last-named district, regarding the origin of the name, the following reply was received:—"From all the information I could obtain it appears that 'Manus' is the Irish anglicised into 'Mago,' or, in some families, 'Mane.' When the father's name is 'Mago,' and a child is called after him, the latter is generally called 'Mane,' to distinguish him from the former. The name is very general in two families in this Barony."

Cases of Incorrect Spelling.

The under-mentioned, amongst others, have been met with :—

Males—Philip	. .	Filip.
—— Sylvester	. .	Cylvester.
Females—Alicia	. .	Alisha, Elisha.
—— Cecily	. .	Sicely.
—— Charlotte	. .	Sharlot, Sharlotte.
—— Elinor	. .	Elnar.
—— Esther	. .	Osther, Easter.
—— Harriett	. .	Hargot, Hargate.
—— Kate	. .	Cate.
—— Magdalene	.	Magdillon.

Peculiar names found in the Indexes.

It only remains in conclusion to refer to some peculiar names, many of them the names of local patron saints, which are liable to be mis-spelt, or otherwise metamorphosed, so as to be thrown out of their proper place in the Indexes. Thus, the name " Ailbe," the patron saint of Emly diocese, has been found in the forms, " Elli," and " Elly," as well as in its proper form " Ailbe."

Two cases recently came under notice in Kilrush Union where the Christian name " Sinon " was given to males. This name is taken from the name of a local saint—St. Senan—and has been met with also in the forms "Senan" and " Synan."

The name " Gourney " for a female was entered in the Register Book of Deaths for Ardrahan District, in Gort Union, County Galway. In reply to a query, the Registrar stated—" This is the only Christian name I could obtain for this woman after a considerable amount of trouble. It is pronounced ' Gurney,' but I believe it is spelt with an ' o.' It is a very uncommon name, but on inquiry I found that St. Gourney is considered the patron saint of a locality not far from here." This name has been reported from Kinvarra District (Gort Union), as " Gurney."

The names " Gillan," " Geelan," and " Keelan," have been reported by the Superintendent Registrar at Mohill, as forms of the name " Kilian," from St. Kilian.

The various forms " Cairn," " Cairan," " Kiaran," " Keiran," " Kieran," and " Kyran," which occur in many parts of Ireland, and are derived from the names of local saints, are very liable to cause confusion in searching. They are sometimes found under the letter " C " and sometimes under the letter " K." Several Registrars report their use under both initial letters in the same locality.

Two entries of birth came under observation in which the name of the child in one and the name of the father in the other were given as " Maur." It was supposed that this was an error in copying for " Maurice," and the Registrar was asked for an explanation. In reply he stated—" Maur, for all I can find out, may be an abbreviation of ' Maurice,' but in this town (Rush), they are looked upon as entirely distinct. Rush, being a fishing village, it was dedicated to St. Maur, who is the patron saint of the place." The Registrar adds that St Maur is the original of the name ' Seymour,' and it might readily assume that form as a Christian name.

A Registrar reports—" Some years ago a man gave me ' Eden' (pronouncing ' E ' like the long English ' A ') as the name of his daughter. I told him I knew no such name. He rather indignantly asked me did I never hear of the Garden of Eden, and said he called her after that." In this case had the Registrar entered the name as pronounced by the informant it would have appeared in the Index as ' Adan ' or ' Aidan,' a well-known male name, and thus, probably, altogether escaped observation.

Other peculiar names have been found, such as " Kado," " Gamuel," " Dill " (in various districts in County Donegal), and "Flan," for males; also "Coosey," and "Afric" (in various parts of Donegal), for females. As, however, such names, if correctly written, do not affect searches, it is unnecessary to refer further to them.

MEMORANDUM EXPLANATORY OF ALPHABETICAL LIST.

IT now remains to add a short explanation of the structure of the Alphabetical List.

It has been compiled from (a) office notes made from time to time for many years past of cases actually coming under observation in the examination of the Records and preparation of the Indexes; (b) from special reports received from the Superintendent Registrars and Registrars of Births, Deaths, and Marriages, and the District Registrars of Marriages, under the 7 and 8 Vic., cap. 81 ; and (c) from the results of a special examination of the printed Indexes in the General Register Office.

The list does not profess to be a complete list of surnames, but only a list of those surnames of which varieties have been met with or reported by local officers to be used in their localities,

The principal names are printed in capitals and numbered throughout consecutively. It is not to be understood that these are the original forms of the names, but the forms which appear to be now most commonly in use.

The names following each of the principal names are the varieties and synonymes of same stated to exist. Where printed in italics they have been reported to be Irish forms (or equivalents) of English names, or *vice versa*. Where a variety is placed in brackets, thus "[Cromie]," it will be found also as a principal name, and where given thus:—

" Archbold or " Snowden (Snedden) "

(Aspell),"

the second name has been reported as a variety of the form of the name immediately preceding it.

It is not intended to convey that the names appearing under the principal names are in all cases forms of the same name, but only that they have been found to have been used interchangeably in the examination of the registration records, or that they have been reported to be so used by local officers.

Neither is it to be inferred that the use of a particular synonyme is general throughout the country. In many cases it is only local. On the other hand, in some cases, the same peculiarities have been observed in many different parts of the country.

Frequently the same name appears as a variety under different principal names. Thus " Cahan " is used as an alias for " Kane," and also for " Keohane."

In many instances numbers have been added after the name to denote the districts from which the variety has been reported. The key to these reference numbers is printed after the list. In cases not so marked, the variety has been met with in the examination of the records in this office.

With the view of curtailing the size of the list, the following will generally be found under one form only:—1. Names ending in ie, y, or ey, as Dempsie . Dempsy . Dempsey. 2. Names terminating with double consonants, as Farrell   Farre

ALPHABETICAL LIST OF SURNAMES WITH THEIR VARIETIES AND SYNONYMES.

No.	Surnames, with Varieties and Synonymes.	No.	Surnames, with Varieties and Synonymes.	No.	Surnames, with Varieties and Synonymes.	No.	Surnames, with Varieties and Synonymes.
1	ABERCROMBIE. Crombie. [Cromie].	16	AISKEW. Askew. Ayscue.	32	ARBUTHNOT. Burthnot. Button. 86.	49	AYLWARD. Ailward. Alyward. Ellard. 526.
2	ABERNETHY. Abernathy. Aberneathy. Benathy. 89. Habernathy. Habernethy.	17	ALDERDICE. Alderdise. Aldridge. 249. Allardice. Allerdice. 249 Elderdice.	33	ARCHDALE. Esdale. 254.	50	AYNSCOUGH. Ainscough. Anscough. Ayscough.
3	ABRAHAM. Abram.	18	ALEXANDER. Elchinder. 59. Elshander. 55. Elshinder. 347. Elshner. 48 (b). Esnor. 112. Kalshander. 9, 210. Macalshender. 112. MacAlshinder. 44, 338. McCalshender. 58. McCalshinder. 75, 494. [McCausland]. 112. M'Clatty. 478. M'Elshender. 204. McElshunder. 60. McKelshenter. 489.	34	ARCHDEACON. [Cady]. 100.		
4	ACHESON. Achison. Aitchison. Atcheson. Atchieson. Atchison. [Atkinson]. 17, 293, 523.			35	ARCHIBALD. Archabald. Archabold. Archbald. Archbold. (Aspell). 435. Archibold. [Aspel]. 436. Aspill. 72, 364. Esbal. 428. Esbald. 234, 254. Esball. 254. Esbel. 19, 313. Esbil. 177. Esble. 59.	51	BACKAS. Bachus. Backhouse. Backis.
5	ACHMUTY. Ahmuty. Amooty. 215. Auchmuty. Aughmuty.					52	BAGNALL. Bagenall. Bagnell. Beglan. 274. Begnall. (Begney). 495. Begnell. Bignel.
6	ACRES. Akers.			36	ARDILL. Ardell. Ardhill.		
7	ADAMS. Adam. [Adamson]. Aidy. 310. [Eadie]. 210.			37	ARMITAGE. Armytage.	53	BAGOT. Baggett. Baggot.
8	ADAMSON. [Adams]. Edimson. 76.	19	ALGIE. Algeo.	38	ARMSTRONG. [Lavery]. 197, 347. Trim – Lavery. 197. Trinlavery. 6, 257, 347. Trun-Lavery. 6.	54	BAIN. Baines. Bayne.
9	ADDY. Addi. Ady. Eaddy. Eady. Edy. Edye.	20	ALLEN. Allan. Alleyne. Allin. [Hallinan]. 510.			55	BAIRD. Beard. Beird.
10	ADRIAN. Adrien. Drain. 450.	21	ALLISON. Alison. Alleson. Allisson. [Ellison]. 374, 429.	39	ASKIN. Asken. Askins. Erskin. 55, 222. Haskins.	56	BALDWIN. Baldin. 488. Baldoon. 262.
11	AGAR. Aigar. [Eagar]. 303.	22	ALTON. Altimes. 287.	40	ASPEL. Archbold. 73, 436. [Archibald].	57	BALLANTINE. Ballantyne. Ballentine. Ballintine. Ballyntyne.
12	AGLISH. Church.	23	ANBOROUGH. Anboro.	41	ATKINS. Aitkins. [Atkinson].	58	BANFIELD. Banfell. 131.
13	AGNEW. Aignew. Egnew.	24	ANDERSON. Andrewson.	42	ATKINSON. [Acheson]. 17, 293, 523. [Atkins].	59	BANNATYNE. Banatyne. Bannytine.
14	AHEARNE. Aheran. Aherin. Aherne. Aheron. [Hearn]. Hearon. Heron. 77. [Herron]. 77.	25	ANGLESEA. Anglesey.	43	ATTERIDGE. Atherage. Atheridge. Attridge.	60	BANNON. Banan. Banin. Bannan. Bannen. Bannin. Banon.
		26	ANKETELL. Ancketell. Ancketill. Ankethill.	44	AUCHINLECK. Achinlec. Achinleck. Aghinlec. Aghinleck. Auchinlec.		
		27	ANKLAND. Ankle. 199.	45	AUL. Auwll. 93.	61	BARKLIE. Barclay. Barcley. Barkley. 426 Bartley. [Berkely].
15	AIKEN. Aicken. Aikin. Aikins. Aitckin. Aitken. Aitkin. Aken. Eaken. Eakin. 159, 374. Eakins. 91. Ekin. 340. Eykin.	28	ANNESLEY. Ainsley. Annsley. Ansla. 73. Ansley.	46	AUNGIER. Danger. 121.	62	BARLOW. Barley. 519.
		29	ANTHONY. Antony.	47	AUSTIN. Astin. 8. Aston. 18. Austen. Auston.	63	BARNES. Bardon. 183. Bearnas. Berrane. 138. [Byron]. 138.
		30	APPLEBY. Appelbe. Appelbey. Applebee.	48	AYLMER. D'Aylmer. Elmer.	64	BARRETT. Barnett. 488. Barratt. Bartnett. 488.
		31	ARBUCKLE. [Buckle]. Buckles. 257.				

No.	Surnames, with Varieties and Synonymes.	No.	Surnames, with Varieties and Synonymes.	No.	Surnames, with Varieties and Synonymes.	No.	Surnames, with Varieties and Synonymes.
65	BARRY. Barrie.	89	BERMINGHAM. Birmingham. Birminghan. Bremigam. 45. Brimage. 424. Brimagum. 386. Brimmagem. 72, 378. Brimmajen. 511. Brimmigan. 511. Brumagem. Brumigem. 401. Brumiger. 40. Brummagem. 72. Brummagen. 473. Caorish. 393. Corish. 28, 393. Korish. 104. MacFeerish. 189. Magorisk. 137. M'Gorish. 319. McGorisk. 127(b).	108	BLAKE. Blavagh. 40. Blakes. 254. Bleach. 469. Blouk. 136. Blowick. 136.	132	BORTHISTLE. Berthistle. Birthistle. Birtwistle. Burthistle.
66	BARTHOLOMEW. Barklimore. 86.			109	BLAKELY. Blackely. Blackley. Bleakley. Bleckley. Bleeks. 478. Blekley.	133	BOTHWELL. Bodel. 238. Bodell 450. [Bodle]. 238, 247. [Bowden]. 210.
67	BARTNETT. Barnidge. 488.						
68	BATES. Baith. 72.					134	BOUCHIER. Boucher. Bourchier.
69	BATTERBERRY. Batter. 431.			110	BLAKENEY. Blakney. Bleakney. Bleak. 131.	135	BOVENIZOR. Bovenizer. Bovinizer. Neazer. Neazor.
70	BAXTER. Bagster.			111	BLANC. Blong. 435.		
71	BAYLY. Bailey. Bailie. Baillie. Baily.			112	BLANCHFIELD. Blanch. 468.	136	BOWDEN. Boden. [Bothwell]. 210.
		90	BERNARD. Barnane. 227. Barnard.	113	BLAYNEY. Blainey. Blaney. Bleaney. Bleney.	137	BOWEN. Bohan. Bohane. 37, 397. Bohanna. 397. Boughan.
72	BEATTY. Beatagh. 329. Beattie. 494. Beaty. [Betty]. 238. 346. M'Caffery. 460. [McCaffry]. 247.	91	BERRY. Bera. 154.	114	BLENNERHASSET. Hassett. 318, 382.	138	BOWLES. Boal. 91. Boale. Boales. Bole. 91. Boles. Bouls. Bowle. Bowls.
		92	BERRYMAN. Bergman. 410.	115	BLESSING. Mulvanerty. 35, 380, 464.		
		93	BERTRAM. Bartrem.	116	BLOXHAM. Bloxsom.		
73	BEAUCHAMP. Beecham. 162.	94	BETTY. [Beatty]. 238, 316. Bettie. [M'Caffry]. 238.	117	BLYTHE. Bligh. Bly. Blyth.	139	BOWMAN. Beaumont. 7.
74	BECHER. Beecher. 488.	95	BEWICK. Beewick.	118	BOAKE. Boakes.	140	BOXWELL. Boxhill.
75	BECK. Bex.	96	BICKERSTAFF. Bicker. 429. Bickers. 429. Bickerstay. 197. Bigger. 429. Biggerstaff. 195. Biggerstaffe. [M'Givern]. 429.	119	BOARDMAN. Boordman. Bordman. Borman.	141	BOYCE. Boice. Boyes. Boyse. Buie. 341. Bwee. 341, 459.
76	BECKETT. Bickett.			120	BOAZ. Boas.		
77	BEDLOE. Bedlow.			121	BODKIN. Zorkin. 40.		
78	BEGGS. Baggs. Begg. Biggs. Bueg. 227.			122	BODLE. Boddle. Bodel. Bodill. [Bothwell]. 238, 247.	142	BOYLAN. Boreland. 19. Boyl. 471. [Boyle]. 471. Bullion. 19.
79	BEGLEY. Bagley. Bigly. [Morrison]. 238, 247.	97	BINGHAM. Bigam. Biggam. Bigham. Byngham.				
		98	BIRCH. Burch. Burdge.	123	BOGUE. Boag. Bogues.	143	BOYLE. Bog. 107. Boal. 83. Foil. 225. Bole. 59. [Boylan]. 471. O'Boyle.
80	BEHAN. Beaghan. Beahan. Bean. Bearkin. 183. Behane. 47, 51.	99	BIRD. [Heany]. 40. Henehan. 119,269. Henekan. 506 [McEneany]. 319.	124	BOHILL. Boyes. 175.		
81	BELCHER. Belsher.			125	BOLAND. Bolan. 454 (b). Bowland. Bullion. 482.	144	BOYNE. Bonny. 497.
82	BELLEW. Bailey. 248.	100	BIRKMYIE. Birkey. 494.			145	BRADLEY. Bradly. O'Brallaghan. 254.
83	BELLINGHAM. Billigam. 59.	101	BIRNEY. Berney. Byrney.	126	BOLGER. Boulger. Bulger. 263.		
84	BENNETT. Bissett. 364. Dimmett. 325.	102	BIRRANE. Byrane. [Byrne]. 266. [Byron]. 266.	127	BOLTON. Balton. 390.	146	BRADSHAW. Bratty. 372.
85	BENSON. Benison. Bennison.	103	BISHOP. Aspig. Aspol. Bisshop. Easping.	128	BONAR. Boner. Bonnar. Bonner. Crampsey. 271. [Crampsie]. 479, 482, &c. Crampsy. 369.	147	BRADY. Briody. 154. [M'Brearty]. 259, 260.
86	BERGIN. Bergan. 68. Bergen. Berrigan. 384. Burgoyne. 473.	104	BLACK. Blackham. 409. [Duff].			148	BRANDON. Brendon.
87	BERKELY. [Barklie]. Berkly.	105	BLACKADDER. Blackender. 86.	129	BONES. Boness. Bownes. 229.	149	BRANNICK. [Walsh]. 506.
88	BERKERRY. Bearkery. Berachry. Berkery. Berkry. Berocry. Biracrea. Biracree.	106	BLACKBURNE. Blackbourne.	130	BORLAND. Boreland. Burland.	150	BRANNIGAN. Branagan. Brangan. 72, 137. Branigan. Brankin. 197. Brennigan. 174.
		107	BLACQUIERE. Blacquire. Blacre. De Blacquiere.	131	BORRISKILL. Bariskill.	151	BRAZIL. Brassil. 47. Brazel.

D

No.	Surnames, with Varieties and Synonymes.	No.	Surnames, with Varieties and Synonymes.	No.	Surnames, with Varieties and Synonymes.	No.	Surnames, with Varieties and Synonymes.
152	BREDIN. Braidon. Breadin. Breadon. Bredon. Breydon.	168	BROSNAHAN. Bresnahan. Bresnane. Bresnehan. Bresnihan. Brosnahen. Brosnahin. Brosnan. 8, 375. Brosnihan. Brusnahan. Brusnehan. Brusnihan.	182	BUICK. Buck. 473.	206	BYRNE. Beirne. 454 (b). Beirnes. Berne. Berrane. 386. Berigin. 396. Beryin. 396. Biern. 35. Bierne. 456. Birne. Birnes. [Birrane . 266. Bourn. Bourne. Burn. 56. Burnes. [Burns]. 358. Byrnes. 358. Byrns. [Byron]. 155. 259. 266. McBrin. 461. McBrinn. 289. 381. Mucbrin. 71. O'Beirne. 410. O'Byrne.
153	BREEN. Brien. 520. Briene. 146.			183	BULLEN. Boleyn. Bullens.		
154	BREHONY. Brehany. Breheny. [Judge]. 105,339, 454 (a), &c.			184	BULLER. Bulla. 358.		
155	BRENNAN. Branan. Braniff. 268. Brannan. 121,432. Brannen. Brannie. 267. Brannon. 385. Branon. Breanon. Brenan. Brennen. Brennon. Brenon. Brinane. 227.	169	BROUGHALL. Broughill. 435.	185	BULLMAN. Baulman. 378.		
		170	BROUGHAM. Broham. Broom. Brugham.	186	BULLOCK. Bulloch.	207	BYRON. [Barnes]. 138. Berrane. 138. [Birrane.] 266. Byran. Byrane. Byrrane. [Byrne]. 155, 259. 266.
		171	BROWN. Broune. Browne.	187	BUNTING. Bunton.		
156	BRERETON. Brearton. Brerton. Bruton. 121,420.	172	BROWNLEE. Brawnlee. [Brownlow]. 154. Burley. 238.	188	BUNYAN. Banane. 142. Binane. 142.	208	BYWATER. Sruffaun. 120.
157	BRESLIN. Bresland. 12. Breslane. 375. Breslaun. 16. Breslawn. 243. Brice. 206. Brislan. Brislane. Brislaun. Brislin. Broslin. Byrce. 259, 260.	173	BROWNLOW. Brimley. 428. [Brownlee]. 154.	189	BURBIDGE. Barbage. Borbidge. Borbridge. Burbage.	209	CADDELL. Caddle. Cadell. Kadell. Keddle.
		174	BRUCE. Brewster. 421. Browster. 41.	190	BURCHELL. Birchill. Bourchill. Burchill. Burtchaell. Burtchell.	210	CADDOW. Caddoo. Cadoo. Kaddow. [McCaddo].
		175	BRUEN. Bruin.	191	BURGESS. Burges. Burgiss.		
158	BRETT. Britt. 393.	176	BRYAN. Brian. 422. Brien. 393. Briens. Brine. Brines. Brion. Bryans. Bryen. Bryne. Brynes. Bryney. [McBrien]. [O'Brien]. 393.	192	BURKE. Bourke. 175. 509.	211	CADOGAN. Cadigan.
159	BRIERY. Bryry.			193	BURKITT. Birkett. Birkitt. Burkett.	212	CAFFREY. Caffary. Caffery. Caffray. [Caulfield]. 350. Kaffrey. M'Caffrey. 505.
160	BRINDLEY. Brendley.	177	BRYSON. Briceson. [Morrison]. 271.	194	BURLEIGH. Burley.		
161	BRITTON. Bretton. Britain. Briton. Brittain. Brittan.	178	BUCHANAN. Bockocan. 401. Bohanan. 318. Bohanna. 92. Bohannon. 55. 233. Bohunnan. 432. Buchanen. Buchannan. Buchannon. Mawhannon. 55. [Mawhinney]. 204. McWhannon. 429. Mewhanan. 347. Mowhannan. 410.	195	BURNELL. Birnell. Bornell. Byrnell.	213	CAHALAN. Cahalin. Cahallane. Cahelan. Cahelin. Cahillane.
				196	BURNISTON. Bonison. 503.		
162	BROADHURST. Brothers. 78.			197	BURNS. [Byrne]. 358. Byrnes. 358. O'Byrne. 206.	214	CAHANE. Cohane. Keohane. O'Cahan.
163	BRODERICK. Brauders. 100. 117. Brodders. 109. Broder. 2. 382. Broderic. Brodrick. Brooder. 117. Broothers. 316. Browder. 65. Bruder. 134. 319. Brudher. 378.	179	BUCKLE. [Arbuckle]. Bookle. Boughal. Buckles. [Buckley].	198	BURRELL. Berrall.	215	CAHEERIN. Keheerin.
				199	BURRIDGE. Berridge. Burage. Burge. Burrage.	216	CAHIR. Kehir. 189.
164	BRODY. Brodie. 509.	180	BUCKLEY. Boughla. 249. Buckely. [Buckle]. Buhilly. 420. Bulkeley. 373. Bulkely.	200	BURROUGHS. Borris. Borroughs. Borrowes. Burriss. Burrowes. Burrows.	217	CAIRNS. Cairn. Cairnes. [Kearns]. 300. Keirans.
165	BRONTE. Brontie. Brunty.			201	BURT. Birt. Byrt.		
166	BROOKE. Brookes. Brookins. Brooks.			202	BURTON. Berton.		
				203	BUSSELL. Bushell. 350.	218	CALDERWOOD. Catherwood. 254.
167	BROPHY. Brofie.	181	BUCKMASTER. Master.	204	BUTLER. Buttler. 422.		
				205	BYERS. Byars.		

No.	Surnames, with Varieties and Synonymes.	No.	Surnames, with Varieties and Synonymes.	No.	Surnames, with Varieties and Synonymes.	No.	Surnames, with Varieties and Synonymes.
219	CALDWELL. Calwell. 58. Cauldwell. Cawldwell. Colavin. 154. Coldwell. Collwell. Colovin. 154. Colwell. 58, 92, &c. Conwell. 58. Cullivan. 49. Horish. 48 (b). Kilwell. 279.	228	CANNING. Caning. [Cannon]. 361, 432, 465. Canon. [Cunnane]. 361. Kenning. 197.	246	CARR. Carre. Karr. 175. Ker. 175. [Kerr]. 19, 213. Kerranc. 258. Kirrane. 5. McElhar. 206. McIlhair. 459. Wilhair. 459.	261	CAULFIELD. [Caffrey]. 350. [Cavanagh]. 461. Cawfield. Colfield. M'Cavanagh. 461. [M'Keown]. 289.
220	CALLAGHAN. Calaghan. Calahan. Callaghen. Callagher. 279. Callaghin. Callahan. Callaughan. Calleghan. Callehan. Calligan. Callighan. Kelaghan. 374. Kellaghan. 374. [Kelly]. 19. [O'Callaghan]. 390.	229	CANNON. Canaan. 72. Cannan. [Canning]. 361, 432, 465. [Cunnane]. 54, 272, &c. Gannon. 174. Kennon. 388. [Kinnane]. 72.	247	CARRAGHER. Caragher. Curaher. 414. Carraher. 414. Kerragher.	262	CAVANAGH. [Caulfield]. 461 [Kavanagh]. 14 516. M'Cavanagh.
		230	CANTILLON. Cantlin. Cantlon.	248	CARRICK. [Craig]. 482. [Rock].	263	CAWLEY. Cowely. Cowley. 231. [Macaulay]. 300
221	CALLAGY. Kellegy.	231	CANTLY. Kentley. 358.	249	CARRIGY. Carrigee. Kerragy.	264	CHADWICK. Chaddick. Chiddick. Sedgwick. 410.
222	CALLAN. [Callanan]. 360. Callen. Callin. Caulin. 178 (a). Cawlin. 495. [Colquhoun]. 399.	232	CANTY. County. 47.	250	CARROLL. [Cardwell]. 210. Caroll. Carrolly. [M'Carroll]. O'Carroll.	265	CHAMBERS. Chalmers. 254.
		233	CAPEL. Caples. [Keppel]. Kepple.			266	CHAYTOR. Cheator.
		234	CAPPLIS. Capples. 65.	251	CARRUTHERS. Carothers. Carrithers. Carrothers. Caruthers. Corathers. 181. Crothers. 213.	267	CHESNEY. Chesnaye.
223	CALLANAN. Calinan. Callaghanan. 373. [Callan]. 360. Callanane. Callinan. Callnan. Calnan.	235	CAPPOCK. Cappack. Cappuck. Kappock. Keappock.			268	CHESTNUTT. Chesnutt. Chessnut.
		236	CARAWAY. Carvey.	252	CARTON. Cartan. Carten. Cartin. [Carty]. 4.	269	CHISHOLM. Chisham. Chishem. Chism. 418. Chisom. 86.
224	CAMAC. Camack. Cammack.	237	CARBERRY. Carbery. Carbry.	253	CARTY. Carthy. 183. [Carton]. 4. Charthy. M'Arthy. [M'Carthy]. 448. [O Carthy]. 525.	270	CHISSELL. Choiseuil. Choiseul—Chisel. 249.
225	CAMLIN. Camblin. Camelin. Cammelin.	238	CARDWELL. Cardell. Cardle. 210. [Carroll]. 210.			271	CHOMONDELEY. Chamley. Chomley. Chumley.
226	CAMPBELL. Cambell. Camble. Camill. Camp. 185. Campble. Campell. Camphill. Cample. Kemp. 185. McCallion. 113, 271, 321. McCallnon. 97. [McCavill]. 216. McCawel. 417. McCowell. 163, 418. M'Guillan. 319	239	CAREY. Carew. 249, 326, &c. Ceary. 286. [Curran]. 520. [Currane]. 520. Karey. Keary. Keary. 167, 517. Keern. 58. Keery. 63. Kirrane. 38.	254	CASEY. Caicey. Cassy. 262. Keacy.	272	CHRISTIE. Christy. (Christian). 348. Chrysty. Cristy.
				255	CASHEN. Casheen. Cashin. Cashion. Cashon. Cassian. Cassin. 420, 496. Keshin.	273	CINNAMON. Cinamon. Cinamond. Cinnamond. Sinemon. Sinnamon.
		240	CARLETON. Carlaton. Carlton.	256	CASS. Coss. 149.	274	CLANCY. Clanchy. Glancy. 515.
		241	CARLISLE. Carley. 86. Carlile. Carlyle.	257	CASSELLS. Cassell. Cassle. Cassles. Castle. Castles. Cushlane.	275	CLARKE. Clairke. Clark. 494. Clarkins. 380. [Cleary]. 238, 506, &c. Clerke. Clerkin. 40, 82, 515, &c. Collery. 485.
		242	CARMODY. Kermode.				
		243	CARNDUFF. Carrinduff.	258	CASSIDY. Casaday. Casidy. Casley. 410. Cassedy. Cassiday. Cassidi. Kessidy. 72.	276	CLASSON. Classan. Claussen. Clausson. Clawson.
227	CANAVAN. Cannavan. Guinevan. 488. Kanavaghan. 181. [Kernaghan]. 410. Kinavan. 36. [Whitehead].	244	CARNEGIE. Carnagie. Carneagy.			277	CLEARY. Clarey. [Clarke]. 238, 506, &c. Cleery. Clery. 317.
		245	CAROLAN. Carlan. 432. Carland. 64, 141. Carlin. 63, 64, 89, 141, 279. Carlon. Carolin. Carollan. Carrolan. Carrolin. Kerlin. Kirland.	259	CATHCART. Kincairt. 374. Kincart. 432.	278	CLEAVER. Cleever.
				260	CATTERSON. Caterson. Keaterson. Keterson.	279	CLEELAND. [Oleland]. Creeland. 381.

No.	Surnames, with Varieties and Synonymes.	No.	Surnames, with Varieties and Synonymes.	No.	Surnames, with Varieties and Synonymes.	No.	Surnames, with Varieties and Synonymes.
280	CLELAND. [Cleeland]. Clelland. Clellond.	296	CODY. [Archdeacon]. 100. Coady. 263. [Cuddihy]. [Cuddy].	307	COLVILLE. Colvan. Colvil. Colvin.	318	CONNIFF. Conneff. [Connor]. 447. Cuniff. Cunniffe. Quinniff.
281	CLEMENTS. Clemens. Clement. Climents. Climons. Clymens. Clymonds. M'Clamon. 254. M'Clement. 254. M'Clements. M'Clymonds. M'Lamond. 19.	297	COFFEY. Coffee.	308	COMERFORD. Comerton. 526. Comford. 120. Comfort. 135. [Comiskey]. 153, 154. Commaskey. 246. Commefort. 72. Cummerford.	319	CONNOLLY. Conally. Coneely. Conelly. 463. [Conlan]. 185, 410, &c. Conley. Conlon. 223, 410. Conly. 14, 112. Connally. Connaly. Conneally. 307. Conneaty. 463. Conneelly. 463. Conneely. 253, 272. [Connell]. [Connellan]. Connelly. 463. Connely. Connoly. Conole. Conolly. Conoly. Cunneely. Kenelly. 119. McIneely. 119. Size. 436.
282	CLENDENNING. Clandinning. Clendenan. Clendennin. Clendining. Clendinning. Clindenning. Clindinnen. Glendinning.	298	COGAN. Coogan. Cooken. [Goggin]. 397. Keogan. 20.				
		299	COGHLAN. Coaghlan. Coghlen. Coghlin. 61. Cohalane. Coholane. 397. Colcloughan. 155. Colin. 498. Collom. 65. Coughlan. 61, 375. Coughlen. Coughlin. 61.	309	COMISKEY. Comaskey. [Comerford]. 153, 154. Comesky. Commaskey. Commerford. 246. Cumaskey. Cumesky. Cumisk. Cumisky. Cummiskey.		
283	CLIBBORN. Clayborne. Clayburn. Clebburn. Cleburne.						
284	CLIFFORD. Cluvane. 8, 377.	300	COHEN. Coan. Coen. [Cowan]. 71. Koen.	310	COMMANE. Commons. 39. Cummane. [Cummins]. 45. [Hurley]. 189, 237, &c.	320	CONNOR. Coner. Conier. Conner. [Conniff]. 447. [Connors]. 100, 183. Conors. Conyer. Conyers. 456. Cunnyer. 240. McCottar. 343. M'Cutter. 53. McNoger. 59. McNogher. 60. McNohor. 343. Menoher. 367. Minochor. 60. Minogher. 60. Minoher. 53. Naugher. 113. Nocher. 175. Nocker. 17. Noghar. 59. Nogher. 71, 137. Noher. 71. O'Conner. [O'Connor]. 100. O'Conor.
285	CLINCH. Clinchey. Clynch.	301	COLE. Coall. Coles. Culle. 318. M'Cole. 259.	311	COMMONS. Coman. Commane. 39, 509. Commins. Common. Cowman. 408. Cummane. 179. [Cumming]. 303. Cummings. [Cummins]. 3, 125, &c.		
286	CLOONEY. Cloney. Clowney. 155. Clowny. 155, 429. Clune. 109. Cluney. McLoonie. 429.	302	COLEMAN. Clovan. 101. Cloven. 468. Colman. 72.				
		303	COLGAN. Coligan. 454 (b). Collagan. Colligan. Culgan. Culgin. Culligan. 308, 318. McColgan. 271. Quiligan. 318. Quilligan. 107.	312	CONATY. Conaghty. Conotty. McConaghy. 211.		
287	CLOTWORTHY. Clitterdy. 503.						
288	CLUGSTON. Cluxton.			313	CONDON. Condron. 420. Coonoon. 488.		
289	CLUSKEY. Clusker. [Cosgrave]. 364. [McCluskey].	304	COLLINS. Colins. [Culhane]. Cullane. [Cullen]. 433, 489. Cullian. 447. Callina. 38. McCallan. 238. O'Cullane. 189. Quillan. 414.	314	CONLAN. Colnan. 103. Conla. 429. Conland. 321. Conlin. 372. Conlon. [Connellan]. 220, 248. 282. [Connolly]. 185, 410, &c.	321	CONNORS. [Connor]. 100, 183. [O'Connor]. 2, 189, &c.
290	CLADESDALE. Clidesdale. Clisdale. Clysdale.					322	CONRAN. Condron. 63.
291	CLYNES. Clyns. 38.	305	COLQUHOUN. Cahoon. 91. Cahoun. Calhoun. [Callan]. 399. Choun. 240. Cohoon. Cohoun. 399. Colhoon. 399. Colhoun. 141. 417. Culhoun. 244. [Cullen]. 244. Colquohoun. 91. Kahoon.	315	CONNAUGHTON. Connaghton. Connerton. 255. Connorton. 3, 255.	323	CONROY. Conary. Conrahy. 68, 457. Conree. [Conry]. 454 (b). Cory. 48 (b). Cunree. 419. [King]. 40, 342. Mulconry. 189.
292	COAKLEY. Coakeley. Cokeley. Colclough. (Cokely). 15. Kehelly. 397. Kehilly. 227. Keily. 397.						
				316	CONNELL. Eally. 145. Conall. [Connellan]. 102, 409. Connelly. 356. [Connolly]. [McConnell]. [O'Connell].		
293	COCHRANE. Caughran. Cockrane. Coghran. [Corcoran]. 72, 410.	306	COLUMB. Collum. Collumb. Colomb. Colum. [McCollum].				
				317	CONNELLAN. [Conlan]. 220, 248, 282. Conley. Conlin. Conlon. 248. [Connell]. 102, 409. Connollan. [Connolly].		
294	COCKBURNE. Cobourn. 450. Cobram. 450. Coburn. 175, 472. Cockbourne. Colborne. Colbourne. Colburne.						
295	CODD. Coade. Code. 109.						

No.	Surnames, with Varieties and Synonymes.	No.	Surnames, with Varieties and Synonymes.	No.	Surnames, with Varieties and Synonymes.	No.	Surnames, with Varieties and Synonymes.
324	CONRY. Connery. 431. [Conroy]. 454 (b). Mulconry. 189.	340	COSGRAVE Clusker. 72,361. [Cluskey]. 361. Coscor. 183. Cosgreave. Cosgreve. Cosgriff. Cosgrive. Cosgroove. Cosgrove. (Cuseo). 33. (Cuskery). 372. Cosker. 412. Coskeran. Coskerry. 111. Coskery. Cossgrove. Crosgrave. Cusker. 274. Cuskor. 104. [M'Cusker]. 429. M'Cuskern. 429.	353	COYNE. Barnacle. 28. Coin. 40,342. Kilcoyne. 136. Kinc. 40,329. [Kyne]. 40,174, &c.	373	CROGHAN. Croan. Crohan. Croughan.
325	CONWAY. Canaway. Conner. 209. Connoway. Conoo. 249. Cunnoo. 249. Gonoude. 249. McConamy. 181. McConaway. McConomy. 159, 418. McConway. 271.			354	CRAHAN. Craan. 72. Creane. 72. [Curran]. 72.	374	CROKE. Croake. Crough. 510. [Crowe]. 320,510.
326	COOKE. Cook. M'Cook. 254.			355	CRAIG. [Carrick]. 482. Crage. 259. Cregg. 34.	375	CROLY. [Crawley]. Crolly. [Crowley].
327	COOLAHAN. Coulehan. Coulihan. Cuolohan. 420.			356	CRAMER. Creamer. Cremor. Krahmer. Kramer.	376	CROMIE. [Abercrombie]. Crombie. Crommie. Cronvy. 185. Crummy. 185.
328	COONEY. Coonahan. Coonan. Coonihan. 224. Coumey. 224. Counihan. 47.	341	COSTELLO. Costellow. Costelo. Costillo. Costily. 316. Costley. 197,381, &c. Costolloe. Costoloe. 309. Cushley. 385.	357	CRAMPSIE. [Bonar]. 479,482, &c. Boner. 271. Bonner. 310,479. Crampsey. Cramsie.	377	CROMWELL. Crummell. Grummell. 521.
329	COOPER. [Cowper].			358	CRAMPTON. Cramp.	378	CRONIN. Cronan. Cronyn.
330	COPELAND. Copelton 414. Copland. Copleton. 55,89, 489.	342	COTTER. M'Cotter. 397.	359	CRANNY. Cranay. Crany. Creaney. 358.	379	CROOKS. Crook. Crookes. [Crozier]. Cruiks.
331	COPPERTHWAITE. Cowperthwaite.	343	COULTER. Coalter. Colter. O'Colter.	360	CRANSTON. Cransen. Cranson.	380	CROOKSHANKS. Crooks-shanks. 429. Cruickshanks. Cruikshanks.
332	COPPLESTONE. Copleton.	344	COURNANE. Courteney. [Courtney]. 111, 303 (b), &c.	361	CRAVEN. Cravin. Creaven.	381	CROSBIE. Crossbie.
333	CORBETT. Combat. 415. Corban. 469. Corbin. 474. Corbitt. Coribeen. 174. Lovett. 352. O'Currobeen. 40.	345	COURTNEY. [Cournane]. 111, 303 (b). &c. Courtenay. (Courneen). 390. Courtency. Courtnay. Curnane. 511, 512. Curneene. 469. M'Courtney. 494.	362	CRAWFORD. Craford. Crauford. Crayford.	382	CROSSAN. Crossen. Crossin. Crosson. [O'Brien]. 332.
334	CORCORAN. [Cochrane]. 72, 410. Corcorin. Corken. 257. Corkeran. Corkerry. 51. Corkoran. Corkran.			363	CRAWLEY. [Croly]. [Crowley]. 304(a).	383	CROWE. [Croke]. 320,510. Crough. 510. MacEuchroe. 189.
		346	COUSINS. Cousin. Cousine. 109. Couzeens. 109. Couzins. Cussen.	364	CREAGH. Cragh. 312. Craigh.	384	CROWLEY. [Crawley]. 304(a). [Croly]. Cronouge. 128. Krowley. 150.
335	CORMACK. Cormick. Cormocan. [M'Cormack]. 3.	347	COWAN. Coan. 71. [Cohen]. 71. Cowen. [Keohane]. 397.	365	CREAN. Crain. Crane. Creaghan. Creen. Crehan.	385	CROZIER. Bachal. [Crooks]. Crosert. Crozert. Grozet. 414.
336	CORNEEN. Curneen. 370. Curnin. 370.	348	COWDEN. Cowdie. 210.	366	CREEDON. Creed. 365.	386	CRUISE. Cruice.
337	CORRIDON. Cordan. 47.	349	COWIE. Coe. Cowey.	367	CREGAN. Craigan. Creegan. Creggan. Crezhan. Creigan.	387	CRUMLEY. Crumlish. 260.
338	CORRIGAN. Carrigan. 82. Courigan. 3. Currigan. 29. [Kerrigan]. 361.	350	COWPER. [Cooper.]			388	CUDDIHY. [Cody]. Cudahoy. Cuddehy. [Cuddy]. 15,452. Cudihy. Quiddihy.
		351	COX. Coxe. 294. Magilly. 460.— M'Gilly.	368	CREIGHTON. Creaton. Creiton. Crichton.		
339	CORRY. Corey. 318. [Curry]. 72,494. O'Curry. 189.	352	COYLE. Coiles. 69. Coole. 319. M'Ilhoyle. 59.	369	CREMIN. Cremen.	389	CUDDY. [Cody]. [Cuddihy]. 15, 452.
				370	CRIBBIN. Cribbon. 435. [Gribben]. [McRobin].	390	CULHANE. Clahane. 131. Clehane. [Collins].
				371	CRILLY. Creely. Creilly. Crelly. 429. Crully. 489.	391	CULKIN. Kulkeen. Quilkin.
				372	CRITCHLEY. Crighley. 98.		

No.	Surnames, with Varieties and Synonymes.	No.	Surnames, with Varieties and Synonymes.	No.	Surnames, with Varieties and Synonymes.	No.	Surnames, with Varieties and Synonymes.
392	CULLEN. Colins. 489. Collen. 17, 410, 489. [Collins]. 433, 489. [Colquhoun]. 244. Culhoun. 244. Culhan. Cullan. Culleeny. 189. Cullin. [Cullinane]. 393. Culliny. Cullion. 356, 459. Culloon. 245. [Cully]. 274. Kulhan. [Quillan]. 154, 194, 246. Quillen. 92.	399	CUNNEEN. Cuneen. Cunihan. 406. Cunion. 172. [Cunnane] Cunnean. Cunneeny. Cunnien. Cunnion 132. Queenane. Quenan. 106. [Rabbit]. 237, 297, &c.	408	CUSACK. Cusac. Cusic. Cusick. Cussac. Cussack. Cussick. Kissick. 204.	426	DAVIS. Davidson. 177. Davies. [Davison]. 177, 489, &c. [Davy]. 381, 432. Davys. 72. [McDaid]. 165.
393	CULLETON. Colleton. Colloton. Cullington. Culliton.	400	CUNNINGHAM. Conyngham. Coon. 96. Coonaghan. 347. Counihan. 42. Crickenham. 274. Cunagum. 386. Cuniam. Cuningham. Cunnahan. 61. Cunniam. 207, 332. Cunnigan. 329. Cunnighan. 216. Cunnyngham. Kinaghan. 214. Kinigam. 346, 372. Kinighan. 42. Kinnegan. 137. Kinnian. 205. Kinnigham 279. McCunnigan. 260.	409	CUSHION. Cushen. 468. Cushing. 468. Cussen. 354.	427	DAVISON. Daveson. Davidson. [Davis]. 177, 489, &c. Davisson. [McDaid].
394	CULLINANE. Culnan. 77, 397. Colothan. 173. Cullanan. [Cullen]. 393. Cullinan. Culnane. Hulnane. 77. Quillenan. Quillinan. 297. Quilnan.			410	CUSHNAHAN. Cushanan. 91.	428	DAVITT. Davits. Devett. [Devitt]. 486. Divitt.
				411	CUTHBERT. Culbert. 19, 89, 374. Curby. Cutbert. Cuthbertson.	429	DAVY. [Davis]. 381, 432.
395	CULLY. [Cullen]. 274. McCully.	401	CURLEY. Corley. 435. Kerly. 249. Kirley. 249.			430	DAWSON. Durrian. 6).
396	CUMMING. [Commons]. 503. Cuming. (Kimins). 42. Cummin. Cummings. [Cummins]. Kimmings. 137. Kimmins. 347.	402	CURRAN. [Carey]. 520. Corn. 289. 481. Corran. 374. Courn. 420. [Crahan]. 72. Crane. 382. Currain. [Currane]. 8, 142. Curreen. 224, 235. &c. Curren. Currin. Kirrane.	412	DALLAS. Dalhouse. 254.	431	DAY. Dea. 2?0.
				413	DALTON. Dawtin. 117.	432	DEANE. Dane. Dean. 290. Deans. Deen. 290. Deens.
				414	DALY. Daily. 223. Dawley. 69, 382, &c. Dawly. 397, 431. Dayley. 224. Dealy. 397. Deely. 360.	433	DEBOYS. Debois. 204.
397	CUMMINS. Comjean. 107. Comjeens. 109. [Commane]. 45. Commins. 101, 408, &c. Common. 109. [Commons]. 3, 125, &c. Comyns. Cowman. 244, 408. Cumin. Cuming. Cumings. Cumins. Cummens [Cumming]. Cummings. 433. Kimmins. 347, 498. McSkimmins. 344. [Misskimmins]. 19.					434	DE COURCY. Courcey. Coursey. D Courcy.
		403	CURRANE. [Carey]. 520. Crane. 304 (n). [Curran]. 8, 142.	415	DALZELL. Dalziell. D'Ell. 267. 279. D.L. 450.	435	DEEGAN. Deighan. Digan. 249, 420. [Duggan]. Duigan. 420.
		404	CURRY. Corr. Corra. Corree. Corrie. [Corry]. 72. 494. Cory. Currie. 91, 250. [McCorry]. 201, 350. McGorry. 515.	416	DANAHER. Danagher. Daniher. Dannaher. [Dennehy]. 45.	436	DEEVEY. [Devereux]. 249. Deverill. 249. Devery. 249.
				417	DANIEL. Daniells. Daniels. Danniel. Danniell. [Donnell]. 328. [O'Donnell]. 171, 328.	437	DELACHEROIS. [Deloohery]. 318.
						438	DELAHOYDE. Delahide. Skinnion. 153.
398	CUNNANE. [Canning]. 361. [Cannon]. 54, 272, &c. [Cunneen]. [Queenan]. 147.	405	CURTAYNE. [Curtin]. Kyerty. 142.	418	DARBY. [McDermott]. 281. 282.	439	DELAHUNTY. Delahunt. Delhunty. Dellunty. Dolohunty. Dulanty. 493. Dulinty. 104. Dullenty. 24?.
		406	CURTIN. Courtayne. 303. Curtan. [Curtayne]. Curten.	419	DARBYSHIRE. Darbishire. Derbyshire.		
				420	D'ARCY. Darcy. Dorcey. 472.	440	DELAMERE. Delamar. 379. Delamore. Delemar. Delmer. D'Lamour. Turbett. 379.
				421	DARGAN. Dergan.		
				422	DARLEY. [Darling]. 172.	441	DELANEY. Delane. 50. Deleany. Deleney. Doolady. 132. Dooladdy. 132. Laney. 305, 324.
				423	DARLING. [Darley]. 172.		
		407	CURTIS. Curteis. Curties.	424	DARRAGH. Daragh. Darah. Darra. Darrah. Darrock. Oak. Oakes. [Oaks].	442	DELAROE. Derow.
				425	DAVENPORT. Devauport. Devonport.	443	DELMEGE. Delmage. Dolmage. Dolmege. Dolmidge.

No.	Surnames, with Varieties and Synonymes.	No.	Surnames, with Varieties and Synonymes.	No.	Surnames, with Varieties and Synonymes.	No.	Surnames, with Varieties and Synonymes.
444	DELOOHERY. [Delachcrois].318. Delohery. Deloorey. Deloughery. Delouhery. Delouri. Delury. Dilloughery. Dillury. [Dilworth]. 99.	459	DEVEREUX. [Deevey]. 249. Deverill. 249. Devery. 249. 420. Duvick. 312.	477	DODSON. Dodgson.	487	DONNELLY. Dannelly. 487. Donaldson. 19. Donelly. Donely. [Donlan]. 271. Donlon. 274. Donly. 448. Donnally. [Donnell]. 72,376. [Donnellan]. 38. Donnely. Donnolly.
445	DEMPSEY. [Dempster]. 87.	460	DEVERS. Diver. 271.	478	DOHENY. Dawney. Deheny. Dogheny. Dohenny. Dohoney. Dougheny. Doughney. Downey. [Duggan]. 189.	488	DONOHOE. Donaghoe. Donaghy. 123. [Donahoe]. Donahy. 447. Donocho. 211. Donoghoe. Donoghue. 509. Donohogue. 451. Donoughoo.
446	DEMPSTER. Deemster. [Dempsey]. 87. Demster. Doomster.	461	DEVINE. Davane. Davin. Davine. Devane. 304 (a). 479. [Devany]. 179,386. Deveen. Deven. 495. Devin. 159. Devon. 416. Diffen. 18. Divane. 382. Diveen. Divin. 240,480,&c. Divine. [O'Devine].				
447	DENEHAN. Deneher. 232.			479	DOHERTY. Daugherty. Dehorty. 529. Dogherty. 355. Dohorty. Dooherty. Doorty. Dougherty. 255. [O'Doherty].355.	489	DONOVAN. Dingavan. 431. [O'Donovan].
448	DENIFFE. Neef. 497.					490	DOODY. [Dowd]. 303 (b).
449	DENISON. [Dennis]. [McDonagh]. 179.	462	DEVITT. [Davitt]. 486.	480	DOLAN. [Doolan]. 246. [Dooly]. 498. [Dowling]. 350, 384.	491	DOOLAN. [Dolan]. 246. Doolen. Doolin. 499. Dooling. 295,382 [Dowling]. 295 498, 511, &c.
450	DENNAN. Denanny. Dennany.	463	DEVLIN. Develin. D'Evelyn. 257,429				
451	DENNEHY. [Danaher]. 45. Danahy. Danihy. 100. Dannahy. Dennhy. Denehy. Dennahy. [Denny]. 242. Donaghey.	464	DIAMOND. Dimond. Dymond.	481	DONAGHY. Donagh. 332. Donaghey. 159. [Duncan]. 216. 417. [McDonagh].350. 423. &c.	492	DOOLY. [Dolan]. 493 Dooley. 457.
		465	DICKSON. Deehan. 79. Deighan. 79. Dixon. 91.	482	DONAHOE. [Donohoe].	493	DORAN. [Dorian]. [Dorran]. 347. Dorran. Dorrian.
452	DENNING. Dening. [Dillon]. 370. Dunion. 161. Durnion. 313.	466	DIFFLEY. Deffely. 454 (b). Diffily. Duffley.	483	DONEGAN. Dinnegan. 3. Domegan. 175. Donagan. Dongan. 72. Donnegan. Dumegan. 175. [Duncan]. 56. Dungan. 72. Dunigan. Dunnegan. Dunnigan. Ounihan. 73. Unehan. 73.	494	DORIAN. Adorian. 411. [Doran]. Dorran. 411. Dorrian. Odarian. 411.
453	DENNIS. Denehy. Denis. [Denison]. Denson. Denys. Dinnis.	467	DILLON. [Denning]. 370. Dillane. 51. 352. Dillion. Dologhan. 59.			495	DORNAN. [Doran.] 347. Durnian. 482. O'Dornan. 112.
454	DENNY. Deanie. Deney. [Dennehy]. 242.	468	DILWORTH. [Deloohery]. 99. Deloorey. 99. Deloughry. 47. Delouri. Dilloughery. 431. Dillworth.	484	DONLAN. Donellan. Donelon. Donlon. Donnallon. Donnelan. [Donnellan]. 298. 508. Donnellon. [Donnelly]. 274. Donnollan.	496	DOUGALL. Dougle. Dugald. M'Dougall.
455	DENROCHE. Dunroche.					497	DOUGLAS. Dougle. 461. Dougs 461.
456	DERMODY. Darmody. Dermoody. [Dermott]. McDermott]. 214. 438. &c.	469	DINEEN. Dynan. 325.				
		470	DINSMORE. Dennismore. Densmore. Densmuir. Dunsmoor.	485	DONNELL. [Daniel]. 328. Danly. 72. Donald. 374. 432. Donnal. [Donnellan]. [Donnelly].72,356. [McDonnell]. [O'Donnell]. 112. O'Donnelly.	498	DOWD. [Doody]. 303 (b). Doud. 307. Dowda. Dowds. 433. [O'Dowd].307,361
457	DERMOTT. Darmody. Dermid. [Dermody]. Dermoty. D'Ermott. Diarmid. Diermott. [McDermott]. O'Dermott.	471	DIVINEY. Duval. 179. Duvalley. 179.			499	DOWDALL. Doudall. Dowdell. Dowdie. [Dowling]. 55.
		472	DOAG. Doake. Doig.				
		473	DOBBIN. Dobbins. Dobbyn. Dobbyns. Dobin. 115. Gubby. 97.	486	DONNELLAN. Donelan. Donellon. Donelon. [Donlan]. 298. 508. Donlon. 274. 298. [Donnell]. Donnellon. [Donnelly]. 38. Donnelon.	500	DOWDICAN. Dudican.
458	DEVANY. Devane. 386. Devann. Devanny. Devenny. Deveny. [Devine]. 179. 386. Devinney. Divenney. Diviney. Dwann	474	DOCKERAY. Dockery. Dockray. Dockry.			501	DOWELL. Doole. [M'Dowell].
		475	DOCKRALL. Dockrell. Dockrill.			502	DOWER. Dore. 353.
		476	DODDS. Dodd. 71. Dods. 71. Douds. 347. Dowds. 381.			503	DOWEY. Dooey. Douey. Douie. Dowie.

No.	Surnames, with Varieties and Synonymes.	No.	Surnames, with Varieties and Synonymes.	No.	Surnames, with Varieties and Synonymes.	No.	Surnames, with Varieties and Synonymes.
504	DOWLER. Dooler.	521	DUFFY. Docy. 76. Doocy. 314, 432. Dooey. 113. [Duff]. 72, 409, 526. O'Diff. 40. [O'Duffy].	538	EADIE. [Adams]. 210.	560	ENNIS. Ennes. Enniss. Inis. Innes. Innis. 433.
505	DOWLING. [Dolan]. 350, 334. [Doolan]. 295, 498, 511, &c. Doolen. Doolin, 51, 72, &c. Dooling. 8. Dooly. 129. [Dowdall]. 55. Dowlan. 30. Dowley. 129. Dowlin. 91. O'Doolan. 189.	522	DUGGAN. [Deegan]. [Doheny]. 189. Doogan. 109, 239, 526. Dougan. 410. Doughan. Dougheny. 189. Dugan. 117, 420, 526. Duggen. O'Doogan. 189. O'Dooghany. 189.	539	EAGAR. [Agar]. 303. Eagars. Eager. 42. Eagers. Egar.	561	ENRIGHT. Enraght. Enwright. Henright.
506	DOWNEY. Dawney. 429. Doona. 309. Downing, 99, 283, 285, &c. Gildowny. 429. McDowney. 429. McGillDowny. 429. Muldowney. 429.	523	DUHIG. Duhy. 235.	540	EATON. Ayton. Aytoun.	562	ENTWISSLE. Antwhistle. Entwhistle. Entwisle. Entwistle.
507	DOYLE. Doil. Dooal. 113. Dyle. 485.	524	DUIGENAN. Deignan. Dignam. Dignan. Digunan. Duigan. Duignam. Duignan. Dygnam.	541	ECCLES. Eckles.	563	ERRINGTON. Ayrington. [Harrington].
508	DRAPER. Draiper. Dreaper.	525	DUKELOW. Ducklow. 80.	542	ECCLESTON. Eagleson. Eagleston. Eccleson. Eggleston. Egleson. Egleston.	564	ERSKINE. Askins. 410.
509	DRELINCOURT. Dredlincourt. Drelingcourt. Drellingcourt. Drillingcourt.	526	DUNCAN. Dinkin. 43. [Donaghy]. 216, 417. [Donegan]. 56. Doonican. 420. Dungan. 56. Dunican. 420. Dunkin.	543	EDEN. Eaden. Eadens. Edens.	565	EUSTACE. Eustice. Ustace.
510	DRENNAN. [Drinan].	527	DUNLEA. Delay. 397. Delea. 134. Dullea. 397.	544	EDGAR. Adger. 433, 503.	566	EVANS. Evens. Evins.
511	DREW. Drough. 63.	528	DUNLEVY. Dunlavy. Dunleavy. Dunleevy.	545	EDMUNDS. Edmond. Edmonds. Esmonde. 103.	567	EVANSON. Evenson.
512	DRINAN. [Drennan]. [Thornton]. 506.	529	DUNLOP. De'ap. 58, 238, 352. Dunlap.	546	EDMUNDSON. Edmondson. Edmonson. Edmonston. Edmunson. Edmunstone. M'Aimon.	568	EVERITT. Everard. 72. (Leveran.) 449. Everett.
513	DRISCOLL. Driscall. Driskell. 107. Driskill. Driskol. Hide. [Hyde]. [O'Driscoll]. Whooley. 164.	530	DUNNE. Dinneen. 142. Dun. 183. Kildunn. 5, 501.	547	EGAN. Aicken. 55. Aikens. 410. Eagan. Eagen. Eakin. [Hagan]. 133, 526. [Keegan]. 312.	569	EWART. Evart.
514	DRISDELL. Drisdale. Drysdale.	531	DUNPHY. Donohue. 109. Dumphy. Dunfy.	548	EGERTON. Edgerton.	570	EYRE. Ayers. Ayre. Ayres.
515	DRUMMOND. Drumm. 154. Drummy. 452.	532	DUNSEATH. Dunseeth. Dunseith. Dunsheath. Dunshee. 58. Dunsheith.	549	EGLINTON. Egglinton. 333. Eglington. 333. Eglintoun.	571	FAGAN. Fagin. Feagan. Feagon. 461. Fegan. 72, 92, &c. Feghan. Feighan. 17. [M'Fadden]. 203.
516	DRURY. Drewry.	533	DUPLEX. Dublack. 30.	550	ELDRED. Aldred. Alldred.	572	FAHY. Faghy. Foy. 38. Vahey. 38.
517	DUANE. Dewane. Divane. Dooan. Duan. Dune. Dwain. Dwan. Dwane.	534	DUPRE. Dupri. Prey. 523.	551	ELLIFFE. Liffe. 152.	573	FAIRCLOUGH. Faircloth. Fairtclough. Fairtlough.
518	DU BOURDIEU. Debouerdieu. Du Boudieu. Dubowdieu.	535	DURHAM. Derham. Dyrham.	552	ELLIOTT. Eliot. Ellot. Ellyett. Elyot.	574	FALCONER. Falchenor. 480. Fealy. 491. Falconder. Falkender. Falkener. Falkiner. Falkner. Faulkener. Faulkner. 159, 254. Faulkney. 136. Foulkard. 181.
519	DUFF. [Black]. Duffin. 526. [Duffy]. 72, 409, 526. McElduff. 417.	536	DURKAN. Durcan. 5. Durkin.	553	ELLIS. Ellies. 421.	575	FALLON. Fallen. Fallin. [Falloon].
520	DUFFERLY. Doorly. 54.	537	DWYER D... Dw... [O'...	554	ELLISON. [Allison]. 374, 429.	576	FALLOON. [Fallon]. Faloon. Faloona.
				555	ELLSMERE. Ellsmoor. Ellsmore.	577	FALVEY. Fallaher. 509.
				556	ELWOOD. Elfred. 40. Ellwood. [Woods]. 381.		
				557	EMMERSON. Amberson. 358. Emberson. Emerson.		
				558	EMMETT. Emmit.		
				559	ENGLISH. [Golagley]. 81. Gology. 312. [Inglis].		

No.	Surnames, with Varieties and Synonymes.	No.	Surnames, with Varieties and Synonymes.	No.	Surnames, with Varieties and Synonymes.	No.	Surnames, with Varieties and Synonymes.
578	FANNING. Fannin. Fannon. Fenning. Finning.	591	FEELY. Fayly. Fealey. Fealy. Feehely. 454 (b). Feehily. Feeley. 329. Fehely. Fehily. 454 (b). Fihily. 329.	604	FIELD. Fields. (Maghery). 97.	623	FITZSIMONS. Fitch. 429. Fitsimmons. Fitsimons. Fitsommons. Fitsummons. Fitz. 282. Fitzimmons. Fitzsimmons. Fitzsimon. (Simon). 54. Fitzsummons. 410.
579	FARLEY. Fairleigh. Fairley. [Farrelly]. 26, 82, 154, &c. Ferly.			605	FIFE. Fyfee. 350.		
		592	FEENEY. Finny. 71.	606	FINCH. Ffinch.		
580	FARMER. M'Scolloy. 319.			607	FINLAY. Fenley. 68. [Fennelly]. 68, 232. Finalay. 409. Findlay. Findley. Finley. Finnally. 68. Finnelly. 332.		Fitzsumons. 246. Simmon. [Simmons]. 436. Simons. 54.
581	FARNAN. Farnand. 417. Farnham. 18.	593	FEIGHERY. Feary. Feehery. Feighan. [Feighney]. [Hunt]. 249.			624	FLACK. Afflack. 429. Affleck. 429. Fleck.
582	FARQUHAR. Farghar. Farker. Farquehar. Farquer. Farquharson. Farquher. Forker. 429, 189. Fourker. 429.	594	FEIGHNEY. Feghany. [Feighery]. Feighry. [Hunt]. 476, 501.	608	FINN. Finne.	625	FLAHAVAN. Flahavin. Flahevan. Flavahan. Flavin. 452.
		595	FENLON. Fendlon. 468. Fenelon. 468.	609	FINNAMORE. Finamore. Finnamure. Finnemor.	626	FLAHERTY. Faherty. 253. Flagherty. 307. [O'Flaherty].
583	FARRAGHER. Faragher. 307. Faraher. 307. Farraher. (Farrahill). 361.	596	FENNELL. Ffennell. Finnell.	610	FINNEGAN. Finigan. Finnigan.		
		597	FENNELLY. Fenelly. Fenley. 68. Finelly. [Finlay]. 68, 232. Finnelly.	611	FINNERTY. Fenaughty. 47. Finerty. 138. Phoenerty. 138.	627	FLAHY. [Lahiff]. 189.
584	FARRELL. [Farrelly.] 72, 515. Ferrall. [O'Farrell]. 390.					628	FLANAGAN. Flang. 37. Flanigan. Flannagan. Flannigan. [O'Flanagan].390
		598	FENTON. Fenaghty. 382. Fenoughty. 309. Foghney. 378. Venton. 128.	612	FINNUCANE. Kinucane. 302.		
585	FARRELLY. Farelly. [Farley]. 26, 82, 154, &c. Farrally. [Farrell]. 72,515. Farrely. Ferly. 401. Ferrall. 56. Varrelly.			613	FIRMAN. Firmin. [Perriman]. 249. Pherman. 249.	629	FLATTLEY. Flatholy.
		599	FERGUSON. Faraday. 364. Farguson. Fargy. 72. 364. Fergie. 267. Fergison. Fergisson. Ferguison. Fergus. 267. Fergusson. Forgay. 60. Forgey. 428, 524. Forgie. 267. Forgy. 71. Hergusson. 364. Vargis. 78. Vargus. 109, 527.	614	FISHER. Bradden. 12. Filcher. 381.	630	FLEMING. Flemon. 427. Flemming. Flemmyng. Flemyng. 427.
				615	FITZALLEN. Fitzalleyn. Fitzallwyn. Fitzalwyn.	631	FLETCHER. Fladger. 503.
586	FARREN. Faran. Faren. Farin. Farnon. 91. Farran. Farron. Ferran. 91.			616	FITZELL. Fizell.	632	FLOOD. Floody. 72, 515. Floyd. 137, 314. McAtilla. 314. O'Thina. 179.
				617	FITZGERALD. Fitz. 189, 329, 448, &c. Fitzerald. Fitzgerrald.	633	FLYNN. Fleens. 72. Flinn. Flyng.
587	FARRER. Ferrar. Ferrer. Ferrers.	600	FERRIER. Ferryar. Ferryer.			634	FOGARTY. Fogaton. 185. Fogerty. [Swift]. 185.
		601	FERRIS. Fairis. 381. Fairy. 381. Faris. 410. Farris. Feris. Ferry. 254. [Fry]. 144. O'Ferry. 254. Pharis. 64.	618	FITZGIBBON. [Gibbon]. 444, 445. Gibbons. 378, 398.	635	FOLEY. Fooley. 453. Fooluiah. 47. [McSharry]. 105, 153, &c. Sharry.
588	FAWCETT. Faucet. Fausit. Fausset. Fawcet. Fossitt.			619	FITZHARRIS. Feeharry. 305. [Fitzhenry]. 526.		
				620	FITZHENRY. [Fitzharris]. 526.	636	FOOTE. Foot. Foots. 381.
589	FAY. Fee. 38. Fey. Fic. 167. Foy. 167, 168, 185, 515, &c. Fye. 482.			621	FITZMAURICE. Fitzmorice. Fitzmorris. 307. Maurice. [Morris]. 456.	637	FORAN. Forehan. 382. Forehane. 199, 303 (b). Forhan. 303 (a). Fourhane. 303 (b).
		602	FETHERSTON. Featherston. Fetherston II. Fetherston-haugh.				
590	FEARON. Faren. Fearen. Fearn. (Fern). 91. Feran. Feron.	603	FFOLLIOTT. Folliett. Folliott.	622	FITZPATRICK. Fitch. 71, 276, 411. Fitchpatrick. Fitz. Paragon. 364. Parrican. 72. Patchy. 292, 293. Patrican. 449. Patrick. 87, 306.	638	FORBES. Forbis. Forbish. 228. Klisham. 189.

No.	Surnames, with Varieties and Synonymes.	No.	Surnames, with Varieties and Synonymes.	No.	Surnames, with Varieties and Synonymes.	No.	Surnames, with Varieties and Synonymes.
639	FORDE. Foard. 40. Forhane. 199. Foorde. 16. Ford. (M'Anare). 48 (*b*).	657	FUDGE. Fuge. 488.	674	GARLAND. Gairlan. Gartlan. Gartland. Gartlin. McGartlan. 72.	691	GEOGHERY. Gohary. 420.
640	FORSTER. Forrester. Foster. 72, 189.	658	FULHAM. Fullam.			692	GERAGHTY. Garahy. 249. Garity. Garrity.
641	FORSYTHE. Forsayeth. Forsithe. Foursides. 429.	659	FULLERTON. Fullarton.	675	GARRAGHAN. Garahan. 54.		Gearty. 454 (*b*). Gerarty. Gernthy. Geraty.
642	FORTUNE. Farshin. 227. [M'Carthy]. 227.	660	FURY. Fleury. 2, 420. Furey.	676	GARRETT. Garratt.		Geraughty. Gerety.
643	FOX. Faux. Foxe. *M'Ashinah.* 165. *M'Shanaghy.* 82. *Shanaghy.* 82, 132, 470. [*Shanahan*]. 152, 153, 206. *Shanahy.* 153. *Shinagh.* 179. *Shinnagh.* 40. *Shinnock.* 393. *Shonoyh.* 174. *Shunagh.* 262. *Shunny.* 393.	661	FYLAND. [Phelan]. 511. Philan. 511.	677	GARVEY. Carway. 124. _Gara. 38. Garveagh. Garven. 456. [Garvin]. 54. O Gara. 38.	693	Gerity. 249. Geroughty. Gerraghty. Gertey. Gerty. Gheraty. Jerety. 152. GERRARD. Gerard. Gerret. 401. Jarrett. Jerrett.
		662	GAFFNEY. Gaffney. Gaffny. 270. Gafney. Gaphney. Gaughney. 234. Gifney.	678	GARVIN. Garven. [Garvey]. 54. Garwin. 69. [Given]. 489.		
				679	GATH. Gaff. 249.	694	GERVIS. Gervais. 17. Jarvis. [Jervis]. 17.
[644	FRACKLETON. Frackletin. Frakleton. Freckleton. Frekleton. Frickelton. Frickleton.	663	GAHAN. Geehan. 526. O'Cahan. 206. [O'Kane]. 206.	680	GAULT. Galt. Gaut. 494.	695	GIBBON. [Fitzgibbon]. 414, 445. Gibben. Gibbings. Gibbins. Gibbons. (Gobin). 156. *O'Kibbon.* 40.
		664	GALBRAITH. Galbreath. Gilbraith. Gilbreath.	681	GAUSSEN. Gasson. 72. Gossan. Gosson.		
645	FRANKLIN. Franklyn.	665	GALLAGHER. Gallagher. Galagher. Gallaher. Gallaugher. 159, 340. Galliher. Gallihur. Gallogher. Gallougher. Goligher. 159. Golliher. 178 (*a*). Gollagher. Gollocher. Gollogher. Golloher. Goloher. 137.	682	GAVAGAN. Gaffikan. Gaffikin. Gavacan. Gaviran. Geffeken.		
646	FRAWLEY. Frehily.			683	GAVIN. [Galvin.] 249. Gavahan. Gavan. Gaven.	696	GIBNEY. Giboney.
647	FRAYNE. Frain. Frane. Frein.					697	GIBSON. Gibsey. 179. *Gibulawn.* 179.
648	FRAZER. Fraisor. Fraizer. Fraizor. Fraser. Frazor. Frizzle. 6, 197, 257.			684	GAYNOR. Gainer. Gaynard. 179. Geanor. Ginnel. 92. [*McGinity*]. 167.	698	GILBEY. Killby. 429. O'Gilbie.
		666	GALLIGAN. [Geoghegan]. 170. Gillgan. [Gilligan]. 92, 246. [White]. 153.	685	GEARY. Gery. 429. Guiry. 437, 488. M'Gerry. 429.	699	GILCHRIST. Gilchreest. Gilchriest. Gilcrest. Gilcriest. Gilcrist. Guilchrist. Kilchreest. 246, 360. Kilchriest. Kilgrist. [Loughlin. 216.
649	FREEBURN. Freebairn. Freebern. Freebirn.			686	GEDDES. Gaddiss. Geddis.		
650	FREEMAN. Free. 296. *Seerey.* 20. *Seery.* 4, 201.	667	GALVIN. Galavan. Galavin. 100. Gallivan. 142, 382, 520. Galvan. Galven. [Gavin]. 249. Glavin. 349.	687	GEE. Ghee. [Magee]. [McGee].	700	GILDEA. Benison. 35. Gay. 298. Kilday. Kildea. 206.
651	FREENY. Frainy. Frany. Freny.			688	GELLETLIE. Galletlie. Gilletlie.	701	GILES. Gilson. Gyles. Jellis. 274. Jiles.
652	FRENCH. Ffrench.	668	GALWAY. Galloway. Gallway. Galwey. Golloway.	689	GELSTON. Galston. Gelson. Ghelson.	702	GILFILLAN. Gilfil'and. Kilfillan.
653	FRIEL. Freal. Freel.	669	GAMBLE. Gambell. Gamel. 397. Gammel.	690	GEOGHEGAN. Gagan. 122, 435. Gahagan. 137, 170, 217. [Galligan]. 170. Gaughan. 337, 373. Gaviran. 429. Geagan. Gegan. 189, 262. Geghan. Gehegan. Geogan. 152. Geoghan. 337. Ghagan. Ghegan. 348. *Houghegan.* 419. [M'Guigan]. 429.	703	GILHOOLEY. Gilhool. 475. Gillooly. Gillowly. Gilooly. Killooley.
654	FRIZELL. Frisell. Frizelle. Frizzel. Frizzell. Frizzle. 19.	670	GANLY. Gantly. 40.				
655	FRY. [Ferris]. 141.	671	GARA. O'Gara. 268.			704	GILKISON. Gilkeson. Gilkieson. Gilkinson. Gilkison. Kilkison. Kilkisson.
656	FRYER. Friar. Frier. Fryarr. 523.	672	GARDINER. Gardner. 91, 435. Garner. 91.				
		673	GARGAN. Garrigan. 26, 72, 332.				

43

No.	Surnames, with Varieties and Synonymes.	No.	Surnames, with Varieties and Synonymes.	No.	Surnames, with Varieties and Synonymes.	No.	Surnames, with Varieties and Synonymes.
705	GILL. Gilliard. 409.	723	GLANN. Glenn. 176. Glennon. Glinn.	743	GOULDSBURY. Gold-berry. Gold-bury. Golds-bury. Golesbery. Gols'erry. Gouldsberry.	761	GREVILLE. Gravell. 274.
706	GILLEN. Gullion. 19. [Killen]. Magauon. 215. McGullian. 357. McGullion. 215.	724	GODSIL. Godson. 199.			762	GRIBBEN. [Cribbin]. Gribbin. Gribbon. [Griffin]. 429. [McRobin].
707	GILLESPIE. Clusby. 214. Galesby. Gelaspy. Gellespey. Gillaspy. Gillesby. 214. Gillispie. Glashby. 13. Glaspy. 407.	725	GODWIN. [O Dea]. 40.179, 505, &c.	744	GOWAN. Gowen. [M'Gowan] [Smith]. 319.	763	GRIFFIN. [Gribben]. 429. Griffen. Griffley. 198. Griffins. [Griffith]. 117. 316.517. Griffly. 302.
708	GILLIGAN. [Galligan].92.246. Gilgan.	726	GOGARTY. Gogerty. Googarty.	745	GOWDY. Goudy.		
709	GILLILAND. Gelland. Gilelin. Gillan. 112. Gilland. Gilleland. Gidilan. Gooly. 55.381. Guililand.	727	GOGGIN. [Cogan]. 397. Gogan. Goggan. Goggins. Gogin. Googan.	746	GRADY. Graddy. 47.490. [O'Grady]. 39.	764	GRIFFITH. Griffeth. [Griffin]. 117,316. 517. Griffiths.
710	GILLIS. Gilis. Gillas. Gilles.	728	GOING. Gowen. 437. Gowing. [Smith]. [Smyth].	747	GRAHAM. Graeme. 415. Grame. Grames. Greaham. Greames. Greham. [Grimes]. 489, 511, &c.	765	GRIMES. [Gormley]. 40. 417.418. [Graham]. 489, 511, &c. [Grehan]. 34.
711	GILMARTIN. Gimartin. [Kilmartin].	729	GOLAGLEY. [English]. 81.	748	GRANT. Granny. 113.271.	766	GRIMLEY. Grumley. 72,364.
712	GILMORE. Gillmore. Gilmer. Gilmour. Killmore.	730	GOLDEN. [Golding]. 99. [Goldrick].106.128 Goulding. 99.488. [Magorlick]. 201. McGoldrick. 128. [McGolrick].	749	GRANVILLE. Grandfield. 203. Granilll. 203. Greenvil. Grenvil. Grenville.	767	GROGAN. Groggan. Groogan.
713	GILSHENAN. Gelshinan. Gilsenan. Gilsenon. Gilshenon. Gunshinan. 215. McGill Shenan. 429. [Nugent]. 214.	731	GOLDIE. [Golding]. 89. Gooley. 381. Gouldy. 381.	750	GRATTAN. Gratten. Grattin. 435.	768	GUERIN. Gearon. [Green]. 329.
714	GILTINANE. Giltenane. [Shannon]. 290, 318, 3.3.	732	GOLDING. Forkin. 506. [Golden]. 99. [Goldie]. 89. Goolden. 199. Goulding. McGouldrick. 175.	751	GRAVES. Greaves. 333. Grieves.	769	GUIDERA. Guider. 457. Guidra. 457.
715	GINITY. Ginaty. 220. Guinnaty. 220.	733	GOLDRICK. Coldrick. 52. [Golden]. 106, 128. Gouldrick. Goulrick.	752	GRAY. Colreary. 132.215, 465. Culreavn. 33.153. 357, &c. Grey.	770	GUIHEN. Guighan. Guihan. Guiheen. Guiken. [Wynne]. 278.371.
716	GIRVIN. Garron. 18.	734	GOODISSON. Godson. Goodison. Goodson.	753	GREEN. Greenan. 464. [Greenaway].409 Greene. Grene. 333. [Guerin]. Honneen. 318.323. Huneen. 299. MacIllesher. 301. McAlasher. 276. McAlesher.238,276 [McGlashan]. 114. 314. McGlashin.114,314 Oonin.	771	GUILFOYLE. Gilfoye. Gilfoyle. Kilfoyle. [Powell]. 509.
717	GITTINGS. Gittons. 101.	735	GOODMAN. Maguigan. 137.			772	GUINANE. Ginnane. Guinan. Kennane. Kinane. 498. Quinane. 498.
718	GIVEN. Garven. 489. [Garvin]. 489. Givan. Giveen. 356. Givin.	736	GOODWIN. [McGolrick]. 417. M'Googan. 254. M'Guiggan. 222.	754	GREENAWAY. [Green]. 409. Greenhaigh. 429. Greenhay. 429. Greenway. 429.	773	GUINEY. Guinea. Guiny.
719	GLANVILLE. Gaun. 63. Glanfield. 63.	737	GORDON. Magournahan. 175. McGournoson. 175.	755	GREENLAW. Grenlaw. Grinlaw.	774	GUINNESS. [McGuinness].
720	GLEASURE. Glazier. 51. Gleazer. 51.	738	GORMAN. Bloomer. 165. [Gormley]. 154, 246, 433. M'Gorman. 319. [O'Gorman].	756	GREENLEES. Greenlee. Grinlee. Grinlees.	775	GUNN. Gilgunn. 238. Gunner. 381. M'Elgunn. 167. McElgunn. 350.
721	GLEESON. Gleason. Glessane. Glissane. 303. 309. Glissawn. Leeson. 249.	739	GORMLEY. [Gorman]. 154, 246, 433. [Grimes]. 40.417, 418. McCormilla. 319.	757	GREER. Greir. Grier. 301,333.	776	GUNNING. Goonan. 107,390, 509. Goonane. 4,9. Gooney. 509. Guning.
722	GLENNY. Glanny. 429.	740	GOSLIN. Gausslin. Gosselin. Gostlin.	758	GREGG. Greig. 410.	777	GURRY. Gorey. 435. Gorry. 435.
		741	GOUGH. Goff. 333.	759	GREHAN. Greyhan. [Grimes]. 34.	778	GUTHRIE. Gutherie. Guttery. 410. [Lahiff]. 189.
		742	GOULD. Goold.	760	GRESHAM. Gressam. 254. Grism. 254. Grissam. Grissom. 197.	779	GWYNNE. Gwyn.

No.	Surnames, with Varieties and Synonymes.	No.	Surnames, with Varieties and Synonymes.	No.	Surnames, with Varieties and Synonymes.	No.	Surnames, with Varieties and Synonymes.
780	HACKETT. Guckian. 128. Guicken. 106. Halckett. M'Gaggy. 223. McGaughy. 163. McGaugie. 372. M'Goggy. 222.	797	HAMMOND. [Hamill]. 72. Whammond.	818	HARDIMAN. Hargaden. 251.	838	HASTINGS. Hastie. 97. Hasting. Hasty. 254. Heasting. Hestin. 361. Hestings. Hestion. 361.
781	HADSKISS. Hadskeath. 381. Haskis.	798	HAMPTON. Hamden. Hampden. Hempton. [Hinton]. 523.	819	HARDMAN. Harman. Harmon. Herdman.	839	HAUGHEY. Haffey. 279. Haghey. Haughan. Haughian. 381. Hoy. 148. M'Heffey. 279.
782	HAGAN. [Egan]. 133, 526. Hagin. Haigan. Haughean. 248. Heagan. Hegans. Hog. 487. [Hogg]. 487. [O'Hagan].17,348.	799	HANAN. Hainen. Hannan. Hannen. Haqnin. Hannon. Hanon. Haynan. Heenan. Henan.	820	HARDWOOD. Harrett. 92.		
				821	HARE. Hair. 342. Haire. Heare. Hegher. Hehir. 189, 318. O'Haire. [O'Hare]. O'Hear.	840	HAUGHTON. Houghton. Houtten. [Hutton]. 76.
783	HAGARTY. Agarty. Hagerty. Haggarty. Haggerty. Hegarty.	800	HANBIDGE. Handbidge. Handridge. Hanvidge.	822	HARNETT. Harknett. Hartnett.	841	HAVERON. Haveren. Havern. Havron. [Heffernan]. Heffron. 433. Hefron.
784	HAHESSY. Ahessy. Hahasy.	801	HANBURY. Hanberry. Hanbery. Handbury.	823	HAROLD. Harel. Harrel. Harrell. Herald. 71. Hirl. 123.	842	HAWES. Fowes.
785	HAINES. Haynes. [Hynes]. 134.	802	HAND. Handy. 511. McClave. 460. M'Lave. 460.	824	HARPUR. Harper.	843	HAWKINS. Haughian. 381.
786	HALDANE. McAldin. 429.	803	HANDCOCK. Hancock. Hancocks. Handcocks.	825	HARREN. Haran. Haren. Harron. [O'Hara]. 201,238, 270.	844	HAWKS. Hawkes.
787	HALES. Hailes.	804	HANDRICK. Hanrick. 468.			845	HAWKSHAW. Hoggshaw.
788	HALFPENNY. Alpin. Halpeny. [Halpin]. 72, 401, &c.	805	HANDSBERY. Hansbury. 356.	826	HARRICKS. Herricks.	846	HAWTHORN. Hathorn. Hawthorne. Haythorne. Henthorn. 383.
		806	HANIFY. Hanafy. Hanephy.	827	HARRINGTON. Airington. Ayrington. Erought. 113. [Errington]. Haroughten. 143. Haroughton. 47. Harrity. 3. Harroughton.112. [Harty]. 3. Irrington.		
789	HALL. Hull. 91.	807	HANLEY. Handly. Hanily. Hanly. 451 (b). Henley.			847	HAYDEN. Haden. Hadian. 329. Haydin. Haydon. Hayten. 305. Headen. 387. Heden. Heydon.
790	HALLIDAY. Halladay. Hallyday. Halyday. Holeday. Holliday.	808	HANLON. [Hallinan]. 134. Handlon. Hanlan. Hanlin. [O'Hanlon].				
791	HALLIGAN. Hilligan. 410. Olligan. 446.	809	HANNA. Hanah. Hannagh. Hannah.	828	HARRIS. Horoho. 486. [Harrison]. 414, 456. Harrisson.	848	HAYES. Hays. Haze. Heys. Hoy. 89. [O'Hea]. 500.
792	HALLINAN. [Allen]. 510. Hallanan. Halnan. Hanlan. 236. [Hanlon]. 134.	810	HANNAWAY. Hanway.	829	HARRISON. [Harris]. 414,456. Horaho. 294.	849	HAYMAN. Heman. Hemans.
793	HALLORAN. Hallaron. Hallorin. Halloron. Holloran. [O'Halloran].	811	HANNON. Hanar. Haneen. 500. Hannan. Hannen. Hannin.	830	HART. Harte. 475. [Harwood]. 523.	850	HAZLEGROVE. Haslegrove.
		812	HANRAHAN. Aurachaun. 488. Handrahan. 130, 442.	831	HARTFORD. Halford. 63. Hardford. Harford.	851	HAZLETON. Haselden. 429. Hasleton. Hazelton. [Hazlett]. 356.
794	HALPIN. Alpin. 241. [Halfpenny]. 72, 401, &c. McAlpin. 325,429.	813	HANRATTY. Ratty. 72.	832	HARTIGAN. Hartican.	852	HAZLETT. Haslett. 256. Hayslip. 410. Hazelett. Hazelitt. [Hazleton]. 356.
795	HAMILL. Hamell. [Hamilton]. 356, 409. Hammel. Hammell. Hammill. [Hammond]. 72. O'Hamill. 112.	814	HANSON. M'Kettrick. 97. [M'Kittrick]. 97.	833	HARTON. Harten. Hartin.		Hazley. 381. Hazlitt. Hazzlett. Heaslett. 256. Heasley. 381. Heazley. 381. Heslitt. Hezlett.
		815	HARBINSON. Harbison. Harvison. [Herbert]. 410. Herbison.	834	HARTY. [Harrington]. 3. Hartry. 488.		
				835	HARVEY. Harrihy. 141. Harvessy. 1.6. Hervy.		
796	HAMILTON. Ham. 397. [Hamill]. 356, 409. Tumbleton. 526.	816	HARCOURT. Harker. 410.	836	HARWOOD. Harrot. 20. [Hart]. 523.	853	HAZLEWOOD. Haslewood. Heazlewood.
		817	HARDEN. M'Dacker. 401.	837	HASSAN. Hasson.		

No.	Surnames, with Varieties and Synonymes.	No.	Surnames, with Varieties and Synonymes.	No.	Surnames, with Varieties and Synonymes.	No.	Surnames, with Varieties and Synonymes.
854	HEACOCK. Haycock. Heathcock. Heycock.	869	HENNESSY. Henesy. Henissy. Hensy. 420, 511. Henzy. 249. Hinsy. 420, 511.	889	HILLAN. Hillen. Hillind.	914	HORAN. Haran. 239. Haren. 390. Harhan. 239, 469. Haughran. 511.
855	HEALY. Heally. Heily. Hely. Hilo. 487. Kerisk. 111, 113. Kerrish. 377. Kerrisk. 303 (b).	870	HENRY. Hendry. 317. Henery. 429. [McElnery]. 429. McHendric. 429. [McHenry]. 429.	890	HILLAS. Heallis. Hilles. Hilliss.	915	HORGAN. Harrigan. 47. [Horrigan]. 283, 431. Horrigon. 431. Horrogan. Organ. 135.
856	HEANY. [Bird]. 40. Hainey. Heeny. Heney.	871	HENSHAW. Henehy. Hinchy.	891	HILLYARD. Hillard. Hilliard. Hilyard.	916	HORRIGAN. Harrigan. [Horgan]. 283, 431.
857	HEAPHY. Havey. 435. Havy. 435. Heify. 51.	872	HERAGHTY. Gerarty. 124. Hanaty. 432.	892	HINDS. [Owens]. 175.	917	HORSFORD. Hosford.
858	HEARD. Hearde. Herd. Hird. Hurd.	873	HERBERT. Harbert. 124. [Harbinson]. 410. Hilbert. 124. [Hobart.] 47.	893	HINTON. [Hampton]. 523. Hanton. 526.	918	HOSKINS. Haskins.
859	HEARN. Ahearn. [Ahearne]. Hearne. 422. [Herron]. 155, 410.	874	HERITAGE. Herrtage.	894	HITCHINS. Hitchens.	919	HOULIHAN. Holahan. Holohan. 187. Holoughan. Hoolaghan. Hoo ahan. Hoolihan. Hoologhan. Houlaghan. Houlahan. Houlehan. Hulihan. Oolahan. Oulahan. 63. Oulihan. Whoolahan. Whoolehan.
860	HEARY. Heery.	875	HERLIHY. Herley. 100.	895	HOARE. Hore. Horohoe. 454 (b).		
861	HEASLIP. Hazlip. Heslip. Heyslip. Hyslop.	876	HERNON. [Heffernan]. 249. Hertnon.	896	HOBART. Hubbert. 142. [Herbert]. 47. Hobert. Hubbard. 365.		
862	HEDNAN. Hedivan. 63. Heduvan. 63.	877	HERRIOTT. Hariott.	897	HODGINS. Hodger. 364.		
863	HEENAN. Heanen. 175. Hennan. 175.	878	HERRON. [Ahearne]. 77. Aherne. 77. Harron. [Hearn]. 155, 410. Herne. Heron. Herran.	898	HODNETT. Hatnet. Hornett. 318.	920	HOURIHAN. Hourihane.
864	HEFFERNAN. Hafferon. Haffron. Hartnane. 144. Hartney. 144. Havern. 429. [Haveron]. Hayfron. Hefferan. Heffernin. Heffernon. Hefferon. Heffron. 25, 155. [Hernon]. 249. Hertnan. 249. Heyfron. 384. Hiffernan.			899	HOEY. Hawey. Hoye.	921	HOUSTON. Houstin. Howison. Hughston. [Huston]. M'Taghlan. 4 3.
		879	HESKETH. Haskett.	900	HOGAN. Houghegan. 262. [Huggins]. 134.	922	HOWARD. Hogart. 59. O'Hare. 189.
		880	HESSION. [Ussher]. 298.	901	HOGG. [Hagan]. 487. Hog.	923	HOWE. Hough. House. 397. Howes.
		881	HETHERINGTON. Hederton.	902	HOLBROOK. Halbrook. Holdbrook.	924	HOWIE. Howay.
		882	HEWSON. Heuson. Hewetson. Hewison. Hewston. Hueson. Hueston. Hugheston. 279. Huson. [Huston]. 279. [McHugh]. 238, 506.	903	HOLDEN. Houldon. 485.	925	HOWLEY. Wholey.
865	HEGARTY. Eagerton. 399. Hagarty. Hagerty. Hegerty. Heggarty. Higerty. Higgerty. Hogarty. 179.			904	HOLDSWORTH. Holesworth. Houldsworth.	926	HOYLE. Hoyles. Hyle. Hyles.
				905	HOLLAND. Hawney. 488. [Mulholland]. 19. Wholihane. 325.	927	HUDDLESTON. Helston. Hillston.
866	HEMPENSTALL. Hemp. 405, 439. Hempe. 333. Hempstall. 333.	883	HEYBURN. Haybrun. Hayburn. Hepburn.	906	HOLLINGSWORTH. Hollinsworth.	928	HUDSON. Hodgin. 76. Hodgson. Hodson.
867	HENDERSON. Hendron. 6, 409.	884	HICKEY. Hickie. 509.	907	HOLLOWAY. Halloway. Hollway. Holoway.	929	HUEY. Huet. 410. Hughey.
868	HENNEBERRY. Heneberry. Henebery. 422. Henebry. 427. Hennebry. Hensbry. 422.	885	HIGGINBOTHAM. Higginbottom. HIGGINS.	908	HOLLY. [Quillan].	930	HUGGINS. [Higgins]. 485. [Hogan]. 134.
		886	Hagans. 267. Haggens. 267. Higgans. Higgens. Higgings. Higins. [Huggins]. 485. [O'Hagan] 178 (b).	909	HOLMES. Cavish. 304. Combes. 142. Homes. McCavish. 138. McCavish. 138.	931	HUGHES. Hews. Hughs.
		887	HILDITCH. Hildage. Hildige.	910	HONE. Owen. 482.	932	HULEATT. Hewlett.
		888	HILL. Heel. 154.	911	HOOKE. Hooks.	933	HUME. Hulme. 91. Humes.
				912	HOPES. Hopps. 274.		
				913	HOPKINS. Habbagan. 3. Hobbikin. 40. Hop. 439.		

No.	Surnames, with Varieties and Synonymes.	No.	Surnames, with Varieties and Synonymes.	No.	Surnames, with Varieties and Synonymes.	No.	Surnames, with Varieties and Synonymes.
934	HUMPHRIES. Humffray. Humfrey. Humphreys. Humphry. Humphrys. 398. Umphries. Umphry.	949	IRONS. Eirons. 91.	965	JOHNSTON. Cheyne. 429. Johnson. 494. Johnstone. 494. Jonson. Mac-Eoin. 512. Mac-Eown. 40. Makeon. 40. McCheyne. 429. [McKeown]. 506. McShan. 216. [McShane]. 18, 153, &c. Shane. 429. Shonahan. 512.	976	KEARNS. [Cairns]. 300. Carns. 155. Cearnes. 218. Kairns. Kearn. 319. Kearnes. [Kearney]. 409. Kearon. 16. Keiran. 319. Keirans. 319. Kerans. Kereen. 403. Kerins. Kerns. Kerons. Kerranc. 330. Kerrins. 448. Kieran. 319. O'Kieran. 319.
935	HUNT. Feghany. 124. Fehoney. 125. [Feighery]. 249. [Feighney]. 476, 501. Feighry. [Hunter]. 242, 409.	950	IRVINE. Ervine. 91. Erwin. Erwin. Irving. [Irwin]. 91.			977	KEATING. Clayton. 431. Keaty. 189, 302.
		951	IRWIN. Erwin. 19. [Irvine]. 91.			978	KEAVENY. Ceevney. Kevney.
936	HUNTER. [Hunt]. 242, 409.	952	ISAAC. Isaacs.	966	JORDAN. Gerdan. Gurdan. 485. Jardan. Jardine. 210, 429. Jerdau. Jorden. Jordine. Jordon. Jourdan. 200. Jourdin. Jurdan. 138.	979	KEEFFE. Keafe. Keefe. [O'Keeffe].
937	HURLEY. [Commane]. 189, 237, 397, &c. Harley. 227, 228. Herley. Herlihy. Herly. Murhilla. 397. O'Herlihy.	953	ISDELL. Easdale. Esdale. Esdel. Isdle.			980	KEEGAN. Cuggeen. [Egan]. 312.
		954	IVERS. Eivers. 333 Evers. 333. Ivors. Jevers.			981	KEELAN. Keelin. Keellin. Killan.
938	HURST. Hearst.			967	JOYCE. Cunnagher. 50. Shoye. 40.	982	KEELY. Kealy. Keeling. 409. Keilly. [Kelly]. 262. Kiely. Kiley.
939	HUSKISSON. Hiskisson. Hoskisson. Huskison.	955	JAGOE. Iago. 40. Jago.	968	JUDGE. Brchenty. 62, 454 (a), 501. [Brchony]. 105, 339, 454 (a), &c.		
940	HUSTON. [Hewson]. 279. [Houston]. [M'Hugh]. 259. [McTaghlin]. 482.	956	JAMES. [Jameson]. 409.	969	JULIAN. Julien.	983	KEENAN. Cainain. 281. Conneen. 3. Keenoy. 38. [Kinahan]. 249. Kinna. 249. Kinnan. Kivneen. 329.
941	HUTCHINSON. Hucheson. Hutchenson. Hutcheson. Hutchison. Hutchisson. Hutson. 274.	957	JAMESON. Jameison. [James]. 409. Jamieson. 390. Jamison. Jemason. Jemison.	970	JURY. Ma-Jury. 494.		
942	HUTTON. [Haughton]. 76.	958	JEFFERS. Gilford. 408. Jeffares. Jeffars. Jumphrey. 489.	971	KANE. Cahan. 210. Cain. Cane. Kain. Kaine. (Cain). 40. Keane. 390. [Kean]. 72, 381. McKane. 216. [O'Kane]. 216, 210, 367.	984	KEIGHTLEY. Keatley. 348. Keitley.
943	HYDE. [Driscoll]. Hide. [O'Driscoll]. 509.	959	JEFFREY. Jallery. Jallrey. Jallries. Jellery. Jeffreys. Mcchanqfry. 267.			985	KEITH. Keat. Keates. Keats.
944	HYLAND. Heelan. 120. 235. Heyland. Highland. Hiland. [Whelan]. 40.	960	JENKINS. Jenkenson. Jenkinson. Jenkison. Jnkins. Junkin. 66.	972	KAVANAGH. Cavan. 144. [Cavanagh]. 14. 516. Cavenagh. 13. Couvane. 47. Kavenagh. Keevane. 142. 144. Kevane. 8. 203. Kevency. Kivrahan. 271.	986	KELLEHER. Kellard. 277. Kellegher. Keller. 100, 199, 376, &c.
945	HYNES. [Haines]. 134. Haynes. 134. Heines. Hinds. 222. Hines. 333. Hoins. 165. Hoynes. 101, 238, 517. Hyndes. Hynds. [Owens]. 82. 238.	961	JENNINGS. Keeneen. 506. Kzoneen. 330. O'Keenen. 40.	973	KEAHERY. Keaghery. 307.	987	KELLOCK. Kelloch. Kellog.
		962	JERMYN. Jarmyn. Jerman.	974	KEAN. Cain. 22, 40, 420. [Kane]. 72. 381.	988	KELLY. [Callaghan]. 19. [Keely]. 262. Kelley. 41. Kiely. 100. [Kilkelly]. 342. [O'Kelly]. 390.
946	IGOE. Igo.	963	JERVIS. Gervaise. Gervase. [Gervis]. 17. Jervaise. Jervois.	975	KEARNEY. Carney. 13, 395. Carny. Karney. [Kearns]. 409. Keherny. Kerney. Kierney. McCarney. 185. O'Caharney. O'Caherney.		
947	INGLIS. [English].					989	KENNA. Kenah. Kinna. 458. [McKenna].
948	INGOLDSBY. Englishby. 13, 214. Gallogly. 214. Inglesby. Insgelby. 402.	964	JILES. Jellis. 274.				

No.	Surnames, with Varieties and Synonymes.	No.	Surnames, with Varieties and Synonymes.	No.	Surnames, with Varieties and Synonymes.	No.	Surnames, with Varieties and Synonymes.
990	KENNEALY. Kenealy. Kenelly. 530. Kenneally. Kennelly. Kinealy. Kinneally. Kinnealy. 530.	1007	KEYS. Kays. Keays. Keyes.	1029	KINGSTON. *Cloughry.* Kingstone. *McCloughry.* 57.	1044	KNOWD. Noud. Nowd.
991	KENNEDY. Kennington. 422. *Minagh.* 132. *Muinagh.* 132.	1008	KIDD. Kiddle. Kydd.	1030	KINNANE. Canaan. 27, 72. Cannan. 72. [Cannon]. 72. Guinane. 498. Kinane. Quinane. 493.	1045	KNOWLES. Knoles. Knowels. Knowls.
992	KENNY. Kenney. 370. Kenny. 370. Kilkenny. 72. Kinney. [McKenny]. [McKinny]. 429.	1009	KIDNEY. Kedney.			1046	KYLE. Kell. 112. M'Suile. 43.
		1010	KIERNAN. Kearan. 72. Keirans. 72. [Kernaghan]. Kernan. 153. Kernon. 153. McKiernan. 153, 246, &c.	1031	KINNEAR. Kinnaird. Kinneard. Kinner. Kinnere. Kinnier.	1047	KYNE. *Barnacle.* 250. [Coyne]. 40, 174. &c.
993	KENRICK. Conderick. 162. Condrick. 162. Kendrick.	1011	KILBRIDE. Macbride. 40. McGill Bride. 429.	1032	KINSELLA. Kenchyla. Kinchela. Kinchella. Kinsela. Kinsellagh. Kinsellah. Kinshela. Kinshelagh. Kinshellagh. Kinslagh. 429.	1048	LACY. Leacy. 244.
994	KEOGH. Cuhy. 15. Kehoe. 448. K'eogh. Keoghoe. 472. Keoghy. 246. Keough. 435. Kough. 295. *McCahugh.* 357. [McKeogh].	1012	KILCLINE. Cline. 54.			1049	LADLEY. Laidley.
		1013	KILFEDDER. Kilfeder.			1050	LAFFAN. Laffen. Laphin. Lapin. Lappin.
		1014	KILGALLEN. Kilcullen. 475.			1051	LAFFERTY. Laferty. [O'Flaherty]. 480.
		1015	KILKELLY. [Kelly]. 342. Killkelly.	1033	KIRBY. Kerbin. 413. Kerby. 413. Kirberry. 413. Kirkby.		
995	KEOHANE. Cahan. [*Cowan*]. *Cowen.* 397. Keoghane. [Keown].	1016	KILLEEN. Killion. 24. 329.			1052	LAHIFF. [Guthrie]. 189. [Flahy]. 189. Lahive. 131.
		1017	KILLEN. [Gillen]. Killian.	1034	KIRKPATRICK. [Kilpatrick]. 43, 175, 271, &c. Kirk. 19, 240. McIlfatrick. 59. McIlfederick. 43.	1053	LAING. Lang. Layng.
996	KEOWN. Cahane. Cohane. [Keohane]. Keon.	1018	KILLOPS. Kellops. Killips. [McKillop].			1054	LAIRD. Layard. Leard.
997	KEPPEL. [Capel]. Kepple.	1019	KILM. Killum. 421.	1035	KIRWAN. Carvin. 495. Keerawin. 427. Kerevan. 295, 316. Kerivan. Kerivin. 130, 442. Kervan. Kerwin. 427. Kierevan. 498. Kiervan. 102. Kirivan. Kirrane. 229. Kirvan. Kirwen. Kirwin.	1055	LAMBERT. Lambart. Lampert.
998	KERIN. Kearin. 382.	1020	KILMARTIN. [Gilmartin]. Guilmartin. 457.			1056	LAMMY. L'Ami. Lamie. Lammie. Lamy. Lemmy.
999	KERLEY. Kirley. McKerlie.	1021	KILPATRICK. Gillpatrick. 429. Killpatrick. [Kirkpatrick].43. 175, 271, &c. Kirpatrick. McGill Patrick. 429. Petherick. 220.			1057	LAMONT. Laman. Lamin. Lammon. Lamon. Lamond. 254. Lemon. 178. (b)
1000	KERLIN. Kirlin. 159.						
1001	KERNAGHAN. [Canavan]. 410. Carnohan. Keernan. Kernahan. (Carnahan). 175. Kernan. Kernohan. Kernon. [Kiernan].	1022	KILROY. Gilroy.	1036	KISSACK. Keesack. Kissick. Kissock.	1058	LANCASTER. Laingster. Langster. Lankester.
		1023	KINAHAN. [Keenan]. 249. Kinna. 249.	1037	KISSANE. Cashman. 47, 309. Coshman. 304(a). Gissane.	1059	LANDERS. Glanders. 120. Landy. 15, 488. Launders.
		1024	KINARNEY. Kinneary. 249.	1038	KITCHEN. Ketchen. 429. [Kitson]. 238, 429. [M'Cutcheon]. 429.	1060	LANE. Layne. 54. Leane. 303. [Lyne]. 329.
1002	KERR. [Carr]. 19, 213.	1025	KINCAID. Kincade. Kinkade. Kinkaid. Kinkead.				
1003	KERRIGAN. Carigan. Carrigan. 238. Comber. 329. Comer. 329. [Corrigan]. 361. Currigan. 361. Keighron. 370. Kergan. Kerigan.	1026	KING. [Conroy]. 40, 342. Conry. 40. *Cunreen.* 485. *Mac-an-Ree.* 40. *McAree.* 175, 319, 460. *M'Keary.* 319. *Muckaree.* 71. *Muckilbouy.* 71.	1039	KITSON. [Kitchen]. 238. 429. Kittson.	1061	LANGLEY. Landy. 243. Langly.
				1040	KNAGGS. Knags. Naggs.	1062	LANGTRY. Langtree. Lanktree. Lantry.
				1041	KNEE. Nee.		
1004	KERRISON. Kearson.	1027	KINGSBURY. Kinsbury.	1042	KNIGHT. [M'Knight]. Neight. Night.	1063	LANNIGAN. Langan. Langin. Lanigan. Lenagan. Lenigan.
1005	KERSHAW. Kearsey. 249.	1028	KINGSLEY. Kinchella. 3. Kinchley. 3. Kinsley.	1043	KNIPE. Nipe.		
1006	KETTLE. Kettyle.						

No.	Surnames, with Varieties and Synonymes.	No.	Surnames, with Varieties and Synonymes.	No.	Surnames, with Varieties and Synonymes.	No.	Surnames, with Varieties and Synonymes.
1064	LARKIN. Larkan. Larken. Larkins. Lorkin.	1082	LEDWICH. Leddy. Ledgwidge. Ledwidge. Ledwitch. Ledwith. 63. Lidwich.	1097	LEONARD. Lenaghan. 319. [Lenane]. 352. 375. Lenard. Lenord. 516. Lennard. [Lennon]. 239. Linane. 375, 101. Lannon. 21, 329. Lynane. 45. McAllingen. 201. McAlinion. 238. McAlinon. 217. Nanany. 454 (b).	1111	LOCKHART. Lock. 523. Lockard. Lockart. Lockheart.
1065	LARMOUR. Laramer. Larimer. Larimor. Larmer. Lorimer. Lorimour. 197. Lormer. Lourimer.	1083	LEE. Leigh. 72. M'Lee. 72.	1098	LESLIE. Lastly. 396. Lussy. 396.	1112	LOFTUS. Loftis. [Loughnane]. 179, 262, 386.
1066	LATHAM. Leadam. 429. Leatham. Leathem. Leedham. Leedom. Leitham. Lethem.	1084	LEECH. Leache. Leetch. Leitch. Lovat. 329. Loocuc. 329. Loogue. 329.	1099	LESTER. Leicester. 429. Leycester. Lister. 429. Lyster. M'Alester. 429.	1113	LOGAN. Lagan. 433. [Loughan]. 307.
1067	LATIMER. Latimore. Latimour. Lattimer. Lattimore. Letimore. Lettimor.	1085	LEES. Alees.	1100	LETSOME. Ledsome. Letsam. Moter. 104. Moton. 457. [Moreton]. 104.	1114	LOGUE. Loag. Loague. [Molloy.] 259, 260.
1068	LAURENCE. Larens. Lawrance. Lawrence.	1086	LEFANU. Lefanu. Leffanue.	1101	LEVEY. Leavy.	1115	LOMAX. Lummacks. 72.
1069	LAVELLE. Lawell. 40.	1087	LEFEVRE. Lefebre.	1102	LEWIS. Lewers. 137, 175. Lowers. 411.	1116	LONERGAN. Ladrigan. 170. Landregan. Londregan. 117 Londrigan. 331. Lundergan. 354.
1070	LAVERTY. O'Laverty. 318.	1088	LEGGATT. Legat. L'gate. (Ligget). 358. Legett. Leget. Leggott. Liggate. Liggot.	1103	LEYBOURNE. Layburn. Leburn. Lyburn.	1117	LONG. Fodha. 488. Longley. 409.
1071	LAVERY. Armstrong]. [197, 347. [Lowry]. [Rafferty]. 410.	1089	LEHANE. Leehane. Leyhane. Lihane. Lyhan. 228. Lyhane. 365. [Lyons]. 226, 325.	1104	LINANE. Lane. 336. Linahan. 249. Linnane.	1118	LONGHILL. Longill.
1072	LAVINS. Levins.	1090	LEIGHTON. Lighton.	1105	LINDEN. Lindin. Lindon. [McAlinden]. 289, 429. M'Linden. 429.	1119	LONICAN. Lunican.
1073	LAWDER. Lauder. Lawther. Louther. Lowther.	1091	LEMON. Lamont. 178 (b). Leeman. Leemon. Lemmon.	1106	LINDSAY. Linchey. 175. Lindesay. Lindsy. Lyndsay.	1120	LONSDALE. Lownsdale. 381. Lownsel. 381.
1074	LAWLESS. [Lawson]. 333. Lillis. 180.	1092	LENANE. Lenahan. 420. [Leonard]. 352, 375. Linahan. 420.	1107	LITTLE. Begg, 124, 219, &c. Beggan. 211, 383. Biggedon, 495. Liddel. 429. [Littleton]. 409. Lytle. 321. Lyttle. 223. [Petit]. 109. Pettit. 109.	1121	LOOBY. Luby. 329.
1075	LAWLOR. Lalor. Lawler.	1093	LENDRUM. Landrum.	1108	LITTLETON. Begane. 508. Biggane. 151, 509. [Little]. 409. Lyttleton.	1122	LOUGHAN. [Logan]. 307. Lohan. 307, 386. [Loughran]. 6.
1076	LAWRENSON. Laurison. Lawrenceson. Lawrinson. Lawrison.	1094	LENIHAN. Lane. 230. Lenaghan. Lenaghen. Lenahan. Leneghan. Lenehan. Lennihan. Linahan. Linighan. Linnahan. Linnehan.	1109	LIVINGSTONE. Levenston. Leveson. 503. Levingstone. Levinson. Levinston. Leviston. 417. Livingstown.	1123	LOUGHEAD. Lougheed.
1077	LAWSON. [Lawless]. 333. Laws. 409.	1095	LENNON. Lannan. 67 Lanon. Lenon. [Leonard]. 239. Linnane. 318. Linnen. 120.	1110	LLOYD. Loyd.	1124	LOUGHLIN. [Gilchrist]. 216. Lachlin. Lacklan. Laghlin. Laughlin. Lochlin. Loghlin. Loghnan. 517. Loughlan. Loughlen. Loughnan. 295. M'Gloughlin. [M'Laughlin]. [O'Loughlin].
1078	LAYCOCK. Lacock. Leacock.	1096	LENNOX. Lenox. Linnox.			1125	LOUGHNANE. [Loftus]. 179, 262, 386. [Loughan]. 6. Loughnan. Lucknawne. 190.
1079	LEAHY. Lahy. 117. 235, 393, &c. Leahey. Leehy. Lehy.					1126	LOUGHRAN. Early. 165. Laugheran. Lochrane. [Loughan]. 76. Lougheran. Loughren.
1080	LEARY. Lairy. Leery. [O'Leary].					1127	LOVETT. Lovat.
1081	LECKY. Lackey. Leaky. Leckie.					1128	LOWNDES. Loundes. Lownes.
						1129	LOWRY. [Lavery]. Loughry. 189. Lowery. 174. Lowroo. 189.
						1130	LUCAS. M'Lucas.

No.	Surnames, with Varieties and Synonymes.	No.	Surnames, with Varieties and Synonymes.	No.	Surnames, with Varieties and Synonymes.	No.	Surnames, with Varieties and Synonymes.
1131	LUKE. Lute. 7.	1148	MACK. [Mac]. Mackaleary. [M'Dermott]. [M'Donald]. [M'Enroe]. 417. [M'Evoy]. [M'Inerney]. [M'Namara]. 345. 430. [M'Namee]. 207. M'Sweeny. 304(a)	1159	MAGILL. MacGill. Mackel. 429. Maguil. 429. M'Gill. Mekill. 429.	1177	MALTSEED. Malseed. Molseed.
1132	LUNDY. Londy. 429. [M'Alinden]. 175.			1160	MAGINN. Maginnis. 409. [M'Ginn]. [M'Guinness].	1178	MANASSES. Manus. 140.
1133	LUNNY. Loney. Lonney. Loony. Luny.			1161	MAGNER. Magnier. Magnir. Magnor. Mingane. 303.	1179	MANGAN. [Magan]. 305. Manghan. Manghen. Mangin. Manion. 63. [Manning]. 182. [Mannion]. 420. Mingane. 303.
1134	LUTTRELL. Lutteral. Lutterel.	1149	MACKEATING. M'Ketian. 481.	1162	MAGORLICK. [Golden]. 201.	1180	MANNERING. Mainwaring. Manron. 73.
1135	LYDEN. Liddane. 131, 419. Ludden. 119. Lydden. Lydon.	1150	MACKENZIE. M'Ilhoney. 59.	1163	MAGRANE. Magahern. 46. Magrean. [M'Grane].	1181	MANNING. [Mangan]. 182. [Mannion]. 215. Meenhan. 322.
1136	LYNAGH. Laney. 432. Linagh. [Lynam.] 286.	1151	MACKEY. Mackay. M'Cay. 19, 60. [M'Gee]. M'Hay. [M'Kay]. 19. [M'Kee]. 189. M'Key. M'Quay. 185.	1164	MAGRATH. Cra. 67. See [M'Grath].	1182	MANNION. [Mangan]. 420. Manion. [Manning]. 215. Mongon. 38.
1137	LYNAM. Lineham. Linham. [Lynagh]. 286. Lynap. 30. Lyneham. Lynham.			1165	MAGUIRE. Macgivir. 40. MacGuire. [M'Guire]. 12.	1183	MANNIX. Manix. [McNiece]. Minogue, 262, 509, &c. [Monaghan]. 469.
1138	LYNAS. Linass. Liness. Lynass. Lyness. M'Aleenan. 524.	1152	MACKINTOSH. Macintosh. M'Entosh. M'Intosh—M'Il-hose. 254. Tosh. 175, 197, &c.	1166	MAHAFFY. Mehaffy.	1184	MANSFIELD. Mansel. 393. [Maunsell]. 203.
				1167	MAHER. Magher. Maheir. 409. Mahier. 410. [Mara]. 514. [Meagher]. 354, 393.	1185	MAPOTHER. Maypowder. 72.
1139	LYNCH. Lynchahan. 113. Lynchy. 515.	1153	MACLISE. Macleese. Macleish. [M'Aleese] M'Cleish. M'Gleish. M'Ilees:. M'Lees. M'Leese. M'Leise. [M'Leish].			1186	MARA. [Maher]. 514. [Meara]. 393. [O'Meara]. 393.
1140	LYNE. [Lane]. 329. Leyne. 8.			1168	MAHON. Maghan. [Mahony]. 57,515. Mann. 81. Maughan. 269, 337. [M'Mahon]. [Mohan]. 269.	1187	MARK. [Markey]. 409. Marks.
1141	LYNN. Lind. 87. Linn. 350.	1154	MADDEN. Maddigan. 367. [M'Avaddy]. 486. M'Evaddy. 119. McEvady. McVady.	1169	MAHONY. Hallissey. 227. [Mahon]. 57,515. Mahoney. 291. (M'Mahon]. 158, 291.	1188	MARKEY [Mark]. 409. Rhyder. [Ryder]. 495.
1142	LYONS. [Lehane]. 226. 325. Leyhane. 325. Lines. Lion. 259. Lions. Lyne. 47. Lyns. [O'Lyons].	1155	MADDOCK. Maddocks. Maddox. Madox. Mayduck. 429.	1170	MAIRS. See [Meares].	1189	MARKHAM. Marcom. Marcum.
				1171	MAJOR. Majur.	1190	MARLEY. Marlay. Marrilly. 259.
1143	LYSAGHT. Lysat.	1156	MAGAN. Magahan. [Mangan]. 305. M'Cahan. [M'Cann]. M'Gahan. M'Gan. [M'Gann]. Megahan. Megan.	1172	MALCOLM. Malkim. 340. Malcom. Meck. 381.	1191	MARMION. Mermont. 310. Merriman. 274. Merryman. 98, 305, 310, &c.
				1173	MALCOLMSON. Malcomson.	1192	MARNANE. Marinane. Mournane. [Murnane]. [Warren]. 283.
				1174	MALLA. Mallew. 137. [Malley]. 174, 312. [O'Malley]. 179.	1193	MARRON. Mearn. 425.
1144	MAC. See Mack.	1157	MAGAURAN. Magawran. Maguran. Magurn. M'Cahern. M'Gaheran. M'Gahran. M'Gaughran. M'Gavern. M'Gouran. [M'Govern]. 82, 238, 270, &c. M'Gowran.	1175	MALLEY. Maley. 370. [Malia]. 174, 342. Malie. Mallagh. 210. Mealia. Mealley. 312. [Melia]. 249, 456. Melly. 208. [O'Malley]. 361, 370. O'Meally.	1194	MARSHALL. Marchal. Marshill.
1145	MACARTNEY. M'Arteney. M'Artney. M'Cartiney. [M'Cartney]. M'Caugherty. 267. Mulhartagh. 69.					1195	MARTIN. Marten. Martyn.
1146	MACAULAY. [Cawley]. 300. Macauley. M'Alay. 60. [M'Auley]. 480. M'Caughley. 197. [M'Cauley]. M'Gawley. 410.	1158	MAGEE. [Gee]. [M'Gee]. M'Ghee. M'Ghie. 481. Wynn. 82. [Wynne]. 82.	1176	MALLON. Mallan. Mailen. Mallin. Mallyn. [Mullen]. 180.	1196	MATEER. Minteer. 175.
1147	MACETAVEY. Tavey. 137.					1197	MATHESON. Mathewson. Mathieson. Mathison. Matson. Mattheson. Matthewson. Matthieson. Mattison.

E

No.	Surnames, with Varieties and Synonymes.	No.	Surnames, with Varieties and Synonymes.	No.	Surnames, with Varieties and Synonymes.	No.	Surnames, with Varieties and Synonymes.
1198	MATHEWS. Mathers. 410. Matthew. Matthews. Mitty. 109.	1212	M'ALLISTER. Macalister. MacEllistram. 47. M'Alasher. 319. M'Alester. M'Allester. M'Callister. 358. M'Clester. M'Ellister. M'Lester. 410.	1227	M'BEAN. M'Bin. 429.	1243	M'CANN. Macan. Mackin. 410. [Magan]. M'Kann. Mecan.
1199	MAUNSELL. Mansel. Mansell. [Mansfield]. 203. Mansill. Monsell. 333.			1228	M'BETH. Macbeth. 141. M'Beath. M'Beith. M'Bey. 480.		
				1229	M'BIRNEY. M'Burney. (Burney). 86.	1244	M'CARROLL. [Carroll]. Mackarel. Mackerel. Mackrell. M'Carrell. M'Garrell. M'Garroll. M'Harroll. M'Kerel. M'Kerrall. Mekerrel.
1200	MAWHINNEY. [Buchanan]. 204. Mahunny. Mawhiney. [M Whinney]. Mewheney. Mewhenney.	1213	M'ALONEY. M'Alunney. M'Luney.	1230	M'BRATNEY. M'Breatney. M'Bretney.		
		1214	M'ALOON. M'Clune. M'Loone. M'Lune. Monday. 82, 350. 460. Mundiiy. 247. 350. Mundu.	1231	M'BREARTY. [Brady]. 259. 260. M'Brairty. M'Mearty. 432. M'Merty. 314.		
1201	MAXWELL. Maxel. 210.			1232	M'BRIDE. Breedeth. 519. M'Gill Bride. 429. Mucklebreed. 97.	1245	M'CARSON. M'Carrison. M'Harrison.
1202	MAY. Mawe. 488. Mea. 40, 188.	1215	M'ALPIN. M'Calpin.				
		1216	M'ARDIE. Macardle. M'Ardell. McCardle. 392.	1233	M'BRIEN. Brien. [Bryan]. M'Brine. M'Bryan. M'Byrne. 163. [O'Brien]. 82. 308. &c. O'Brine. 270.	1246	M'CARTHY. Carthy. 100. [Carty]. 448. Cremeen. 79. Cremin. 79. Crimmeen. 79. Farshin. 227. [Fortune]. 227. Macarha or Carha. 397. MacCarthy. M'Arthy. M'Artie. 199. [M'Cagherty]. 210. [M'Cartney]. 410. M'Cartie. 288. M'Carty. M'Caugherty. 267. [Quirk]. 500.
1203	MAYBERRY. Maberry. Maybury. 283. Meberry.	1217	M'AREAVY. M'Arevy. M'Gill Reavy. 429. [M'Greevy].		
1204	MAYNE. Main. Mains. Maynes. [M'Manus]. 238, 247.	1218	M'ARTHUR. M'Carter. M'Carthur.		
		1219	M'ASEY. Macasey. Mackessy. M'Assie. M'Casey.	1234	M'CABE. Macabe. Maccabe.		
1205	MAZE. Maise. Maize. Mayes. Mays. Mayze. Mease. Meaze.	1220	M'ASKIE. Caskey. M'Caskie.	1235	M'CADDEN. Muckedan. 63.		
		1221	M'ATAMNEY. M'Ataminey. M'Atimeny. M'Atimney. M'Tamney.	1236	M'CADDO. [Caddow]. M'Ado. M'Adoo. M'Cadoo.		
1206	M ADAM. M'Adams. M Cadam. M'Caddam. M'Cudden. 492.	1222	M'ATEER. Mateer. M'Atear. M'Atier. M'Cateer. M'Entyre. 223. [M'Intyre]. 177, 223, 421. M'Teer. M'Tier.	1237	M'CAFFRY. [Bratty]. 247. [Betty]. 238. Cafferty. 82. Caffery. 82. M'Cafferty. 70. M'Caffery. 70. M'Caffray. M'Caffrey. 70. M'Cafry.	1247	M'CARTNEY. Cartin. 159. [Macartney]. M'Carten. 381. [M'Carthy]. 410. M'Carton. 175. Mulhartagh. 41, 70.
1207	M'AFEE. Macfie. M'Affee. M'Affie. M'Fee. M'Haffy.			1238	M'CAGHERTY. M'Caharty. M'Caherty. M'Cangherty. [M'Carthy]. 210.	1248	M'CAUGHEY. M'Aghy. 17. M'Caghey. M'Cahy. McCahon. 321. [M'Caughin]. 202 M'Coughey. [M Gahcy]. 256. M'Gahy. M'Gaughey. (McGaughy). 256
1208	M'ALEE. M'Lee.	1223	M'AULEY. [Macaulay]. 480. MacAuly. MacAwly. M'Aulay. M'Aully. M'Awley. M'Calla. 411. M'Caulay. 71. [M'Cauley]. 208, 259. M'Caully. M'Cawley. 340. M'Cawly. M'Gaulay. M'Gauley. M'Gawlay. M'Gawley.	1239	M'CALL. M'All. 279. M'Calla. 372. M'Caul. 279. M'Cawell. M'Cawl. M'Gall. M'Hall. Megall.		
1209	M'ALEESE. M'Aleece. (M'Lice). 363. [Maclise].			1240	M'CALLION. M'Kellan. 418. M'Killion. 417.	1249	M'CAUGHLEY. M'Cally. 348.
1210	M'ALINDEN. [Linden]. 289, 429, 478. [Lundy]. 175. MacLinden. 478. M'Alindon. M'Clinton. M'Linden. 478. M'Lindon. M'Linton.			1241	M'CALMONT. M'Cammon. M'Cammond. M'Colman. 429. M'Kemmin. 429.	1250	M'CAUL. M'Coll. 91.
						1251	M'CAULEY. [Macaulay]. M'Aulay. [M'Auley]. 208, 259. M'Camley. 381. M'Comley. 197.
		1224	M'AVADDY. [Madden]. 486. M'Evaddy. 486.	1242	M'CANDLESS. M'Andless. 358. M'Anliss. M'Candlass. M'Candleish. M'Candliss. M'Canlis.		
1211	M'ALLEN. Macallon. M'Alen. M'Alin. M'Allion. M'Allon. M'Callion. M'Killian.	1225	M'AVEY. M'Ileboy. 175. M'Ilwee. 523.			1252	M'CAUSLAND. [Alexander]. 112 M'Caslan. 18. M'Casland.
		1226	M'AWEENY. M'Weeny.				

No.	Surnames, with Varieties and Synonyms.	No.	Surnames, with Varieties and Synonyms.	No.	Surnames, with Varieties and Synonyms.	No.	Surnames, with Varieties and Synonyms.
1253	M'CAVILL. [Campbell]. 216. M'Caufield. 480.	1268	M'CONKEY. Maconchie. McConohy. 265. M'Konkey.	1284	M'CREANOR. M'Crainor. M'Grenor. Treanor. 367.	1297	M'DERMOTT. [Darby]. 281, 282. Darmody. 117, 427, &c. De Ermot. 177. Dermott. 343,482. [Dermody]. 214, 438, &c. Dermond. 161. [Dermott]. De Yermond. 344. Deyermott. 271, 356, 478, &c. Diarmid. 341, 381, 432. Diarmod. 271. Diarmond. 314. Diermott. 240,260. Diurmagh. 391. Durmody. 295. Dyermott. 374. Macdermott. [Mack]. M'Diarmod. [Mulrooney]. 29, 125.
1254	M'CLAFFERTY. M'Cafferty. 259.	1269	M'CONN. M'Ilchon. 175.	1285	M'CREERY. M'Creary. M'Reery.		
1255	M'CLARY. M'Alary. 19. M'Lary. 19.	1270	M'CONNELL. [Connell]. M'Conell. M'Connon. 214. M'Conol. [M'Conville]. 461. [M'Donnell]. 276. M'Gonnell.	1286	M'CRORY. Macrory. M'Arory. McRoary. 95. McRory. 95. Rodger Rodgers. 18, 418, &c. [Rogers]. 97, 222, 423, &c.		
1256	M'CLEAN. Maclean. M'Alean. M'Clain. M'Clane. M'Laine. M'Lane. [M'Lean]. 420.						
1257	M'CLEARY. M'Aleery. M'Cleery. M'Eleary. M'Learey. M'Leary. M'Leery.	1271	M'CONNELLOGUE. Conlogue. 447.	1287	M'CRUM. M'Crumb. M'Rum. 489.		
		1272	M,CONVILLE. [M'Connell]. 461.	1288	M'CUE. [M'Hugh]. 259, 341, &c.		
		1273	M'CORKELL. M'Corkill M'Corkle. M'Corrikle.	1289	M'CULLAGH. Bour. 124. Bower. 125. M'Collough. M'Cull. 16. M'Culla. M'Cullah. M'Culloch. 159. M'Cullogh. M'Cullough. M'Cullow. 423.	1298	M'DEVITT. MacDevettie. M'Dade. 434. [M'Daid]. 314, 356, &c.
1258	M'CLELLAND. M'Clellan. 494. M'Leland. M'Lellan. 83. M'Lelland.	1274	M'CORMACK. Cormac. 448. [Cormack]. 3. Cormick. MacCormack. M'Comick. 410. M'Cormac. M'Cormick. (Cormican). 6.				
1259	M'CLEMENT. M'Clements. M'Clemonts. M'Climent. M'Climond. 175. M'Climont. M'Clymon. 267. M'Lamond. 19. M'Lement. M'Limont.	1275	M'CORQUODALE. M'Corcadale. M'Corcodale. M'Quorcodale.	1290	M'CUMESKY. Cumberford. 289. M'Comiskey. M'Comoskey. M'Cumisky.	1299	M'DONAGH. [Denison]. 179. Donaghey. 159. [Donaghy]. 350, 423, &c. Donogh. Macdona. MacDonagh. MacDonough. M'Dona. M'Donnagh. M'Donogh. M'Donough.
		1276	M'CORRY. [Curry]. 201, 350. M'Curry. M'Gorry. M'Gurry.	1291	M'CUNE. MacEwen. M'Ewan. M'Ewen. M'Keon. [M'Keown]. 429.		
1260	M'CLENAGHAN. Clenaghan. M'Clenahan. M'Cleneghan. M'Clenighan. M'Clennon. [M'Lenaghan].	1277	M'COSKER. M'Coskar.	1292	M'CURDY. M'Kurdy.	1300	M'DONALD. [Mack]. [M'Daniel]. 214, 472. [M'Donnell]. 214, 281, 410, &c.
		1278	M'COUBREY. Macoubrey. M'Cobric. M'Covera. M'Cubrae. M'Oubery. M'Oubrey.	1293	M'CUSKER. [Cosgrave]. 429. Cosgrove. 132, 153, 429, &c. Cuskern. 367. M'Cuskern. 429. M'Kusćar. M'Kusker. M'Oscar. 367, 429. M'Usker.	1301	M'DONNELL. Donald. 432. [Donnell]. MacDonald. MacDonnell. [M'Connell]. 276. [M'Daniel]. 214, 467, 472, &c. [M'Donald]. 214, 281, 410, &c. [O'Donnell]. 352,
1261	M'CLINTOCK. M Clyntock. M Lintock. 321.						
1262	M'CLOY. Maloy. 19.	1279	M'COWLEY. M'Cownley. 69.				
1263	M'CLURE. M'Lure. 432.	1280	M'COY. Macoy. M'Cay. 216. [M'Kay]. 383, 410. M'Kie. 69. M'Koy.	1294	M'CUTCHEON. [Kitchen]. 429. M'Cutchan. M'Cutchon.	1302	M'DOWELL. [Dowell]. Macdowell. Madole. 381. Madowell. 461. Maydole. M'Dole. 95. M'Dool. M'Dougal. M'Dowall. M'Dugal. Medole. 197. [Muldoon]. 92.
1264	M'CLUSKEY. Clusker. [Cluskey]. Macloskey. M'Closkey. M'Losky. 209. 240. M'Luskey. M'Trustry. 85.			1295	M'DAID. [Davis]. 165. [Davison]. M'Dade. M'David. M'Davitt. [M'Devitt]. 314, 356, &c. M'Divitt. 271.		
1265	M'COLLUM. [Columb]. M'Calum. M'Collom. M'Colum. M'Cullum.	1281	M'CRANN. Rinn. [Wrenn]. 128.			1303	M DWYER. M'Dire. 259.
		1282	M'CREA. M'Cray. M'Rae. M'Ray. M'Wray.	1296	M'DANIEL. M'Daniall. [M'Donald]. 214, 472. [M'Donnell]. 214, 467, 472, &c.	1304	M'ELDOWNEY. Ildowney. 429. M'Gill Downey. 429. M'Ildowney. 429.
1266	M'COMBS. M'Comb. M'Combes.						
1267	M'CONAGHY. Conaty. 211. M'Conachie. M'Conaughty. 367. M'Connaghy. M'Connaughey. M'Connerty. 367. [Quinn]. 319.	1283	M'CREADY. Macready. M'Aready. 254. M'Conready. 254. M'Creedy. M'Ready. M'Reedy. Mecredy.				

No.	Surnames, with Varieties and Synonymes.	No.	Surnames, with Varieties and Synonymes.	No.	Surnames, with Varieties and Synonymes.	No.	Surnames, with Varieties and Synonymes.
1305	M'ELERNEY. M'Lerney. 137	1321	M'EWAN. MacEwan. 91. M'Ewen. 91.	1336	M'GEEHAN. Mageahan. Mageehan. Mageen. M'Gean. M'Gechin. M'Gehan. M'Gihen.	1354	M'GOLRICK. [Golden]. [Goodwin]. 417. Goulding. 175. Gouldrick. M'Goldrick. M'Golric. M'Gorlick. M'Gouldrick.
1306	M'ELHINNEY. Ilhinney. M'Elhenny. M'Elheny. M'Ilhenny.	1322	M'FADDEN. [Fagan]. 206. Faggy. 139, 206. M'Faddin. M'Faddon. M'Faden. M'Fadian. M'Fadzen. 13. M'Feddan. [M'Padden]. M'Phadden.			1355	M'GONIGLE. MacCongail. M'Gonagle. M'Gonegal. M'Gonegle. M'Gonigal. (Magon). 59. M'Gonnigle.
1307	M'ELMEEL. M'Meel. 256.			1337	M'GEOGHEGAN. M'Gaffigan. 169.		
1308	M'FLREAVY. M'Ilravy. 19.			1338	M'GETTIGAN. Gaitens. 206. Gattins. 314.		
1309	M'ELROY. M'Alroy. M'Gill Roy. 429. [M'Ilroy]. 59. 87. 410. M'Leroy. M'Lroy. 358. Roy. 154, 413.	1323	M'FALL. M'Falls.	1339	M'GILLOWAY. [M'Elwee]. 483.	1356	M'GOUGH. M'Geough. M'Golf.
		1324	M'FARLAND. M'Farlaine. M'Farlane. [M'Parland]. M'Parlin. M'Partland. 238. M'Pharland.	1340	M'GILLYCUDDY. M'Elcuddy. M'Elhuddy. M'Elleuddy. M'Gillicuddy. M'Illicuddy.	1357	M'GOVERN. [Magauran]. 82, 238, 270. &c. Magaurn. 264. Magawran. 246. Magoveran. Magovern. M'Gauran. 82. 238, 381, &c. M'Gaurn. 264. [M'Givern]. 381. M'Govran.
1310	M'ELWEE. Ilwee. Magillowy. 432. [M'Gilloway]483 M'Gillowy. 161. M'Gilway. 161. M'Ilwee.	1325	M'FATE. M'Feat.	1341	M'GIMPSEY. M'Jimpsey.		
		1326	M'FETRIDGE. M'Fatridge. M'Fattrick. M'Fattridge. M'Fetrick. M'Fetrish. M'Fettridge. M'Phettridge.	1342	M'GING. M'Gin. 119.		
1311	M'ENDOO. M'Indoo.			1343	M'GINITY. Gainer. 167. [Gaynor]. 167. Maginnetty. [M'Entee]. 319. M'Ginety. M'Ginnety. M'Ginnitty. M'Ginnitty. 137.	1358	M'GOWAN. [Gowan]. Mageown. Magowan. 370. Magovern. 35. 505. Magowen. Magurn. 201. M'Ghoon. 49. M'Gowen. M'Gown. Mc owan. Megowan. [Smith]. 165, 222, 515. [Smith]. 165.
1312	M'ENEANY. [Bird]. 319. MacEneany. MacNeney. M'Aneany. M'Aneeny. M'Aneny.	1327	M'GAFFIN. M'Guffin. 416.				
1313	M'ENERY. [Henry]. 429. [M'Eniry]. [M'Henry]. 117.	1328	M'GAHEY. [M'Caughey]. 256. M'Gahy. M'Gaughey. 159. 256. M'Gaughy. 256.	1344	M'GINLEY. Magenley. 259. M'Ginly.		
1314	M'ENIRY. MacEnerney. 235. Mac Eniry. [M'Enery].			1345	M'GINN. Ginn. [Macinn]. [M'Glynn.] 434. Megginn.		
1315	M'ENROE. [Mack]. 416.	1329	M'GANN. [Magan]. Magann. 54. M'Gahan. Magan.	1346	M'GIRR. M'Gerr. [Short]. 163. 117, &c.	1359	M'GRANAHAN. M'Grenahan.
1316	M'ENTEE. M'Atee. 13. M'Enteer. M'Entire. 246. [M'Ginity]. 319. M'Intee. M'Kenty. M'Kinty.	1330	M'GARRAN. M'Gurn. 238.	1347	M'GIVERN. [Beckerstaff]. 129. Magiveran. Magaverin. 358. Maeivern. M'Giveran. M'Giverin. [M'Govern]. 381. [Montgomery]. 175.	1360	M'GRANE. [Magrane].
		1331	M'GARRELL. M'Gerroll. M'Girl. M'Gorl. M'Gurl.			1361	M'GRANN. M'Graun. M'Krann. M'Rann. 443.
1317	M'ENTEGART. MacEntaggert. M'Entagert. M'Entaggart. M'Intagert. M'Intaggart. [M'Intyre]. 42. M'Taggart. M'Tegart. Teg. 413. Teggarty. 42. Tiger. 305.	1332	M'GARRIGLE. M'Argle. M'Frigle. M'Garrical.	1348	M'GIVNEY. M'Avinue. 308. M'Evinie. 92. M'Givena. 332. [Smith]. 212.	1362	M'GRATH. Magra. Magragh. [Magrath]. Magraw. 481. M'Craith. 235. M'Gra. 19. M'Gragh. M'Grau. 210. Megrath. Megraw. 175, 267.
		1333	M'GARRITY. M'Garaty. M'Garity. M'Gerety. M'Gerraghty. M'Gerrity. Me arrity. Me arty.	1349	M'GLADDERY. M'Glade. 469. M'Gladery. M'Glathery.		
				1350	M'GLASHAN. [Green]. 114, 314. M'Glashin.	1363	M'GREEVY. Magreevy. Magreevy. [M'Areavy]. M'Creavy. M'Crevy. M'Grievy. M'Reavy.
1318	M'ERLANE. M'Erlain. M'Erlean. M'Erleen.	1334	M'GERRY. Garry. 323. Magarry. Maharry. M'Carrie. M'Geary. 38. M'Gherry. M'Harry. Me arry. 38. 347.	1351	M'GLEW. M'Cleod. 364. M'Cloud. 364.		
1319	M'EVINNEY. M'Eviniogh. 137.			1352	M'GLOIN. M'Glone. 124. 370.		
1320	M'EVOY. Bwee. 381. Evoy. MacAvoy. MacEvoy. [Mack]. Mackeu. 312. M'Avoy. 195. M'Ilboy. 55. 293. M'Ilbwee. 381.	1335	M'GEE. [Gee]. [Mackey]. [Maceo]. Wynn. 82. [Wynne]. 82.	1353	M'GLINN. Glan. 417. Glynn. 417 [M'Ginn]. 434. M'Glin.	1364	M'GREGOR. M'Gregar. M'Greggor. M'Grigor.

No.	Surnames. with Varieties and Synonymes.	No.	Surnames. with Varieties and Synonymes.	No.	Surnames. with Varieties and Synonymes.	No.	Surnames, with Varieties and Synonymes.
1365	M'GRILLAN. Magrillan. Migrillan.	1376	M'HUGH. Cue. 397. [Hewson]. 238, 506. Hue. Hutson. 506. [Huston]. 259. Machue. MacHugh. M'Coo. [M'Cue]. 259, 341, &c. M'Hue. M'Hugo. 330. M'Kew. 332.	1389	M'INTYRE. Macantyre. M'Antire. 155. [M'Ateer]. 177, 223, 421. M'Enteer. 26. [M'Entegart]. 42. M'Entire. M'Entyre. M'Intee. 246. M'Inteer. 309. M'Intire.	1400	M'KENNA. Gennagh. 352. Ginna. 309. Ginnane. Ginnaw. 51, 114. Gna. 8. Guina. 303. Guinna. 303. [Kenna]. Kennah. 431. M'Hinny. [M'Kenny]. M'Kinney. 113.
1366	M'GRORY. Magrory. M'Rory, 374. Rodgers. 292. [Rogers]. 153. 238. 292.					1401	M'KENNY. [Kenny]. [M'Kenna]. [M'Kinny]. 19.
1367	M'GUCKIAN. M'Gookin. M'Guckin. M'Gughian. M'Guickian. [M'Guigan].	1377	M'ILDOWIE. M'Gill Dowie. 429.	1390	M'IVOR. Maciver. Mackiver. M'Ever. M'Iver. M'Ivers. [M'Keever]. 223. 367. 385, &c. M'Keevor. 410. M'Kevor. 42. M'Kiever.	1402	M'KENZIE. Kinghan. 466. Mackenzie. Makenzy. M'Kensie. M'Kinney. 95. M'Kinnie. 86. M'Kinzie.
1368	M'GUIGAN. Fidgeon, 205. Gavigan. 429. [Geoghegan]. 429. Guigan. Maguigan. M'Googan. M'Gookin. 87. [M'Guckian]. M'Guiggan. M'Quiggan. M'Wiggan. M'Wigrin. Meguiggan. [Pidgeon]. 205. Wigan.	1378	M'ILHARRY. M'Elharry. M'Gilharry. M'Harry.				
		1379	M'ILHATTON. Hatton. 367. Macklehattan. M'Clatton. M'Elhatton. M'Hatton. 367. M'Illhatton.	1391	M'KAY. Mackay. [Mackey]. 19. M'Cay. 19, 358. [M'Coy] 383. 410. [M'Kee]. 410. M'Key. 358. M'Quay. M'Quey.	1403	M'KEOGH. Keghan. 312. Kehoe. [Keogh]. M'Keo. M'Keough. M'Kough.
1369	M'GUINNESS. [Guinness]. Magenis. Magennis. Maginess. [Maginn]. Maginness. Maginnis. (M'Creesh). 248. Magrecce. 276. Maguiness. Maguinis. Maguinness. M'Creech. 248. M'Creesh. 388. 414. M'Gennis. 370. M'Genniss. M'Giniss. M'Ginness. M'Ginnis. 370. Meginniss.	1380	M'ILHERRON. M'Klern.			1404	M'KEOWN. [Caulfield]. 289. Geon. Johnson. 506. [Johnston]. 506. Mackeown. 512. Magone. 524. [M'Cune]. 429. M'Ewen. 210. 429. M'Geown. 524. M'Keoan. M'Keon. M'Keowen. M'Kewen. M'Kewn. M'Koen. 332. M'Kone. 137. [M'Owen].
		1381	M'ILMOYLE. Macklemoyle. M'Elmoyle. M'Ilmoil.	1392	M'KEAG. Keag. Keague. M'Aig. M'Cague. M'Caig. M'Caigue. M'Haig. M'Kage. M'Kague. M'Kaige. M'Kaigue. M'Keague. M'Keigue.		
		1382	M'ILMURRAY. Kilmurry. M'Elmurray. M'Kilmurray.				
		1383	M'ILPATRICK. M'Elfatrick. M'Gilpatrick.				
		1384	M'ILROY. Ilroy. 137. Macelroi. MacElroy. MacIlroy. [M'Elroy]. 59, 87, 410. Roy. 137.	1393	M'KEAN. M'Cain. M'Kain. 358.— Muckian. 127 (a).	1405	M'KERNAN. M'Carnon. M'Harnon. M'Eiernan.
1370	M'GUIRE. . Guare. 318. [Maguire]. 12.	1385	M'ILVEEN. M'Elvaine. M'Elveen. M'Kilveen.	1394	M'KEANY. Keany. 238.	1406	M'KIBBIN. M'Gibben. M'Gibbon. M'Kibben. M'Kibbon.
1371	M'GURK. Maguirke. M'Guirk. M'Gurke. M'Quirk.	1386	M'ILWAINE. Mackelwaine. M'Elwain. M'Elwane. M'Elwean. M'Illwain.	1395	M'KEE. Mackay. 189. [Mackey]. 189. [M'Kay]. 410.	1407	M'KILLEN. M'Callion. M'Kellan. M'Killian.
1372	M'GURRAN. M'Kivirking. 524.	1387	M'ILWRATH. Macklewraith. M'Elreath. M'Elwreath. Rath. 254.	1396	M'KEEVER. Keevers. 214. Keeves. M'Iver. 254. [M'Ivor]. 223, 367, 385. &c. M'Keaver. M'Keiver.	1408	M'KILLOP. [Killops]. M'Kellop. M'Killip. M'Killopps.
1373	M'HARG. M'Carg. M'Karg.						
1374	M'HENRY. [Henry]. 429. MacHenry. M'Endry. [M'Enery]. 117. M'Hendry. M'Henery. [M'Kendry]. 367. 410. &c. M'Kenery. M'Kennery.	1388	M'INERNEY. Connerney. 21. Keverny. 469. Kinerney. 389. Kiniry. 431. Macinerney. [Mack]. M'Anern. M'Anerney. M'Enerny. M'Enery. 445. M'Innerney. M'Keniry.	1397	M'KEITH. Mackheath. M'Heath.	1409	M'KIMMON. Mackimmon. M'Keeman. M'Keemon.
				1398	M'KELVEY. Kilvey. M'Calvey. M'Celvey. M'Elvee. M'Elvie. M'Gilvie. M'Kilvie.	1410	M'KINLEY. M'Gindle. 154. M'Kinlay.
1375	M'HINCH. M'Aninch. M'Inch. M'Kinch.					1411	M'KINNY. [Kenny]. 429. [M'Kenny]. 19.
				1399	M'KENDRY. [M'Henry]. 367, 410, &c.	1412	M'KINSTRY. M'Kinestry. M'Nestry.

No.	Surnames, with Varieties and Synonymes.	No.	Surnames, with Varieties and Synonymes.	No.	Surnames, with Varieties and Synonymes.	No.	Surnames, with Varieties and Synonymes.
1413	M'KISSOCK. M'Kussack.	1426	M'MAHON. Maghan. [Mahon]. [Mahony]. 158, 291. M'Machon. M'Maghen. M'Maghon. M'Maghone. M'Mahan. M'Mann. M'Mechan. 411.	1438	M'MURRAY. M'Elmurray. 238. M'Morray. M'Morrow. 370. M'Morry. M'Murry. [Murray].	1454	M'NEILLY. Maneely. Maneilly. 66. M'Nealey. M'Neally. [M'Neely]. M'Nielly. Meneely. Mineely.
1414	M'KITTRICK. [Hanson].· 97. M'Ketterick. M'Kettrick. M'Kirtrick. M'Kitterick. Munkettrick. Munkittrick.						
				1439	M'MURTRY. M'Murtery. M'Murthry.·	1455	M'NELIS. Manelis. 12, 259.
1415	M'KNIGHT. [Knight]. M'Kneight. M'Naghten. 358. M'Naught. 432. M'Neight. 494. M'Night. 358. M'Nite. M'Ruddery, 483. Menautt. 347. Minett. 310. Minnitt. 429.			1440	M'NABB. M'Anabb. M'Nabo. 275.	1456	M'NERLAND. M'Nerlin. 19.
		1427	M'MANUS. Manus. 457. [Mayne]. 238, 247. M'Manis. M'Mannus.	1441	M'NABOE. M'Nabo. (M'Nabb). 275. M'Nabow. Monaboe. 154. [Victory]. 154, 265, 470, &c.	1457	M'NERNEY. M'Nertney. M'Nirny.
						1458	M'NIECE. Manice. Mannice. [Mannix]. M'Neece. 359. M'Neese. Mencese. 411. Meneiss. Miniece. 429. Minnis. 429.
		1428	M'MATH. M'Ma. 344. M'Magh. 19.				
1416	M'LARNEY. Larney. 282.	1429	M'MEEKIN. M'Machan. M'Meckan. M'Meckin.· M'Meechan. M'Meekan. M'Meeken M'Meichan. M'Michan. Mecmeckin.	1442	M'NABOOLA. Benbo. 464.		
1417	M'LARNON. M'Clarnon. M'Clearnon. M'Clernon. M'Larenon. M'Larinon. M'Learnon. M'Lernon. M'Lorinan. 433.			1443	M'NAIRN. M'Nern.		
				1444	M'NALLY. Canally. 312. Mackinaul. 72. Manally, 17. M'Anally. 17. 87, 367, &c. M'Anaul. 364. M'Anily. M'Annally. M'Anulla. 367. M'Enally. M'Inally. [Nally].	1459	M'NIFF. M'Kniff. M'Kniff.
						1460	M'NISH. Minnish. 429.
		1430	M'MENAMIN. M'Manamon. M'Meenamon. M'Menamen. M'Menamon. M'Menemen. M'Menim. 418. M'Menimin. M'Vanamy. 48(a) Menemin.			1461	M'NUFF. M'Anuff.
						1462	M'NULTY. M'Anulty. 91. McKnulty. [M'Nalty].
1418	M'LAUGHLIN. [Loughlin]. MacLaughlin. 355. Macloghlin. MacLoughlin. M'Clachlin. M'Glaughlin. 358. M'Gloughlin. M'Lachlin. M'Laghlan. M'Lauchlin. M'Lochlin. M'Loghlen. M'Loghlin. M'Loughlan. M'Loughlen. [M'Loughlin]. Meglaughlin,223.			1445	M'NALTY. M'Analty. [M'Nulty]. [Nalty].	1463	M'OWEN. M'Cone. M'Keon. [M'Keown].
		1431	M'MENEMY. M'Menamy. M'Menimey. M'Minamy.	1446	M'NAMA. M'Ma. 106.		
				1447	M'NAMANAMEE. M'Munaway. 105.	1464	M'PADDEN. [M'Fadden]. M'Paddan. M'Paden. M'Padgen. M'Padan.
		1432	M'MICHAEL. M'Michalin. M'Michall. M'Mighael.	1448	M'NAMARA. Kilmary. 344. [Mack]. 345, 430. M'Nama. 128, 380. M'Namarra. M'Namorrow. 267. Morin. 380. [Sheedy]. 509.		
		1433	M'MILLAN. M'Millen. M'Millin. [M'Mullan]. 177, 350, 466.			1465	M'PARLAND. [M'Farland]. M'Partlan. 410.
						1466	M'PEAKE. M'Pake.
1419	M'LEAN. MacLean. [M'Clean]. 420. Muckeen. 38.					1467	M'PHELAN. M'Flinn. 385. [Phelan].
		1434	M'MONAGLE. M'Monegal. M'Monigal. M'Monigle. M'Munigal.	1449	M'NAMEE. [Mack]. 207. Mee. 248.		
1420	M'LEISH. [Maclise]. M'Leesh.			1450	M'NAUGHTEN. MacNaughten. M'Naghten. M'Naughton. M'Night. 433. [Naughton].	1468	M'PHERSON. Macpherson. M'Farson. M'Ferson. M'Pharson. Pherson.
1421	M'LENAGHAN. [M'Clenaghan]. M'Lenahan. M'Leneghan. M'Lenigan. M'Lennon.	1435	M'MORDIE. M'Murdy. 210. Murdy. 210.				
		1436	M'MORRAN. [Moran]. M'Moran. M'Morin. M'Mouran. M'Murran. M'Murren. M'Murrin.			1469	M'QUADE. M'Aragh. 275. M'Quaid. 137. M'Quaide. M'Quoid. 254 M'Wade. 175 (a). Quaide. [Wade]. 215.
1422	M'LEOD. MacLeod. M'Cleod. M'Cloud. 72.			1451	M'NAY. M'Nea. M'Neagh. M'Nee. M'Neigh.		
1423	M'LINNEY. M'Aleney. M'Lehenny. M'Lehinney. M'Lhinney.			1452	M'NEELY. M'Avady. 119. [M'Neilly].	1470	M'QUESTON. M'Question. M'Quiston. M'Whiston.
		1437	M'MULLAN. MacMullen. [M'Millan]. 177. 350, 466. M'Millen. 350. M'Millin. 466. M'Mullen. M'Mullon. [Mullan]. [Mullen].	1453	M'NEILL. M'Nail. M'Nalo. M'Neal. M'Neel. M'Neile.		
1424	M'LOONE. M'Loon. Munday. 259, 260.					1471	M'QUILKIN. M'Quilquane. M'Wilkin.
1425	M'LOUGHLIN. See [M'Laughlin].						

No.	Surnames, with Varieties and Synonymes.	No.	Surnames, with Varieties and Synonymes.	No.	Surnames, with Varieties and Synonymes.	No.	Surnames, with Varieties and Synonymes.
1472	M'QUILLAN. M'Cullen. 495, 515. M'Cullion. 351. M'Quilin. M'Quillen. 351. M'Quillian. M'Quillon. [M'Williams]. 410. [Quillan]. 137.	1491	M'VICKER. M'Vicar. M'Vickar.	1510	MELEADY. Malady. 332. Meledy. Melledy. Mulleady.	1530	MITCHELL. Michael. Michal. Michel. Mitchael. [Mulvihill]. 147, 528.
1473	M'QUINN. Maqueen. M'Queen. M'Quin. M'Whin.	1492	M'VITTY. Mavity. M'Veety. M'Veity. M'Vity.	1511	MELIA. [Malley]. 249, 456. Mealia. Meally. [O'Malley]. 72, 128, 506, &c.	1531	MITTEN. Mythen. 109.
1474	M'QUITTY. M'Whitty. M'Witty.	1493	M'WALTER. MacQualter. MacWalter. M'Qualter. Qualter. 506, 507.	1512	MELLETT. Mellet. 40. Mellitt. Mellot. Mellott. 40. Mylott. 174, 179. Mylotte. 40.	1532	MOCKLER. Muckler. 108.
1475	M'RICHARD. Crickard. 175. Cricket. 175.	1494	M'WATTERS. M'Quatters.			1533	MOFFATT. Moffett. Moffitt.
1476	M'ROBERTS. MacRoberts, M'Croberts.	1495	M'WHA. M'Qua. M'Quagh. M'Waugh. M'Whaugh. Mewha.	1513	MELVILLE. Blehein. 36. [Melvin]. 175. Mulavill. 262. [Mulvihill]. 318.	1534	MOHAN. [Mahon]. 269. Moan. 42, 110. Moen. 42. Moghan. Moughan. Mowen.
1477	M'ROBIN. [Cribbin]. [Gribben].	1496	M'WHINNEY. [Mawhinney]. M'Quiney. M'Quinney. M'Weeny. M'Whinny. M'Winey. M'Winney.	1514	MELVIN. Bleheen. 330. Bleheine. 298. [Melville]. 175.	1535	MOLES. Moulds. Mowlds. Mowles.
1478	M'SHANE. [Johnston]. 18, 153, &c. M'Shan. Shane.			1515	MENARY. Manary. Menairy. Menarry.	1536	MOLLOY. [Logue]. 259, 260. Maloy. Meloy. Moloy. Mullee. 157 (a). Mullock. 249. [Mulloy]. Muloy. [Mulvihill]. 47. Sloey. 167. Slowey. 167.
1479	M'SHARRY. Feley. 371. [Foley]. 105, 153, &c.	1497	M'WHIRTER. Mawhirter. M'Wherter. Mewherter. Mewhirter. 281.	1516	MENTON. Mintin.		
1480	M'SORLEY. M'Soreley. M'Sorely.	1498	M'WILLIAMS. M'Collyums. 503. M'Cullyam. 55. [M'Quillan]. 410. M'Quilliams. 385. M'William.	1517	MERCER. Massa. 17.	1537	MOLONY. Malloney. Mallowney. 231. Mallowny. Malony. Malowny. Mollony. Mollowney. Mologhney. Moloney. 398. Molowny. Molumby. 354. Mulloney. Mullowney. 147, 337. Muloney.
1481	M'SPADDIN. M'Speddin. 358.	1499	M'WILLIE. M'Quilly.	1518	MEREDITH. Merdiff. 401. Merdith. Merdy. 411. Meredyth.		
1482	M'SPARRAN. MacAsparran.	1500	MEADE. Maid. 410.	1519	METCALF. Medcalf. Metkiff.		
1483	M'SWEENY. MacSweeny. M'Sweney. M'Swine. [M'Swiney]. 77, 366. [Sweeny]. 182, 301 (a). 309. [Swiney].	1501	MEAGHER. Magher. 104. [Maher]. 354, 393.	1520	MEYRICK. Mayrick. Merrick.	1538	MOLYNEUX. Moleyneux. Mollyneux Molyneaux. Mullinex. Mullinix.
		1502	MEANY. Many.	1521	MILFORD. Minford. 494.		
1484	M'SWIGGAN. M'Swiggin. M'Swigin.	1503	MEARA. [Mara]. 393. [O'Meara]. 393.	1522	MILLEA. Melay. 316.	1539	MONAGHAN. [Mannix]. 469. Menaght. 267. Minogue. 330, 469. Monachan. Monahan. Monehan. [Monks]. 364. [Moynihan]. 304 (a), 429.
1485	M'SWINEY. [M'Sweeny]. 77, 366. [Sweeny]. 283.	1504	MEARES. Maires. [Mairs]. Mares. Mayers. Mears.	1523	MILLEN. Millan. 429. Milne. 429.		
				1524	MILLER. Millar. 159.		
1486	M'TAGHLIN. [Huston]. 482. M'A'Taghlin.	1505	MEEAN. Maybin. 112.	1525	MILLIGAN. Miligan. Millican. 254. Milligen. Millikan. Milliken. 90. Millikin. [Mulligan]. 18, 381, 410.	1540	MONEYPENNY. Monypenny. Monypeny.
1487	M'TAGUE. M'Teague. M'Tegue. M'Teigue. M'Tigue. [Montague]. 381. [Tighe]. 46, 82.	1506	MEDLICOTT. Medlycott.			1541	MONKS. [Monaghan]. 364. Monck. Monk.
		1507	MEEHAN. Mee. 409. Meeghan. Meegan. 137. Meehen. Meekin. 87. Meghan. Mehan. Meighan. 117, 316, 410. Myhan. 117. O'Meehon. 237.	1526	MILLING. Millin. 267.		
1488	M'TERNAN. M'Tiernan. 217.			1527	MISKELL. Mescel. Miskella.	1542	MONNELLY. Monley. 301.
1489	M'VEIGH. M'Avey. 477. M'Bay. M'Vay. M'Vea. M'Veagh. [M'Vey]. Vahy. 28. Veigh.	1508	MEGAW. Magaw. McGaw.	1528	MISKELLY. Miscella.	1543	MONTAGUE. [M'Tague]. 381. Tague. 97, 423. Teague. 163, 216. Teigue. 165.
1490	M'VEY. See [M'Veigh].	1509	MELDON. [Muldoon]. 19, 249.	1529	MISSKIMMINS. [Cummins]. 19. M'Commings. 358. Maskimon. Meskimmon. Miskimmin. Miskimmon. Moskimmon.		

No.	Surnames, with Varieties and Synonymes.	No.	Surnames, with Varieties and Synonymes.	No.	Surnames, with Varieties and Synonymes.	No.	Surnames, with Varieties and Synonymes.
1544	MONTEITH. Menteith. Minteith. Monteeth.	1558	MORRISSEY. Moresay. Morisey. Morissy. Morressy. Morresy. [Morris]. 142, 303 (b). Morrisey. [Morrison]. 488. Morrissee. Morrossey. 91.	1576	MULLAN. [M'Mullan]. Mollan. 410. [Mullen]. [Mulligan.] 409. Mullin. 48 (b).	1594	MUNNS. Monds. Munce. Munds. Muntz. Munze.
1545	MONTFORD. Minford. 112. Montfort. Mountiford. Mountifort. Munford.			1577	MULLARKEY. Malarky. Melarkey.	1595	MUNROE. Monroe. Munrow.
				1578	MULLAVIN. Mallavin. 152. M'Lavin. 152.	1596	MURCHISON. Murchan. Murchisson. Murkin.
1546	MONTGOMERY. Gomory. Goonery. 274. Goonry. 505. Maglamery. 18. Maglammery. 429. [M'Givern]. 175. Meglamry. 429. Mongney. 467.	1559	MORROW. Morrogh. 72. Morrough. 72. Morrowson. Murrough. Murrow.	1579	MULLBRIDE. Millbride.	1597	MURDOCK. Murdoch. 91,494. Murdough. 91. Murdow. [Murtagh]. 210, 429.
		1560	MORTIMER. Mortagh. 40. Mortimor. Mortimore. Mortymer.	1580	MULLEN. [Mallon]. 180. [M'Mullen]. Mellon. 180. Millane. 253. Mulhane. [Mullan]. Mullane. Mullin. 159. [Mullins]. Mullon. 159.	1598	MURLAND. [Moreland]. 175, 267. Muirland. 267.
1547	MOONEY. Moany. 410. Money. 76. Moyney. 249.					1599	MURNANE. [Marnane]. Marrinane. 80. Murnain. Murnan. Murney. [Warren]. 288.
		1561	MOSS. Malmona. 276. Mulmona. 421.				
1548	MOORE. Moir. 91. More. Moreen. 304 (b). Morey. 134. Muir. 91.	1562	MOUNTAIN. Montane. 488. Montang. 488. Montangue. 488.	1581	MULLIGAN. [Milligan]. 18,381, 410. Milligen. 18. Milliken. 433. Mulgan. Mullagan. [Mullan]. 409. Mullogan. [Mulqueen]. 131.		
		1563	MOWBRAY. Moabray. Moobray.			1600	MURPHY. Molphy. 484. Murricohu. 65. O'Muracha. 40.
1549	MOORHEAD. Moorehead. Mooreheed. Morehead. Muirhead.	1564	MOYERS. [Myers].			1601	MURRANE. Merna. 440.
		1565	MOYNIHAN. [Monaghan]. 304 (a),429. Monahan. 186. Monehan. 186. Monohan. 304 (a). Moynahan. Moynan. 249.			1602	MURRAY. Kilmurray. 238. M'Elmurray. 238, 418. [M'Murray]. Murrihy. 291. Murry.
1550	MORAN. [M'Morran]. Moarn. Moeran. Moren. Morin. Morrin. 73, 209. Mourn. Muran. 400.			1582	MULLINS. De'Moleyns. 318. Mullane. 365. [Mullen]. O'Mullane. 189.		
		1566	MUCKADY. Moughty. 63.	1583	MULLOY. See [Molloy].	1603	MURRIN. Murn. Murren.
		1567	MUCKARAN. Magabaran. 308.	1584	MULLREAVY. Milreavy.	1604	MURTAGH. [Moriarty]. 125. Murdoch. 210,429. [Murdock]. 210, 429. Murt. 429. Murta. Murtaugh. Murtha.
1551	MORELAND. M'Murlan. 71. Morland. Mortland. [Murland]. 175, 267. Murtland.	1568	MULCAHY. Cahy. 429. Caughy. 429. M'Cahy. 429. Vulcougha. 488.	1585	MULQUEEN. [Mulligan]. 131.		
				1586	MULRENAN. Mulreany. 154. Mulrenin. Mulrennan. Mulrennin. Renan. 429.		
		1569	MULCREEVY. Creevey. Mulgrievey. 267.				
1552	MORETON. [Letsome]. 104. Morton.	1570	MULDOON. [M'Dowell]. 92. [Meldon]. 19, 249. Muldon. 72.	1587	MULROE. Melroy. 119. Monroe. 269. Mulrow. 174. [Mulroy]. 119.	1605	MUSE. Muise. 91.
1553	MORIARTY. Morey. 19.. [Murtagh]. 125.					1606	MUSGRAVE. Mosgrove. Musgrove.
1554	MORLEY. Marley. 109. Morrolly. 50.	1571	MULDOWNEY. Dawney. 429.	1588	MULROONEY. [McDermott]. 29, 125. Mulrony. [Rooney].	1607	MYALL. Miall. Myhill.
		1572	MULGRAVE. Mulgroo. 279.			1608	MYERS. Meere. 509. Miers. [Moyers]. Myres.
1555	MORONEY. Moroony. Morroney.	1573	MULHALL. Halley. 519.	1589	MULROY. Milroy. [Mulroe]. 119.		
1556	MORRIS. [Fitzmaurice]. 456. Maurice. 515. Morice. Moris. Moriss. 91. Morris-Roe. [Morrissey.] 142, 303 (b).	1574	MULHERN. Mulhearn. Mulheeran. Mulheran. Mulheren. Mulherrin. Mulherron. Mulkhearn.	1590	MULVANY. Mulvanny. [Mulvey]. 221.	1609	MYLES. Miles. Moyles. 31.
				1591	MULVEY. [Mulvany]. 221.		
				1592	MULVIHILL. [Melville]. 318. [Mitchell]. 147, 528. [Molloy]. 47. Mullvihill. Mulvehill. Mulvihil.	1610	NAGLE. Neagle.
						1611	NALLY. M'Inally. [M'Nally].
1557	MORRISON. [Begley]. 238, 247. [Bryson]. 271. Morison. Morisson. [Morrissey]. 488. Morrisson.	1575	MULHOLLAND. [Holland]. 19. Mahollum. 381. Maholm, 18, 429, 461. Mulhollum. 429. Mulholm. 83. Mulholn.	1593	MUMFORD. Mimnagh. 215.	1612	NALTY. [M'Nalty]. Naulty. Nolty. Nulty.

No.	Surnames, with Varieties and Synonymes.	No.	Surnames, with Varieties and Synonymes.	No.	Surnames, with Varieties and Synonymes.	No.	Surnames, with Varieties and Synonymes.
1613	NAPIER. Naper. 429. Neeper. 175,381, 429. Neiper. 76. Neper. 429,489.	1631	NICHOLL. Nichol. 91. Nicholds. Nicholls. Nichols. [Nicholson]. 489. Nickelson. Nickle. 421. Nickles. Nicol. 91. Nicoll. Nicolls. Nicols.	1645	O'CLOHESSY. O'Cloghessy. O'Clussey.	1668	O'HARE. Hair. 348. [Hare]. *O'Garriga.* 450. O'Haire. O'Hear. 76.
1614	NASH. Naish. 390.			1646	O'CONNELL. [Connell]. Connelly. 478.	1669	O'HEA. [Hayes]. 500.
1615	NAUGHTER: Naugher. Nocher. Nocter. 261. Nogher.			1647	O'CONNOR. [Connor]. 100. [Connors]. 2, 189, &c.	1670	O'KANE. [Gahan]. 206. [Kane]. 216, 240, 367. O'Cahan. 206, 254. O'Caughan. 19. O'Keane.
1616	NAUGHTON. Behane. 352. Connaughton. Knockton. McNaghten. 23. [M'Naughten]. Naghten. 23. Naghton. Naughtan. Naughten. 23. Nochtin. Nockton. Nocton. 307,419. Norton. 63, 307, 351, &c. Noughton. 23.	1632	NICHOLSON. [Nicholl]. 489. Nichols. 409.	1648	O'DEA. Day. [*Godwin*]. 40, 179, 506, &c.		
		1633	NIXON. Nickson.	1649	ODLUM. Adlum. 74.	1671	O'KEEFFE. [Keeffe]. O'Keefe.
		1634	NOLAN. *Hoolihan.* 54. *Houlahan.* 485. *Hulahun.* 82. *Hultaghan.* 238, 247, 350. *Hultahan.* 154. Noland. Nolans. Nowlan. 437,448.	1650	O'DEVINE. [Devine].	1672	O'KELLY. [Kelly]. 390.
				1651	O'DOHERTY. [Doherty]. 355. O'Dougherty.	1673	O'LEARY. [Leary].
1617	NAVIN. Neaphsey. 501. [Nevin].			1652	O'DONNELL. [Daniel]. 171,328. [Donnell]. 112. MacDonnell. [M'Donnell]. 352.	1674	O'LOUGHLIN. Loughlan. 116. [Loughlin]. O'Loughlan.
1618	NAYLOR. Nailer. Nailor. Nealer.	1635	NOONAN. Neenan. 283. Newnan. Noonane. Nunan. 303. Nunun. 469.	1653	O'DONOVAN. [Donovan].	1675	O'LYONS. Holian. 40. [Lyons].
1619	NEALON. [Neilan]. 301.			1654	O'DOWD. Doud. 307. [Dowd]. 307,361. O'Doud.	1676	O'MALLEY. [Malia]. 179. Malie. 40. Mallia. Mallew. 137. [Malley]. 361,370. Mealia. 72,128. Mealy. 128. [Melia]. 72, 128, 506, &c. Millea. 120. O'Mealue. 128. O'Mealy. 398.
1620	NEARY. Nary. 485.	1636	NORRIS. Northridge. 164. Noury. 19. Nowry. 19. Nurse. 142.	1655	O DRISCOLL. [Driscoll]. [Hyde]. 509.		
1621	NEENAN. Neehan. 134.			1656	O'DUFFY. [Duffy].		
1622	NEILAN. [Nealon]. Nelan. Neylon. 455. Nilan. Nilon.	1637	NORTH. *Ultagh.* 312.	1657	O'DWYER. [Dwyer]. O'Dheer. 378.		
		1638	NORWOOD. Norrit. 55,411.			1677	O'MEARA. [Mara]. [Meara]. 393. O'Mara.
		1639	NUGENT. *Gilsenan.* 214. [*Gilshenan*]. 214.	1658	O'FARRELL. [Farrell]. 390.		
1623	NEILANDS. Kneeland. Knilans. Neiland. Neyland.			1659	O'FLAHERTY. [Flaherty]. [Lafferty]. 480.	1678	O'NEILL. Neal. [Neill]. 16. O'Neal.
				1660	O'FLANAGAN. [Flanagan]. 390.	1679	ORCHARD. Auher. 135.
1624	NEILL. Nail. 381. Neal. 457. Neale. Niell. [O'Neill]. 16.	1640	OAKS. [*Darragh*]. *McAdarra.* 220. *McAdarrah.* 450. *M'Dara.* 450. Oak. Oakes.	1661	O'GILVIE. Gillbee. O'Gilbie. Ogilby.	1680	O'REILLY. O'Reiley. O'Rielly. [Reilly]. 17,413.
		1641	OATES. Oats. [*Quirk*]. 36, 386.	1662	O'GORMAN. [Gorman].	1681	O'RIORDAN. Reardon. [Riordan].
1625	NEILSON. Nealson. Nelson. 197,204. Nielson.			1663	O'GRADY. [Grady]. 390. Gready. O'Gready.	1682	O'RORKE. O'Roarke. O'Rourke. Roragh. 383. Rorke. [Rourke]. 61. Rurk. 189
		1642	O'BRIEN. Brian. 468. Brien. 393,468. Briens. Brine. Brines. [Bryan]. 393. [Crossan]. 332. [M'Brien]. 82, 308, &c. M'Brine. 270,276. O'Brian. O'Bryan. O'Bryen.	1664	O'HAGAN. [Hagan]. 17.348. Haghen. 185. Hegan. 185. [Higgins]. 178 (*b*). O'Hegan.		
1626	NELIS. M'Grillish. 166.			1665	O'HALLORAN. [Halloran]. O'Hallaran. O'Halleran. O'Halleron.	1683	OSBORNE. Osbourne. Osburne.
1627	NESBITT. Nesbett. Nisbett. Nisbit.			1666	O'HANLON. [Hanlon].	1684	O'SHAUGHNESSY. O'Shanesy. O'Shoughnessy. Shanessy. [Shaughnessy].
1628	NEVIN. [Navin]. Neavin. Neven. Nevins. Nivin.			1667	O'HARA. Haran. Haren. 238. [Harren]. 201, 238, 270. O'Harra. O'Hora.	1685	O'SHEA. Shay. [Shea]. 244, 393. Shee. 393.
1629	NEWCOMEN. Newcomb. 72. Newcome. 72.	1643	O'CALLAGHAN. [Callaghan]. 390. O'Callahan.			1686	O'SULLIVAN. [Sullivan].
1630	NEWELL. Newells. Newill.	1644	O'CARTHY. [Carty]. 525. Charthy. 525.				

No.	Surnames, with Varieties and Synonymes.	No.	Surnames, with Varieties and Synonymes.	No.	Surnames, with Varieties and Synonymes.	No.	Surnames, with Varieties and Synonymes.
1687	O TOOLE. Toal. 222. [Toole]. 223. Tooley. 175.	1707	PENDER. Pendy. 203. [Prendergast]. 32, 207, 229, &c.	1725	PIDGEON. Fidgeon. 205. [M'Guigan]. 205. Pigeon.	1744	PURCELL. Pureill. Pursell. Purtill. 318.
1688	OTTLEY. Arkley. 435.	1708	PENDLETON. Pendelton. Penleton.	1726	PIGOTT. Pickett. Piggott.	1745	PURDON. Perdou. Purdy. 83.
1689	OVENDEN. Hovenden. Ovington.	1709	PENNYCOOK. Pennycuik. Penycook.	1727	PINDAR. Findars. 249.	1746	PURFIELD. Purtle. 72.
1690	OWENS. [Hinds]. 175. Hoins. 71, 216. Hoynes. 238. [Hynes]. 82, 238. Oins. 429. Owen.	1710	PEPPER. Peppard. 72. [Piper]. 243.	1728	PINKERTON. Pinkey. 524. Pinky. 55.		
		1711	PERRIMAN. [Firman]. 249. Pherman. 249.	1729	PIPER. [Pepper]. 243. Pyper.	1747	QUAID. Coid. 91. Coyd. 91. Quade. 91. Quoid. 91.
		1712	PERROTT. Parrette. Parrott.	1730	POGUE. Poag. [Pollock]. 10, 175, 383, &c.	1748	QUAN. Quann. Whan.
1691	PAGE. Peg. 523.	1713	PERRY. Penny. 86. Pirie. 91. Pirrie. 91. 356.	1731	POLAND. M'Polin. 410. Polin. 410.	1749	QUEALE. Quaile. Qwail.
1692	PAGET. Pagett. Patchet. 155.			1732	POLLOCK. Poag. 9, 411. [Pogue]. 10, 175, 383, &c. Poke. 234, 482. Polk. 254. Pollick.	1750	QUEENAN. Cuinane. 138. [Cunnane]. 147. Cunnaim. 105.
1693	PAISLEY. Pasley. Pazley. Peasley.	1714	PETERS. Peter. Petre. Petres.			1751	QUIGLEY. Cogley. 243, 245. Kegley. 383. Twigley. 87, 433.
1694	PAKENHAM. Packenham. Pagnam. 217. Pegnam. 238. Pegnim. 247.	1715	PETIT. [Little]. 109. Petite. Pettitt. Petty.	1733	POMFRET. Pumfrey.	1752	QUILLAN. [Cullen]. 154, 194, 246. [Holln]. [M'Quillan]. 137.
1695	PARK. Parkes.	1716	PETTIGREW. Peticrew. Petticrew. Pettycrew.	1734	PONSONBY. Punch. 483.		
1696	PARKINSON. Parkenson. Parkison. Perkinson.	1717	PEYTON. Paten. Paton. [Patton]. 429. Payton. Peton.	1735	POWELL. [Guilfoyle]. 509. Pole. 253. Poole. 429.	1753	QUINLAN. Quinlivan. 131, 193.
1697	PARLE. Parill. 245.			1736	POWER. Poer. 109, 473. Poor. 316.	1754	QUINLISK. Cunlick. Quinlish.
1698	PARNELL. Parlon. 458.	1718	PHAIR. Fair. 350. Fare. Fayre. Phayer. Phayre.	1737	PRENDERGAST. [Pender]. 32, 207, 229, &c. Pendergast. Pendergrass. 273. Penders. 373. Pendy. 65, 511. Pinder. 120, 274. Pinders. 249. Pindy. 142. Prender. 67, 229, 242, &c. Prindergast. Shearhoon. 144.	1755	QUINN. Cunnea. 126, 259. Cunny. 5. [M'Conaghy]. 319. Queen. 383. Quenn. 17. Whin. 292. Whinn. 461.
1699	PATTERSON. Cussane. 157(b), 229, 528. Paterson. 90. Patison. 429. Pattersen. Patteson. Pattison.	1719	PHELAN. Fealan. 443. Felan. Fylan. [Fyland]. 511. [M'Phelan]. Phelon. Philan. 511. Phylan. [Whelan]. 40, 101, 117, &c.			1756	QUINTON. Quintin. Winton.
1700	PATTON. Paten. Paton. Patten. Pattin. Patty. 381. [Peyton]. 429.					1757	QUIRK. Kirk. 431, 488. [M'Carthy]. 500. [Oats]. 36, 386. Querk. Quick, 325.
1701	PAULETT. Pollett. Powlett.	1720	PHIBBS. Hipps. 436.	1738	PRENDEVILLE. Pendy. 151, 352. Pindy. 304(a). Prenderville. Prendible. 443. Prendivill. Prendiville. Prendy. 249, 352. Prindeville. Prindiville.		
1702	PEARSE. Pearce. Peirce. Percy. 249. Pierce. 47. Pierse. 47. Piersse.	1721	PHILBIN. Filbin. 40. MacPhilbin. O'Filbin. 40. Philban. [Phillips]. 507. [Whelan]. 252.				
				1739	PRICE. Pryce. Pryse.	1758	RABBIT. Conheeny. 386. Cuneen. 136, 189, 307. Cunnane. 38. [Cunneen]. 237, 297, &c. Cunneeny. 386. Cunnion. 132. Kinneen. 360. Rabbett.
1703	PEARSON. Person. Pierson. 333.	1722	PHILEMON. Philomy. 55.				
1704	PEAVEY. Pavy.	1723	PHILIPSON. Filson. Phillippson. Phillipson. Philson.	1740	PRIESTLEY. Pressly. 175.		
1705	PEDEN. Paden. Padon. Paiden. Pedian.	1724	PHILLIPS. [Philbin]. 507. Philipin. 276. Philips. Phillipin. 233.	1741	PRIOR. Friary. 470.	1759	RADCLIFFE. Ratcliffe. Ratliff. Ratty. 368.
				1742	PRUNTY. Brunty. 359.		
1706	PEEL. Peile.			1743	PRYALL. Priall. 301.		

No.	Surnames, with Varieties and Synonymes.	No.	Surnames, with Varieties and Synonymes.	No.	Surnames, with Varieties and Synonymes.	No.	Surnames, with Varieties and Synonymes.
1760	RAFFERTY. [Lavery]. 410. O'Rafferty. Raferty. Raltery. 63. Raverty. 348.	1781	REDMOND. Redmon. Redmont. Redmun. Rodman. 177, 433. Rodmont. 177.	1795	RIORDAN. [O'Riordan]. Reardan. Rearden. [Reardon]. 303. Reirdon. Reordan. Reordon. Rierdan. Rierdon. Riorden.	1809	RONAYNE. Ronane. Roughneen. Roynane.
1761	RAFTER. Raftiss. 117. Wrafter.	1782	REDPATH. Reppet. 429. Rippet. 76, 429, 489. Rippit. 75.			1810	ROONEY. [Mulrooney]. Rhoney. Roney. 71. Roohan. 334. Rooneen. 371. Roonoo. 189. Rowney. 410. Ruineen. 370. Runey. Runian. 41.
1762	RAHILL. Rall. 154	1783	REID. Maddery. 259, 260. Read. Reede.	1796	RITCHIE. Richey. 348.		
1763	RAINEY. Raney. Reany. Reiny. Rennie. 410. Reyney.	1784	REIGHILL. Rekle. 351.	1797	ROBERTS. [Robertson].		
1764	RAINSFORD. Ransford.	1785	REILLY. [O'Reilly]. 17,413. Reily. Rieley. Rielly. Riley. 435. Rilly. Ryely. 1. Ryley.	1798	ROBERTSON. [Roberts]. [Robinson]. 136, 276, 338.	1811	ROSEINGRAVE. Rosey. 262.
1765	RALEIGH. Rahlly. Rally. 391. Rawleigh.			1799	ROBINSON. MacRoberts. 338. MacRubs. 338. M'Crub. 60. Robbinson. [Robertson]. 136, 276, 338. Robins. 409. Robison. Robisson. Robson. 87, 267, 385.	1812	ROSSBOROUGH. Rosborough. Rosbrow. Rosebery. 254. Rosebrough. 240 Rosmond. 128. Rossboro. 91. Rossburrow. Roxberry. 254. Roxborough (Rosebrough). 254. Russboro.
1766	RALPH. Rafe. Rolfe. Rolph.	1786	REINHARDT. Raynard. Renard. Reynard Rheynard. Rhynhart. Rynard.				
1767	RANKIN. Renken. Renkin.	1787	RENAHAN. Ranaghan. 196. Renaghan. Renehan (Ferns). 96. Renihan. Rhuneon. Rinaghan. Rinahan. Ronaghan. 196.	1800	ROCHE. Roache. Rostig.	1813	ROSSBOTHAM. Robotham. Rosbottom. Rossbottam.
1768	RATHBORNE. Rathbone. Rathburne.			1801	ROCHFORD. Rashford. 133, 526. Rochefort. Rochfort. Rochneen. 327. Rouchneen. 486. Rushford. 173.	1814	ROSSITER. Rositer. Rosseter. Rossitor. Rosster.
1769	RATIGAN. Ratean. Ratican. Rattigan. Rhategan. Rhatigan.	1788	RENNICKS. Rennick. Rennix. Rennox. Renwicks. Reynick. Reynicks.	1802	ROCK. [Carrick]. Cregg.	1815	ROTHERAM. Rotherham. Rotherum.
1770	RAWLINSON. Rallinson. Rowlendson.	1789	REYNOLDS. Gronel. 40. M'Gronan. 18, 97. M'Ranald. 254. M'Rannal. 429. M'Reynold. 429. Randalson. 185. Rannals. Ranolds. Renolds. 91. Reynalds. Reynoldson. 185. Ronaldson. 185.	1803	RODDY. [Reddy]. Reidy. Rhoddy. Roddie. Rody. Ruddy.	1816	ROTHWELL. Radwill 468. Rathwell. 468.
1771	REA. Craigh. 97. Rae. Ray. 417 Reigh. 109. [Wray]. 417.			1804	RODEN. M'Crudden. 429. Rodan. Rodin. [Rudden]. 46. Ruddon. 429.	1817	ROULSTON. Rolestone. Rollestone. Rollstone. Rolston. Rowlston.
1772	REAMSBOTHAM. Ramsbottom. 249. Reams. 249. Reamsbottom.	1790	RIALL. Rile. Ryall. Ryle.	1805	ROE. M'Enroe. Rowe.	1818	ROUGHAN. Rohan. 469.
1773	REARDON. See [Riordan].	1791	RICE. Roice. 109.	1806	ROGERS. Macrory. 153. Magrory. 153. [M'Crory]. 97, 222, 423, &c., [M'Grory]. 153, 238, 292. M'Rory. 165, 209. Rodger. Rodgers. 509. Roger.	1819	ROUNTREE. Roantree. Roundtree. 332. Rowantree.
1774	REAVENY. Ravy. 485.	1792	RICHARDS. Richard. [Rickards].			1820	ROURKE. [O'Rorke]. 61. O'Rourke. 61. Roark. Roarke, 61. Roorke. Rorke. 61, 370 Ruirk. Ruarke. 61. Ruorke.
1775	REBURN. Rayburn. Reyburn. Wrayburn.	1793	RICKARDS. Racards. 526. Ricards. [Richards]. Rickard.	1807	ROGERSON. Rorison. 59.		
1776	REDDING. Riding. Ryding.	1794	RING. Reen. 100, 199. Wren. 186. [Wrenn]. 186.	1808	ROLANDS. Rawlings. Rawlins. Rollins. Rowlandson. Rowlins.	1821	ROWAN. Rewan. Roan. Roane. 30. Roon. Rowen. Ruan.
1777	REDDINGTON. Mulderrig. 300.					1822	ROYCROFT. Raycraft. Raycroft. Reycroft. Roycraft. Rycroft.
1778	REDDY. Readdy. Ready. 518. Redy. Rheady. [Roddy].					1823	ROYSE. Roice. Royce.
1779	REDEHAN. Redahan. Rodaughan. 484. Rudican. 484.						
1780	REDERY. Edery. 431. Hedery. 431.						

60

No.	Surnames, with Varieties and Synonymes.	No.	Surnames, with Varieties and Synonymes.	No.	Surnames, with Varieties and Synonymes.	No.	Surnames, with Varieties and Synonymes.
1824	ROYSTON. Roy. 409.	1846	SCANLON. Scandlon. [Scanlan]. Scanlen. Scanlin.	1863	SHAUGHNESSY. [O'Shaughnessy] Shanessy. Shaughness. 232, 435. Shaughnesy. Shaunessy. Shocknesy. Shoughnesey. Shoughnessy.	1879	SHOEMAKER. Schumacker. 287.
1825	RUANE. [Ryan]. 38, 337.					1880	SHORT. M'Gerr. 18. 97. [M'Girr]. 163,417, &c.
1826	RUDDEN. Roddon. [Roden]. 46. Ruddan. Ruddin.	1847	SCHOALES. Scholes. Schoules. Scoales. Scoles.			1881	SHORTALL. Shortell. Shorthall. Shortle. 526. Surtill.
1827	RUSSELL. Russle.	1848	SCHOFIELD. Scholefield. Scofield. Scolefield.	1864	SHEA. See [O'Shea].		
1828	RUTH. Roth. Rothe. Routh.			1865	SHEEDY. [M'Namara]. 509. Silk. 262.	1882	SHOLDICE. Sholdies. Sholdise. Shouldice.
1829	RUTHVEN. Reven. 498.	1849	SCULLION. Skoolin. 58.	1866	SHEEHAN. Shane. Sheahan. Shean. Sheean. Sheen. Shehan. Shine. 329.	1883	SIMCOX. Simcocks. Symcox.
1830	RUTLEDGE. Routledge. Rutlege. Ruttledge. Ruttlege.	1850	SEARIGHT. Seawright.			1884	SIMMONS. [Fitzsimons].436. Simmonds. Simonds. Simons. Symonds.
1831	RYAN. Mulryan. 380. O'Ryan. Rouane. 502. Royan. 147. Ruan. 3. [Ruane]. 38, 337.	1851	SEGRAVE. Seagrave. Seagrove. Segre. 332. [Sugrue].	1867	SHELLY. Shelloe. 438.		
		1852	SEMPLE. Sample. Simple.	1868	SHEPPARD. Shephard. 333. Shepherd. 333. Shepperd.	1885	SIMMS. [Simpson]. 409. Sims. Symes. Symms. Syms.
1832	RYDER. [Markey]. 495. Rhyder.	1853	SERGISON. Sarges-on. Sargisson. Sergerson. Sergeson. Sergesson. Sergisson. Surgesson.	1869	SHERA. Sheera. Shirra.	1886	SIMPSON. [Simms]. 409. Simson. Sympson.
				1870	SHERIDAN. Sheirdan. Sherden. Sherdian. 35. Sherdon. Sheredan. Shereden. Sheriden. Sherodan. Sherridan. [Shilliday]. 175. Shirdan. Shurden. 319.	1887	SINCLAIR. Cairaie. 191. Sinclare. Sincler. St. Clair.
1833	SALISBURY. Salisberry. Salisbry. Sa-:lisbury. Solesbury. Solisberry. Sollsbury.	1854	SERRAGE. Serridge.			1888	SINNOTT. Sinott. Synnott.
		1855	SEWELL. Shuell. Suel.			1889	SKIFFINGTON. Skeffington. Skifenton. Skifington. Skivington.
1834	SALMON. Sammon.	1856	SEXTON. Tackney. 515.	1871	SHERLOCK. Scurlock. 474. Shearlock. Shirlock.	1890	SKILLET. Skellet.
1835	SANDS. Sandes. Sandys.	1857	SEYMOUR. Emo. 94. 153. Seaver. 184. Semore. Semour. Seymore.	1872	SHERRARD. Shearer. 204,240. Sherard. Sherra. 343. Sherrar. 343. Sherrerd.		
1836	SARGENT. Sargeant. Sargint. Sergeant. Sergent.	1858	SHACKLETON. Shakleton. Sheckleton. Shekelton. Shekleton.	1873	SHERWIN. Sharvin. 72.	1891	SLATOR. Slater. Sleater. Sleator.
1837	SARSFIELD. Archfield. 224. Sarseil. 40. Sausheil. 40.	1859	SHANAHAN. [Fox]. 152, 153, 506. Shanaghan. Shanahen. Shanan. 408. Shanihan. Shannahan. Shannihan. [Shannon]. 408.	1874	SHIELDS. Shails. 59. Shales. Sheales. Sheals. 358. Sheil. Sheils. Sheles. Shiel. 420. Shiells. Shiels. Shiles.	1892	SLEVIN. Slamon. 249. Slavin. 249, 319. Sleavin. Sleevin. Slevan.
1838	SAULTERS. Salters. 91.					1893	SLOAN. Slane. 483. Sloane. Slone. Slown.
1839	SAUNDERSON. Sanderson. Saunders.						
1840	SAURIN. [Soden]. 281. Sodin. 281.	1860	SHANNON. Giltenane. 318, 323. [Giltinane]. 299, 318, 323. [Shanahan]. 408. Shannagh. Shanny. Shanon. Sheenan. 168.	1875	SHILLIDAY. Shelliday. [Sheridan]. 175. Shillady. 71. Shilliady. 279. Shillidy.	1894	SLOWEY. Sloy. 211.
1841	SAVAGE. Sage. 94, 219, 474.					1895	SLY. Sleigh. Sligh.
1842	SAWAY. Sawey. Sie, 71. Soy. 71.			1876	SHILLITOE. Sillitoe.	1896	SMALL. Gilkie. 53. Keeltagh. 175. Keiltogh. 175. Kielt. 254. Kielty. 180, 181, 289. Kilkey. 234. O'Kielt. 254. Smalls.
1843	SAWYER. Sawer. Sawier. Sawyers.	1861	SHARKEY. Sharket.	1877	SHIRE. Sheir. Shier.		
1844	SCALLY. Skally. Skelly. 57, 394.	1862	SHARPE. Gearn, 260 Gearns. 259. Shairp.	1878	SHOEBOTTOM. Shubottom.		
1845	SCANLAN. See [Scanlon].						

No.	Surnames, with Varieties and Synonymes.	No.	Surnames, with Varieties and Synonymes.	No.	Surnames. with Varieties and Synonymes.	No.	Surnames, with Varieties and Synonymes.
1897	SMITH. Goan. 97, 238, &c. Going. Gow. 416, 515. [Gowan]. 319. Magough. 40. M'Cona. 271. [M'Givney]. 212. [M'Gowan]. 165, 222, 515. O'Gowan. 221. Smeeth. [Smyth]. 494. Smythe. 494.	1914	SPROULE. Sprool. 91. Sprowle.	1930	STRAHAN. Strachan. Straghan. Strain. 429.	1947	SWORDS. Claveen. 179.
		1915	STACKPOOLE. Stacpole.	1931	STRAYHORN. Streahorn.		
		1916	STAFFORD. M'Astocker. 433.	1932	STRETTON. Stratten. Stratton. Streaton. Streatton. 429. Streeten. 429.	1948	TAAFFE. Taff.
		1917	STAPLETON. Stapelton. Stapylton.			1949	TAGGART. M'Ateggart. 478. M'Integgart. M'Taggart. 201. M'Teggart. Tagart. Tagert. Taggert. Tegart. Teggart. 201.
		1918	STARRET. Staratt. Starrat. Starrett. 91. Starritt. Steritt. Sterritt. Stirratt. 91. Stirrett. 91. Stirrit.	1933	STUART. See [Stewart].		
1898	SMOLLEN. Smallen. Smollan. Smullen.			1934	STUDDERT. [Stoddart]. 410. Studdart.		
1899	SMYLIE. Smiley. Smillie. Smily.			1935	SUGRUE. [Segrave]. Sughrue. Sugrew.	1950	TARPEY. Torpy.
						1951	TATE. Tait. Taite.
1900	SMYRL. Smerle. Smirell. Smurell. Smyrrell.	1919	STAUNTON. M'Evely. 501. Stanton. Stenton. Stinton.	1936	SULLIVAN. Guilavan. 397. [O'Sullivan]. Shorelahan. 480. Soolivan. 109. [Soraghan]. 92, 383. Sulavan. Sulevan. Sulivan. Sullahan. Sullevan.	1952	TAYLOR. Tayler. Taylour. Tyler. 29.
		1920	STAVELY. Steavely. Stevely. Stively.			1953	TEAGUE. Tague. 350.
1901	SMYTH. See [Smith].					1954	TEASE. Taise. Teaze.
1902	SNODDEN. Snoddon. Snoden. Snodon. Snowden (Snedden). 9.	1921	STEAD. Steads. Steed. Steid.				
		1922	STEPHENS. [Stephenson].185. Stevens. 333.	1937	SUMMERLY. O'Summachan. 40.	1955	TEMPLETON. Templetown.
1903	SODEN. [Saurin]. 281. Sodan. Sodin.	1923	STEPHENSON. Steamson. Steen. 489, 515. Steenson. 185,489, &c. Steinson. 58. Stenson. 63, 515. Stepenson. [Stephens]. 185. Steven. Stevenson. Stevinson. Stinson. 97, 494, &c.	1938	SUMMERS. Hourican. 470. [Somers]. 72.	1956	THOMPSON. McAvish. 191. M'Cavish. 60. M'Tavish. 60. Thomson. 494. Tompson. Tomson. Tonson. 65.
1904	SOMERS. Hourican. 264. Sommers. Sonahaun. 329. Sumahean. 329. [Summers]. 72.			1939	SURGENOR. Surgener. Surgeoner. Surgeonor. Surginer. Surginor.		
				1940	SURPLICE. Serplice. Serplus.	1957	THORNBERRY. Thornburgh. 511.
1905	SOMERSET. Sommersett. Summersett.			1941	SUTCLIFFE. Sitcliff. Sitliff. Sutliffe.	1958	THORNTON. Dreinan. 40. [Drinan]. 506. Drinane. 419. M'Sheaghan. 319. M'Skean. 383. Meenagh. 40. Skehan. 13. Tarrant. 100, 199. Thorn. 72.
1906	SOMERVILLE. Simvil. 233. Sommerville. Sumeril. 489. Sumerly. 174. Summerville.	1924	STERLING. Stirling. (Stern). 91.	1942	SUTHERLAND. Southerland. Sunderland. 472. Surley. 197. Suthern. 311.		
1907	SORAGHAN. Sorahan. Soran. [Sullivan]. 92, 383.	1925	STEWART. Steuart. 374. Steward. [Stuart]. 454 (b)	1943	SWANWICK. Swanick.		
				1944	SWEENY. MacSweeny. 309 (a). [M'Sweeny]. 182, 304, 309. M'Swine. 114, 374, &c. [M'Swiney]. 283. O'Sevnagh. 40. Sweny. [Swiney]. 314, 374.	1959	TIERNAN. Ternan. 72. Terney. Tierney. 390.
1908	SOUGHLEY. Suckley.	1926	ST. JOHN. Cingen. 117. Singen. 315, 393, 498. Singin. 25. Sinjohn. Sinjun. 316.			1960	TIGHE. Kangley. 211. [M'Tague]. 46, 82. M'Teague. 46. M'Teigue. 82. Tee. 183. Tye. Tyghe. 183.
1909	SOUTTAR. Shuiter. Shuter. Suter. Sutor.						
		1927	ST. LEGER. Lyster. 273. Sallanger. 508. Sallenger. 273. Sallinger. 472, 497, 509. Selenger. 473. Sellinger. St. Ledger.				
1910	SPEERS. Spear. Spears. Speer.			1945	SWIFT. Fodaghan. 413. [Fogarty]. 185. Fogaton. 185. Foody. 138, 528. O'Foodhy. 40. Speed. 50.	1961	TIMMONS. Tummon. 413. Tymmins. Tymmons.
1911	SPELMAN. Spellman. Spollen. 455.					1962	TIMOTHY. [Tumelty]. 528.
1912	SPENCE. Spense. Spince.					1963	TINCKLER. Tinkler. 435.
1913	SPILLANE. Spalane. Spelessy. 8. Spellane. Spilane. Spillessy. 142. Splaine. 77.	1928	STODDART. Stothart. Stotherg. 410. Stothers. [Studdert]. 410.	1946	SWINEY. [M'Sweeny]. M'Swine. [Sweeny]. 314, 374. Swine. 349.	1964	TITTERINGTON. Titterton. 381.
		1929	STOKES. Stoakes.			1965	TOAL. Toale. Tohall. 97. [Toole]. 97, 223.

62

No.	Surnames, with Varieties and Synonymes.	No.	Surnames, with Varieties and Synonymes.	No.	Surnames, with Varieties and Synonymes.	No.	Surnames, with Varieties and Synonymes.
1966	TOBIN. Tobyn.	1989	TULLY. Tally. 215.	2008	URQUHART. Urkuhart. Urquahart. Urquehart.	2027	WALSH. Branagh. 174. Brannagh. 40. [Brannick]. 506. Brannock. 51. Brawnick. 179. Brennagh. 483. Coon. 50. [Wallace]. 118, 253. Wallsh. Welch. 91. Welsh. 91, 259.
1967	TODD. Shinnahan. 191.	1990	TUMELTY. [Timothy]. 528. Tomilty. Tumalti. Tumblety. Tumiltey. Tumilty.	2009	USSHER. [Hession]. 298. Ushart. 254. Usher. 254.		
1968	TOGHILL. Toal. 97. Tohill. Tohull. 97. Toughill.						
1969	TOLAN. Toland. 432.	1991	TUOHIG. Toohig. Towhig. Twohig.			2028	WARD. M'Award. M'Ward.
1970	TOMKINS. Tomkin. Toompane. 131.	1992	TUOHY. Tooey. Toohy. Touhy. Tuhy. Twohy. Twoohy.	2010	VAIL. M'Phail. 422.	2029	WARREN. [Marnane]. 283. Mournane. [Murnane]. 288. Waring. 513. Warrenne. Warrin. Warring.
1971	TOMLINSON. Tumblinson. 59.			2011	VAKINS. Veakins. 335.		
1972	TOOLE. [O'Toole]. 223. [Toal]. 97, 223. Tuhill. 189.	1993	TURKINGTON. Torkington. 333. Turk. 83, 201, &c. Turkinton.	2012	VALENTINE. Vallantine. Vallentine.	2030	WARWICK. Warick. Warreck. 429. Warrick. 429.
1973	TOPPING. Tipping. 58.			2013	VALLELY. Vally. 344. [Varrilly]. 160.		
1974	TORLEY. Turley.	1994	TURNER. Turnor. Turnour.	2014	VANDELEUR. Vandaleur. Vandelleur.	2031	WATERS. Toorish. 482. Toorisk. 419. Turish. 161, 483. Uske. 40. Waterson. 52, 522. Watters (Whorriskey). 504.
1975	TORRENS. Teerry. 254. Terry. 254. Torrance. Torrans. Torrence. Torrins. Torry. 254.	1995	TUTHILL. Tothill. Tuttell. Tuttil. Tuttle. Tutty. 333.	2015	VARRILLY. [Vallely]. 160. Vallily. 362. Varily. 160. Varley. 39, 160, 174, &c.		
		1996	TWAMLEY. Twomley.	2016	VAUGHAN. Moghan. 316. Moughan. 117.	2032	WATSON. Watch. 329.
1976	TOWNSEND. Townshend. [Townsley]. 89.	1997	TWEEDY. Tweedie.	2017	VESEY. Veasy. Vessey. Vezey.	2033	WATTERSON. Waterson. Winterson.
1977	TOWNSLEY. Tinsley. 76. [Townsend]. 89.	1998	TWIGG. Quigg. 88.				
1978	TRACY. Treacy. Tracey. 174. Tressy.	1999	TWINAM. Twinem. Twinim. Twynam. Twynem. Twynim.	2018	VICKERS. Vicars. Vickars. Vikers.	2034	WAUCHOPE. Wachop. Wauchob. Wauhope.
1979	TRAVERS. Travors. Trevors. Trower. 370.	2000	TWOHILL. Toohill. Toomey. 91. Toughall. Towell. Towill. Tuohill.	2019	VICTORY. M'Nabo. 26, 153. &c. [M'Naboe]. 154, 265, 470, &c. Monaboe. 154.	2035	WAUGH. Vaugh. 128.
1980	TRAYNOR. Trainor. 256. Tranor. Trayner. Treanor. 256. Trenor. 429.					2036	WEADICK. Waddick. Waddock. 16. Wadick. Wadock. 16. Weadock. 16.
		2001	TWOMEY. Toomey. Towmey. Tuomy. Twoomy.	2020	VINCENT. M'Avinchy. 385.		
1981	TROUSDALE. Troosel. Trousdell. Truesdall. Trusdale. Trusdell. Trusdill. Trusill.	2002	TYMMANY. Timmin. 397.			2037	WEATHERHEAD. Wethered.
		2003	TYNAN. Tinin. 211. Tynnan. 32.			2038	WEBBER. Weber. Wiber. Wyber. 219.
1982	TROUTON. Troughton. Trouten. Trowtan.	2004	TYNDALL. Tindal. Tyndell.	2021	WADDEN. Wadding. 526, 527.	2039	WEEKES. Weaks. Weeks. Wicks.
1983	TROWLAND. Troland. 367. Trolen. 367.			2022	WADE. [M'Quade]. 215. Waid. Waide.	2040	WEIR. Corra. Wear. Weere. Were. Wier. Wire. 146. Wyer. 146.
1984	TROY. Trehy. 457.	2005	UBANK. Eubank. Ewbank.	2023	WADSWORTH. Wadworth. Wodsworth.		
1985	TUBMAN. Tugman.	2006	UNCLES. Unckles. Unkles.	2024	WAITE. Waites. Waytes. Whaite.	2041	WELDON. Veldon. 72, 364.
1986	TUBRIDY. Tubrit. 509.	2007	UPRICHARD. Bridget. 381, 523. Prichard. 6, 381. Pritchard, 381, 413.	2025	WALLACE. Wallice. Wallis. 214, 389 [Walsh]. 118, 253.	2042	WELLESLEY. Welsley. Wesley.
1987	TUITE. Chute.					2043	WELLWOOD. Walwood. Welwood.
1988	TUKE. Chooke. Took. Tooke.			2026	WALMSLEY. Wamsley.	2044	WHALLEY. Whaley. Whealy.

No.	Surnames, with Varieties and Synonyms.	No.	Surnames, with Varieties and Synonyms.	No.	Surnames, with Varieties and Synonyms.	No.	Surnames, with Varieties and Synonyms.
2045	WHARTON. Faughton. 303(b). Warton. Werton. Wherton.	2054	WHITTAKER. Whitaker. 333. Whiteacre. Whiteaker. Whitegar. Whittacre. Whittegar.	2068	WINTER. M'Alivery. 216. Winters. Wintour. Wynter.	2078	WREFORD. Rayford. Reford. Reyford. Wrayford.
2046	WHEATLY. Whately. Wheately. Whitly. Whittley.	2055	WHOLY. Holey.	2069	WISEHEART. Wisehart. Wishart.	2079	WRENN. M'Crann. 123. Reen. 280. [Ring]. 186. Rynn. 48 (a). Wrynn. 465.
2047	WHELAN.· [Hyland]. 40. Peelan. Pelan. 306. [Phelan]. 40, 101. 117. &c. [Philbin]. 252. Whalan. Whalen. Whealan. Whealon. Wheelahan. Wheelan. Whelahan. 172, 249, 291. Whelezhan. 312. Whelehan. 136. Whelen. Whelon.	2056	WHORISKEY. Horisky.	2070	WOGAN. Ogan. 495. Oogan. 364, 495. Ougan. 72, 178(a).	2080	WRIGHT. Kincart. 301.
		2057	WHYTE. See [White].	2071	WOLFE. Nix. 11, 404. Wolff. Woulfe-Nix. 405.	2081	WRIGLEY. Rigley.
		2058	WIDDICOMB. Widdecombe. Withecomb.	2072	WOLSELEY. Wolsey. Wolsley. Woolsey.	2082	WRIXON. Rixon.
		2059	WIGHTMAN. Whiteman.	2073	WOODROOFFE. Woodroofe. Woodruff.	2083	WYBRANTS. Whybron.
		2060	WILDE. Wild. Wildes. Wyld. Wylde.	2074	WOODROW. Wither. 254.	2084	WYLIE. Wiley. 95, 250, 494. Wilie Wily.
		2061	WILKINSON. M'Quilkan. 43. M'Quilkin. 44. Wilkie. 55. Wilkison.⁵ Wilkisson.	2075	WOODS. Ellwood. 381. [Elwood]. 381. Killimith. 152. Kilmet. 152. M'Elhill. 216. M'Ihone. 60. M'Ilhone. 60, 97. M'Ilhun. 59. Smallwoods. 53.	2085	WYMBS. Wimbs. 125.
2048	WHIGHAM. Whigam. Wiggam.	2062	WILLIAMS. [Williamson].			2086	WYNNE. Guiheen. 123. [Guihen]. 278, 371. [Magee]. 82. [M'Gee]. 82. M'Guiehan. 212. Winn. Wyn.
2049	WHITE. Banane. 501. Baun. 488. Bawn. 76, 136, 210. [Galligan]. 153. Whight. [Whyte]. 393.	2063	WILLIAMSON. [Williams].	2076	WORRALL. Warrell. Worald. World. Worrell.		
		2064	WILLOUGHBY. Wilby. 102.			2087	WYSE. Wise. Wize.
2050	WHITEHEAD. [Canavan].	2065	WILMOT. Willmott. Wilmitt. Wilmont. 177.	2077	WRAY. Rae. Ray. 417. [Rea]. 417. Reay. Reigh.		
2051	WHITELY. Whitla. 112. Whitley. 346.	2066	WILSON. Willison. Willson.			2088	YEATES. Yates. Yeats.
2052	WHITESIDE. Whitsitt. 429.	2067	WINGFIELD. Winfield. Winnfield. Wynfield. Wynnfield.			2089	YIELDING. Yeilding.
2053	WHITFIELD. Whitfle. 249.					2090	YOUNG. Yonge.
						2091	YOURELL. Eurell. Urrell. 152.

KEY TO REFERENCE NUMBERS IN ALPHABETICAL LIST OF NAMES.

N.B.—Where the Union name only appears, the variety has been reported by the Superintendent Registrar or Registrar of Marriages (7 & 8 Vic., cap. 81).

Reference Numbers.	Names of Registrars' Districts.	Unions in which situated.	Reference Numbers.	Names of Registrars' Districts.	Unions in which situated.
1	Abbey, ...	Tuam.	57	Ballymahon. ..	Ballymahon.
2	Abbeyfeale. ...	Newcastle.	58	— ...	Ballymena.
3	Abbeyshrule. ...	Ballymahon.	59	Ballymoney, ...	Ballymoney.
4	Achill, ...	Westport.	60	— ...	„
5	Aclare, ...	Tobercurry.	61	Ballymore. ...	Ballymahon.
6	Aghalee, ...	Lurgan.	62	Ballymote. ...	Sligo.
7	Ahoghill, ...	Ballymena.	63	Ballynacargy, ...	Mullingar.
8	Anascall. ...	Dingle.	64	Ballynahinch. ...	Downpatrick.
9	Annahilt. ...	Lisburn.	65	Ballynoe. ..	Fermoy.
10	— ...	Antrim.	66	Ballynure. ...	Larne.
11	Ardagh. ...	Newcastle.	67	Ballyragget, ...	Castlecomer.
12	Ardara. ...	Glenties.	68	Ballyroan. ...	Abbeyleix.
13	— ...	Ardee.	69	— ...	Ballyshannon.
14	Ardee, ...	„	70	Ballyshannon, ...	„
15	Ardmore, ...	Youghal.	71	Ballyward, ...	Banbridge.
16	Arklow, ...	Rathdrum.	72	— ...	Balrothery.
17	Armagh. ...	Armagh.	73	— ...	Baltinglass.
18	— ...	Armagh.	74	Banagher. ...	Birr.
19	Articlave, ..	Coleraine.	75	— ...	Banbridge.
20	Arvagh, ...	Cavan.	76	Banbridge, ...	„
21	Athenry, ...	Loughrea.	77	Bandon, ...	Bandon.
22	Athleague, ...	Roscommon.	78	Bannow, ...	Wexford.
23	Athlone, No. 2, ...	Athlone	79	— ...	Bantry.
24	— ...	„	80	Bantry, ...	„
25	— ...	Athy.	81	Barronstown, ...	Dundalk.
26	— ...	Bailieborough.	82	— ...	Bawnboy.
			83	Belfast, No. 1, ...	Belfast.
			84	„ No. 2, ...	„
			85	„ No. 3, ...	„
			86	Belfast Rural, No. 4,	„
27	Balbriggan, ...	Balrothery.	87	Belfast, No. 6, ...	„
28	Balla, ...	Castlebar.	88	„ No. 7, ...	„
29	Ballaghaderreen,	Castlerea.	89	„ No. 9, ...	„
30	Ballickmoyler and Newtown,	Carlow.	90	„ No. 11, ...	„
31	Ballina, ...	Ballina.	91	— ...	„
32	Ballinakill, ...	Abbeyleix.	92	Bellananagh, ...	Cavan.
33	Ballinalee, ...	Granard.	93	Bellarena, ...	Limavady.
34	Ballinameen, ...	Boyle.	94	Belturbet, ...	Cavan.
35	Ballinamore, ...	Bawnboy.	95	Benburb, ...	Dungannon.
36	— ...	Ballinasloe.	96	Birr, ...	Birr.
37	Ballincollig, ...	Cork.	97	Blackwatertown,	Armagh.
38	Ballindine, ...	Claremorris.	98	Blanchardstown and Castle-knock,	Dublin, North.
39	— ...	Ballinrobe.			
40	Ballinrobe, ...	„	99	Blarney, ..	Cork.
41	Ballintra, ...	Ballyshannon.	100	Boherboy, ...	Kanturk.
42	Ballybay, ...	Castleblayney.	101	Borris, ...	Carlow.
43	— ...	Ballycastle.	102	Borris-in-Ossory,	Roscrea.
44	Ballycastle. ...	Killala	103	— ...	Borrisokane.
45	Ballyclough, ...	Mallow.	104	Bourney, ...	Roscrea.
46	Ballyconnell, ...	Bawnboy.	105	— ...	Boyle.
47	Ballyduff, ...	Listowel.	106	Boyle. ...	„
48(a)	Ballyfarnon, No. 1,	Boyle.	107	Bridgetown, ...	Wexford.
48(b)	Ballygawley, ...	Clogher.	108	Broadford, ...	Newcastle.
49	Ballyhaise. ...	Cavan.	109	Broadway, ...	Wexford.
50	Ballyhaunis, ...	Claremorris.	110	Brookeborough,	Lisnaskea.
51	Ballyhorgan, ...	Listowel.	111	Brosna, No. 2, ...	Tralee.
52	Ballyjamesduff,	Oldcastle.	112	Broughshane, ...	Ballymena.
53	Ballykelly, ...	Limavady.	113	Buncrana, ...	Inishowen.
54	Ballyleague, ...	Roscommon.	114	Burt, ...	Londonderry.
55	Ballylesson, ...	Lisburn.	115	Bushmills, ...	Ballymoney.
56	— ...	Ballymahon.			

Reference Numbers.	Names of Registrars' Districts.	Unions in which situated.	Reference Numbers.	Names of Registrars' Districts.	Unions in which situated.
116	Caher, ...	Clogheen.	190	Creagh, ...	Ballinasloe.
117	— ...	Callan.	191	Croagh, ...	Ballycastle.
118	Callan, ...	„	192	Croom, ...	Croom.
119	Cappaghduff, ...	Ballinrobe.	193	— ...	
120	Cappoquin, ...	Lismore.	194	Crossakeel, ...	Oldcastle.
121	Carbury, ...	Edenderry.	195	Crossgar, ...	Banbridge.
122	Carlow.	Carlow.	196	Crossmaglen, ...	Castleblayney.
123	Carndonagh, ...	Inishowen.	197	Crumlin, ...	Antrim.
124	Carney, No. 1, ...	Sligo.	198	Crusheen, ...	Ennis.
125	„ No. 2, ...	„	199	Cullen, ...	Millstreet.
126	Carrick, ...	Glenties.			
127(a)	— ...	Carrickmacross.			
127(b)	Carrickmacross,	„			
128	— ...	Carrick-on-Shan-non	200	Delvin, ...	Delvin.
			201	Derrylin, ...	Lisnaskea.
129	Carrick-on-Suir,	Carrick-on-Suir.	202	Dervock, ...	Ballymoney.
130	— ...	„	203	Dingle, ...	Dingle.
131	Carrigaholt, ...	Kilrush.	204	Doagh, ...	Antrim.
132	Carrigallen, ...	Mohill.	205	Donaghmoyne,...	Carrickmacross.
133	Carrigbyrne, ...	New Ross.	206	Donegal, ...	Donegal.
134	Carrignavar, No. 1	Cork.	207	Donnybrook, ...	Dublin, South.
135	— ...	Cashel.	208	Doocharry, ...	Glenties.
136	— ...	Castlebar.	209	Draperstown, ...	Magherafelt.
137	Castleblayney,...	Castleblayney.	210	Dromore, ...	Banbridge.
138	Castleconor, ...	Dromore West.	211	Drum, ...	Cootehill.
139	. — ...	Castlederg.	212	Drumahaire, ...	Manorhamilton.
140	Castlederg and Killeter, No. 1,...		213	Drumbeg, ...	Lisburn.
			214	Drumconrath, ...	Ardee.
141	Castlefin, ...	Strabane.	215	Drumlish, ...	Longford.
142	Castlegregory,...	Dingle.	216	Drumquin, ...	Castlederg.
143	Castleisland, ...	Tralee.	217	Drumshambo, ...	Carrick-on-Shan-non.
144	Castlemaine, ...				
145	Castlemartyr, ...	Midleton.			
146	Castlepollard, ...	Delvin.	218	Dublin, North, No. 1, W.	Dublin, North.
147	Castlerea, ...	Castlerea.			
148	Castlereagh, No.2,	Belfast.	219	Dublin, North, No. 3.	„
149	Castletown, ...	Abbeyleix.	220	. — ...	Dundalk.
150	„ ...	Castletown.	221	Dundrum and Glencullen,No.2,	Rathdown.
151	„ ...	Croom.			
152	Castletown Geo-ghegan, ...	Mullingar.	222	—	Dungannon.
			223	Dungannon, ...	„
153	— ...	Cavan.	224	— ...	Dungarvan.
154	Cavan, ...	„	225	Dungloe, No. 1,...	Glenties.
155	— ...	Celbridge.	226	Dunkineely, ...	Donegal.
156	Church Hill, ...	Ballyshannon.	227	— ...	Dunmanway.
157(a)	— ...	Claremorris.	228	Dunmanway, ,...	„
157(b)	Claremorris, ...	„	229	Dunmore, ...	Glenamaddy.
158	Clarina, ...	Limerick.	230	Dunnamanagh,...	Strabane.
159	Claudy, ...	Londonderry.			
160	— ...	Clifden.			
161	Cloghan, ...	Stranorlar.			
162	— ...	Clogheen.	231	Easky, ...	Dromore, West.
163	Clogher, ...	Clogher.	232	Edenderry, ...	Edenderry.
164	Clonakilty, ...	Clonakilty.	233	Ederney, ...	Irvinestown.
165	Clonavaddy, ...	Dungannon.	234	Eglinton, ...	Londonderry.
166	Clonelly, ...	Irvinestown.	235	Emly, ...	Tipperary.
167	— ...	Clones.	236	Ennis, No. 1, ...	Ennis.
168	Clones, ...	„	237	— ...	„
169	Clonmany, ...	Inishowen.	238	— ...	Enniskillen.
170	— ...	Clonmel.			
171	Clonmel, ...	„			
172	Clonmellon, ...	Delvin.			
173	Clonroche, ...	Enniscorthy.	239	Feakle, ...	Scarriff.'
174	Cloonbur, No. 1,	Oughterard.	240	Feeny, ...	Limavady.
175	Clough, ...	Downpatrick.	241	Fenagh and My-shall, ..	Carlow.
176	— ...	Coleraine.			
177	Coleraine, ...	„	242	— ...	Fermoy.
178(a)	Collon, No. 1, ...	Ardee.	243	Ferns, ...	Enniscorthy.
178(b)	Comber, ...	Newtownards.	244	Fethard, No. 1, ...	New Ross.
179	Cong, ...	Ballinrobe.	245	Fethard, No. 2,...	„
180	— ...	Cookstown.	246	Finnea, ...	Granard.
181	Cookstown, ...	„	247	Florencecourt, ...	Enniskillen.
182	Coolacasey, ...	Limerick.	248	Forkhill, ...	Newry.
183	Coolgreany, ...	Gorey.	249	Frankford, ...	Parsonstown.
184	Coolrain, ...	Mountmellick.			
185	— ...	Cootehill.			
186	Coom, ...	Killarney.	250	Galgorm, ...	Ballymena.
187	Cork, Urban,No. 2,	Cork.	251	— ...	Galway.
188	Cork, Urban,No. 7,	„	252	Galway, No. 1, ...	„
189	Corrofin, ...	Corrofin.	253	Galway, No. 3, ...	„

G

Reference Numbers.	Names of Registrars' Districts.	Unions in which situated.	Reference Numbers.	Names of Registrars' Districts.	Unions in which situated.
254	Garvagh, ...	Coleraine.	322	Kilrush, ...	Kilrush.
255	Glassan, ...	Athlone.	323	— ...	
256	Glasslough, ...	Monaghan.	324	Kilsallaghan, ...	Balrothery.
257	Glenavy, ...	Lisburn.	325	Kilshannig, ...	Mallow.
258	Glennamaddy, ...	Glenamaddy.	326	Kilsheelan, ...	Clonmel.
259	— ...	Glenties.	327	Kiltimagh, ...	Swineford.
260	Glenties, ...		328	Kiltinan, ...	Clonmel.
261	Gorey, ..	Gorey.	329	Kiltoom, ...	Athlone.
262	— ...	Gort.	330	Kiltormer, ...	Ballinasloe.
263	Gowran, ...	Kilkenny.	331	Kilworth, ...	Fermoy.
264	— ...	Granard	332	Kingscourt, ...	Bailieborough
265	Granard, ...	Granard.	333	Kingstown, No. 2.	Rathdown.
266	Grean, ...	Tipperary.	334	Kinlough, ...	Ballyshannon.
267	Grey Abbey, ...	Newtownards.	335	Kinsale, ...	Kinsale.
268	Gurteen, ...	Boyle.	336	Kinvarra, ...	Gort.
			337	Knocknalower,...	Belmullet.
269	Hollymount. ...	Ballinrobe.			
270	Holywell, ...	Enniskillen.	338	Larne. ...	Larne.
271	— ...	Inishowen.	339	Leitrim, ...	Car.-on-Shannon.
			340	— ...	Letterkenny.
			341	Letterkenny, ...	"
272	Inishbofin, ...	Clifden.	342	Lettermore. ...	Oughterard.
273	Inistioge, ...	Thomastown.	343	— ...	Limavady.
274	Innfield, ...	Trim.	344	Limavady. ...	
275	Irvinestown, ...	Irvinestown.	345	Limerick, No. 2.	Limerick.
276	— ...	"	346	Lisbellaw, ...	Enniskillen.
			347	— ...	Lisburn.
			348	Lisburn, ...	"
			349	Lismore, ...	Lismore.
277	Kanturk, ...	Kanturk.	350	— ...	Lisnaskea.
278	Keadue, ...	Boyle.	351	Lisnaskea, ...	
279	Keady, ...	Armagh.	352	— ...	Listowel.
280	Kealkill, ...	Bantry.	353	Listowel, ...	
281	— ...	Kells.	354	Littleton, ...	Thurles.
282	Kells, ...	"	355	Londonderry Urban, No. 2. ...	Londonderry.
283	— ...	Kenmare.			
284	Kilbeggan, ...	Tullamore.	356	— ...	Londonderry.
285	Kilcatherine, ...	Castletown.	357	— ...	Longford.
286	Kilcock, ...	Celbridge.	358	Loughbrickland, ...	Banbridge.
287	Kilfinane, ...	Kilmallock.	359	Loughgall, ...	Armagh.
288	Kilgarvan, ..	Kenmare.	360	— ...	Loughrea.
289	— ...	Kilkeel.	361	Louisburgh, No. 1,	Westport.
290	Kilgobban, ...	Tralee.	362	" No. 2,	"
291	Kilkee, ...	Kilrush.	363	Lurgan, No. 2. ...	Lurgan.
292	Kilkeel, No. 1, ...	Kilkeel.	364	Lusk, ...	Balrothery.
293	" No. 2, ...				
294	Kilkelly, ...	Swineford.			
295	— ...	Kilkenny.	365	Macroom, ...	Macroom.
296	Kilkenny, No. 2, ...	Kilkenny.	366	— ...	
297	Kilkishen, ...	Tulla.	367	Maghera, ...	Magherafelt.
298	Killaan, ...	Ballinasloe.	368	Malahide, ...	Balrothery
299	— ...	Killadysert.	369	Malin, ...	Inishowen.
300	Killala, ...	Killala.	370	Manorhamilton, ...	Manorhamilton.
301	— ...	Killala.	371	— ...	Manorhamilton.
302	Killanniv, ...	Ennis.	372	Markethill, ...	Armagh.
303(a)	— ...	Killarney.	373	Maryborough, ...	Mountmellick.
303(b)	Killarney, No. 1...	Killarney.	374	— ...	Milford.
304	Killeagh, ...	Youghal.	375	Milford, ...	Kanturk.
305	Killeen, ...	Dunshaughlin.	376	— ...	Millstreet.
306	Killenagh and Wells.	Gorey.	377	Milltown. ...	Killarney.
307	Killeroran, ...	Mountbellew.	378	— ...	Mitchelstown.
308	Killeshandra, ...	Cavan.	379	— ...	Mohill.
309	Killorglin, ...	Killarney.'	380	Mohill, ...	"
310	Killough, ...	Downpatrick.	381	Moira, ...	Lurgan.
311	Killoughy, ...	Tullamore.	382	Molahiffe, ...	Killarney.
312	Killucan, ...	Mullingar.	383	— ...	Monaghan.
313	Killygordon, ...	Stranorlar.	384	Monasterevan, ...	Athy.
314	Kilmacrenan and Milford.	Milford.	385	Moneymore, ...	Magherafelt.
315	— ...	Kilmacthomas.	386	— ...	Mountbellew.
316	Kilmaganny, ...	Callan.	387	Mountmellick, ...	Mountmellick.
317	Kilmallock, ...	Kilmallock.	388	Mountnorris, ...	Newry
318	Kilmihil, ...	Kilrush.	389	Mountrath, ...	Mountmellick.
319	Kilmore, ...	Monaghan.	390	Mountshannon, ...	Scarriff.
320	Kilpatrick, ...	Oashel.	391	Moville, ...	Inishowen.
321	Kilrea, ...	Coleraine	392	Mullaghglass, ...	Newry.
			393	Mullinahone, ...	Callan.

Reference Numbers.	Names of Registrars' Districts.	Unions in which situated.	Reference Numbers.	Names of Registrars' Districts.	Unions in which situated.
394	Mullingar, ...	Mullingar.	462	Roundstone, No. 1,	Clifden.
395	— ...	„	463	„ No. 2,	„
396	Multyfarnham,	„	464	Rowan, ...	Mohill.
397	Murragh, ...	Bandon.	465	Rynn, ...	„
398	Murroe, ...	Limerick.			
			466	Saintfield, ...	Lisburn.
399	Naas & Carragh,	Naas.	467	St. Mary's, ...	Drogheda.
400	— ...	„	468	St. Mullin's, ...	New Ross.
401	— ...	Navan.	469	— ...	Scarriff.
402	Navan, ...	„	470	Scrabby, ...	Granard.
403	Nenagh, ...	Nenagh.	471	Shercock, ...	Bailieborough.
404	— ...	Newcastle.	472	— ...	Shillelagh.
405	Newcastle, ...	Rathdrum.	473	Shinrone, ...	Roscrea.
406	Newport, ...	Nenagh.	474	Silvermines, ...	Nenagh.
407	„ ...	Westport.	475	Skreen, ...	Dromore West.
408	New Ross, ...	New Ross.	476	— ...	Sligo.
409	Newry, No. 1, ...	Newry.	477	Sligo, No. 2, ...	„
410	„ No. 2, ...	„	478	Stewartstown, ...	Cookstown.
411	Newtownards, ...	Newtownards.	479	— ...	Strabane.
412	Newtownbarry,	Enniscorthy.	480	Strabane, ...	Strabane.
413	Newtownbutler,	Clones.	481	Strangford, ...	Downpatrick.
414	Newtownhamilton.	Castleblayney.	482	— ...	Stranorlar.
			483	Stranorlar, ...	„
415	Newtownstewart,	Strabane.	484	Street, No. 1, ...	Granard.
			485	— ...	Strokestown.
			486	— ...	Swineford.
416	Oldcastle,, ...	Oldcastle.	487	Swords, ...	Balrothery.
417	— ...	Omagh.			
418	Omagh, No. 2, ...		488	Tallow, ...	Lismore.
419	— ...	Oughterard.	489	Tanderagee, ...	Banbridge.
420	— ...	Parsonstown.	490	Tarbert, No. 1, ...	Listowel.
			491	„ No. 2, ...	„
421	Pettigoe, ...	Donegal.	492	Tartaraghan, ...	Lurgan.
422	Pilltown, ...	Carrick-on-Suir.	493	Templemore, ...	Thurles.
423	Plumb Bridge, ...	Strabane.	494	Templepatrick,...	Antrim.
424	Pomeroy, ...	Cookstown.	495	Termonfeckin, ...	Drogheda.
425	Portaferry, ...	Downpatrick.	496	Terryglass, ...	Borrisokane.
426	Portglenone, ...	Ballymena.	497	— ...	Thomastown.
427	Portlaw, ...	Carrick-on-Suir.	498	— ...	Thurles.
428	Portrush, ...	Coleraine.	499	Thurles, ...	„
429	Poyntzpass, ...	Newry.	500	Timoleague, ...	Clonakilty.
			501	— ...	Tobercurry.
			502	Tobercurry, ...	„
430	Quin, ...	Tulla.	503	Toome, ...	Ballymena.
			504	Tory Island, ...	Dunfanaghy.
			505	Trim, ...	Trim.
431	Rahan, ...	Mallow.	506	Tuam, No. 1, ...	Tuam.
432	Ramelton, ...	Milford.	507	„ No. 2, ...	„
433	Randalstown, ...	Antrim.	508	Tulla, ...	Tulla.
434	Raphoe, ...	Strabane.	509	— ...	„
435	Rathangan, ...	Edenderry.	510	Tullamain, ...	Cashel.
436	Rathcoole, ...	Celbridge.	511	— ...	Tullamore.
437	Rathcormack, ...	Fermoy.	512	Tullamore, ...	„
438	Rathdowney, ...	Abbeyleix.	513	Tullaroan, ...	Kilkenny.
439	— ...	Rathdrum.	514	Tullow, ...	Carlow.
440	Rathdrum, ...	„	515	Tullyvin, ...	Cootehill.
441	Rathfriland, ...	Newry.	516	Turloughmore,...	Galway.
442	Rathgormuck, ...	Carrick-on-Suir.	517	— ...	Urlingford.
443	— ...	Rathkeale.			
444	Rathkeale, No. 1,	„	518	Ullid, ...	Waterford.
445	„ No. 2,	„	519	Urlingford, ...	Urlingford.
446	Rathmore, ...	Naas.			
447	Rathmullan, ...	Milford.	520	Valencia, ...	Caherciveen.
448	Rathvilly, ...	Baltinglass.	521	Ventry, ...	Dingle.
449	Ratoath, ...	Dunshaughlin.	522	Virginia, ...	Oldcastle.
450	Ravensdale, ...	Dundalk.			
451	Rhode, ...	Edenderry.	523	Waringstown, ...	Lurgan.
452	Ringville, ...	Dungarvan.	524	Warrenpoint, ...	Newry.
453	Riverstown, ...	Parsonstown.	525	— ...	Waterford.
454(a)	Riverstown, ...	Sligo.	526	— ...	Wexford.
454(b)	Roosky, ...	Strokestown.	527	Wexford, ...	„
455	Roscommon, ...	Roscommon.	528	Williamstown, ...	Glennamaddy.
456	— ...	„	529	Woodstown, ...	Waterford.
457	Roscrea, No. 1, ...	Roscrea.			
458	„ No. 2, ...	„	530	Youghal, ...	Youghal
459	Rosguill, ...	Milford.			
460	Rosslea, ...	Clones.			
461	Rostrevor, ...	Kilkeel.			

INDEX TO ALPHABETICAL LIST OF SURNAMES, WITH THEIR VARIETIES AND SYNONYMES.

N.B.—The number following each name refers to the number of the principal name under which it will be found in the Alphabetical List.

Surname and Reference No.	Surname and Reference No.	Surname and Reference No.	Surname and Reference No.
Baun, 2049.	Bex, 75.	Blessing, 115.	Bourke, 192.
Bawn, 2049.	Bicker, 96.	Bligh, 117.	Bourn, 206.
Baxter, 70.	Bickers, 96.	Blong, 111.	Bourne, 206.
Bayly, 71.	Bickerstaff, 96, 1347.	Bloomer, 738.	Bovenizer, 135.
Bayne, 54.	Bickerstay, 96.	Blouk, 108.	Bovenizor, 135.
Beaghan, 80.	Bickett, 76.	Blowick, 108.	Bovinizer, 135.
Beahan, 80.	Biern, 206.	Bloxham, 116.	Bowden, 133, 136.
Bean, 80.	Bierne, 206.	Bloxsom, 116.	Bowen, 137.
Beard, 55.	Bigam, 97.	Bly, 117.	Bower, 1289.
Bearkery, 88.	Biggam, 97.	Blyth, 117.	Bowland, 125.
Bearkin, 80.	Biggane, 1108.	Blythe, 117.	Bowle, 138.
Bearnas, 63.	Biggedon, 1107.	Boag, 123.	Bowles, 138.
Beatagh, 72.	Bigger, 96.	Boake, 118.	Bowls, 138.
Beattie, 72.	Biggerstaff, 96.	Boakes, 118.	Bowman, 139.
Beatty, 72, 94, 1237.	Biggerstaffe, 96.	Boal, 138, 143.	Bownes, 129.
Beaty, 72.	Biggs, 78.	Boale, 138.	Boxhill, 140.
Beauchamp, 73.	Bigham, 97.	Boales, 138.	Boxwell, 140.
Beaumont, 139.	Bigly, 79.	Boar, 1289.	Boyce, 141.
Becher, 74.	Bignel, 52.	Boardman, 119.	Boyes, 124, 141.
Beck, 75.	Billigam, 83.	Boas, 120.	Boyl, 142.
Beckett, 76.	Binane, 188.	Boaz, 120.	Boylan, 142, 143.
Bedloe, 77.	Bingham, 97.	Bockocan, 178.	Boyle, 142, 143.
Bedlow, 77.	Biracrea, 88.	Boddle, 122.	Boyne, 144.
Beecham, 73.	Biracree, 88.	Bodel, 122, 133.	Boyse, 141.
Beecher, 74.	Birch, 98.	Bodell, 133.	Bradden, 614.
Beewick, 95.	Birchill, 190.	Boden, 136.	Bradley, 145.
Begane, 1108.	Bird, 99, 856, 1312.	Bodill, 122.	Bradly, 145.
Begg, 78, 1107.	Birkett, 193.	Bodkin, 121.	Bradshaw, 146.
Beggan, 1107.	Birkey, 100.	Bodle, 122, 133.	Brady, 147, 1231.
Beggs, 78.	Birkitt, 193.	Bog, 143.	Braidon, 152.
Beglan, 52.	Birkmyre, 100.	Bogue, 123.	Branagan, 150.
Begley, 79, 1557.	Birmingham, 89.	Bogues, 123.	Branagh, 2027.
Begnall, 52.	Birminghan, 89.	Bohan, 137.	Branan, 155.
Begnell, 52.	Birne, 206.	Bohanan, 178.	Brandon, 148.
Begney, 52.	Birnell, 195.	Bohane, 137.	Brangan, 150.
Behan, 80.	Birnes, 206.	Bohanna, 137, 178.	Braniff, 155.
Behane, 80, 1616.	Birney, 101.	Bohannon, 178.	Branigan, 150.
Beird, 55.	Birrane, 102, 206, 207.	Bohill, 124.	Brankin, 150.
Beirne, 206.	Birt, 201.	Bohunnan, 178.	Brannagh, 2027.
Beirnes, 206.	Birthistle, 132.	Boice, 141.	Brannan, 155.
Belcher, 81.	Birtwistle, 132.	Boil, 143.	Brannen, 155.
Bellew, 82.	Bishop, 103.	Bolan, 125.	Brannick, 149, 2027.
Bellingham, 83.	Bissett, 84.	Boland, 125.	Brannie, 155.
Belsher, 81.	Bisshop, 103.	Bole, 138, 143.	Brannigan, 150.
Benathy, 2.	Blacagh, 108.	Boles, 138.	Brannock, 2027.
Benbo, 1442.	Black, 104, 519.	Boleyn, 183.	Brannon, 155.
Benison, 85, 700.	Blackadder, 105.	Bolger, 126.	Branon, 155.
Bennett, 84.	Blackbourne, 106.	Bolton, 127.	Brassil, 151.
Bennison, 85.	Blackburne, 106.	Bonar, 128, 357.	Bratty, 146.
Benson, 85.	Blackely, 109.	Boner, 128, 357.	Brauders, 163.
Bera, 91.	Blackender, 105.	Bones, 129.	Brawnick, 2027.
Berachry, 88.	Blackham, 104.	Boness, 129.	Brawnlee, 172.
Bergan, 86.	Blackley, 109.	Bonison, 196.	Brazel, 151.
Bergen, 86.	Blacquiere, 107.	Bonnar, 128.	Brazil, 151.
Bergin, 86.	Blacquire, 107.	Bonner, 128, 357.	Breadin, 152.
Bergman, 92.	Blacre, 107.	Bonny, 144.	Breadon, 152.
Berigan, 206.	Blainey, 113.	Bookle, 179.	Breanon, 155.
Berkeley, 61, 87.	Blake, 108.	Boordman, 119.	Brearton, 156.
Berkerry, 88.	Blakely, 109.	Borbidge, 189.	Bredin, 152.
Berkery, 88.	Blakeney, 110.	Borbridge, 189.	Bredon, 152.
Berkly, 87.	Blakes, 108.	Bordman, 119.	Breedeth, 1232.
Berkry, 88.	Blakney, 110.	Boreland, 130, 142.	Breen, 153.
Bermingham, 89.	Blanc, 111.	Borland, 130.	Brehany, 154.
Bernard, 90.	Blanch, 112.	Borman, 119.	Breheny, 154, 968.
Berne, 206.	Blanchfield, 112.	Bornell, 195.	Brehony, 154, 968.
Berney, 101.	Blaney, 113.	Borris, 200.	Bremigam, 89.
Berocry, 88.	Blayney, 113.	Borriskill, 131.	Brenan, 155.
Berrall, 198.	Bleach, 108.	Borroughs, 200.	Brendley, 160.
Berrane, 63, 206, 207.	Bleak, 110.	Borrowes, 200.	Brendon, 148.
Berridge, 199, 206, 207.	Bleakley, 109.	Borthistle, 132.	Brennagh, 2027.
Berrigan, 86.	Bleakney, 110.	Bothwell, 122, 133, 136.	Brennan, 155.
Berry, 91.	Bleaney, 113.	Boucher, 134.	Brennen, 155.
Berryman, 92.	Bleckley, 109.	Bouchier, 134.	Brennigan, 150.
Berthistle, 132.	Bleeks, 109.	Boughal, 179.	Brennon, 155.
Berton, 202.	Bleheen, 1514.	Boughan, 137.	Brenon, 155.
Bertram, 93.	Blehein, 1513.	Boughla, 180.	Brereton, 156.
Beryin, 206.	Bleheine, 1514.	Boulger, 126.	Brerton, 156.
Bettie, 94.	Blekley, 109.	Bouls, 138.	Bresland, 157.
Betty, 72, 94, 1237.	Bleney, 113.	Bourchier, 134.	Breslane, 157.
Bewick, 95.	Blennerhasset, 114.	Bourchill, 190.	Breslaun, 157.

70

Surname and Reference No.	Surname and Reference No.	Surname and Reference No.	Surname and Reference No.
Breslawn, 157.	Brudher, 163.	Burrows, 200.	Callahan, 220.
Breslin, 157.	Bruen, 175.	Burt, 201.	Callan, 222, 223, 305.
Bresnahan, 168.	Brugham, 170.	Burtchaell, 190.	Callanan, 222, 223.
Bresnane, 168.	Bruin, 175.	Burtchell, 190.	Callanane, 223.
Bresnehau, 168.	Brumagem, 89.	Burthistle, 132.	Callaughan, 220.
Bresnihan, 168.	Brumigem, 89,	Burthnot, 32.	Calleghan, 220.
Brett, 158.	Brumiger, 89.	Burton, 202.	Callehan, 220.
Bretton, 161.	Brummagem, 89.	Bushell, 203.	Callen, 222.
Brewster, 174.	Brummagen, 89.	Bussell, 203.	Calligan, 220.
Breydon, 152.	Brunty, 165, 1742.	Butler, 204.	Callighan, 220.
Brian, 176, 1642.	Brusnahan, 168.	Buttler, 204.	Callin, 222.
Brice, 157.	Brusnehan 168.	Button, 32.	Callinan, 223.
Briceson, 177.	Brusnihan, 168.	Bwee, 141, 1320.	Callnan, 223.
Bridget, 2007.	Bruton, 156.	Byars, 205.	Calnan, 223, 394.
Brien, 153, 176, 1233, 1642.	Bryan, 176, 1233, 1642.	Byers, 205.	Calwell, 219.
Briene, 153.	Bryans, 176.	Byngham, 97.	Camac, 224.
Briens, 176, 1642.	Bryen, 176.	Byran, 207.	Camack, 224.
Briery, 159.	Bryne, 176.	Byrane, 102, 207.	Cambell, 226.
Brimage, 89.	Brynes, 176.	Byrce, 157.	Camble, 226.
Brimagum, 89.	Bryney, 176.	Byrne, 102, 197, 206, 207.	Camblin,225.
Brimley, 173.	Bryry, 159.	Byrnell, 195.	Camelin, 225.
Brimmagem, 89.	Bryson, 177, 1557.	Byrnes, 197, 206.	Camill, 226.
Brimmajen, 89.	Buchanan, 178, 1200.	Byrney, 101.	Camlin, 225.
Brimmigan, 89.	Buchanen, 178.	Byrns, 206.	Cammack, 224.
Brinane, 155.	Buchannan, 178.	Byron, 63, 102, 206, 207.	Cammelin, 225.
Brindley, 160.	Buchannon, 178.	Byrrane, 207.	Camp, 226.
Brine, 176, 1642.	Buck, 182.	Byrt, 201.	Campbell, 226, 1253.
Brines, 176, 1642.	Buckely, 180.	Bywater, 208.	Campble, 226.
Briody, 147.	Buckle, 31, 179, 180.		Campell, 226.
Brion, 176.	Buckles, 31, 179.		Camphill, 226.
Brislan, 157.	Buckley, 179, 180.		Cample, 226.
Brislane, 157.	Buckmaster, 181.		Canaan, 229, 1030.
Brislaun, 157.	Bueg, 78.		Canally, 1444.
Brislin, 157.	Buhilly, 180.	Caddell, 209.	Canavan, 227, 1001, 2050.
Britain, 161.	Buick. 182.	Caddle, 209.	Canaway, 325.
Briton, 161.	Buie, 141.	Caddoo, 210.	Cane, 971.
Britt, 158.	Bulger, 126.	Caddow, 210, 1236.	Caning, 228.
Brittain, 161.	Bulkeley, 180.	Cadell, 209.	Cannan, 229, 1030.
Brittan, 161.	Bulkely, 180.	Cadigan, 211.	Cannavan, 227.
Britton, 161.	Bulla, 184.	Cadogan, 211.	Cannaway, 299.
Broadhurst, 162.	Bullen, 183.	Cadoo, 210.	Canning, 228, 229, 398.
Brodders, 163.	Bullens, 183.	Caffary, 212.	Cannon, 228, 229, 398, 1030.
Broder, 163.	Buller, 184.	Cafferty, 1237.	Canon, 228.
Broderic, 163.	Bullion, 125, 142.	Caffery, 212, 1237.	Cantillon, 230.
Broderick, 163.	Bullman, 185.	Caffray, 212.	Cantlin, 230.
Brodie, 164.	Bulloch, 186.	Caffrey, 212, 261.	Cantlon, 230.
Brodrick, 163.	Bullock, 186.	Cahalan, 213.	Cantly, 231.
Brody, 164.	Bunting, 187.	Cahalin, 213.	Canty, 232.
Brofle, 167.	Bunton, 187.	Cahallane, 213.	Caorish, 89.
Broham, 170.	Bunyan, 188.	Cahan, 971, 995.	Capel, 233, 997.
Bronte, 165.	Burage, 199.	Cahane, 214, 996.	Caples, 233.
Brontie, 165.	Burbage, 189.	Caheerin, 215.	Cappack, 235.
Brooder, 163.	Burbidge, 189.	Cahelan, 213.	Capples, 234.
Brooke, 166.	Burch, 98.	Cahelin, 213.	Capplis, 234.
Brookes, 166.	Burchell, 190.	Cahillane, 213.	Cappock, 235.
Brookins, 166.	Burchill, 190.	Cahir, 216.	Cappuck, 235.
Brooks, 166.	Burdge, 93.	Cahoon, 305.	Caragher, 247.
Broom, 170.	Burge, 199.	Cahoun, 305.	Caraher, 247.
Broothers, 163.	Burges, 191.	Cahy, 1568.	Caraway, 236.
Brophy, 167.	Burgess, 191.	Caicey, 254.	Carberry, 237.
Broslin, 157.	Burgiss, 191.	Cain, 971, 974.	Carbery, 237.
Brosnahan, 168.	Burgoyne, 86.	Cainan, 983.	Carbry, 237.
Brosnahen, 168.	Burke, 192.	Cairdie, 1887.	Cardell, 238.
Brosnahin, 168.	Burkett, 193.	Cairn, 217.	Cardle, 238.
Brosnan, 168.	Burkitt, 193.	Cairnes, 217.	Cardwell, 238, 250.
Brosnihan, 168.	Burland, 130.	Cairns, 217, 976.	Carew, 239.
Brothers, 162.	Burleigh, 194.	Calaghan, 220.	Carey, 239, 402, 403.
Broughall, 169.	Burley, 172, 194.	Calahan, 220.	Carha, 1246.
Brougham, 170.	Burn, 206.	Calderwood, 218.	Carigan, 1003.
Broughill, 169.	Burnell, 195.	Caldwell, 219.	Carlan, 245.
Broune, 171.	Burnes, 206.	Calhoun, 305.	Carland, 245.
Browder, 163.	Burney, 1229.	Calinan, 223.	Carlaton, 240.
Brown, 171.	Burniston, 196.	Callaghan, 220, 988, 1643.	Carleton, 240.
Browne, 171.	Burns, 197, 206.	Callaghanan. 223.	Carley, 241.
Brownlee, 172, 173.	Burrage, 199.	Callaghen, 220.	Carlile, 241.
Brownlow, 172, 173.	Burrell, 198.	Callagher, 220, 665.	Carlin, 245.
Browster, 174.	Burridge, 199.	Callaghin, 220.	Carlisle, 241.
Bruce, 174.	Burriss, 200.	Callagy, 221.	Carlon, 245.
Bruder, 163.	Burroughs, 200.		
	Burrowes, 200.		

Surname and Reference No.	Surname and Reference No.	Surname and Reference No.	Surname and Reference No.
Carlton, 240.	Cavanagh, 261, 262, 972.	Clemens, 281.	Cohoon, 305.
Carlyle, 241.	Cavenagh. 972.	Clement, 281.	Cohoun, 305.
Carmody, 242.	Cavish. 909.	Clements, 281.	Coid, 1747.
Carnagie, 244.	Cawfield, 261.	Clenaghan, 1260.	Coiles, 352.
Carnahan, 1001.	Cawldwell, 219.	Clendenan, 282.	Coin, 353.
Carnduff, 243.	Cawley, 263, 1146.	Clendennin, 282.	Cokeley, 292.
Carneagy, 244.	Cawlin, 222.	Clendenning, 282.	Cokely, 292.
Carnegie, 244.	Cearnes, 976.	Clendining, 282.	Colavin, 219.
Carney, 975.	Ceary, 239.	Clendinning, 282.	Colborne, 294.
Carnohan. 1001.	Ceevney, 978.	Clerke, 275.	Colbourne, 294.
Carns, 976.	Chaddick, 264.	Clerkin, 275.	Colburne, 294.
Carny, 975.	Chadwick, 264.	Clery,. 277	Colclough, 292.
Carolan, 245.	Chalmers, 265.	Clibborn, 283.	Colcloughan, 299.
Carolin, 245.	Chambers, 265.	Clidesdale, 290.	Coldrick, 733.
Caroll, 250.	Chamley, 271.	Clifford, 284.	Coldwell, 219.
Carollan, 245.	Charthy, 253, 1644.	Climents, 281.	Cole, 301.
Carothers, 251.	Chaytor, 266.	Climons, 281.	Coleman, 302.
Carr, 246, 1002.	Cheator. 266.	Clinch, 285.	Coles, 301.
Carragher, 247.	Chesnaye, 267.	Clinchey, 285.	Colfield, 261.
Carraher, 247.	Chesney, 267.	Clindenning, 282.	Colgan, 303.
Carre, 246.	Chesnutt, 268.	Clindinnen, 282.	Colhoon, 305.
Carrick, 248, 355, 1802.	Chessnut. 268.	Cline, 1012.	Colhoun, 305.
Carrigan, 338, 1003.	Chestnutt, 268.	Clisdale, 290.	Coligan, 303.
Carrigee. 249.	Cheyne. 965.	Clitterdy, 287.	Colin, 299.
Carrigy, 249.	Chiddick, 264.	Cloney, 286.	Colins, 304, 392.
Carrinduff, 243.	Chisel, 270.	Clooney, 286.	Collagan, 303.
Carrithers. 251.	Chisham, 269.	Clotworthy, 287.	Collen, 392.
Carrolan, 245.	Chishem, 269.	Cloughry, 1029.	Collery, 275.
Carrolin, 245.	Chisholm, 269.	Clovan, 302.	Colleton, 393.
Carroll, 238. 250, 1244.	Chism, 269.	Cloven, 302.	Colligan, 303.
Carrolly, 250.	Chisom, 269.	Clowney, 286.	Collins, 304, 390, 392.
Carrothers, 251.	Chissell. 270.	Clowny, 286.	Collom, 299.
Carruthers, 251.	Choiseuil, 270.	Clugston, 288.	Colloton, 393.
Cartan, 252.	Choiseul, 270.	Clune, 286.	Collum, 306.
Carten, 252.	Cholmondeley. 271.	Cluney, 286.	Collumb, 306.
Carthy, 253, 1246.	Chomley, 271.	Clusby, 707.	Collwell, 219.
Cartin, 252, 1247.	Chooke, 1988.	Clusker, 289, 340, 1264.	Colman, 302.
Carton, 252, 253.	Choun, 305.	Cluskey, 289, 340, 1264.	Colnan, 314.
Carty, 252, 253, 1246, 1644.	Christian, 272.	Cluvane, 281.	Colomb, 306.
Caruthers, 251.	Christie, 272.	Cluxton, 288.	Colothan, 394.
Carvey, 236.	Christy, 272.	Clydesdale, 290.	Colovin, 219.
Carvin, 1035.	Chrysty, 272.	Clymens, 281.	Colquhoun, 222, 305, 392.
Carway, 677.	Chumley, 271.	Clymonds, 281.	Colquohoun, 305.
Casaday, 258.	Church, 12.	Clynch, 285.	Colreavy, 752.
Casey, 254.	Chute. 1987.	Clynes, 291.	Colter, 343.
Casheen, 255.	Cinamon, 273.	Clyns, 291.	Colum, 306.
Cashen, 255.	Cinamond, 273.	Clysdale, 290.	Columb, 306, 1265.
Cashin, 255.	Cingen, 1926.	Coade, 295.	Colvan. 307.
Cashion, 255.	Cinnamon. 273.	Coady, 296.	Colvil. 307.
Cashman, 1037.	Cinnamond, 273.	Coaghlan, 299.	Colville, 307.
Cashon, 255.	Clahane, 390.	Coakeley, 292.	Colvin, 307.
Casidy, 258.	Clairke, 275.	Coakley, 292.	Colwell, 219.
Caskey, 1220.	Clanchy, 274.	Coall, 301.	Coman, 311.
Casley, 258.	Clancy, 274.	Coalter, 343.	Comaskey, 309.
Cass, 256.	Clandinning, 282.	Coan, 300. 347, 2027.	Comba, 333.
Cassedy, 258.	Clarey, 277.	Cobourn, 294.	Comber, 1003.
Cassell, 257.	Clark, 275.	Cobram, 294.	Combes, 909.
Cassells, 257.	Clarke, 275, 277.	Coburn, 294.	Comer, 1003.
Cassian, 255.	Clarkins, 275.	Cochrane, 293, 334.	Comerford, 308, 309.
Cassiday, 258.	Classan, 276.	Cockbourne, 294.	Comerton, 308.
Cassidi, 258.	Classon, 276.	Cockburne, 294.	Comesky, 309.
Cassidy, 258.	Claussen, 276.	Cockrane, 293.	Comford, 308.
Cassin, 255.	Clausson, 276.	Codd, 295.	Comfort, 308.
Cassle, 257.	Claveen, 1947.	Code, 295.	Comiskey, 308, 309.
Cassles, 257.	Clawson, 276.	Cody, 34, 296, 388, 389.	Comjean, 397.
Cassy, 254.	Clayborne, 283.	Coe, 349.	Comjeens. 397.
Castle, 257.	Clayburn, 283.	Coen, 300.	Commane, 310, 311, 397, 937.
Castles, 257.	Clayton, 977.	Coffee, 297.	Commaskey, 308, 309.
Caterson, 260.	Cleary, 275, 277.	Coffey, 297.	Commefort, 308.
Cathcart, 259.	Cleaver, 278.	Cogan, 298, 727.	Commerford, 309.
Catherwood, 218.	Clebburn, 283.	Coghlan, 299.	Commins, 311, 397.
Catterson, 260.	Cleburne, 283.	Coghlen, 299.	Common, 311, 397.
Caughran, 293	Cleeland, 279, 280.	Coghlin, 299.	Commons, 310, 311, 396, 397.
Caughy, 1568.	Cleery, 277.	Coghran, 293.	Comyns, 397.
Cauldwell, 219.	Cleever, 278.	Cogley, 1751.	Conaghty, 312.
Caulfield, 212, 261, 262, 1404.	Clehane, 390.	Cohalane. 299.	Conall, 316.
Caulin, 222.	Cleland, 279, 280.	Cohane, 214, 996.	Conally, 319.
Cavan, 972.	Clelland, 280.	Cohen, 300, 347.	
	Clellond, 280.	Coholane, 299.	

Surname and Reference No.	Surname and Reference No.	Surname and Reference No.	Surname and Reference No.
Conary, 323.	Coonoon, 313.	Coursey, 434.	Creilly, 371.
Conaty, 312, 1267.	Cooper, 329. 350.	Courtayne, 406.	Creiton, 368.
Conderick, 993.	Copeland, 330.	Courtenay, 345:	Crelly, 371.
Condon, 313.	Copelton, 330.	Courteney, 344, 345.	Cremeen, 1246.
Condrick, 993.	Copland, 330.	Courtnay, 345.	Cremen, 369.
Condron, 313, 322.	Copleton, 330, 332.	Courtney, 344, 345.	Cremin, 369, 1246.
Coneely, 319.	Copperthwaite, 331.	Cousin, 346.	Cremor, 356.
Conelly, 319.	Copplestone, 332.	Cousine, 346.	Cribbin, 370. 762.
Coner, 320.	Corathers, 251.	Cousins, 346.	1477.
Conheeny, 1758.	Corban, 333.	Couvane, 972.	Cribbon, 370.
Conier, 320.	Corbett, 333.	Couzeens, 346.	Crichton, 368.
Conla, 314.	Corbin, 333.	Couzins, 346.	Crickard, 1475.
Conlan, 314, 317, 319.	Corbitt, 333.	Cowan, 300. 347, 995.	Crickenham, 400.
Conland, 314.	Corcoran, 293, 334.	Cowden, 318.	Cricket, 1475.
Conley, 317, 319.	Corcorin, 334.	Cowdie, 348.	Crigley, 372.
Conlin, 314, 317.	Cordan, 337,	Cowely, 263.	Crilly, 371.
Conlogue, 1271.	Corey, 339.	Cowen, 347, 995.	Crimmeen, 1246.
Conlon, 314, 317, 319.	Coribeen, 333.	Cowey, 349.	Cristy, 272.
Conly, 319.	Corish, 89.	Cowie, 349.	Critchley, 372.
Conmee, 325.	Corken, 334.	Cowley, 263.	Croake, 374.
Connaghton, 315.	Corkeran, 334.	Cowman, 311, 397.	Croan, 373.
Connally, 319.	Corkerry, 334.	Cowper, 329, 350.	Croghan, 373.
Connaly. 319.	Corkoran, 334.	Cowperthwaite, 331.	Crohan, 373.
Connaughton, 315, 1616.	Corkran, 334.	Cox. 351.	Croke, 374, 383.
Conneally, 319.	Corley, 401.	Coxe, 351.	Crolly, 375.
Connealy, 319.	Cormac, 1274.	Coyd, 1747.	Croly, 363, 375, 384.
Conneelly, 319.	Cormack, 335, 1274.	Coyle, 352.	Crombie, 1, 376.
Conneely, 319.	Cormican, 1274.	Coyne, 353, 1047.	Cromie, 1, 376.
Conneff, 318.	Cormick, 335. 1274.	Cra, 1164.	Crommie, 376.
Connell, 316, 317, 319,	Cormocan, 335.	Craan, 354.	Cromwell, 377.
1270, 1646.	Corn, 402.	Craford, 362.	Cronan, 378.
Connellan, 314, 316,	Corneen, 336.	Crage, 355.	Cronin, 378.
317, 319.	Corr, 404.	Cragh, 364.	Cronouge, 384.
Connelly, 316. 319,	Corra, 404, 2040.	Crahan, 354, 402.	Cronvy, 376.
1646.	Curran, 402.	Craig, 248, 355.	Cronyn, 378.
Connely, 319.	Corree, 404.	Craigan, 367.	Crook, 379.
Conner, 320.	Corridon, 337.	Craigh, 364, 1771.	Crookes, 379.
Connerney, 1388.	Corrie, 404.	Crain, 365.	Crooks, 379, 385.
Connerton, 315.	Corrigan, 338, 1003.	Cramer, 356.	Crookshanks, 380.
Connery, 324.	Corry, 339, 404.	Cramp, 358.	Crooks-Shanks, 380.
Conniff, 318, 320.	Cory, 323, 404.	Crampsey, 128, 357.	Crosbie, 381.
Connollan, 317.	Coscor, 340.	Crampsie, 128, 357.	Crosert, 385.
Connolly, 314, 316,	Cosgrave. 289, 340,	Crampsy, 128.	Crosgrave, 340.
317, 319.	1293.	Crampton, 358.	Crossan, 382, 1642.
Connoly, 319.	Cosgreave, 340.	Cramsie, 357.	Crossbie, 381.
Connor, 318, 320, 321,	Cosgreve, 340.	Cranay, 359.	Crossen, 382.
1647.	Cosgriff, 340.	Crane. 365, 402, 403.	Crossin, 382.
Connors, 320, 321,	Cosgrive, 340.	Cranny, 359.	Crosson, 382.
1647.	Cosgroove, 340.	Cransen, 360.	Crothers, 251.
Connorton. 315.	Cosgrove, 340, 1293.	Cranson, 360.	Crough, 374, 383.
Connoway. 325.	Coshman, 1037.	Cranston, 360.	Croughan, 373.
Conole, 319.	Cosker, 340.	Crany, 359.	Crowe, 374. 383.
Conolly, 319.	Coskeran, 340.	Crauford, 362.	Crowley, 363, 375, 384.
Conoly. 319.	Coskery, 340.	Craven, 361.	Crozert, 385.
Conoo, 325.	Coskerry, 340.	Cravin, 361.	Crozier, 379, 385.
Conors, 320.	Coss, 256.	Crawford, 362.	Cruice, 386.
Conotty, 312.	Cossgrove, 340.	Crawley, 363, 375, 384.	Cruickshanks, 380.
Conrahy, 323.	Costello, 341.	Crayford, 362.	Cruiks, 379.
Conran, 322.	Costellow, 341.	Creagh, 364.	Cruikshanks, 380.
Conree, 323.	Costelo, 341.	Creaghan, 365.	Cruise, 336.
Conroy, 323, 324. 1026.	Costillo, 341.	Creamer, 356.	Crully, 371.
Conry, 323, 324. 1026.	Costily, 341.	Crean, 365.	Crumley, 387.
Conway, 325.	Costley. 341.	Creane, 354.	Crumlish, 387.
Conwell, 219.	Costolloe, 341.	Creaney, 359.	Crummell, 377.
Conyeen, 983.	Costoloe, 341.	Creaton, 368.	Crummy, 376.
Conyer, 320.	Cotter. 342.	Creaven, 361.	Cudahey, 388.
Conyers, 320.	Coughlan, 299.	Creed, 366.	Cuddehy, 388.
Conyngham, 400.	Coughlen, 299.	Creedon, 366.	Cuddihy, 296, 388, 389.
Coogan, 298.	Coughlin, 299.	Creegan, 367.	Cuddy, 296, 888, 889.
Cook, 326.	Coulehan 327.,	Creeland, 279.	Cudihy, 388.
Cooke, 326.	Coulihan, 327.	Creely, 371.	Cue, 1376.
Cooken, 298.	Coulter, 343.	Creen, 365.	Cuggeen, 960.
Coolahan, 327.	Coumey, 328.	Creevey, 1569.	Cuhy, 994.
Coole, 352.	Counihan, 328, 400.	Cregan, 367.	Cuinane, 1750.
Coon, 400.	County, 232.	Cregg, 355, 1802.	Culbert, 411.
Coonaghan, 400.	Courcey, 434.	Creggan, 367.	Culgan, 303.
Coonahan, 328.	Courigan, 338.	Creghan, 367.	Culgin, 303.
Coonan, 328.	Courn, 402.	Crehan, 365.	Culhan, 392.
Cooney, 328.	Cournane. 344, 345.	Creigan, 367.	Culhane, 304, 390.
Coonihan, 328.	Courneen, 345.	Creighton, 368.	Culhoun, 305, 392.

Surname and Reference No.	Surname and Reference No.	Surname and Reference No.	Surname and Reference No.
Culkin, 391.	Curnane, 345.	Darling. 422. 423.	Delmege,443.
Cullan, 392.	Curneen, 336.	Darmody.456,457,1297.	Delmer, 440.
Cullanan, 394.	Curneene. 345.	Darra, 424.	Delohery, 444.
Cullane. 304.	Curnin. 336.	Darragh, 424, 1640.	Deloohery, 437, 444, 468.
Culle, 301.	Currain, 402.	Darrah, 424.	
Culleeny, 392.	Curran, 239, 354, 402, 403.	Darrock, 424.	Deloorey, 444, 468.
Cullen. 304, 305, 392, 394, 395, 1752.	Currane, 239, 402, 403.	Daugherty, 479.	Deloughery, 444.
Culleton, 393.	Curreen, 402.	Davane, 461.	Deloughry, 468.
Cullian, 304.	Curren, 402.	Davenport, 425.	Delouhery, 444.
Culligan, 303.	Currie, 404.	Daveson, 427,	Delouri, 444, 468.
Cullin, 392.	Currigan, 338, 1003.	Davidson, 426, 427.	Delury, 444.
Cullina, 304.	Currin, 402.	Davies, 426.	DeMoleyns, 1582.
Cullinan, 394.	Curry, 339, 404, 1278.	Davin, 461.	Dempsey, 445, 446.
Cullinane, 392.	Curtan, 406. 1276.	Davine, 461.	Dempster, 445, 446.
Cullington, 393.	Curtayne, 405, 406.	Davis, 426, 427, 429, 1295.	Demster, 446.
Culliny, 392.	Curteis, 407.	Davison, 426, 427, 1295.	Denahy, 451.
Cullion, 392.	Curten, 406.	Davisson, 427.	Denanny, 450.
Culliton, 393.	Curties, 407.	Davits, 428.	Denehan, 447.
Cullivan, 219.	Curtin, 405, 406.	Davitt, 428, 462.	Deneher, 447.
Culloon, 392.	Curtis, 407.	Davy, 426, 429.	Denehy. 451, 453.
Cully, 392, 395.	Cusac, 408.	Davys, 426.	Deney, 454.
Culnane, 394.	Cusack, 403.	Dawley, 414.	Deniffe, 448.
Culreavy, 752.	Cusco, 340.	Dawlin, 505.	Dening, 452.
Cumaskey, 309.	Cushanan, 410.	Dawly, 414.	Denis, 453.
Cumberford. 1290.	Cushen, 409.	Dawney, 478, 506, 1571.	Denison, 449, 453, 1299.
Cumesky, 309.	Cushing, 409.	Dawson, 430.	Dennahy, 451.
Cumin, 397.	Cushion, 409.	Dawtin, 413.	Dennan, 450.
Cuming, 396, 397.	Cushlane, 257.	Day, 431, 1648.	Dennany, 450.
Cumings, 397.	Cushley, 341.	Dayley, 414.	Dennehy, 416, 451, 454.
Cumins, 397.	Cushnahan, 410.	D'Aylmer, 48.	
Cumisk, 309.	Cusic. 408.	D'Courcy, 434.	Denning, 452, 467.
Cumisky. 309.	Cusick, 408.	Dea, 431.	Dennis, 449, 453.
Cummane, 310, 311.	Cusker, 340.	Dealy, 414.	Dennismore, 470.
Cummens, 397.	Cuskern, 1293.	Dean, 432.	Denny, 451, 454.
Cummerford. 303.	Cuskery, 310.	Deane, 432.	Denroche, 455.
Cummin, 396.	Cuskor, 340.	Deanie, 454.	Densmore, 470.
Cumming, 311, 396, 397,	Cussac, 408.	Deans, 432.	Densmuir, 470.
	Cussack, 408.	De Blacquiere, 107.	Denson, 453.
Cummings, 311, 396, 397.	Cussane, 1699.	Debois, 433.	Denys, 453.
	Cussen, 346, 409.	Debouerdieu, 518.	Derbyshire, 419.
Cummins, 310, 311, 396, 397. 1529.	Cussick, 408.	Deboys, 433.	Dergan, 421.
	Cutbert, 411.	De Courcy, 434.	Derham, 535.
Cummiskey. 309.	Cuthbert, 411.	Deegan, 435, 522.	Dermid, 457.
Cunagum, 400.	Cuthbertson, 411.	Deehan, 465.	Dermody, 456, 457, 1297.
Cuneen, 399, 1758.		Deely, 414.	
Cuniam, 400.		Deemster, 446.	Dermond, 1297.
Cuniff, 318.		Deen, 432.	Dermoody, 456.
Cunihan, 399.	Daily, 414.	Deens, 432.	Dermott, 456, 457, 1297·
Cuningham, 400.	Dalhouse, 412.	DeErmot, 1297.	D'Ermott, 457.
Cunion, 399.	Dallas, 412.	Deérmott. 1297.	Dermoty, 457.
Cunlick. 1754.	Dalton, 413.	Deevey, 436, 459.	Derow, 442.
Cunnagher, 967.	Daly, 414.	Deffely, 466.	Devane, 458, 461.
Cunnahan, 400.	Dalzell 415.	Deheny, 478.	Devann, 458.
Cunnaim, 1750.	Dalziell, 415.	Dehorty, 479.	Devanny, 458.
Cunnane, 228, 229, 398, 399, 1750, 1758.	Danagher, 416.	Deighan, 435, 465.	Devanport, 425.
	Danaher, 416, 451.	Deignan, 524.	Devany, 458, 461.
Cunnea, 1755.	Danahy, 451.	Delacherois, 437, 444.	Deveen, 461.
Cunnean. 399.	Dane, 432.	Delahide. 438.	Develin, 463.
Cunneely, 319.	Danger, 46.	Delahoyde, 438.	D'Evelyn, 463.
Cunneen, 398, 399, 1758.	Daniel, 417, 485, 1652.	Delahunt, 439.	Deven, 461.
	Daniells, 417.	Delahunty, 439.	Devenny, 458.
Cunneeny, 399, 1758.	Daniels, 417.	Delamar, 440.	Deveny, 458.
Cunniam. 400, 1642.	Daniher, 416.	Delamere, 440.	Devereux, 436, 459.
Cunnien, 399.	Danihy, 451.	Delamore, 440.	Deverill, 436, 459.
Cunniffe, 318.	Danly, 485.	Delane, 441.	Devers, 460.
Cunnigan, 400.	Dannaher, 416.	Delaney, 441.	Devery, 436, 459.
Cunnighan, 400.	Dannahy, 451.	Delap, 529.	Devett, 428.
Cunningham, 400.	Dannelly, 487.	Delaroe, 442.	Devin, 461.
Cunnion, 399, 1758.	Danniel, 417.	Delay, 527.	Devine, 458, 461, 1650.
Cunnoo, 325.	Danniell, 417.	Delea, 527.	Devinney, 458.
Cunny, 1755.	Daragh, 424.	Deleany, 441.	Devitt, 428, 462.
Cunnyer, 320.	Darah, 424.	Delemar, 440.	Devlin, 463.
Cunnyngham, 400.	Darbishire, 419.	Deleney, 441.	Devon, 461.
Cunree, 323.	Darby, 418, 1297.	Delhunty, 439.	Devonport, 425.
Cunreen, 1026.	Darbyshire, 419.	D'Ell, 415.	Dewane, 517.
Cunvane, 1750.	Darcy, 420.	Dellunty, 439.	De Yermond, 1297.
Cuolohan, 327.	D'Arcy, 420.	Delmage, 443.	Deyermott, 1297.
Curby, 411.	Dargan,421.		Diamond, 464.
Curley. 401.	Darley, 422, 423.		Diarmid, 457, 1297.

Surname and Reference No.	Surname and Reference No.	Surname and Reference No.	Surname and Reference No.
Diarmod, 1297.	Donaghoe, 488.	Dougheny, 478, 522.	Dulinty, 439.
Diarmond, 1297.	Donaghy, 481, 488, 526, 1299.	Dougherty, 479.	Dullea, 527.
Dickson, 465.	Donahoe, 482, 488.	Doughney, 478.	Dullenty, 439.
Diermott, 457, 1297.	Donahy, 488.	Douglas, 497.	Dumegan, 483.
Diffen, 461.	Donald, 485, 1301.	Dougle, 496, 497.	Dumphy, 531.
Diffley, 466.	Donaldson, 487.	Dougs, 497.	Dun, 530.
Diffily, 466.	Donegan, 483, 526.	Douie, 503.	Duncan, 481, 483, 526.
Digan, 435.	Donelan, 486.	Dowd, 490, 498, 1654.	Dune, 517.
Dignam, 524.	Donellan, 484.	Dowda, 498.	Dunfy, 531.
Dignan, 524.	Donellon, 486.	Dowdall, 499, 505.	Dungan, 483, 526.
Digunan, 524.	Donelly, 487.	Dowdell, 499.	Dunican, 526.
Dillane, 467.	Donelon, 484, 486.	Dowdican, 500.	Dunigan, 483.
Dillion, 467.	Donely, 487.	Dowdle, 499.	Dunion, 452.
Dillon, 452, 467.	Dongan, 483.	Dowds, 476, 498.	Dunkin, 526.
Dilloughery, 444, 468.	Donigan, 483.	Dowell, 501, 1302.	Dunlap, 529.
Dillury, 444.	Donlan, 484, 486, 487.	Dower, 502.	Dunlavy, 528.
Dillworth, 468.	Donlon, 484, 486, 487.	Dowey, 503.	Dunlea, 527.
Dilworth, 444, 468.	Donly, 487.	Dowie, 503.	Dunleavy, 528.
Dimmett, 84.	Donnal, 485.	Dowlan, 505.	Dunleevy, 528.
Dimond, 464.	Donnallon, 484.	Dowler, 504.	Dunlevy, 528.
Dineen, 469.	Donnelly, 487.	Dowley, 505.	Dunlop, 529.
Dingavan, 489.	Donnegan, 483.	Dowlin, 505.	Dunne, 530.
Dinkin, 526.	Donnelan, 484.	Dowling, 480, 491, 499, 505.	Dunnegan, 483.
Dinneen, 530.	Donnell, 417, 485, 486, 487, 1301, 1652.	Downey, 478, 506.	Dunnigan, 483.
Dinnegan, 483.	Donellan, 484, 485, 486, 487.	Downing, 506.	Dunphy, 531.
Dinnis, 453.	Donnellon, 484, 486.	Doyle, 507.	Dunroche, 455.
Dinsmore, 470.	Donnelly, 484, 485, 486, 487.	Drain, 10.	Dunseath, 532.
Diurmagh, 1297.	Donnelon, 486.	Draiper, 508.	Dunseeth, 532.
Divane, 461, 517.	Donnely, 487.	Draper, 508.	Dunseith, 532.
Diveen, 461.	Donnollan, 484.	Dreaper, 508.	Dunsheath, 532.
Divenney, 458.	Donnolly, 487.	Dredlincourt, 509.	Dunshee, 532.
Diver, 460.	Donocho, 488.	Dreinan, 1958.	Dunsheith, 532-
Divin, 461.	Donogh, 1299.	Drelincourt, 509.	Dunsmoor, 470.
Divine, 461.	Donoghoe, 488.	Drelingcourt, 509.	Duplex, 533.
Diviney, 458, 471.	Donoghue, 483.	Drellingcourt, 509.	Dupré, 534.
Divitt, 428.	Donohoe, 482, 488.	Drennan, 510, 512.	Dupri, 534.
Dixon, 465.	Donohogue, 488.	Drew, 511.	Durcan, 536.
D.L., 415.	Donohue, 531.	Drewry, 516.	Durham, 535.
D'Lamour, 440.	Donoughoo, 488.	Drillingcourt, 509.	Durkan, 536.
Doag, 472.	Donovan, 489, 1653.	Drinan, 510, 512, 1958.	Durkin, 536.
Doake, 472.	Dooal, 507.	Drinane, 1958.	Durmody, 1297.
Dobbin, 473.	Dooan, 517.	Driscall, 513.	Durnian, 495.
Dobbins, 473.	Doocy, 521.	Driscoll, 513, 913, 1655.	Durnion, 452.
Dobbyn, 473.	Doody, 490, 498.	Drisdale, 514.	Durrian, 430.
Dobbyns, 473.	Dooey, 503, 521.	Drisdell, 514.	Duval, 471.
Dobin, 473.	Doogan, 522.	Driskell, 513.	Duvalley, 471.
Dockeray, 474.	Dooherty, 479.	Driskill, 513.	Duvick, 459.
Dockery, 474.	Dooladdy, 441.	Driskol, 513.	Dwain, 517.
Dockrall, 475.	Doolady, 441.	Drough, 511.	Dwan, 517.
Dockray, 474.	Doolan, 480, 491, 505.	Drumm, 515.	Dwane, 517.
Dockrell, 475.	Doole, 501.	Drummond, 515.	Dwann, 458.
Dockrill, 475.	Doolen, 491, 505.	Drummy, 515.	Dwire, 537.
Dockry, 474.	Dooler, 504.	Drury, 516.	Dwyer, 537, 1567.
Docy, 521.	Dooley, 492.	Drysdale, 514.	Dwyre, 537.
Dodd, 476.	Doolin, 491, 505.	Duan, 517.	Dyermott, 1297.
Dodds, 476.	Dooling, 491, 505.	Duane, 517.	Dygnam, 524.
Dodgson, 477.	Dooly, 480, 492, 505.	Dublack, 533.	Dyle, 507.
Dods, 476.	Doomster, 446.	Du Boudieu, 518.	Dymond, 464.
Dodson, 477.	Doona, 506.	Du Bourdieu, 518.	Dynan, 469.
Dogheny, 478.	Doonican, 526.	Dubowdieu, 518.	Dyrham, 535.
Dogherty, 479.	Doorly, 520.	Ducklow, 525.	
Dohenny, 478.	Doorty, 479.	Dudican, 500.	
Doheny, 478, 522.	Doran, 493, 494, 495.	Duff, 104, 519, 521.	
Doherty, 479, 1651.	Dorcey, 420.	Dufferly, 520.	
Dohoney, 478.	Dore, 502.	Duffin, 519.	
Dohorty, 479.	Dorian, 493, 494.	Duffley, 466.	
Doig, 472.	Dornan, 493, 495.	Duffy, 519, 521, 1656.	Eaddy, 9.
Doil, 507.	Dorran, 493, 494.	Dugald, 496.	Eaden, 543.
Dolan, 480, 491, 492, 505.	Dorrian, 493, 494.	Dugan, 522.	Eadens, 543.
Dolmage, 443.	Doud, 498, 1654.	Duggan, 435, 478, 522.	Eadie, 7, 538.
Dolmege, 443.	Doudall, 499.	Duggen, 522.	Eady, 9.
Dolmidge, 443.	Douds, 476.	Duhig, 523.	Eagan, 547.
Dologhan, 467.	Douey, 503.	Duhy, 523.	Eagar, 11, 539.
Dolohunty, 439.	Dougall, 496.	Duigan, 435, 524.	Eagars, 539.
Domegan, 483.	Dougan, 522.	Duigenan, 524.	Eagen, 547.
Donagan, 483.	Doughan, 522.	Duignam, 524.	Eager, 539.
Donagh, 481.		Duignan, 524.	Eagers, 539.
Donaghey, 451, 481, 1299.		Dukelow, 525.	Eagerton, 865.
		Dulanty, 439.	Eagleson, 542.
			Eagleston, 542.

Surname and Reference No.	Surname and Reference No.	Surname and Reference No.	Surname and Reference No.
Eaken, 15.	Entwisle, 562.	Faragher, 583.	Fenaughty. 611.
Eakin, 15, 547.	Entwissle, 562.	Faraher, 583.	Fendlon, 595.
Eakins, 15.	Entwistle, 562.	Faran, 586.	Fenelly, 597.
Early. 1126.	Enwright, 561.	Fare, 1718.	Fenelon, 595.
Easdale, 953.	Erought, 827.	Farelly, 585.	Fenley, 597, 607.
Easping, 103.	Errington, 563, 827.	Faren, 586, 590.	Fenlon, 595.
Eaton, 540.	Erskin, 39.	Farghar, 582.	Fennell, 596.
Eccles, 541.	Erskine, 564.	Farguson, 599.	Fennelly, 597, 607.
Eccleson, 542.	Ervine. 950.	Fargy, 599.	Fenning, 578.
Eccleston, 542.	Erwin, 950, 951.	Farin, 586.	Fenoughty, 598.
Eckles, 541.	Esbal, 35.	Faris, 601.	Fenton, 598.
Eden, 543.	Esbald, 35.	Farker, 582.	Feoghney, 598.
Edens, 543.	Esball, 35.	Farley, 579, 585.	Feran, 590.
Edery, 1780.	Esbel, 35.	Farmer, 580.	Fergie, 599.
Edgar. 544.	Esbil, 35.	Farnan, 581.	Fergison, 599.
Edgerton, 548.	Esble, 35.	Farnand, 581.	Fergisson, 599.
Edimson, 8.	Esdale, 33, 953.	Farnham, 581.	Ferguison, 599.
Edmond, 545.	Esdel, 953.	Farnon. 586.	Fergus, 599.
Edmonds, 545.	Esmonde, 545.	Farquehar, 582.	Ferguson, 599.
Edmondson, 546.	Esnor, 18.	Farquer, 582.	Fergusson, 599.
Edmonson, 546.	Eubank, 2005.	Farquhar, 582.	Feris, 601.
Edmonston, 546.	Eurell, 2091.	Farquharson, 582.	Ferly, 579, 585.
Edmunds, 545.	Eustace, 565.	Farquher, 582.	Fern, 590.
Edmundson, 546.	Eustice, 565.	Farragher, 583.	Ferns, 1787.
Edmunson, 546.	Evans, 566.	Farraher. 583.	Feron, 590.
Edmunstone, 546.	Evanson, 567.	Farrahill. 583.	Ferrall, 584, 585.
Edy, 9.	Evart, 569.	Farrally, 585.	Ferran, 586.
Edye, 9.	Evens, 566.	Farran, 586.	Ferrar, 587.
Egan, 547, 782, 980.	Evenson, 567.	Farrell, 584, 585, 1658.	Ferrer. 587.
Egar, 539.	Everard, 568.	Farrelly, 579, 584, 585.	Ferrers, 587.
Egerton, 548.	Everett, 568.	Farrely, 585.	Ferrier, 600.
Eggleston, 542.	Everitt, 568.	Farren, 586.	Ferris, 601, 655.
Egglinton, 549.	Evers, 954.	Farrer, 587.	Ferry, 601.
Egleson, 542.	Evins, 566.	Farris, 601.	Ferryar, 600.
Egleston, 542.	Evoy, 1320.	Farron, 586.	Ferryer. 600.
Eglington, 549.	Ewart, 569.	Farshin, 642, 1246.	Fetherston, 602.
Eglinton, 549.	Ewbank, 2005.	Faucet, 588.	Fetherston H., 602.
Eglintoun, 549.	Eykin, 15.	Faughton, 2045.	Fetherstonhaugh,
Egnew, 13.	Eyre, 570.	Faulkener, 574.	602.
Eirons, 949.		Faulkner, 574.	Fey, 589.
Eivers, 954.		Faulkney, 574.	Ffennell, 596.
Ekin, 15.		Fausit, 588.	Ffinch, 606.
Elchinder, 18.		Fausset, 588.	Ffolliott, 603.
Elderdice, 17.		Faux, 643.	Ffrench, 652.
Eldred, 550.		Fawcet, 588.	Fidgeon, 1368, 1725.
Elfred, 556.		Fawcett, 588.	Fie, 589.
Eliot, 552.	Fagan, 571, 1322.	Fay. 589.	Field, 604.
Ellard, 49.	Faggy, 1322.	Fayly, 591.	Fields, 604.
Ellies, 553.	Faghy, 572.	Fayre, 1718.	Fife, 605.
Elliffe, 551.	Fagin, 571.	Feagan, 571.	Fihily, 591.
Elliott, 552.	Faherty, 626.	Feagon, 571.	Filbin, 1721.
Ellis, 553.	Fahy, 572.	Fealan, 1719.	Filcher, 614.
Ellison, 21, 554.	Fair, 1718.	Fealey, 591.	Filson, 1723.
Ellot, 552.	Faircloth, 573.	Fealy, 574, 591.	Finalay, 607.
Ellsmere, 555.	Fairclough, 573.	Fearen, 590.	Finamore, 609.
Ellsmoor, 555.	Fairis, 601.	Fearn, 590.	Finch, 606.
Ellsmore, 555.	Fairleigh, 579.	Fearon, 590.	Findlay, 607.
Ellwood, 556, 2075.	Fairley, 579.	Feary, 593.	Findley, 607.
Ellyett, 552.	Fairtclough, 573.	Featherston, 602.	Finelly, 597.
Elmer, 48.	Fairtlough, 573.	Fee, 589.	Finerty, 611.
Elshander, 18.	Fairy, 601.	Feeharry, 619.	Finigan, 610.
Elshinder, 18.	Falchenor, 574.	Feehely, 591.	Finlay, 597, 607.
Elshner, 18.	Falconder, 574.	Feehery, 593.	Finley, 607.
Elward, 49.	Falconer, 574.	Feehily, 591.	Finn, 608.
Elwood, 556, 2075.	Falkender, 574.	Feeley, 591.	Finnally, 607.
Elyot, 552.	Falkener, 574.	Feely, 591.	Finnamore, 609.
Emberson, 557.	Falkiner, 574.	Feeney, 592.	Finnamure, 609.
Emerson, 557.	Falkner, 574.	Fegan, 571.	Finne, 608.
Emmerson, 557.	Fallaher, 577.	Feghan, 571.	Finnegan, 610.
Emmett, 558.	Fallen, 575.	Feghany, 594, 935.	Finnell, 596.
Emmit, 558.	Fallin. 575.	Fehely, 591.	Finnelly, 597, 607.
Emo, 1857.	Fallon, 575, 576.	Fehily, 591.	Finnemor. 609.
English, 559, 729, 947.	Falloon, 575, 576.	Fehoney, 935.	Finnerty, 611.
Englishby, 948.	Faloon, 576.	Feighan, 571, 593.	Finnigan, 610.
Ennes, 560.	Faloona, 576.	Feighery, 593, 594, 935.	Finning, 578.
Ennis, 560.	Falvey, 577.	Feighney, 593, 594, 935.	Finnucane, 612.
Enniss, 560.	Fannin, 578.	Feighry, 594, 935.	Finny, 592.
Enraght, 561.	Fanning, 578.	Felan, 1719.	Firman, 613, 1711.
Enright, 561.	Fannon, 578.	Feley. 1479.	Firmin, 613.
Entwhistle, 562.	Faraday, 599.	Fenaghty, 598.	Fisher, 614.

Surname and Reference No.	Surname and Reference No.	Surname and Reference No.	Surname and Reference No.
Fitch, 622, 623.	Forbish, 638.	Fullerton, 659.	Garveagh, 677.
Fitchpatrick, 622.	Ford-M'Anare, 639.	Furey, 660.	Garven, 677. 678, 718.
Fitsimmons, 623.	Forde, 639.	Fury, 660.	Garvey, 677, 678.
Fitsimons, 623.	Forehan, 637.	Fylan, 1719.	Garvin, 677, 678.
Fitsommons, 623.	Forehane, 637.	Fyland, 661, 1719.	Garwin, 678.
Fitsummons, 623.	Forgay, 599.	Fye, 589.	Gasson, 681.
Fitz, 617, 622, 623.	Forgey, 599.	Fyfee, 605.	Gath, 679.
Fitzallen, 615.	Forgie, 599.		Gattins, 1338.
Fitzalleyn, 615.	Forgy, 599.		Gaughan, 690.
Fitzallwyn, 615.	Forhan, 637.		Gaughney, 662.
Fitzalwyn, 615.	Forhane, 639.		Gault, 680.
Fitzell, 616.	Forker, 582.		Gaussen, 681.
Fitzerald, 617.	Forkin, 732.	Gaddiss, 686.	Gausslin, 740.
Fitzgerald, 617.	Forrester, 640.	Gaff, 679.	Gaut, 680.
Fitzgerrald, 617.	Forsayeth, 641.	Gaffikan, 682.	Gavacan, 682.
Fitzgibbon, 618, 695.	Forsithe, 641.	Gaffikin, 682.	Gavagan, 682.
Fitzharris, 619, 620.	Forster, 640.	Gaffiny, 662.	Gavahan, 683.
Fitzhenry, 619, 620.	Forsythe, 641.	Gaffney, 662.	Gavan, 683.
Fitzimmons, 623.	Fortune, 612, 1246.	Gafiney, 662.	Gaven, 683.
Fitzmaurice, 621, 1556.	Fossitt, 588.	Gafney, 662.	Gavigan, 682, 690, 1368.
Fitzmorice, 621.	Foster, 640.	Gagan, 690.	Gavin, 667, 683.
Fitzmorris, 621.	Foulkard, 574.	Gahagan, 690.	Gay, 700.
Fitzpatrick, 622.	Fourhane, 637.	Gahan, 663, 1670.	Gaynard, 684.
Fitzsimmons, 623.	Fourker, 582.	Gainer, 684, 1343.	Gaynor, 684, 1343.
Fitzsimon, 623.	Foursides, 641.	Gairlan, 674.	Geagan, 690.
Fitzsimons, 623, 1884.	Fox, 643, 1859.	Gaitens, 1338.	Geanor, 684.
Fitzsummons, 623.	Foxe, 643.	Galagher, 665.	Gearn, 1862.
Fitzsumons, 623.	Foy, 572, 589.	Galavan, 667.	Gearns, 1862.
Fizell, 616.	Frackletin, 644.	Galavin, 667.	Gearon, 768.
Flack, 624.	Frackleton, 644.	Galbraith, 664.	Gearty, 692.
Fladger, 631.	Frain, 647.	Galbreath, 664.	Geary, 685.
Flagherty, 626.	Frainy, 651.	Galesby, 707.	Geddes, 686.
Flahavan, 625.	Fraisor, 648.	Gallagher, 665.	Geddis, 686.
Flahavin, 625.	Fraizer, 648.	Gallaher, 665.	Gee, 687, 1158, 1335.
Flaherty, 626, 1659.	Fraizor, 648.	Gallaugher, 665.	Geehan, 663.
Flahevan, 625.	Frakleton, 644.	Galletlie, 688.	Geffeken, 682.
Flahy, 627, 1052.	Frane, 647.	Galligan, 666, 690, 708,	Gegan, 690.
Flanagan, 628, 1660.	Franklin, 645.	2049.	Geghan, 690.
Flang, 628.	Franklyn, 645.	Galliher, 665.	Gehegan, 690.
Flanigan, 628.	Frany, 651.	Gallihur, 665.	Gelaspy, 707.
Flannagan, 628.	Fraser, 648.	Gallivan, 667.	Gelland, 709.
Flannigan, 628.	Frawley, 646.	Gallogher, 665.	Gellespey, 707.
Flatholy, 629.	Frayne, 647.	Gallogly, 948.	Gelletlie, 688.
Flattley, 629.	Frazer, 648.	Gallougher, 665.	Gelshinan, 713.
Flavahan, 625.	Frazor, 648.	Galloway, 668.	Gelson, 689.
Flavin, 625.	Freal, 653.	Gallway, 668.	Gelston, 689.
Fleck, 624.	Freckleton, 644.	Galston, 689.	Gennagh, 1400.
Fleens, 633.	Free, 650.	Galt, 680.	Geogan, 690.
Fleming, 630.	Freebairn, 649.	Galvan, 667.	Geoghan, 690.
Flemming, 630.	Freebern, 649.	Galven, 667.	Geoghegan, 666, 690,
Flemmyng, 630.	Freebirn, 649.	Galvin, 667, 683.	1368.
Flemon, 630.	Freeburn, 649.	Galway, 668.	Geoghery, 691.
Flemyng, 630.	Freel, 653.	Galwey, 668.	Geon, 1404.
Fletcher, 631.	Freeman, 650.	Gambell, 669.	Geraghty, 692.
Fleury, 660.	Freeny, 651.	Gamble, 669.	Gerard, 693.
Flinn, 633.	Frehily, 646.	Gamel, 669.	Gerarty, 692, 872.
Flood, 632.	Frein, 647.	Gammel, 669.	Gerathy, 692.
Floody, 632.	Frekleton, 644.	Ganly, 670.	Geraty, 692.
Floyd, 632.	French, 652.	Gannon, 229.	Geraughty, 692.
Flyng, 633.	Freny, 651.	Gantly, 670.	Gerdan, 966.
Flynn, 633.	Friar, 656.	Gaphney, 662.	Gerety, 692.
Foard, 639.	Friary, 1741.	Gara, 671, 677.	Gerity, 692.
Fodaghan, 1945.	Frickelton, 644.	Garahan, 675.	Geroughty, 692.
Fodha, 1117.	Frickleton, 644.	Garahy, 692.	Gerraghty, 692.
Fogarty, 634, 1945.	Friel, 653.	Gardiner, 672.	Gerrard, 693.
Fogaton, 634, 1945.	Frier, 656.	Gardner, 672.	Gerret, 693.
Fogerty, 634.	Frisell, 654.	Gargan, 673.	Gertey, 692.
Foley, 635, 1479.	Frizell, 654.	Garity, 692.	Gerty, 692.
Folliett, 603.	Frizelle, 654.	Garland, 674.	Gervais, 694.
Folliott, 603.	Frizzel, 654.	Garner, 672.	Gervaise, 963.
Foody, 1945.	Frizzell, 654.	Garraghan, 675.	Gervase, 963.
Fooley, 635.	Frizzle, 648, 654.	Garratt, 676.	Gervis, 694, 963.
Fooluiah, 635.	Fry, 601, 655.	Garrett, 676.	Gery, 685.
Foorde, 639.	Fryarr, 656.	Garrigan, 673.	Ghagan, 690.
Foot, 636.	Fryer, 656.	Garrity, 692.	Ghee, 687.
Foote, 636.	Fudge, 657.	Garron, 716.	Ghegan, 690.
Foots, 636.	Fuge, 657.	Garry, 1334.	Ghelson, 689.
Foran, 637.	Fulham, 658.	Gartlan, 674.	Gheraty, 692.
Forbes, 638.	Fullam, 658.	Gartland, 674.	Gibben, 695.
Forbis, 638.	Fullarton, 659.	Gartlin, 674.	Gibbings, 695.

Surname and Reference No.	Surname and Reference No.	Surname and Reference No.	Surname and Reference No.
Gibbins, 695.	Ginnel, 684.	Goonan, 776.	Gribbin, 762.
Gibbon, 618, 695.	Girvin, 716.	Goonane, 776.	Gribbon, 762.
Gibbons, 618, 695.	Gissane, 1037.	Goonery, 1546.	Grier, 757.
Gibney, 696.	Gittings, 717.	Gooney, 776.	Grieves, 751.
Giboney, 696.	Gittons, 717.	Goonry, 1546.	Griffen, 763.
Gibsey, 697.	Givan, 718.	Gordon, 787.	Griffeth, 764.
Gibson, 697.	Giveen, 718.	Gorey, 777.	Griffey, 763.
Gibulawn, 697.	Given, 678, 718.	Gorman, 738, 739, 1662,	Griffin, 762, 763, 764.
Gifford, 958.	Givin, 718.	Gormley, 738, 739, 765.	Griffins, 763.
Gifney, 662.	Glan, 719, 1353	Gorry, 777.	Griffith, 763, 764.
Gilbey, 698.	Glancy, 274.	Goslin, 740.	Griffiths, 764.
Gilbraith, 664.	Glanders, 1059.	Gossan, 681.	Griffy, 763.
Gilbreath, 664.	Glanfield, 719.	Gosselin, 740.	Grimes, 739, 747, 759,
Gilchreest, 699.	Glanny, 722.	Gosson, 681.	765.
Gilchriest, 699.	Glanville, 719.	Gostlin, 740.	Grimley, 766.
Gilchrist, 699, 1124.	Glashby, 707.	Goudy, 745.	Grinlaw, 755.
Gilcrest, 699.	Glaspy, 707.	Gough, 741.	Grinlee, 756.
Gilcriest, 699.	Glavin, 667.	Gould, 742.	Grinlees, 756.
Gilcrist, 699.	Glazier, 720.	Goulding, 730, 732,	Grism, 760.
Gildea, 700.	Gleason, 721.	1354.	Grissam, 760.
Gildowny, 506.	Gleasure, 720.	Gouldrick, 733, 1354.	Grissom, 760.
Gilelin, 709.	Gleazer, 720.	Gouldsberry, 743.	Grogan, 767.
Giles, 701.	Gleeson, 721.	Gouldsbury, 743.	Groggan, 767.
Gilfillan, 702.	Glendinning, 282.	Gouldy, 731.	Gronel, 1789.
Gilfilland, 702.	Glenn, 723.	Goulrick, 733.	Groogan, 767.
Gilfoye, 771.	Glennon, 723.	Gow, 1897.	Grozet, 385.
Gilfoyle, 771.	Glenny, 722.	Gowan, 744, 1358, 1897.	Grumley, 766.
Gilgan, 708.	Glessane, 721.	Gowdy, 745.	Grummell, 377.
Gilgunn, 775.	Glinn, 723.	Gowen, 728, 744.	Guare, 1370.
Gilhool, 703.	Glissane, 721.	Gowing, 728.	Gubby, 473.
Gilhooley, 703	Glissawn, 721.	Graddy, 746.	Guckian, 780.
Gilis, 710.	Glynn, 723, 1353.	Grady, 746, 1663.	Guerin, 753, 768.
Gilkeson, 704.	Gna, 1400.	Graeme, 747.	Guicken, 780.
Gilkie, 1896.	Goan, 1897.	Graham, 747, 765.	Guider, 769.
Gilkieson, 704.	Gobin, 695.	Grame, 747.	Guidera, 769.
Gilkinson, 704.	Godsil, 724.	Grames, 747.	Guidra, 769.
Gilkison, 704.	Godson, 724, 734.	Grandfield, 749.	Guigan, 1368.
Gilkisson, 704.	Godwin, 725, 1648.	Granfill, 749.	Guighan, 770.
Gill, 705.	Goff, 741.	Granny, 748.	Guihan, 770.
Gillan, 709.	Gogan, 727.	Grant, 748.	Guiheen, 770, 2086.
Gilland, 709.	Gogarty, 726.	Granville, 749.	Guihen, 770, 2086.
Gillas, 710.	Gogerty, 726.	Grattan, 750.	Guiken, 770.
Gillaspy, 707.	Goggan, 727.	Gratten, 750.	Guilavan, 1936.
Gillbee, 1661.	Goggin, 298, 727.	Grattin, 750.	Guilchrist, 699.
Gilleland, 709.	Goggins, 727.	Gravell, 761.	Guilfoyle, 771, 1735.
Gillen, 706, 1017.	Gogin, 727.	Graves, 751.	Guilliland, 709.
Gilles, 710.	Gohary, 691.	Gray, 752.	Guilmartin, 711, 1020.
Gillesby, 707.	Going, 728, 1897.	Gready, 1663.	Guina, 1400.
Gillespie, 707.	Golagley, 559, 729.	Greaham, 747.	Guinan, 772.
Gilletlie, 688.	Golden, 730, 732, 733,	Greames, 747.	Guinane, 772, 1030.
Gillgan, 666.	1162, 1354.	Greaves, 751.	Guinea, 773.
Gilliard, 705.	Goldie, 731, 732.	Green, 753, 754, 768,	Guinevan, 227.
Gilligan, 666, 708.	Golding, 730, 731, 732.	1350.	Guiney, 773.
Gillilan, 709.	Goldrick, 730, 733.	Greenan, 753.	Guinna, 1400.
Gilliland, 709.	Goldsberry, 743.	Greenaway, 753, 754.	Guinnaty, 715.
Gillis, 710.	Goldsbury, 743.	Greene, 753.	Guinness, 774, 1369.
Gillispie, 707.	Golesbery, 743.	Greenhaigh, 754.	Guiny, 773.
Gillmore, 712.	Goligher, 665.	Greenhay, 754.	Guiry, 685.
Gillooly, 703.	Gollagher, 665.	Greenlaw, 755.	Gullion, 706.
Gillowly, 703.	Golliher, 665.	Greenlee, 756.	Guning, 776.
Gillpatrick, 1021.	Gollocher, 665.	Greenlees, 756.	Gunn, 775.
Gilmartin, 711, 1020.	Gollogher, 665.	Greenvil, 749.	Gunner, 775.
Gilmer, 712.	Golloher, 665.	Greenway, 754.	Gunning, 776
Gilmore, 712.	Golloway, 668.	Greer, 757.	Gunshinan, 713.
Gilmour, 712.	Gology, 559.	Gregg, 758.	Gurdan, 966.
Gilooly, 703.	Goloher, 665.	Greham, 747.	Gurry, 777.
Gilroy, 1022.	Golsberry, 743.	Grehan, 759, 765.	Gutherie, 778.
Gilsenan, 713, 1639.	Gomory, 1546.	Greig, 758.	Guthrie, 778, 1052.
Gilsenon, 713.	Gonoude, 325.	Greir, 757.	Guttery, 778.
Gilshenan, 713, 1639.	Goodison, 734.	Grene, 753.	Gwyn, 779.
Gilshenon, 713.	Goodisson, 734.	Grenlaw, 755.	Gwynne, 779.
Gilson, 701.	Goodman, 735.	Grenvil, 749.	Gyles, 701.
Giltenane, 714, 1860.	Goodson, 734.	Grenville, 749.	
Giltinane, 714, 1860.	Goodwin, 736, 1354.	Gresham, 760.	
Ginaty, 715.	Googan, 727.	Gressam, 760.	
Ginity, 715.	Googarty, 726.	Greville, 761.	
Ginn, 1345.	Goold, 742.	Grey, 752.	
Ginna, 1400.	Goolden, 732.	Greyhan, 759.	Habbagan, 913.
Ginnane, 772, 1400.	Gooley, 731.	Gribben, 370, 762, 763,	Habbert, 896.
Ginnaw, 1400.	Gooly, 709.	1477.	Habernathy, 2.
			Habernethy, 2.

Surname and Reference No.	Surname and Reference No.	Surname and Reference No.	Surname and Reference No.
Hackett, 780.	Handlon, 808.	Hartford, 831.	Headen, 847.
Haden, 847.	Handly, 807.	Hartican, 832.	Heagan, 782.
Hadian, 847.	Handrahan, 812.	Hartigan, 832.	Heally, 855.
Hadnet, 898.	Handrick, 801.	Hartin, 833.	Healy, 855.
Hadskeath, 781.	Handridge, 800.	Hartmane, 861.	Heanen, 863.
Hadskiss, 781.	Handsbery, 805.	Hartnett, 822.	Heany, 99, 856.
Hafferon, 864.	Handy, 802.	Hartney, 864.	Heard, 858.
Haffey, 839.	Haneen, 811.	Harton, 833.	Hearde, 858.
Hafford, 831.	Hanephy, 806.	Hartry, 834.	Heare, 821.
Haffron, 864.	Hanity, 806.	Harty, 827, 834.	Hearn, 14, 859, 878.
Hagan, 547, 782, 901, 1664.	Hanily, 807.	Harvessy, 835.	Hearne, 859.
Hagans, 886, 782.	Hanlan, 792, 808.	Harvey, 835.	Hearon, 14.
Hagarty, 782, 865.	Hanley, 807.	Harvison, 815.	Hearst, 938.
Hagerty, 783, 865.	Hanlin, 808.	Harwood, 830, 836.	Henry, 860.
Haggarty, 783.	Hanlon, 792, 808, 1666.	Haselden, 851.	Heaslett, 852.
Haggens, 886.	Hanly, 807.	Haskett, 879.	Heasley, 852.
Haggerty, 783.	Hanna, 809.	Haskins, 39, 918.	Heaslip, 861.
Haghen, 1664.	Hannagh, 809.	Haskis, 781.	Heasting, 838.
Haghey, 839.	Hannah, 809.	Haslegrove, 850.	Heaphy, 857.
Hagin, 782.	Hannan, 799, 811.	Hasleton, 851.	Heathcock, 854.
Hahasy, 784.	Hannaway, 810.	Haslett, 852.	Heazlewood, 853.
Hahessy, 784.	Hannen, 799, 811.	Haslewood, 853.	Heazley, 852.
Haigan, 782.	Hannin, 799, 811.	Hassan, 837.	Heden, 847.
Hailes, 787.	Hannon, 799, 811	Hassett, 814.	Hederton, 881.
Hainen, 799.	Hanon, 799.	Hasson, 837.	Hedery, 1780.
Haines, 785, 945.	Hanrahan, 812.	Hastie, 838.	Hedivan, 862.
Hainey, 856.	Hanratty, 813.	Hasting, 838.	Hednan, 862.
Hair, 821, 1668.	Hanrick, 804.	Hastings, 838.	Heduvan, 862.
Haire, 821.	Hansbury, 805.	Hasty, 838.	Heel, 888.
Halbrook, 902.	Hanson, 814, 1414.	Hathorn, 846.	Heelan, 944.
Halckett, 780.	Hanton, 893.	Hatton, 1379.	Heenau, 799, 863.
Haldane, 786.	Hanvidge, 800.	Haughan, 839.	Heeny, 856.
Hales, 787.	Hanway, 810.	Haughean, 782.	Heery, 860.
Halfpenny, 788, 794.	Haran, 825, 914, 1667.	Haughey, 839.	Hefferan, 864.
Hall, 789.	Harbert, 873.	Haughlin, 839, 843.	Heffernan, 841, 864, 876
Halladay, 790.	Harbinson, 815, 873.	Haughran, 914.	Heffernin, 864.
Hallanan, 792.	Harbison, 815.	Haughton, 840, 942.	Heffernon, 864.
Hallaron, 793.	Harcourt, 816.	Haveren, 841.	Hefferon, 864.
Halley, 1573.	Harden, 817.	Havern, 841, 864.	Heffron, 841, 864.
Halliday, 790.	Hardford, 831.	Haveron, 841, 864.	Hefron, 841.
Halligan, 791.	Hardiman, 818.	Havey, 857.	Hegan, 1664.
Hallinan, 20, 792, 808.	Hardman, 819.	Havron, 841.	Hegans, 782.
Hallissey, 1169.	Hardwood, 820.	Havy, 857.	Hegarty, 783, 865.
Halloran, 793, 1665.	Hare, 821, 1668.	Hawes, 842.	Hegerty, 865.
Hallorin, 793.	Harel, 824.	Hawey, 899.	Heggarty, 865.
Halloron, 793.	Haren, 825, 914, 1667.	Hawkes, 844.	Hegher, 821.
Halloway, 907.	Harford, 831.	Hawkins, 843.	Hehir, 821.
Hallyday, 790.	Hargaden, 818.	Hawks, 844.	Heify, 857.
Halnan, 792.	Harhan, 914.	Hawkshaw, 845.	Heilis, 890.
Halpeny, 788.	Hariott, 877.	Hawney, 905.	Heily, 855.
Halpin, 788, 794.	Harker, 816.	Hawthorn, 846.	Heines, 945.
Halyday, 790.	Harknett, 822.	Hawthorne, 846.	Helston, 927.
Ham, 796.	Harley, 937.	Haybrun, 883.	Hely, 855.
Hamden, 798.	Harman, 819.	Hayburn, 883.	Heman, 849.
Hamell, 795.	Harmon, 819.	Haycock, 854.	Hemans, 849.
Hamill, 795, 796, 797.	Harnett, 822.	Hayden, 847.	Hemp, 866.
Hamilton, 795, 796.	Harold, 823.	Haydin, 847.	Hempe, 366.
Hammel, 795.	Haroughten, 827.	Haydon, 847.	Hempenstall, 866.
Hammell, 795.	Haroughton, 827.	Hayes, 848, 1669.	Hempstall, 866.
Hammill, 795.	Harper, 824.	Hayfron, 864.	Hempton, 798.
Hammond, 795, 797.	Harpur, 824	Hayman, 849.	Henan, 799.
Hampden, 798.	Harrel, 823.	Haynan, 799.	Henchy, 871.
Hampton, 798, 893.	Harrell, 823.	Haynes, 785, 945.	Henderson, 867.
Hanafy, 806.	Harren, 825, 1667	Hays, 848.	Hendron, 867.
Hanah, 809.	Harrett, 820.	Hayslip, 852.	Hendry, 870.
Hanan, 799.	Harricks, 826.	Hayten, 847.	Heneberry, 868.
Hanar, 811.	Harrigan, 915, 916.	Haythorne, 846.	Henebery, 868.
Hanaty, 872.	Harrihy, 835.	Haze, 848.	Henebry, 868.
Hanberry, 801.	Harrington, 563, 827, 834.	Hazelett, 852.	Henehan, 99.
Hanbery, 801.	Harris, 828, 829.	Hazelett, 852.	Henekan, 99.
Hanbidge, 800.	Harrison, 828, 829.	Hazelton, 851.	Henery, 870.
Hanbury, 801.	Harrisson, 828.	Hazlegrove, 850.	Henesy, 869.
Hancock, 803.	Harrity, 827.	Hazleton, 851, 852.	Heney, 856.
Hancocks, 803.	Harron, 825, 878.	Hazlett, 851, 852.	Henissy, 869.
Hand, 802.	Harrot, 836.	Hazlewood, 853.	Henley, 807.
Handbidge, 800.	Harroughton, 827.	Hazley, 852.	Hennan, 863.
Handbury, 801.	Hart, 830, 836.	Hazlip, 861.	Henneberry, 868.
Handcock, 803.	Harte, 830.	Hazlitt, 852.	Hennebry, 868.
Handcocks, 803.	Harten, 833.	Hazzlett, 852.	Hennessy, 869.
		Heacock, 854.	Henright, 561.

Surname and Reference No.	Surname and Reference No.	Surname and Reference No.	Surname and Reference No.
Henry, 870, 1313, 1374.	Hilliss, 890.	Hosford, 917.	Hutchisson, 941.
Hensbry, 868.	Hillston, 927.	Hoskins, 918.	Hutson, 941.
Henshaw, 871.	Hillyard, 891.	Hoskisson, 939.	Hutton, 840, 942.
Hensy, 869.	Hilo, 855.	Hough, 923.	Hyde, 513, 943, 1655.
Henthorn, 846.	Hilyard, 831.	Houghegan, 690, 900.	Hyland, 944, 2047.
Henzy, 869.	Hinchy, 871.	Houghton, 840.	Hyle, 926.
Heraghty, 872.	Hinds, 892. 945, 1690.	Houlaghan, 919.	Hyles, 926.
Herald, 823.	Hines, 945.	Houldon, 903.	Hyndes, 945.
Herbert, 815, 873, 896.	Hinsy, 869.	Houlehan, 919.	Hynds, 945.
Herbison, 815.	Hinton, 798, 893.	Houldsworth. 904.	Hynes, 785, 945, 1690.
Herd, 858.	Hipps, 1720.	Houlahan, 919. 1634.	Hyslop, 861.
Herdman, 819.	Hird, 858.	Houlehan, 919.	
Hergusson, 599.	Hirl. 823.	Houneen, 753.	
Heritage, 874.	Hiskisson, 939.	Hourican, 1904, 1938.	
Herley, 875. 937.	Hitchens, 894.	Hourihan, 920.	
Herlihy. 875, 937.	Hitchins, 894.	Hourihane, 920.	
Herly, 937.	Hoare, 895.	House, 923.	Iago, 955.
Herne, 878.	Hobart. 873, 896	Houstin, 921.	Igo, 946.
Hernon, 864, 876.	Hobbikin, 913.	Houston 921, 910.	Igoe, 946.
Heron, 14, 878.	Hobert, 896.	Houtten. 840.	Ildowney, 1304.
Herran, 878.	Hodger, 897.	Hovenden. 1689.	Ilhinney, 1306.
Herricks, 826.	Hodgin, 928.	Howard, 922.	Ilroy, 1384.
Herriott, 877.	Hodgins, 897.	Howay, 924.	Ilwee. 1310.
Herron, 14, 859, 878.	Hodgson. 928.	Howe, 923.	Inglesby, 948.
Herrtage, 874.	Hodnett. 898.	Howes. 842, 923.	Inglis, 559, 947.
Hertnan, 864.	Hodson. 928.	Howie, 924.	Ingoldsby, 948.
Hertnon. 876.	Hoey, 899.	Howison, 921.	Inis, 560.
Hervy, 835.	Hog, 782, 901.	Howley, 925.	Innes, 560.
Hesketh, 879.	Hogan, 900, 930.	Hoy, 839. 848.	Innis, 560.
Heslip, 861.	Hogart, 922.	Hoye, 899.	Insgelby, 948.
Heslitt. 852.	Hogarty. 865.	Hoyle, 926.	Irons, 949.
Hession. 880, 2009.	Hogg, 901.	Hoyles, 926.	Irrington, 827.
Hestin, 838.	Hoggshaw, 845.	Hoynes, 945, 1690.	Irvine, 950, 951.
Hestings, 838.	Hoins, 945, 1690.	Hubbard, 896.	Irving, 950.
Hestion, 838.	Holahan, 919.	Hucheson, 941.	Irwin, 950, 951.
Hetherington, 881.	Holbrook, 902.	Huddleston, 927.	Isaac, 952.
Heuson, 882.	Holdbrook. 902.	Hudson, 928.	Isaacs, 952.
Hewetson, 882.	Holden, 903.	Hue, 1376.	Isdell, 953.
Hewison, 882.	Holdsworth. 904.	Hueson, 882. 1376.	Isdle, 953.
Hewlett, 932.	Holeday, 790.	Hueston. 882.	Ivers, 954.
Hews, 931.	Holesworth, 904.	Huet, 929.	Ivors, 954.
Hewson, 882, 940, 1376.	Holey, 2055.	Huey. 929.	
Hewston, 882.	Holian, 1675.	Huggins. 886. 900, 930.	
Heyburn, 883.	Holland, 905, 1575.	Hughes. 931.	
Heycock, 854.	Holliday, 790.	Hugheston. 882.	
Heydon, 847.	Hollingsworth, 906.	Hughey. 929.	
Heyfron, 864.	Hollinsworth, 906.	Hughs. 931.	
Heyland, 914.	Holloran, 793.	Hughston, 921.	Jaffery, 959.
Heys, 848.	Holloway. 907.	Hulahun, 1634.	Jaffrey, 959.
Heyslip 861.	Hollway. 907.	Huleatt, 932.	Jaffries, 959.
Hezlett, 852.	Holly. 908, 1752.	Hulihan, 919.	Jago, 955.
Hickey, 884.	Holmes, 909.	Hull, 789.	Jagoe, 955.
Hickie, 884.	Holohan, 919.	Hulme. 933.	Jameison, 957.
Hide, 513, 943.	Holoughan. 919.	Hulnane, 394.	James, 956, 957.
Hiffernan, 864.	Holoway. 907.	Hultaghan, 1634.	Jameson, 956, 957.
Higerty, 865.	Homes, 909.	Hultahan. 1634.	Jamieson, 957.
Higgans, 886.	Hone, 910.	Hume, 933.	Jamison, 957.
Higgens. 886.	Hooke, 911.	Humes, 933.	Jardan, 966.
Higgerty, 865.	Hooks, 911.	Humffray, 934.	Jardine, 966.
Higginbotham, 885.	Hoolaghan, 919.	Humfrey, 934.	Jarmyn, 962.
Higginbottom, 885.	Hoolahan, 919.	Humphreys. 934.	Jarrett, 693.
Higgings. 886.	Hoolihan, 919, 1634.	Humphries. 934.	Jarvis, 694.
Higgins, 886, 930, 1664.	Hoologhan, 919.	Humphry, 934.	Jeffares, 958.
Highland, 914.	Hop, 913.	Humphrys. 934.	Jeffars, 958.
Higins 886.	Hopes, 912.	Hunecn. 753.	Jeffers, 958.
Hiland, 914.	Hopkins. 913.	Hunt, 593, 594, 935, 936.	Jeffery, 959.
Hilbert, 873.	Hopps, 912.		Jeffrey, 959.
Hildage, 887.	Horaho, 829.	Hunter. 935, 936.	Jeffreys, 959.
Hildige, 887.	Horan, 914.	Hurd, 858.	Jellis, 701, 964.
Hilditch, 887.	Hore, 895.	Hurley, 310, 937.	Jemason. 957.
Hill, 888	Horgan, 915, 916.	Hurst, 938.	Jemison, 957.
Hillan, 889.	Horish, 219.	Huskison, 939.	Jenkenson, 960.
Hillard, 891.	Horisky, 2056.	Huskisson, 939.	Jenkins, 960.
Hillas, 890.	Hornett, 898.	Huson, 882.	Jenkinson, 960.
Hillen, 889.	Horoho, 828.	Huston, 882, 921, 940, 1376, 1486.	Jenkison, 960.
Hilles, 890.	Horohoe, 895.		Jennings, 961.
Hilliard, 891.	Horrigan, 915, 916.	Hutchenson, 941.	Jerdan, 966.
Hilligan, 791.	Horrigon, 915.	Hutcheson, 941.	Jerety, 692.
Hillind, 889.	Horrogan, 915.	Hutchinson, 941.	Jerman, 962.
	Horsford, 917.	Hutchison, 941.	Jermyn, 962.

80

Surname and Reference No.	Surname and Reference No.	Surname and Reference No.	Surname and Reference No.
Jerrett. 693.	Keddle. 209.	Keon, 996.	Kilfoyle, 771.
Jervaise. 963.	Kedney. 1009.	Keoneen. 961.	Kilgallen. 1014.
Jervis. 694. 963.	Keefe. 979.	Keough. 994.	Kilgrist, 699.
Jervois. 963.	Keeffe. 979. 1671.	Keown. 995. 996.	Kilkelly, 988. 1015.
Jevers. 954.	Keegan, 547. 980.	Keppel. 233. 997.	Kilkenny. 992.
Jiles. 701. 964.	Keelan. 981.	Kepple. 233. 997.	Kilkey. 1896.
Jinkins, 960.	Keelin. 981.	Ker. 246.	Kilkison. 704.
Johnson, 965. 1404.	Keeling. 982.	Kerans, 976.	Kilkisson. 704.
Johnston. 965, 1404, 1478.	Keellin, 981.	Kerbin. 1033.	Killan. 981.
Johnstone. 965.	Keeltagh. 1896.	Kerby. 1033.	Killby. 698.
Jonson, 965.	Keely. 982. 988.	Kereen, 976.	Killeen. 1016.
Jordan, 966.	Keenan, 983. 1023.	Kerevan. 1035.	Killen, 706, 1017.
Jorden. 966.	Keenoy. 983.	Kergan. 1003.	Killian. 1017.
Jordine. 966.	Keerawin. 1035.	Kerigan. 1003.	Killimith. 2075.
Jordon. 966.	Keern. 239.	Kerin, 998.	Killion, 1016.
Jourdan. 966.	Keernan. 1001.	Kerins. 976.	Killips. 1018.
Jourdin. 966.	Keery. 239.	Kerisk. 855.	Killkelly. 1015.
Joyce, 967.	Keesack, 1036.	Kerivan. 1035.	Killmore. 712.
Judge. 154, 968.	Keevane. 972.	Kerivin. 1035.	Killooley. 703.
Julian, 969.	Keevers. 1396.	Kerley. 999.	Killops. 1018. 1408.
Julien, 969.	Keeves. 1396.	Kerlin. 245, 1000.	Killpatrick. 1021.
Jumphrey, 958.	Keghan. 1403.	Kerly. 401.	Killum. 1019.
Junkin, 960.	Kegley, 1751.	Kermode. 242.	Kilm, 1019.
Jurdan. 966.	Keheerin. 215.	Kernaghan, 227, 1001, 1010.	Kilmartin. 711. 1020.
Jury, 970, 1078.	Kehelly. 292.	Kernahan. 1001.	Kilmary. 1448.
	Keherny. 975.	Kernan, 1001. 1010.	Kilmet, 2075.
	Kehilly. 292.	Kerney, 975.	Kilmurray. 1602.
	Kehir. 216.	Kernohan. 1001.	Kilmurry, 1382.
	Kehoe, 994. 1403.	Kernon. 1001, 1010.	Kilpatrick. 1021, 1034.
	Keighron, 1003.	Kerns. 976.	Kilroy, 1022.
	Keightley. 984.	Kerons, 976.	Kilvey. 1398.
Kaddow, 210.	Keilly. 982.	Kerr. 246. 1002.	Kilwell, 219.
Kadell, 209.	Keiltogh. 1896.	Kerragher, 247.	Kimins. 396.
Kaffrey, 212.	Keily. 292.	Kerragy, 249.	Kimmings. 396.
Kahoon, 305.	Keiran, 976	Kerrane, 246. 976.	Kimmins, 396. 397.
Kain, 971.	Keirans. 217, 976. 1010.	Kerrigan, 338, 1003.	Kinaghan, 400.
Kaine, 971.	Keith, 985.	Kerrins, 976.	Kinahan, 983, 1023.
Kairns, 976.	Keitley, 984.	Kerrish, 855.	Kinane, 772, 1030.
Kalshander, 18.	Kelaghan, 220.	Kerrisk, 855.	Kinarney, 1024.
Kanavaghan, 227.	Kell, 1046.	Kerrison, 1004.	Kinavan, 227.
Kane, 971, 974. 1670	Kellaghan, 220.	Kershaw, 1005.	Kincade, 1025.
Kangley. 1960	Kellard, 986.	Kervan, 1035.	Kincaid. 1025.
Kappock, 235.	Kellegher, 986	Kerwin, 1035.	Kincairt, 259.
Karey, 239.	Kellegy, 221.	Keshin, 255.	Kincart, 259, 2080.
Karney, 975.	Kelleher. 986.	Kessidy, 258.	Kinchela, 1032.
Karr, 246.	Keller, 986.	Ketchen, 1038.	Kinchella, 1028, 1032.
Kavanagh, 262, 972	Kelley, 988.	Keterson, 260.	Kinchley, 1028.
Kavenagh, 972.	Kelloch, 987.	Kettle, 1006.	Kine, 353.
Kays, 1007.	Kellock, 987.	Kettyle, 1006.	Kinealy, 990.
Keacy, 254.	Kellog, 987.	Kevane, 972.	Kinerney, 1388.
Keafe, 979.	Kellops, 1018.	Keveney, 972.	King, 323, 1026.
Keag, 1392.	Kelly, 220, 982, 988, 1015, 1672.	Keverny, 1388.	Kinghan, 1402.
Keaghery, 973.	Kemp, 226.	Kevney, 978.	Kingsbury, 1027.
Keague, 1392.	Kenah, 989.	Keyes, 1007.	Kingsley, 1028.
Keahery. 973.	Kenchyla, 1032.	Keys, 1007.	Kingston, 1029.
Kealy, 982.	Kendrick, 993.	Kidd. 1008.	Kingstone, 1029.
Kean, 971, 974.	Kenealy, 990.	Kiddle. 1008.	Kinigam, 400.
Keane, 971.	Kenelly. 319. 990.	Kidney, 1009.	Kinighan, 400.
Keaney, 992.	Kenna, 989, 1400	Kielt, 1896.	Kiniry. 1388.
Keany, 992, 1394.	Kennah, 1400	Kielty, 1896.	Kinkade, 1025.
Keappock, 235.	Kennane, 772.	Kiely, 982, 988.	Kinkaid, 1025
Kearan, 1010.	Kenneally, 990.	Kieran, 976.	Kinkead, 1025.
Kearin, 998.	Kenneally, 990.	Kierevan, 1035.	Kinna, 983, 989, 1023.
Kearn, 976.	Kennedy, 991.	Kiernan, 1001, 1010.	Kinnan, 983.
Kearnes, 976.	Kennelly, 990.	Kierney, 975.	Kinnane, 229, 1030.
Kearney, 975, 976.	Kenning, 228.	Kiervan, 1035.	Kinneally, 990.
Kearns, 217, 975, 976.	Kennington, 991.	Kilbride, 1011.	Kinnealy, 990.
Kearon, 976.	Kennon, 229.	Kilchreest, 699.	Kinnear, 1031.
Kearsey, 1005.	Kenny, 992, 1401, 1411.	Kilchriest. 699.	Kinneard, 1031.
Kearson, 1004.	Kenrick, 993.	Kilcline, 1012.	Kinneary, 1024.
Keary. 239.	Kentley, 231.	Kilcoyne, 353.	Kinneen, 1758.
Keat, 985.	Keogan, 298.	Kilcullen, 1014.	Kinnegan, 400.
Keaterson, 260.	Keogh, 994, 1403.	Kilday, 700.	Kinner. 1031.
Keates, 985.	Keogh, 994.	Kildea, 700.	Kinnere, 1031.
Keating, 977.	Keoghane, 995.	Kildunn, 530.	Kinney, 992.
Keatley, 984.	Keoghoe, 994.	Kiley, 982.	Kinnian, 400.
Keats, 985.	Keoghy. 994.	Kilfedder, 1013.	Kinnier, 1031.
Keaty, 977.	Keohane, 214, 347, 995, 996.	Kilfeder, 1013.	Kinnigham, 400.
Keaveny, 978.		Kilfillan, 702.	
Keays, 1007.			

Surname and Reference No.	Surname and Reference No.	Surname and Reference No.	Surname and Reference No.
Kinsbury, 1027.	Lagan, 1113.	Lawder. 1073.	Lenane, 1092, 1097.
Kinsela, 1032.	Laghlin. 1124.	Lawell, 1069.	Lenard, 1097.
Kinsella, 1032.	Lahiff, 627, 778, 1052.	Lawler, 1075.	Lendrum, 1093.
Kinsellagh, 1032.	Lahive. 1052.	Lawless, 1074, 1077.	Leneghan, 1094.
Kinsellah, 1032.	Lahy, 1079.	Lawlor. 1075.	Lenehan, 1094.
Kinshela, 1032.	Laidley. 1049.	Lawrance, 1068.	Lenigan, 1063.
Kinshelagh, 1032.	Laing, 1053.	Lawrence, 1068.	Lenihan. 1094.
Kinshellagh, 1032.	Laingster. 1058.	Lawrenceson. 1076.	Lennard. 1097.
Kinslagh, 1032.	Laird, 1054.	Lawrenson. 1076.	Lennihan. 1094.
Kinsley, 1028.	Lairy, 1080.	Lawrinson. 1076.	Lennon. 1095. 1097.
Kinucane. 612.	Lalor, 1075.	Lawrison. 1076.	Lennox. 1096.
Kirberry. 1033.	Laman, 1057.	Laws, 1077.	Lenon, 1095.
Kirby, 1033.	Lambart, 1055.	Lawson, 1074, 1077.	Lenord, 1097.
Kirk, 1034, 1757.	Lambert. 1055.	Lawther. 1073.	Lenox, 1096.
Kirkby, 1033.	L'ami, 1056.	Layard, 1054.	Leonard, 1092, 1095.
Kirivan, 1035.	Lamie, 1056.	Layburn, 1103.	1097
Kirkpatrick, 1021,1034.	Lamin, 1057.	Laycock, 1078.	Leslie, 1098.
Kirland. 245.	Lammie, 1056.	Layne, 1060.	Lester, 1099.
Kirley, 401. 999.	Lammon. 1057.	Layng, 1053.	Lethem, 1066.
Kirlin, 1000.	Lammy, 1056.	Leache, 1084.	Letimore, 1067.
Kirpatrick. 1021, 1034.	Lamon, 1057.	Leacock, 1078.	Letsam, 1100.
Kirrane, 239, 246, 402,	Lamond, 1057	Leacy, 1048.	Letsome, 1100, 1552.
1035.	Lamont, 1057. 1091.	Leadam, 1066.	Lettimor, 1067.
Kirvan, 1035.	Lampert, 1055.	Leahey, 1079.	Levenston, 1109.
Kirwan, 1035.	Lamy, 1056.	Leahy, 1079.	Leveran, 568.
Kirwen, 1035.	Lancaster, 1058.	Leaky, 1081.	Leveson, 1109.
Kirwin, 1035.	Landers, 1059.	Leane, 1060.	Levey, 1101
Kissack, 1036.	Landregan, 1116.	Leard, 1054.	Levingstone, 1109.
Kissane, 1037.	Landrum, 1093.	Leary, 1080, 1673.	Levins, 1072.
Kissick, 408, 1036.	Landy. 1059, 1061.	Leatham, 1066.	Levinson, 1109.
Kissock, 1036.	Lane, 1060, 1094, 1104,	Leathem. 1066.	Levinston, 1109.
Kitchen, 1038, 1039,	1140.	Leavy, 1101.	Leviston, 1109.
1294.	Laney, 441, 1136.	Leburn, 1103.	Lewers, 1102.
Kitson, 1038, 1039.	Lang, 1053.	Leckie, 1081.	Lewis, 1102.
Kittson, 1039.	Langan, 1063.	Lecky, 1081.	Leybourne, 1103.
Kivnahan, 972.	Langin, 1063.	Leddy, 1082.	Leycester, 1099.
Kivneen, 983.	Langley, 1061.	Ledgwidge, 1082.	Leyhane, 1089, 1142.
Klisham, 638.	Langly, 1061.	Ledsome, 1100.	Leyne, 1140.
Knaggs, 1040.	Langster, 1058.	Ledwich, 1082.	Liddane, 1135.
Knags, 1040.	Langtree, 1062.	Ledwidge, 1082.	Liddel, 1107.
Knee, 1041.	Langtry, 1062.	Ledwitch. 1082.	Lidwich, 1082.
Kneeland, 1623.	Lanigan, 1063.	Ledwith, 1082.	Liffe, 551.
Knight, 1042, 1415.	Lankester, 1058.	Lee, 1083.	Liggate, 1088.
Knilans, 1623.	Lanktree, 1062.	Leech, 1084.	Ligget, 1088.
Knipe, 1043.	Lannan, 1095.	Leedham, 1066.	Liggot, 1088.
Knockton, 1616.	Lannigan, 1063.	Leedom, 1066.	Lighton, 1090.
Knoles, 1045.	Lanon, 1095.	Leehane, 1089.	Lihane, 1089.
Knowd, 1044.	Lantry, 1062.	Leehy, 1079.	Lillis, 1074.
Knowels, 1045.	Laphin, 1050.	Leeman, 1091.	Linagh, 1136.
Knowles, 1045.	Lapin, 1050.	Leemon, 1091.	Linahan, 1092, 1094,
Knowls, 1045.	Lappin, 1050.	Leery, 1080.	1104.
Koen, 300.	Laramer. 1065.	Lees, 1085.	Linane, 1097, 1104.
Korish, 89.	Larens, 1068.	Leeson, 721.	Linass. 1138.
Kough, 994.	Larimer, 1065.	Leetch, 1084.	Linchey, 1106.
Krahmer, 356.	Larimor, 1065.	Le Fanu, 1086.	Lind, 1141.
Kramer, 356.	Larkan, 1064.	Lefanu, 1086,	Linden, 1105, 1210,
Krowley. 384.	Larken, 1064.	Lefebre, 1087.	1212.
Kulhan, 392.	Larkin, 1064.	Lefevre, 1087.	Lindesay, 1106.
Kulkeen. 391.	Larkins, 1064.	Leffanue, 1086.	Lindin, 1105.
Kydd, 1008.	Larmer, 1065.	Legat, 1088.	Lindon, 1105.
Kyerty, 405.	Larmour, 1065.	Legate, 1088.	Lindsay, 1106.
Kyle, 1046.	Larney, 1416.	Leget, 1088.	Lindsy, 1106.
Kyne, 353, 1047.	Lastly, 1098.	Legett, 1088.	Lineham, 1137.
Kzoneen, 961.	Latham, 1066.	Leggatt, 1088.	Lines, 1142.
	Latimer, 1067.	Legget, 1088.	Liness, 1138.
	Latimore, 1067.	Leggott, 1088.	Linham, 1095.
	Latimour, 1067.	Lehane, 1089, 1142.	Linighan, 1094.
	Lattimer, 1067.	Lehy, 1079.	Linn, 1141.
	Lattimore. 1067.	Leicester, 1099.	Linnahan, 1094.
Lachlin, 1124	Lauder, 1073.	Leigh, 1083.	Linnane, 1095, 1104.
Lackey, 1081.	Laugheran, 1126.	Leighton, 1090.	Linnehan, 1094.
Lacklan, 1124.	Laughlin, 1124.	Leitch, 1084.	Linnen, 1095.
Lacock, 1078.	Launders, 1059.	Leitham, 1066	Linnox, 1096.
Lacy, 1048.	Laurence, 1068,	Lemmon, 1091.	Lion, 1142.
Ladley, 1049.	Laurison, 1076.	Lemmy, 1056.	Lions, 1142.
Ladrigan, 1116.	Lavelle, 1069.	Lemon, 1057, 1091.	Lister, 1099.
Laferty, 1051.	Laverty, 1070.	Lenagan, 1063.	Little. 1107, 1108, 1715.
Laffan, 1050.	Lavery, 38, 1071, 1129,	Lenaghan, 1094, 1097,	Littleton, 1107, 1108.
Laffen, 1050.	1760.	Lenaghen, 1094.	Livingstone, 1109.
Lafferty, 1051, 1659.	Lavins. 1072,	Lenahan, 1092, 1094.	Livingstown, 1109.

Surname and Reference No.	Surname and Reference No.	Surname and Reference No.	Surname and Reference No.
Lloyd, 1110.	Lute, 1131.	Mac Eown, 965.	Maddox, 1155.
Loag, 1114.	Lutteral, 1134.	Mac Etavey, 1147.	Madole, 1302.
Loague, 1114.	Lutterel, 1134.	Mac Euchroe, 383.	Madowell, 1302.
Lochlin, 1124.	Luttrell, 1134.	Mac Evoy, 1320.	Madox, 1155.
Lochrane, 1126.	Lyburn, 1103.	Mac Ewan, 1321.	Magahan, 1156.
Lock, 1111.	Lydden, 1135.	Mac Ewen, 1291.	Magaharan, 1567.
Lockard, 1111.	Lyden, 1135.	Mac Feerish, 89.	Magahern, 1163.
Lockart, 1111.	Lydon, 1135.	Macfie, 1207.	Magan, 1156, 1179, 1243, 1329.
Lockhart, 1111.	Lyhan, 1089.	Mac Gill, 1159.	Magann, 1329.
Lockheart, 1111.	Lyhane, 1089.	Macgivir, 1165.	Magarry, 1334.
Loftis, 1112.	Lynagh, 1136, 1137.	Mac Guire, 1165.	Magauran, 1157, 1357.
Loftus, 1112, 1125.	Lynam, 1136, 1137.	Machamfry, 959.	Magaurn, 1357.
Logan, 1113, 1122.	Lynane, 1097.	Mac Henry, 1374.	Magaw, 1508.
Loghlin, 1124.	Lynap, 1137.	Machue, 1376.	Magawran, 1157, 1357.
Loghnan, 1124.	Lynas, 1138.	Mac Hugh, 1376.	Magcahan, 1336.
Logue, 1114, 1536.	Lynass, 1138.	Mac Illesher, 753.	Magee, 657, 1158, 1335, 2086
Lohan, 1122.	Lynch, 1139.	MacIlroy, 1384.	
Lomax, 1115.	Lynchahan, 1139.	Macinerney, 1388.	Magcehan, 1336.
Londregan, 1116.	Lynchy, 1139.	Macintosh, 1152.	Mageen, 1336.
Londrigan, 1116.	Lyndsay, 1106.	Maciver, 1390.	Magenis, 1369.
Londy, 1132.	Lyne, 1000, 1140, 1142.	Mack, 1144, 1148, 1297, 1300, 1315, 1320, 1388, 1148, 1149.	Magennis, 1369.
Lonergan, 1116.	Lyncham, 1137.		Mageown, 1358.
Loney, 1133.	Lyness, 1138.		Maghan, 1168, 1426.
Long, 1117.	Lynham, 1137.	Mackaleary, 1148.	Magher, 1167, 1501.
Longhill, 1118.	Lynn, 1141.	Mackarel, 1244.	Maghery, 604.
Longill, 1118.	Lyns, 1142.	Mackay, 1151, 1391, 1395.	Magill, 1159.
Longley, 1117.	Lyons, 1089, 1142, 1675.		Magillowy, 1310.
Lonican, 1119.	Lysaght, 1143.	Mac Keating, 1149.	Magilly, 351.
Lonney, 1133.	Lysat, 1143.	Mackel, 1049.	Maginess, 1369.
Lonsdale, 1120.	Lyster, 1099, 1927.	Mackelwaine, 1386.	Maginley, 1314.
Looby, 1121.	Lytle, 1107.	Macken, 1320.	Maginn, 1160, 1345, 1369.
Loogue, 1084.	Lyttle, 1107.	Mackenzie, 1150, 1402.	
Loony, 1133.	Lyttleton, 1108.	Mackeown, 1401.	Maginnes, 1369.
Lorimer, 1065.		Mackerel, 1244.	Maginnotty, 1313.
Lorimour, 1065.		Mackessy, 1249.	Maginnis, 1160, 1369
Lorkin, 1064.		Mackey, 1151, 1335, 1391, 1395.	Magiveran, 1317.
Lormer, 1065.	Maberry, 1203.		Magiverin, 1317.
Loughan, 1113, 1122, 1125, 1126.	Mac, 1144, 1148.	Mackheath, 1397.	Magivern, 1347
	Macabo, 1234.	Mackimmon, 1409.	Maglamery, 1546.
Loughead, 1123.	Macalister, 1212.	Mackin, 1213.	Maglammery, 1546.
Lougheed, 1123.	Macallon, 1211.	Mackinaul, 1444.	Magner, 1161.
Lougheran, 1126.	Macalshender, 18.	Mackintosh, 1152.	Magnier, 1161.
Loughlan, 1124, 1674.	Mac Alshinder, 18.	Mackiver, 1390.	Magnir, 1161.
Loughlen, 1124.	Macan, 1243.	Macklehattan, 1379.	Magnor, 1161.
Loughlin, 699, 1124, 1418, 1674.	Mac-an-Ree, 1026.	Macklemoyle, 1381.	Magon, 1355.
	Macantyre, 1389.	Macklewraith, 1387.	Magone, 1101.
Loughnan, 1124, 1125.	Macardle, 1216.	Mackrell, 1244.	Magorisk, 89.
Loughnane, 1112, 1125.	Macarha, 1216.	Macleaghlin, 1418.	Magorlick, 730, 1162.
Loughran, 1122, 1126.	Macartney, 1145, 1247.	Maclean, 1256.	Magough, 1897.
Loughren, 1126.	Macasey, 1219.	Mac Lean, 1419.	Magourmahan, 737.
Loughry, 1129.	Mac Asparran, 1182.	Macleese, 1153.	Magoveran, 1357.
Loundes, 1128.	Macaulay, 263, 1116, 1223, 1251.	Macleish, 1153.	Magoverin, 1357.
Lourimer, 1065.		Mac Leod, 1122.	Magovern, 1357, 1358.
Louther, 1073.	Macauley, 1146.	Mac Linden, 1210.	Magowan, 1358.
Lovat, 1084, 1127.	Mac Auly, 1223.	Maclise, 1153, 1209, 1420.	Magowen, 1358.
Lovett, 333, 1127.	Mac Avoy, 1320.		Magra, 1362.
Lowers, 1102.	Mac Awly, 1223.	Macloghlin, 1418.	Magragh, 1362.
Lowery, 1129.	Macbeth, 1228.	Macloskey, 1264	Magrane, 1163, 1360.
Lowndes, 1128.	Macbride, 1011.	Mac Loughlin, 1418.	Magrath, 1164, 1362.
Lownes, 1128.	Maccabe, 1234.	Mac Mullen, 1437.	Magraw, 1362.
Lownsdale, 1120.	Mac Carthy, 1246.	Mac Naughten, 1450.	Magrean, 1163.
Lownsel, 1120.	Mac Congail, 1355.	Maconchie 1268.	Macreavy, 1363.
Lowroo, 1129.	Mac Cormack, 1274.	Macoubrey, 1278.	Macreece, 1369.
Lowry, 1071, 1129.	Macdermott, 1297.	Macoy, 1280.	Macreevy, 1363.
Lowther, 1073.	Mac Devettie, 1298.	Macpherson, 1468.	Magrillan, 1365.
Loyd, 1110.	Macdona, 1299.	Mac Philbin, 1721.	Magrory, 1366, 1806.
Luby, 1121.	Mac Donagh, 1299.	Mac Qualter, 1493.	Maguigan, 735, 1368.
Lucas, 1130.	Mac Donald, 1301.	Macready, 1283.	Maguil, 1159.
Lucknawne, 1125.	Mac Donnell, 1301, 1652.	Mac Roberts, 1476, 1793.	Maguiness, 1369.
Ludden, 1135.			Maguinis, 1369.
Luke, 1131.	Mac Donough, 1299.	Macrory, 1286, 1806.	Maguinness, 1369.
Lummacks, 1115.	Macdowell, 1302.	Mac Rubs, 1799.	Maguire, 1165, 1370.
Lundergan, 1116.	Mac Ellistram, 1212.	Mac Sweeny, 1483, 1914.	Maguirke, 1371.
Lundy, 1132, 1210.	Macelroi, 1384.		Magullion, 706.
Lunican, 1119.	Mac Elroy, 1384.	Mac Walter, 1493.	Maguran, 1157.
Lunneen, 1097.	Mac Eneany, 1312.	Madden, 1154, 1224.	Magurn, 1157, 1358.
Lunny, 1133.	Mac Enerney, 1314.	Maddigan, 1154.	Mahaffy, 1166.
Luny, 1133.	Mac Eniry, 1314.	Maddock, 1155.	Maharry, 1334.
Luogue, 1084.	Mac Entaggert, 1317.	Maddocks, 1155.	Maheir, 1167.
Lussy, 1098.	Mac Eoin, 965.		

83

Surname and Reference No.	Surname and Reference No.	Surname and Reference No.	Surname and Reference No.
Maher, 1167. 1186, 1501.	Manus, 1178, 1427	M'Affee. 1207.	M'Atee, 1316.
Mahier, 1167.	Many. 1502.	M'Affie. 1207.	M'Ateer, 1222. 1389.
Mahollum, 1575.	Mapother, 1185.	M'Aghy. 1248.	M'Ateggart, 1949.
Maholm, 1575.	Maqueen. 1473.	M'Aig. 1392.	M'Atier, 1222.
Mahon,1168,1169,1426,	Mara. 1167, 1186, 1593.	M'Aimon. 546.	M'Atilla. 632.
1534.	1677.	M'Alary, 1255.	M'Atimeny, 1221.
Mahoney, 1169.	Marchal. 1194.	M'Alasher. 753. 1212.	M'Atimney, 1221.
Mahony, 1168, 1169.	Marcom. 1189.	M'Alay. 1146.	M'Aulay, 1223. 1251.
1426.	Marcum, 1189.	M'Aldin. 786.	M'Auley, 1146. 1223,
Mahunny, 1200.	Mares, 1504.	M'Alean. 1256.	1251.
Maid, 1500.	Marinane. 1192.	M'Alee. 1208.	M'Aully. 1223.
Maikim, 1172.	Mark, 1187, 1188.	M'Aleece, 1209.	M'Avaddy. 1154, 1224
Main, 1204.	Markey, 1187, 1188,	M'Alcenan. 1138.	M'Avady. 1452.
Mains, 1204.	1832.	M'Aleery, 1257.	M'Avey. 1225. 1489.
Mainwaring, 1180.	Markham, 1189.	M'Aleese. 1153. 1209.	M'Avinchy, 2020.
Maires, 1504.	Marks, 1187.	M'Alen. 1211.	M'Avinue. 1348.
Mairs, 1170, 1504.	Marlay, 1190.	M'Aleney, 1423.	M'Avish. 909. 1956.
Maise, 1205.	Marley, 1190, 1554.	M'Alesher. 753.	M'Avoy. 1320,
Maize, 1205.	Marmion, 1191.	M'Alester. 1039. 1212.	M'Award, 2028.
Major, 1171.	Marnane, 1192, 1599,	M'Alin. 1211.	M'Aweeny. 1226.
Majur, 1171.	2029.	M'Alinden. 1105, 1132,	M'Awley, 1223.
Ma Jury, 970.	Marrilly, 1190.	1210, 1212.	M'Bay. 1489.
Makenzy, 1402.	Marrinane. 1599.	M'Alindon, 1210, 1212.	M'Bean. 1227.
Makeon, 965.	Marron. 1193.	M'Alingen. 1097.	M'Beath, 1228.
Malady, 1510.	Marshall, 1194.	M'Alinion, 1097.	M Beith. 1228.
Malarky, 1577.	Marshill. 1194.	M'Alinon. 1097.	M'Beth, 1228.
Malcolm, 1172.	Marten. 1195.	M'Alish, 1153.	M'Bey, 1228.
Malcolmson. 1173.	Martin. 1195.	M'Alivery. 2068.	M'Bin, 1227.
Malcom, 1172.	Martyn. 1195.	M'All, 1239.	M'Birney, 1229.
Malcomson, 1173.	Maskimon, 1529.	M'Allen, 1211.	M'Brairty, 1231.
Maley, 1175.	Massa. 1517.	M'Allester, 1212.	M'Bratney, 1230.
Malia, 1174. 1175, 1676.	Master. 181.	M'Allion. 1211.	M'Brearty, 147, 1231.
Malie. 1175, 1676.	Mateer, 1196. 1222.	M'Allister, 1212.	M'Breatney. 1230.
Mallagh. 1175.	Mathers. 1198.	M'Alton, 1211.	M'Bretney, 1230.
Mallan, 1176.	Matheson, 1197.	M'Aloney, 1213.	M'Bride, 1232.
Mallavin, 1578.	Mathews, 1198.	M'Aloon, 1214.	M'Brien, 176,1233,1642.
Mallen, 1176.	Mathewson, 1197.	M'Alpin, 794, 1215.	M'Brin. 206.
Mallew, 1174, 1676.	Mathieson. 1197.	M'Alroy, 1309.	M'Brine, 1233, 1642.
Malley, 1174, 1175,1511,	Mathison. 1197.	M'Alunney. 1213.	M'Brinn, 205
1676.	Matson, 1197.	M'Anabb. 1440.	M'Bryan, 1233.
Mallia, 1676.	Mattheson, 1197.	M'Anally, 1444.	M'Burney. 1229.
Mallin, 1176.	Matthew, 1198.	M'Analty, 1445.	M'Byrne, 1233.
Mallon, 1176. 1580.	Matthews, 1198.	M'Anaul, 1444.	M'Cabe, 1234.
Malloney, 1537.	Matthewson. 1197.	M'Andless, 1242.	M'Cadam, 1206.
Mallowney, 1537.	Matthieson, 1197.	M'Aneany, 1312.	M'Caddam, 1206.
Mallowny, 1537.	Mattison, 1197.	M'Aneeny, 1312.	M'Cadden, 1235.
Mallyn, 1176.	Maughan, 1168.	M'Aneny, 1312.	M'Caddo, 210, 1236.
Malmona, 1561.	Maunsell. 1184. 1199.	M'Anern, 1388.	M'Cadoo, 1236.
Malony, 1537.	Maurice, 621, 1556.	M'Anerney, 1388.	M'Cafferty, 1237, 1254.
Malowny, 1537.	Mavity, 1492.	M'Anilly, 1444.	M'Caffery, 72, 1237.
Maloy, 1262, 1536.	Mawe, 1202.	M'Aninch, 1375.	M'Caffray, 1237.
Malseed. 1177.	Mawhannon. 178.	M'Anliss. 1242.	M'Caffrey, 212, 1237.
Maltseed, 1177.	Mawhiney, 1200.	M'Annally, 1444.	M'Caffry, 72, 94, 1237.
Manally, 1444.	Mawhinney, 178, 1200,	M'Antire, 1389.	M'Cafry, 1237.
Manary. 1515.	1496.	M'Anuff, 1461.	M'Cagherty. 1238, 1246.
Manasses, 1178.	Mawhirter, 1497.	M'Anulla, 1444.	M'Caghey, 1248.
Manceely, 1454.	Maxel, 1201.	M'Anulty, 1462.	M'Cague, 1392.
Maneilly, 1454.	Maxwell, 1201.	M'Aragh, 1469.	M'Cahan, 1156.
Manelis, 1455.	May. 1202.	M'Ardell, 1217.	M'Caharty, 1238.
Mangan, 1156, 1179,	Mayberry, 1203.	M'Ardle, 1216.	M'Cahern, 1157.
1181, 1182.	Maybin, 1505.	M'Aready, 1283.	M'Caherty, 1238.
Manghan, 1179.	Maybury, 1203.	M'Areavy. 1217, 1363.	M'Cahon, 1248.
Manghen, 1179.	Maydole, 1302.	M'Aree. 1026.	M'Cahugh, 994.
Mangin, 1179.	Mayduck, 1155.	M'Arevy, 1217.	M'Cahy, 1248, 1568.
Manice, 1458.	Mayers, 1504.	M'Argle, 1332.	M'Caig, 1392.
Manion, 1179, 1182.	Mayes, 1205.	M'Arory. 1286.	M'Caigue, 1392.
Manix, 1183, 1539.	Mayne, 1204, 1427.	M'Arteney, 1145.	M'Cain, 1393.
Mann, 1168,	Maynes. 1204.	M'Arthur, 1218.	M'Call, 1239.
Mannering, 1180.	Maypowder, 1185.	M'Arthy, 253, 1246.	M'Calla, 1223, 1239.
Mannice, 1458.	Mayrick, 1520.	M'Artie, 1246.	M'Callan, 304.
Manning, 1179, 1181,	Mays, 1205.	M'Artney, 1145.	M'Callion, 226, 1211,
1182.	Mayze, 1205.	M'Asey, 1219.	1240, 1407.
Mannion, 1179, 1181,	Maze, 1205.	M'Ashinah, 643.	M'Callister, 1212.
1182.	M'Adam, 1206.	M'Askie, 1220.	M'Callnon, 226.
Mannix, 1183, 1458.	M'Adams, 1206.	M'Assie, 1219.	M'Cally, 1249.
Manron, 1180.	M'Adarra, 1640.	M'Astocker, 1916.	M'Calmont, 1241.
Mansel, 1184, 1199.	M'Adarrah, 1640.	M'A'Taghlin, 1486.	M'Calpin, 1215.
Mansell, 1199.	M'Ado, 1236.	M'Ataminey, 1221.	M'Calshender, 18.
Mansfield, 1184, 1199.	M'Adoo, 1236.	M'Atamney, 1221.	M'Calshinder 18.
Mansill, 1199.	M'Afee, 1207.	M'Atear, 1222.	M'Calum, 1265.

Surname and Reference No.	Surname and Reference No.	Surname and Reference No.	Surname and Reference No.
M'Calvey, 1398.	M'Clemonts, 1259.	M'Corry, 404, 1276.	M'Donagh, 449, 481, 1299.
M'Camley, 1251.	M'Clenaghan, 1260, 1421.	M'Coskar, 1277.	M'Donald, 1148, 1296, 1300, 1301.
M'Cammon, 1241.	M'Clenahan, 1260.	M'Cosker, 1277.	M'Donnagh, 1299.
M'Cammond, 1241.	M'Cleneghan, 1260.	M'Cottar, 320.	M'Donnell, 485, 1270, 1296, 1300, 1301, 1652.
M'Candlass, 1242.	M'Clenighan, 1260.	M'Cotter, 342.	M'Donogh, 1299.
M'Candleish, 1242.	M'Clennon, 1260.	M'Cottier, 320.	M'Donough, 1299.
M'Candless, 1242.	M'Cleod, 1351, 1422.	M'Coubrey, 1278.	M'Dool, 1302.
M'Candliss, 1242.	M'Clernon, 1417.	M'Coughey, 1248.	M'Dougal, 1302.
M'Cangherty. 1238.	M'Clester, 1212.	M'Courtney, 345.	M'Dougall, 496.
M'Canlis, 1242.	M'Climent, 1259.	M'Covera, 1278.	M'Dowall, 1302.
M'Cann, 1156, 1243.	M'Climond, 1259.	M'Cowell, 226.	M'Dowell, 501, 1302, 1570.
M'Cardle, 1216.	M'Climont, 1259.	M'Cowley, 1279.	M'Downey, 506.
M'Carg, 1373.	M'Clintock, 1261.	M'Cownley, 1279.	M'Dugal, 1302.
M'Carney, 975.	M'Clinton, 1210.	M'Coy, 1280, 1391.	M'Dwyer, 1303.
M'Carnon, 1405.	M'Closkey, 1264.	M'Crainor. 1284.	M'Elcuddy, 1340.
M'Carrell, 1244	M'Cloud, 1351, 1422.	M'Craith, 1362.	M'Eldowney, 1304.
M'Carrie, 1334.	M'Cloughry. 1029.	M'Crann, 1281, 2079.	M'Elduff, 519.
M'Carrison, 1245.	M'Cloy, 1262.	M'Cray, 1282.	M'Eleary, 1257.
M'Carroll, 250, 1244.	M'Clune, 1214.	M'Crea, 1282.	M'Elerney, 1305.
M'Carson, 1245.	M'Clure, 1263.	M'Cready, 1283.	M'Elfatrick, 1383.
M'Carten, 1247.	M'Cluskey, 289, 1264.	M'Creanor. 1284.	M'Elgun, 775.
M'Carter, 1218.	M'Clymon, 1259.	M'Creary, 1285.	M'Elgunn, 775.
M'Carthur, 1218.	M'Clymonds, 281.	M'Creavy, 1363.	M'Elhar, 246.
M'Carthy, 253, 642. 1238, 1246, 1247, 1757.	M'Clyntock. 1261.	M'Creech, 1369.	M'Elharry, 1378.
M'Cartie, 1246.	M'Cobrie, 1278.	M'Creedy, 1283.	M'Elhatton, 1379.
M'Cartiney, 1145.	M'Cole, 301.	M'Creery, 1285.	M'Elhenny, 1306.
M'Cartney, 1145, 1246, 1247.	M'Colgan, 303.	M'Creesh, 1369.	M'Elheny, 1306.
M'Carton, 1247.	M'Coll, 1250.	M'Creevy, 1363.	M'Elhill, 2075.
M'Carty, 1246.	M'Collom, 1265.	M'Crevey, 1363.	M'Elhinney, 1306.
M'Casey, 1219.	M'Collough, 1289.	M'Croberts, 1476.	M'Elhuddy, 1340.
M'Caskie, 1220.	M'Collum, 306, 1265.	M'Crory, 1286, 1806.	M'Ellecuddy, 1340.
M'Caslan, 1252.	M'Collyums, 1498.	M'Crub, 1799.	M'Ellister, 1212.
M'Casland, 1252.	M'Colman, 1241.	M'Crudden, 1804.	M'Elmeel, 1307.
M'Cateer, 1222.	M'Colum, 1265.	M'Crum, 1287.	M'Elmoyle, 1381.
M'Caufield, 1253.	M,Comb, 1266.	M'Crumb, 1287.	M'Elmurray, 1382, 1438, 1602.
M'Caugherty, 1145, 1246.	M'Combes, 1266.	M'Cubrae, 1278.	M'Elreath, 1387.
M'Caughey, 1248, 1328.	M'Combs, 1266.	M'Cudden, 1206.	M'Elreavy, 1308.
M'Caughin, 1248.	M'Comick, 1274.	M'Cue, 1288, 1376.	M'Elroy, 1309, 1384.
M'Caughley, 1146, 1249.	M'Comiskey, 1290.	M'Cull, 1289.	M'Elshender, 18.
M'Caul, 1239,1250.	M'Comley, 1251.	M'Culla, 1289.	M'Elshunder, 18.
M'Caulay, 1223.	M'Comming, 1529.	M'Cullagh, 1289.	M'Elvaine, 1385.
M'Cauley, 1146, 1223, 1251.	M'Comoskey, 1290.	M'Cullah, 1289.	M'Elvee, 1398
M'Caully, 1223.	M'Cona, 1897.	M'Cullen, 1472.	M'Elveen, 1385.
M'Causland, 18, 1252.	M'Conachie, 1267.	M'Cullion, 1472.	M'Elvie, 1398.
M'Cavanagh, 261, 262.	M'Conaghy, 312, 1267, 1755.	M'Culloch, 1289.	M'Elwain, 1386.
M'Cavill, 226, 1253.	M'Conamy, 325.	M'Cullogh, 1289.	M'Elwane, 1386.
M'Cavish, 909, 1956.	M'Conaughty, 1267.	M'Cullough, 1289.	M'Elwean, 1386.
M'Cawel, 226.	M'Conaway, 325.	M'Cullow, 1289.	M'Elwee, 1310, 1339.
M'Cawell, 1239.	M'Cone, 1463.	M'Cullum, 1265.	M'Elwreath, 1387.
M'Cawl, 1239.	M'Conell, 1270.	M'Cully, 395.	M'Enally, 1444.
M'Cawley, 1223.	M'Conkey, 1268.	M'Cullyam, 1498.	M'Endoo, 1311.
M'Cawly, 1223.	M'Conn, 1269.	M'Cumesky, 1290.	M'Endry, 1374.
M'Cay, 1151, 1280, 1391.	M'Connaghy, 1267.	M'Cumisky, 1290.	M'Eneany, 99, 1312.
M'Celvey, 1398.	M'Connaughey, 1267.	M'Cune. 1291, 1404.	M'Enerny, 1388.
M'Cheyne, 965.	M'Connell, 316, 1270. 1272, 1301.	M'Cunnigan, 400.	M'Enery, 870, 1313 1314, 1374, 1388.
M'Clachlin, 1418.	M'Connellogue. 1271.	M'Curdy, 1292.	M'Eniry, 1313, 1314.
M'Clafferty. 1254.	M'Connerty, 1267.	M'Curry, 1276.	M'Enroe, 1148, 1315, 1805.
M'Clain, 1256.	M'Connon, 1270.	M'Cusker, 340, 1293.	M'Entagert. 1317.
M'Clamon, 281.	M'Conohy, 1264.	M'Cuskern. 340, 1293.	M'Entaggart. 1317.
M'Clane, 1256	M'Conol, 1270.	M'Cutchan, 1294.	M'Entee, 1316, 1343.
M'Clarnon, 1417.	M'Conomy, 325.	M'Cutcheon, 1038, 1294.	M'Enteer, 1316. 1389.
M'Clary, 1255.	M'Conready, 1283.	M'Cutchon, 1294.	M'Entegart, 1317, 1389.
M'Clatton. 1379.	M'Conville, 1270, 1272.	M'Dacker, 817.	M'Entire, 1316, 1389.
M'Clatty, 18.	M'Conway. 325.	M'Dade, 1295, 1298.	M'Entosh, 1152.
M'Clave, 802.	M'Coo. 1376.	M'Daid, 426, 427, 1295, 1298.	M'Entyre, 1222, 1389.
M'Clean, 1256, 1419.	M'Cook. 326.	M'Daniall, 1296.	M'Erlain, 1318.
M'Clearnon, 1417.	M'Corcadale, 1275.	M'Daniel, 1296, 1300, 1301.	M'Erlane, 1318.
M'Cleary, 1257.	M'Corcodale. 1275.	M'Dara, 1640.	M'Erlean, 1318.
M'Cleery, 1257.	M'Corkell, 1273.	M'David, 1295.	M'Erleen, 1318.
M'Cleish, 1153.	M'Corkill, 1273.	M'Davitt, 1295.	M'Errigle, 1332.
M'Clellan, 1258.	M'Corkle, 1273.	M'Dermott, 418, 456, 457, 1148, 1297, 1588.	M'Evaddy, 1154, 1224.
M'Clelland, 1258.	M'Cormac, 1274.	M'Devitt, 1295, 1298.	M'Evady, 1154.
M'Clement, 281, 1259.	M'Cormack, 335, 1274.	M'Diarmod, 1297.	M'Evely, 1919.
M'Clements, 281, 1259.	M'Cormick, 1274.	M'Dire, 1303.	
	M'Cormilla, 739.	M'Divitt, 1295.	
	M'Corquodale, 1275.	M'Dole, 1302.	
	M'Corrikle, 1273.	M'Dona, 1299.	

Surname and Reference No.	Surname and Reference No.	Surname and Reference No.	Surname and Reference No.
M'Keigue, 1392.	M'Konkey, 1268.	M'Maghen, 1426.	M'Nally, 1444. 1611.
M'Keith, 1397.	M'Kough. 1403.	M'Maghon, 1426.	M'Nalty, 1445, 1462, 1612.
M'Keiver, 1396.	M'Koy, 1280.	M'Maghone. 1426.	M'Nama, 1446, 1448.
M'Kellan, 1240, 1407.	M'Krann. 1361.	M'Mahan, 1426.	M'Namanamee. 1447.
M'Kellop, 1408.	M'Kurdy, 1292.	M'Mahon, 1168, 1169, 1426.	M'Namara, 1148. 1448. 1865.
M'Kelshenter. 18.	M'Kuscar. 1293.	M'Manamon. 1430.	M'Namarra, 1448.
M'Kelvey, 1398.	M'Kusker. 1293.	M'Manis, 1427.	M'Namee. 1148. 1449.
M'Kemmin. 1241.	M'Kussack. 1413.	M'Mann. 1426.	M'Namorrow. 1448.
M'Kendry, 1374, 1399.	M'Lachlin, 1418.	M'Mannus. 1427.	M'Naught. 1415.
M'Kenery, 1374.	M'Laghlan. 1418.	M'Manus. 1204, 1427.	M'Naughten, 1450, 1616.
M'Keniry, 1388.	M'Laine, 1256.	M'Math. 1428.	M'Naughton, 1450.
M'Kenna, 989, 1400. 1401.	M'Lamond. 281. 1259.	M'Mearty. 1231.	M'Nay, 1451.
M'Kennery, 1374.	M'Lane, 1256.	M'Mechan. 1426.	M'Nea, 1451.
M'Kenny. 992, 1400. 1401, 1411.	M'Larenon. 1417.	M'Meckan. 1429.	M'Neagh. 1451.
M'Kensie, 1402.	M'Larinon. 1417.	M'Meckin, 1429.	M'Neal. 1453.
M'Kenty, 1316.	M'Larney, 1416.	M'Meechan, 1429.	M'Nealey, 1454.
M'Kenzie. 1402.	M'Larnon. 1417.	M'Meekan, 1429.	M'Neally. 1454.
M'Keo, 1403.	M'Lary. 1255.	M'Meeken. 1429.	M'Nee, 1451.
M'Keoan. 1404.	M'Lauchlin, 1418.	M'Meekin. 1429.	M'Neece. 1458.
M'Keogh, 994, 1403.	M'Laughlin, 1124, 1418, 1425.	M'Meel, 1307.	M'Neel. 1453.
M'Keon, 1291, 1404, 1463.	M'Lave. 802.	M'Meenamon. 1430.	M'Neese, 1458.
M'Keough, 1403.	M'Lavin, 1578.	M'Meichan. 1429	M'Neigh. 1451.
M'Keowen, 1404.	M'Lean, 1256. 1419.	M'Menamen. 1430.	M'Neight. 1415.
M'Keown, 261, 965, 1291, 1404, 1463.	M'Learey, 1257.	M'Menamin. 1430	M'Neile, 1453.
M'Kerel, 1244.	M'Learnon. 1417.	M'Menamon. 1430.	M'Neill, 1453.
M'Kerlie. 999.	M'Leary. 1257.	M'Menamy, 1431.	M'Neilly. 1452, 1454.
M'Kernan, 1405.	M'Lee. 1083, 1208.	M'Menemen. 1430.	M'Nelis, 1455.
M'Kerrall, 1244.	M'Leery, 1257.	M'Menemy. 1431.	M'Nerland, 1456.
M'Ketian. 1149.	M'Lees. 1153.	M'Menim, 1430.	M'Nerlin, 1456.
M'Ketterick. 1414.	M'Leese, 1153.	M'Menimey. 1431.	M'Nern, 1443.
M'Kettrick, 814, 1414.	M'Leesh, 1420.	M'Menimin. 1430.	M'Nerney, 1457.
M'Kevor, 1390.	M'Lehenny, 1423.	M'Merty, 1231.	M'Nertney, 1457.
M'Kew, 1376.	M'Lehinney, 1423.	M'Michael, 1432.	M'Nestry. 1412.
M'Kewen. 1404.	M'Leise, 1153.	M'Michalin, 1432.	M'Niece, 1183, 1458.
M'Kewn, 1404.	M'Leish. 1153. 1420.	M'Michall, 1432.	M'Nielly. 1454.
M'Key, 1151, 1391.	M'Leland, 1258	M'Michan, 1429.	M'Niff. 1459.
M'Kibben, 1406.	M'Lellan, 1258.	M'Mighael, 1432.	M'Night, 1415, 1450.
M'Kibbin, 1406.	M'Lelland, 1258.	M'Millan, 1433, 1437.	M'Nirny, 1457.
M'Kibbon, 1406.	M'Lement, 1259.	M'Millen, 1433, 1437.	M'Nish, 1460.
M'Kie, 1280.	M'Lenaghan, 1260, 1421.	M'Millin, 1433. 1437.	M'Nite, 1415.
M'Kiernan, 1010, 1405.	M'Lenahan, 1421.	M'Minamy, 1431.	M'Noger, 320.
M'Kiever, 1390.	M'Leneghan, 1421.	M'Monagle, 1434.	M'Nogher, 320.
M'Killen, 1407.	M'Lenigan. 1421.	M'Monegal, 1434.	M'Nohor, 320.
M'Killian, 1211, 1407.	M'Lennon. 1421.	M'Monigal, 1434.	M'Nuff. 1161.
M'Killion, 1240.	M'Leod, 1422.	M'Monigle, 1434.	M'Nulty, 1445, 1462.
M'Killip, 1408.	M'Lerney, 1305.	M'Moran, 1436.	M'Oscar, 1293.
M'Killop, 1018, 1408.	M'Lernon, 1417.	M'Mordie. 1135.	M'Oubery, 1278.
M'Killopps, 1408.	M'Leroy, 1309.	M'Morin, 1436.	M'Oubrey, 1278.
M'Kilmurray, 1382.	M'Lester, 1212.	M Morran, 1436, 1550.	M'Owen. 1404, 1463.
M'Kilveen, 1385.	M'Lhinney. 1423.	M'Morray, 1438.	M'Paddan. 1164.
M'Kilvie, 1398.	M'Lice, 1209.	M'Morrow. 1438.	M'Padden. 1322, 1164.
M'Kimmon, 1409.	M'Limont, 1259.	M'Morry, 1438.	M'Paden, 1464.
M'Kinch, 1375.	M'Linden, 1105, 1210.	M'Mouran, 1436.	M'Padgen, 1464.
M'Kinestry, 1412.	M'Lindon, 1210.	M'Mullan, 1433, 1437, 1576.	M'Padian, 1464.
M'Kiniff, 1459.	M'Linney, 1423.	M'Mullen, 1437, 1580.	M'Pake, 1466.
M'Kinlay, 1410.	M'Lintock, 1261.	M'Mullon, 1437.	M'Parland, 1324, 1465.
M'Kinley, 1410.	M'Linton, 1210.	M'Munaway. 1447.	M'Parlin, 1324.
M'Kinney, 1400, 1402.	M'Lochlin, 1418.	M'Munigal, 1434.	M'Partlan, 1465.
M'Kinnie, 1402.	M'Loghlen, 1418.	M'Murdy, 1435.	M'Partland, 1324.
M'Kinny, 992, 1401, 1411.	M'Loghlin, 1418.	M'Murlan, 1551.	M'Peake, 1466.
M'Kinstry, 1412.	M'Loon, 1424.	M'Murran, 1436.	M'Phadden, 1322.
M'Kinty, 1316.	M'Loone, 1214, 1424.	M'Murray, 1438, 1602.	M'Phail, 2010.
M'Kinzie. 1402.	M'Loonie, 286.	M'Murren, 1436.	M'Pharland, 1324.
M'Kirtrick, 1414.	M'Lorinan, 1417.	M'Murrin, 1436.	M'Pharson, 1468.
M'Kissock, 1413.	M'Losky, 1264.	M'Murry, 1438.	M'Phelan, 1467. 1719.
M'Kitterick. 1414.	M'Loughlan, 1418.	M'Murtery, 1439.	M'Pherson, 1468.
M'Kittrick, 814, 1414.	M'Loughlen, 1418.	M'Murthry, 1439.	M'Phettridge, 1326.
M'Kivirking, 1372.	M'Loughlin, 1418, 1425.	M'Murtry, 1439.	M'Polin, 1731.
M'Klern, 1380.	M'Lroy, 1309	M'Nabb, 1440, 1441.	M'Qua, 1495.
M'Kneight, 1415.	M'Lucas, 1130.	M'Nabo, 1440, 1441 2019.	M'Quade, 1469, 2022.
M'Kniff. 1459.	M'Lune, 1214.	M'Naboe. 1441, 2019.	M'Quagh, 1495.
M'Knight, 1012, 1415.	M'Luney, 1213.	M'Naboola. 1442.	M'Quaid, 1469.
M'Knulty, 1462.	M'Lure, 1263.	M'Nabow, 1441.	M'Quaide, 1469.
M'Koen, 1404.	M'Luskey, 1264.	M'Naghten, 1415, 1616.	M'Qualter, 1493.
M'Kone, 1404.	M'Ma, 1428, 1446.	M'Naghton, 1450.	M'Quatters, 1494.
	M'Machan, 1429.	M'Nail. 1453.	M'Quay, 1151, 1391.
	M'Machon, 1426	M'Nairn. 1443.	
	M'Magh, 1428.	M'Nale, 1453.	

Surname and Reference No.	Surname and Reference No.	Surname and Reference No.	Surname and Reference No.
M'Queen. 1473.	M'Ternan, 1488.	Meere, 1608.	Miers, 1608.
M'Question. 1470.	M'Tier. 1222.	Megahan, 1156.	Migrillan, 1365.
M'Queston. 1470.	M'Tiernan, 1488.	Megall, 1239.	Miles, 1609.
M'Quey. 1391.	M'Tigue, 1487.	Megan, 1156.	Milford, 1521.
M'Quiggan. 1368.	M Trustry. 1264.	Megarrity. 1333	Miligan, 1525.
M'Quilin, 1472.	M'Usker. 1293.	Megarry, 1334	Millan, 1523.
M'Quilkan. 2061.	M'Vady. 1154.	Megarty, 1333.	Millane. 1580.
M'Quilkin, 1471. 2061.	M'Vanamy. 1430.	Megaw, 1508.	Millar, 1524.
M'Quillan, 1472, 1498.	M'Vay, 1489.	Megginn, 1345.	Millbride, 1579.
1752.	M'Vea, 1489.	Meghan, 1507	Millea, 1522. 1676.
M'Quillen. 1472.	M'Veagh, 1489.	Meginniss, 1369.	Millen, 1523.
M'Quilliams. 1498.	M'Veety, 1492.	Meglamry. 1546.	Miller, 1524.
M'Quillian, 1472.	M'Veigh. 1489. 1490.	Meglaughlin. 1418.	Millican, 1525.
M'Quillon. 1472.	M'Veity. 1492.	Megowan, 1358.	Milligan, 1525, 1581.
M'Quilly. 1499.	M'Vey, 1489. 1490.	Megrath, 1362.	Milligen, 1525, 1581.
M'Quilquane, 1471.	M'Vicar, 1491.	Megraw, 1362.	Millikan, 1525.
M'Quin. 1473.	M'Vickar, 1491.	Meguiggan. 1368.	Milliken, 1525, 1581.
M'Quiney. 1496.	M'Vicker. 1491.	Mehatty, 1166.	Millikin, 1525.
M'Quinn. 1473.	M'Vitty, 1492.	Mehan, 1507.	Millin, 1526.
M'Quinney. 1496.	M'Vity, 1492.	Meighan, 1507.	Milling, 1526.
M'Quirk, 1371.	M'Wade, 1469.	Mekerrel, 1244.	Milne, 1523.
M'Quiston. 1470.	M'Walter. 1493	Mekill. 1159.	Milreavy, 1584.
M'Quitty. 1474.	M'Ward. 2028.	Melarkey, 1577.	Milroy, 1589.
M'Quoid. 1469.	M'Watters. 1494.	Melay. 1522.	Mimnagh, 1593.
M'Quorcodale. 1275.	M'Waugh, 1495.	Meldon, 1509. 1570.	Minagh, 991.
M'Rae. 1282.	M'Weeny. 1226, 1496.	Meleady, 1510.	Mineely, 1454.
M'Ranald. 1789.	M'Wha, 1495.	Meledy, 1510.	Minett. 1415.
M'Rann, 1361.	M'Whannon. 178	Melia. 1175. 1511, 1676.	Minford, 1521, 1545.
M'Rannal, 1789.	M'Whaugh. 1495.	Melledy. 1510.	Mingane, 1179.
M'Ray. 1282.	M'Wherter. 1497.	Mellet. 1512.	Miniece, 1458.
M'Ready, 1283.	M Whin, 1473.	Mellett. 1512.	Minnis. 1458.
M'Reavy, 1363.	M'Whinney. 1290, 1496.	Mellitt. 1512.	Minnish, 1460.
M'Reedy. 1283.	M'Whinny. 1496.	Mellon. 1580.	Minnitt, 1415.
M'Reery. 1285.	M'Whirter. 1497.	Mellot. 1512.	Minochor, 320.
M'Reynold. 1789.	M'Whiston. 1470.	Mellott. 1512.	Minogher, 320.
M'Richard. 1475.	M'Whitty. 1474.	Melly. 1175.	Minogue, 1183, 1539.
M'Roary. 1286.	M'Wiggan, 1368.	Meloy, 1536.	Minoher, 320.
M'Roberts. 1476.	M'Wiggin, 1368.	Melroy, 1587.	Minteer. 1196.
M'Robin. 370. 762. 1477.	M'Wilkin, 1471.	Melville, 1513, 1514,	Minteith. 1544.
M'Rory. 1286. 1366.	M'William, 1498.	1592.	Mintin, 1516.
1806.	M Williams. 1472. 1498	Melvin, 1513. 1514.	Miscella, 1528.
M'Ruddery. 1415.	M'Willie, 1499.	Menaght. 1539.	Miskell, 1527.
M'Rum. 1287.	M'Winey. 1496.	Menairy. 1515.	Miskella, 1527.
M'Scollog, 580.	M'Winney, 1496.	Menarry. 1515.	Miskelly, 1528.
M'Shan. 965. 1478.	M'Witty. 1474.	Menary. 1515.	Miskimmin, 1529.
M'Shanaghy, 643.	M'Wray, 1282.	Menautt. 1415.	Miskimmon, 1529.
M Shane. 965. 1478.	Mea. 1202.	Meneely. 1454.	M sskimmins, 397,
M'Sharry, 635. 1479.	Meade. 1500.	Menease. 1458	1529.
M'Sheaghan, 1958.	Meagher. 1167. 1501.	Meneiss. 1458.	Mitchael, 1530.
M'Skean. 1958.	Mealia. 1175. 1511. 1676.	Menemin. 1430.	Mitchell. 1530. 1592.
M'Skimmins. 397.	Mealley. 1175.	Menocher. 320.	Mitten. 1531.
M'Soreley, 1480.	Meally. 1511.	Menteith. 1544.	Mitty. 1198.
M'Sorely. 1480.	Mealy. 1676.	Menton. 1516.	Moabray. 1563.
M'Sorley, 1480.	Meany. 1502	Mercer. 1517.	Moan. 1534.
M'Spaddin. 1481.	Meara. 1186. 1503.	Merditt. 1518.	Moany, 1547.
M'Sparran, 1482.	1677.	Merdith. 1518.	Moarn, 1550.
M'Speddin. 1481.	Meares. 1170, 1504.	Merdy. 1518.	Moekler. 1532.
M'Suile. 1046.	Mearn. 1193.	Meredith, 1518.	Moen, 1534.
M'Sweeny. 1148. 1483.	Mears. 1504.	Meredyth. 1518.	Moeran, 1550.
1485. 1944, 1946.	Mease. 1205.	Mermont. 1191.	Moffatt, 1533.
M'Sweney. 1483.	Meaze. 1205.	Merna. 1601.	Moffett. 1533.
M'Swiggan. 1484.	Meban. 1505.	Merrick. 1520.	Moffitt. 1533.
M'Swigin. 1484.	Meberry. 1203.	Merriman. 1191.	Moghan. 1534. 2016.
M'Swigin, 1484.	Mecan. 1243.	Merryman. 1191.	Mohan. 1168, 1534.
M'Swine. 1483, 1944.	Mecmeckin. 1429	Mescel. 1527.	Moir. 1548.
1946.	Mecowan. 1358.	Meskimmon, 1529	Moles. 1535.
M'Swiney. 1483. 1485.	Mecredy. 1283.	Metcalf. 1519.	Moleyneux, 1538.
1944.	Medcalf. 1519.	Metkiff, 1519.	Mollan, 1576.
M'Taggart. 1317, 1949.	Medlicott. 1306.	Mewha. 1495.	Mollony, 1537.
M'Taghlan. 921.	Medlycott. 1306.	Mewhanan. 178	Mollowney. 1537.
M Taghlin. 940 1486.	Medole. 1302	Mewheney, 1200	Molloy, 1114, 1536,
M'Tague. 1487. 1543	Mee, 1449. 1507.	Mewhenney. 1200.	1583, 1592.
1960.	Meegan. 1507	Mewherter. 1497	Mollyneux. 1538.
M'Tamney. 1221.	Meeghan. 1507.	Mewhirter. 1497.	Mologhnev. 1537.
M'Tavish, 1956.	Meehan. 1507.	Meyers. 1504.	Moloney. 1357.
M'Teague. 1487. 1960.	Meehen. 1507.	Meyrick. 1520.	Molony, 1537.
M'Teer. 1222.	Meek. 1172.	Miall. 1607.	Molowny. 1537.
M'Teggart. 1317, 1949.	Meekin. 1507.	Michael, 1530.	Moloy. 1536.
M'Tegue, 1487.	Meenagh. 1958.	Michal. 1530.	Molphy, 1600.
M'Teigue, 1487, 1960.	Meenhan, 1181.	Michel. 1530.	Molseed, 1177.

Surname and Reference No.	Surname and Reference No.	Surname and Reference No.	Surname and Reference No.
Molumby, 1537.	Morrow, 1559.	Mullan, 1437, 1576, 1580, 1581.	Murray, 1438, 1602.
Molyneaux, 1538.	Morrowson, 1559.	Mullano, 1580, 1582.	Murron, 1603.
Molyneux, 1538.	Mortagh, 1560.	Mullarkey, 1577.	Murricohu, 1600.
Monaboe, 1441, 2019.	Mortimer, 1560.	Mullavin, 1578.	Murrihy, 1602.
Monachan, 1539.	Mortimor, 1560.	Mullbrido, 1579.	Murrin, 1603.
Monaghan, 1183, 1539, 1541, 1565.	Mortimore, 1562.	Mulleady, 1510.	Murrough, 1559.
Monahan, 1539, 1565.	Mortland, 1551.	Mulleo, 1536.	Murrow, 1559.
Monck, 1541.	Morton, 1552.	Mullen, 1176, 1437, 1576, 1580, 1582.	Murry, 1602.
Monday, 1214.	Mortymer, 1560.	Mulligan, 1525, 1576, 1581, 1585.	Murt, 1604.
Monds, 1594.	Mosgrove, 1606.		Murta, 1604.
Monehan, 1539, 1565.	Moskimmon, 1529.	Mullin, 1576, 1580.	Murtagh, 1553, 1597, 1604.
Money, 1547.	Moss, 1561.	Mullinox, 1538.	Murtaugh, 1604.
Moneypenny, 1540.	Moter, 1100.	Mullinix, 1538.	Murtha, 1604.
Mongney, 1546.	Moton, 1100.	Mullins, 1580, 1582.	Murtland, 1551.
Mongon, 1182.	Moughan, 1534, 2016.	Mullock, 1356.	Murvano, 2029.
Monk, 1541.	Moughty, 1566.	Mullogan, 1581.	Muse, 1605.
Monks, 1539, 1541.	Moulds, 1535.	Mullon, 1580.	Musgrave, 1606.
Monley, 1542.	Mountain, 1562.	Mulloney, 1537.	Musgrove, 1606.
Monnelly, 1542.	Mountiford, 1545.	Mullowney, 1537.	Myall, 1607.
Monohan, 1565.	Mountifort, 1545.	Mulloy, 1356, 1583.	Myers, 1564, 1603.
Monroe, 1587, 1595.	Mourn, 1550.	Mullreavy, 1584.	Myhan, 1507.
Monsell, 1199.	Mournane, 1192, 2029.	Mullvihill, 1592.	Myhill, 1607.
Montague, 1487, 1543.	Mowbray, 1563.	Mulmona, 1561.	Myles, 1609.
Montane, 1562.	Mowen, 1531.	Muloney, 1537.	Mylott, 1512.
Montang, 1562.	Mowhannan, 178.	Muloy, 1536.	Mylotte, 1512.
Montangue, 1562.	Mowlds, 1535.	Mulqueen, 1581, 1585.	Myres, 1608.
Monteeth, 1544.	Mowles, 1535.	Mulreany, 1586.	Mythen, 1531.
Monteith, 1544.	Moyers, 1564, 1608.	Mulrenan, 1586.	
Montford, 1545.	Moyles, 1609.	Mulrenin, 1586.	
Montfort, 1545.	Moynahan, 1565.	Mulrennan, 1586.	
Montgomery, 1347, 1546.	Moynan, 1565.	Mulrennin, 1586.	
Monypenny, 1540.	Moyney, 1547.	Mulroe, 1587, 1589.	
Monypeny, 1540.	Moynihan, 1539, 1565.	Mulrony, 1588.	Naggs, 1040.
Moobray, 1563.	Mucbrin, 206.	Mulrooney, 1297, 1588, 1810.	Naghten, 1616.
Mooney, 1547.	Muckady, 1566.		Naghton, 1616.
Moore, 1548.	Muckaran, 1567.	Mulrow, 1587.	Nagle, 1610.
Moorehead, 1549.	Muckaree, 1026.	Mulroy, 1587, 1589.	Nail, 1624.
Mooreheed, 1549.	Muckedan, 1225.	Mulryan, 1831.	Nailer, 1618.
Moorhead, 1549.	Muckeen, 1419.	Mulvanerty, 115.	Nailor, 1618.
Moran, 1436, 1550.	Muckian, 1393.	Mulvanny, 1590.	Naish, 1614.
More, 1548.	Muckilbouy, 1026.	Mulvany, 1590, 1591.	Nally, 1444, 1611.
Moreen, 1548.	Mucklebreed, 1232.	Mulvehill, 1592.	Nalty, 1445, 1612.
Morehead, 1549.	Muckler, 1532.	Mulvey, 1590, 1591.	Nanany, 1097.
Moreland, 1551, 1598.	Mugan, 1329.	Mulvihil, 1592.	Naper, 1613.
Moren, 1550.	Muinagh, 991.	Mulvihill, 1513, 1530, 1536, 1592.	Napier, 1613.
Moresay, 1558.	Muir, 1548.		Nary, 1620.
Moreton, 1100, 1552.	Muirhead, 1549.	Mumford, 1593.	Nash, 1614.
Morey, 1548, 1553.	Muirland, 1598.	Munce, 1594.	Naugher, 320, 1615.
Moriarty, 1553, 1604.	Muise, 1605.	Munday, 1214, 1424.	Naughtan, 1616.
Morice, 1556.	Mulavill, 1513.	Munds, 1594.	Naughten, 1616.
Morin, 1448, 1550.	Mulcahy, 1568.	Mundy, 1214.	Naughter, 1615.
Moris, 1556.	Mulconry, 323, 324.	Munford, 1545.	Naughton, 1420, 1616.
Morisey, 1558.	Mulcreevy, 1569.	Munkettrick, 1414.	Naulty, 1612.
Morison, 1557.	Mulderg, 1783.	Munkittrick, 1414.	Navin, 1617, 1628.
Moriss, 1556.	Mulderrig, 1777.	Munns, 1794.	Naylor, 1618.
Morisson, 1557.	Muldon, 1570.	Munroe, 1595.	Neagle, 1610.
Morissy, 1558.	Muldoon, 1302, 1509, 1570.	Munrow, 1595.	Neal, 1624, 1678.
Morland, 1551.	Muldowney, 506, 1571.	Muntz, 1594.	Neale, 1624.
Morley, 1554.	Mulgan, 1581.	Munze, 1594.	Nealer, 1618.
Moroney, 1555.	Mulgrave, 1572.	Muran, 1550.	Nealon, 1619, 1622.
Moroony, 1555.	Mulgrievey, 1569.	Murchan, 1596.	Nealson, 1625.
Morressy, 1558.	Mulgroo, 1572.	Murchison, 1596.	Neaphsey, 1617.
Morresy, 1558.	Mulhall, 1573.	Murchisson, 1596.	Neary, 1620.
Morrin, 1550.	Mulhane, 1580.	Murdoch, 1597, 1604.	Neavin, 1628.
Morris, 621, 1556, 1558.	Mulbartagh, 1145, 1247.	Murdock, 1597, 1604.	Neazer, 135.
Morrisey, 1558.	Mulhearn, 1574.	Murdough, 1597.	Neazor, 135.
Morrison, 79, 177, 1557, 1558.	Mulheeran, 1574.	Murdow, 1597.	Nee, 1041.
Morris-Roe, 1556.	Mulheran, 1574.	Murdy, 1435.	Neef, 448.
Morrissee, 1558.	Mulheren, 1574.	Murhilla, 937.	Neehan, 1621.
Morrissey, 1556, 1557, 1558.	Mulhern, 1574.	Murkin, 1593.	Neenan, 1621, 1635.
Morrisson, 1557.	Mulherrin, 1574.	Murland, 155, 1598.	Neeper, 1613.
Morrogh, 1559.	Mulherron, 1574.	Murn, 1603.	Neight, 1042.
Morrolly, 1554.	Mulholland, 905, 1575.	Murnain, 1599.	Neilan, 1619, 1622.
Morroney, 1555.	Mulhollum, 1575.	Murnan, 1599.	Neiland, 1623.
Morrossey, 1558.	Mulholm, 1575.	Murnane, 1192, 1599.	Neilands, 1623.
Morrough, 1559.	Mulholn, 1575.	Murney, 1599.	Neill, 1624, 1678.
	Mulkhearn, 1574.	Murphy, 1600.	Neilson, 1625.
	Mullagan, 1581.	Murrane, 1601.	Neiper, 1613.

Surname and Reference No.	Surname and Reference No.	Surname and Reference No.	Surname and Reference No.
Nelan, 1622.	Oak, 424. 1640.	O'Halleran, 1665.	Packenham, 1694.
Nelis, 1626.	Oakes, 424. 1640.	O'Halleron, 1665.	Paden, 1705.
Nelson, 1625.	Oaks, 424. 1640.	O'Halloran, 793, 1665.	Padon, 1705.
Neper, 1613.	Oates, 1641.	O'Hamill, 795.	Page, 1691.
Nesbett, 1627.	Oats, 1641, 1757.	O'Hanlon, 808, 1666.	Paget, 1692.
Nesbitt, 1627.	O'Beirne, 206.	O'Hara, 825, 1667.	Pagett, 1692.
Neven, 1628.	O'Boyle, 143.	O'Hare, 821, 1668.	Pagnam, 1694.
Nevin, 1617. 1628.	O'Brallaghan, 145.	O'Harra, 1667.	Paiden, 1705.
Nevins, 1628.	O'Brian, 1642.	O'Hea, 848, 1669.	Paisley, 1693.
Newcomb, 1629.	O'Brien, 176, 382, 1233, 1642.	O'Hear, 821, 1668.	Pakenham, 1694.
Newcome, 1629.	O'Brine, 1233.	O'Hegan, 1664.	Paragon, 622.
Newcomen, 1629.	O'Bryan, 1642.	O'Herlihy, 937	Parill, 1697.
Newell, 1630.	O'Bryen, 1642.	O'Hora, 1667.	Park, 1695
Newells, 1630.	O'Byrne, 197, 206.	O'Hure, 922.	Parkenson, 1696.
Newill, 1630.	O'Cahan, 214, 663, 1670.	Oins, 1690.	Parkes, 1695.
Newnan, 1635.	O'Caharney, 975	O'Kane, 663, 971, 1670.	Parkinson, 1696.
Neyland, 1623.	O'Caherney, 975.	O'Keane, 1670.	Parkison, 1696.
Neylon, 1622.	O'Callaghan, 220, 1643.	O'Keefe, 1671.	Parle, 1697.
Nichol, 1631.	O'Callahan, 1643.	O'Keeffe, 979, 1671.	Parlon, 1698.
Nicholds, 1631.	O'Carroll, 250.	O'Kelly, 988, 1672.	Parnell, 1698.
Nicholl, 1631, 1632.	O'Carthy, 253. 1644.	O Keoneen, 961.	Parrette, 1712.
Nicholls, 1631.	O'Caughan, 1670.	O'Kibbon, 695.	Parrican 622.
Nichols, 1631, 1632.	O Cloghessy, 1645.	O'Kielt, 1896.	Parrott, 1712.
Nicholson, 1631, 1632.	O'Clohessy, 1645.	O'Kieran, 976.	Pasley, 1693.
Nickelson, 1631.	O'Clussey, 1645.	O'Laverty, 1670.	Patchet, 1692.
Nickle, 1631.	O'Colter, 343.	O'Leary, 1080, 1673.	Patchy, 622.
Nickles, 1631.	O'Connell, 316, 1646.	Olligan, 791.	Paten, 1700. 1717.
Nickson, 1633.	O'Conner, 320.	O'Loughlan, 1674.	Paterson, 1699.
Nicol, 1631.	O'Connor, 320, 321, 1647.	O'Loughlin, 1124, 1674	Patison, 1699.
Nicoll, 1631.	O'Conor, 320.	O'Lyons, 1142, 1675.	Paton, 1700. 1717.
Nicolls, 1631.	O'Cullane, 304.	O'Mallev, 1174, 1175, 1511, 1676.	Patrican, 622.
Nicols, 1631.	O'Currobeen, 333.	O'Mara, 1677.	Patrick, 622.
Niell, 1624.	O'Curry, 339.	O'Meally, 1175.	Patten, 1700.
Nielson, 1625.	Odarian, 494.	O'Mealue, 1676.	Pattersen, 1699.
Night, 1042.	O'Dea, 725, 1648.	O'Mealy, 1676.	Patterson, 1699.
Nilan, 1622.	O Dermott, 457.	O'Meara, 1186, 1503, 1677.	Patteson, 1699.
Nilon, 1622.	O'Devine, 461, 1650.	O'Meehon, 1507.	Pattin, 1700.
Nipe, 1043.	O'Dheer, 1657.	O'Mullane, 1582.	Pattison, 1699.
Nisbett, 1627	O'Diff, 521.	O'Muracha, 1600.	Patton, 1700, 1717.
Nisbit, 1627.	Odlum, 1649.	O'Neal, 1690.	Patty, 1700.
Nivin, 1628.	O'Doherty, 479, 1651.	O'Neill, 1624, 1678.	Paulett, 1701.
Nix, 2071.	O'Donnell, 417, 485, 1301, 1652.	Oogan, 2070.	Pavy, 1704.
Nixon, 1633.	O'Donnelly, 485.	Oolahan, 919.	Payton, 1717.
Nocher, 320, 1615.	O'Donovan, 489, 1653.	Oonin, 753.	Pazley, 1693.
Nochtin, 1616.	O'Doogan, 522.	O'Rafferty, 1760.	Pearce, 1702.
Nocker, 320.	O'Dooghany, 522.	Orchard, 1679.	Pearse, 1702.
Nockton, 1616.	O'Doolan, 505.	O'Reiley, 1680.	Pearson, 1703.
Nocter, 1615.	O'Dornan, 495.	O'Reilly, 1680, 1785.	Peasley, 1693.
Nocton, 1616.	O'Doud, 1654.	Organ, 915.	Peavey, 1704.
Noghar, 320.	O'Dougherty, 1651.	O'Rielly, 1680.	Peden, 1705.
Nogher, 320, 1615.	O'Dowd, 498, 1654.	O'Riordan, 1681, 1795.	Pedian, 1705.
Noher, 320.	O'Driscoll, 513, 943, 1655.	O'Roarke, 1682.	Peel, 1706.
Nolan, 1634.	O'Duffy, 521, 1656.	O'Rorke, 1682, 1820.	Peelan, 2047.
Noland, 1634.	O'Dwyer, 537, 1657.	O'Rourke, 1682, 1820	Peg, 1691
Nolans, 1634.	O'Farrell, 584, 1658.	O'Ryan, 1831	Pegnam, 1694.
Nolty, 1612.	O'Ferry, 601.	Osborne, 1683.	Pegnim, 1694.
Noonan, 1635.	O'Filbin, 1721.	Osbourne, 1683.	Peile, 1706.
Noonane, 1635.	O'Flaherty, 626, 1051, 1659.	Osburne, 1683.	Peirce, 1702.
Norris, 1636.	O'Flanagan, 628, 1660.	O'Sevnagh, 1944.	Pelan, 2047.
Norrit, 1638.	O'Foodhy, 1945.	O,Shanesy, 1684.	Pendelton, 1708.
North, 1637.	Ogan, 2070.	O'Shaughnessy, 1684, 1863.	Pender, 1707, 1737.
Northridge, 1636.	O'Gara, 671, 677.	O'Shea, 1685, 1864.	Pendergast, 1737.
Norton, 1616.	O'Garriga, 1668.	O'Shoughnessy, 1684.	Pendergrass, 1737.
Norwood, 1638.	O'Gilbie, 698, 1661.	O'Sullivan, 1686, 1936.	Penders, 1737.
Noud, 1044.	Ogilby, 1661.	O'Summachan, 1937.	Pendleton, 1708.
Noughton, 1616.	O'Gilvie, 1661.	O'Thina, 632.	Pendy, 1707, 1737, 1738
Nourv, 1636.	O'Gorman, 738, 1662.	O'Toole, 1687. 1972.	Penleton, 1708.
Nowd, 1044.	O'Gowan, 1897.	Ottley, 1688.	Penny, 1713.
Nowlan, 1634.	O'Grady, 746, 1663.	Ougan, 2070.	Pennycook, 1709.
Nowry, 1636.	O'Gready, 1663.	Oulahan, 919.	Pennycuik, 1709.
Nugent, 713, 1639.	O'Hagan, 782, 886, 1664.	Oulihan, 919.	Penycook, 1709.
Nulty, 1612	O'Haire, 821, 1668.	Ounihan, 483.	Peppard, 1710.
Nunan, 1635.	O'Hallaran, 1665.	Ovenden, 1689.	Pepper, 1710, 1729.
Nunun, 1635.		Ovington, 1689.	Percy, 1702.
Nurse, 1636.		Owen, 910, 1690.	Perdon, 1745.
		Owens, 892, 945, 1690.	Perkinson, 1696.
			Perriman 613, 1711.
			Perrott, 1712.
			Perry, 1713.

K

Surname and Reference No.	Surname and Reference No.	Surname and Reference No.	Surname and Reference No.
Person, 1703.	Powlett, 1701.	Rabbett, 1758.	Redmun, 1781.
Peter, 1714.	Prender, 1737.	Rabbit, 399, 1758.	Redpath, 1782.
Peters, 1714.	Prendergast, 1707, 1737.	Racards, 1793.	Reede, 1783.
Petherick, 1021.	Prenderville, 1738.	Radcliffe, 1759.	Reen, 1794, 2079.
Peticrew, 1716.	Prendeville, 1738.	Radwill, 1816	Reford, 2078.
Petit, 1107. 1715.	Prendible, 1738.	Rae, 1771. 2077.	Reid, 1783.
Petite, 1715.	Prendivill, 1738.	Rafe, 1766.	Reidy, 1803.
Peton, 1717.	Prendiville, 1738.	Raferty, 1760	Reigh, 1772, 2077.
Petre, 1714.	Prendy, 1738.	Rafferty, 1071, 1760.	Reighill, 1784.
Petres, 1714.	Pressly, 1740.	Rafter, 1761.	Reilly, 1680, 1785.
Petticrew, 1716.	Prey, 534.	Raftery, 1760.	Reily, 1785.
Pettigrew, 1716.	Priall, 1743.	Raftiss, 1761.	Reinhardt, 1786.
Pettit, 1107.	Price, 1739.	Rahill, 1762.	Reiny, 1763.
Pettitt, 1715	Prichard, 2007.	Rahlly, 1765.	Reirdon, 1795.
Petty, 1715.	Priestley, 1740.	Rainey, 1763.	Rekle, 1784.
Pettycrew, 1716.	Prindergast, 1737.	Rainsford, 1764.	Renaghan, 1787.
Peyton, 1700, 1717.	Prindeville, 1738.	Raleigh, 1765.	Renahan, 1787.
Phair, 1718.	Prindiville, 1738.	Rall, 1762.	Renan, 1586.
Pharis, 601.	Prior, 1741.	Rallinson, 1770.	Renard, 1786.
Phayer, 1718.	Pritchard, 2007.	Rally, 1765.	Renehan, 1787.
Phayre, 1718.	Prunty, 1742.	Ralph, 1766.	Renihan, 1787.
Phelan, 661, 1467 1719, 2047.	Pryall, 1743.	Ramsbottom. 1772.	Renken, 1767.
Phelon, 1719.	Pryce, 1739.	Ranaghan, 1787.	Renkin, 1767.
Pherman. 613 1711.	Pryse, 1739.	Randalson, 1789.	Rennick, 1788.
Pherson, 1468.	Pumfrey, 1733.	Raney, 1763.	Rennicks, 1788.
Phibbs, 1720.	Punch, 1734.	Rankin, 1767.	Rennie, 1763.
Philan, 661, 1719.	Purcell, 1744.	Rannals, 1789.	Rennix, 1788.
Fhilban, 1721.	Purcill, 1744.	Ranolds, 1789.	Rennox, 1788.
Philbin, 1721, 1724, 2047.	Purdon, 1745.	Ransford, 1764.	Renolds, 1789.
Philemon. 1722.	Purdy, 1745.	Rashford, 1801.	Renwicks, 1788.
Philipin, 1724.	Purfield. 1746.	Ratecan, 1769.	Reordan, 1795.
Philips, 1724.	Pursell, 1744.	Rath. 1387.	Reordon, 1795.
Philipson, 1723.	Purtill, 1744.	Rathbone, 1768.	Reppet, 1782.
Phillipin, 1724.	Purtle, 1746.	Rathborne, 1768.	Reven, 1829.
Phillippson, 1723.	Pyper, 1729.	Rathburne. 1768.	Rewan, 1821.
Phillips, 1721, 1724.		Rathwell, 1816.	Reyburn, 1775.
Phillipson. 1723.		Ratican, 1769	Reycroft, 1822.
Philomy, 1722.		Ratigan. 1769.	Reyford, 2078.
Philson, 1723		Ratliff. 1759.	Reynalds. 1789.
Phoenerty, 611.	Quade, 1747.	Rattigan, 1769.	Reynard, 1786.
Phylan, 1719.	Quaid, 1747.	Ratty. 813. 1759.	Reyney, 1763.
Pickett, 1726.	Quaide, 1469.	Raverty. 1760.	Reynick, 1788.
Pidgeon, 1368, 1725.	Quaile. 1749.	Ravery. 1760.	Reynicks, 1788.
Pierce, 1702.	Qualter, 1493.	Ravy. 1774.	Reynolds, 1789.
Pierse, 1702.	Quan. 1748.	Rawleigh, 1765.	Reynoldson. 1789.
Pierson, 1703.	Quann. 1748.	Rawlings. 1808.	Rhategan, 1769.
Piersse, 1702.	Queale. 1749.	Rawlins. 1808.	Rhatigan, 1769.
Pigeon, 1725.	Queen. 1755.	Rawlinson. 1770.	Rheady, 1778.
Piggott, 1726.	Queenan. 398. 1750.	Ray, 1771. 2077.	Rheynard. 1786.
Pigott, 1726.	Queenane. 399.	Rayburn. 1775.	Rhoddy, 1803.
Pindar, 1727.	Quenan. 399.	Raycraft, 1822	Rhoney, 1810.
Pindars, 1727.	Quenn. 1755.	Raycroft. 1822.	Rhuneon. 1787.
Pinder, 1737.	Querk. 1757.	Rayford. 2078.	Rhyder, 1188. 1832.
Pinders, 1737.	Quick. 1757.	Raynard. 1786.	Rhynhart, 1786.
Pindy, 1737. 1738.	Quiddihy. 388	Rea. 1771. 2077.	Riall, 1790.
Pinkerton, 1728.	Quigg. 1998.	Read. 1783.	Ricards, 1793.
Pinkey, 1728.	Quigley, 1751.	Readdy. 1778.	Rice, 1791.
Pinky, 1728.	Quiligan. 303.	Ready, 1778.	Richard, 1792.
Piper, 1710, 1729.	Quilkin. 391.	Reams. 1772.	Richards. 1792, 1793.
Pirie, 1713.	Quillan. 304, 392, 908, 1472, 1752.	Reamsbotham. 1772.	Richey. 1796.
Pirrie. 1713.	Quillen. 392.	Reamsbottom. 1772.	Rickard. 1793.
Poag, 1730, 1732.	Quillenan. 394.	Reany. 1763.	Rickards, 1792, 1793.
Poer, 1736.	Quilligan. 303.	Reardan, 1795.	Ridd, 1783.
Pogue, 1730, 1732.	Quillinan. 394.	Rearden. 1795.	Riding, 1776.
Poke, 1732.	Quilnan. 394.	Reardon, 1681, 1773, 1795.	Rieley, 1785.
Poland, 1731.	Quinane. 772. 1030.	Reaveny. 1774.	Rielly, 1785.
Pole, 1735.	Quinlan, 1753.	Reay. 2077.	Rierdan, 1795.
Polin, 1731.	Quinlish. 1754.	Reburn. 1775.	Rierdon. 1795.
Polk, 1732.	Quinlisk. 1754.	Redahan. 1779.	Rigley, 2081.
Pollett, 1701.	Quinlivan. 1753.	Redding. 1776.	Rile, 1790.
Pollick, 1732.	Quinn. 1267. 1755.	Reddington. 1777.	Riley, 1785.
Pollock, 1730, 1732.	Quinniff. 318.	Reddy, 1778, 1803.	Rilly, 1785.
Pomfret, 1733.	Quintin. 1756.	Redehan. 1779.	Rinaghan. 1787.
Ponsonby, 1734.	Quinton, 1756.	Redery, 1780.	Rinahan, 1787.
Poole, 1735.	Quirk, 1246, 1641, 1757.	Redy, 1778.	Ring, 1794, 2079.
Poor, 1736.	Quoid, 1747.	Redmon, 1781.	Rinn, 1281.
Powell, 771, 1735.	Qwail, 1749.	Redmond, 1781.	Riordan, 1681, 1773, 1795.
Power, 1736.		Redmont, 1781.	Riorden, 1795.
			Rippet, 1782.

Surname and Reference No.	Surname and Reference No.	Surname and Reference No.	Surname and Reference No.
Rippit, 1782.	Rosseter, 1814.	Salisbury, 1833.	Shackleton, 1858.
Ritchie, 1796.	Rossiter, 1814.	Sallanger, 1927.	Shails, 1874.
Rixon, 2082.	Rossitor. 1814.	Sallenger, 1927.	Shairp, 1862.
Roache, 1800.	Rosster, 1814.	Sallinger. 1927.	Shakleton, 1858.
Roan, 1821.	Rostig, 1800.	Salmon, 1834.	Shales, 1874.
Roane, 1821.	Roth, 1828.	Salters, 1838.	Shanaghan, 1859.
Roantree, 1819.	Rothe, 1828.	Sammon, 1834.	Shanaghy, 613.
Roark. 1820.	Rotheram, 1815.	Sample, 1852.	Shanahan, 643, 1859,
Roarke. 1820.	Rotherham. 1815.	Sanderson, 1839.	1860.
Robbinson, 1799.	Rotherum. 1815.	Sandes. 1835.	Shanahen, 1859.
Roberts, 1797. 1798.	Rothweil, 1816.	Sands, 1835.	Shanahy, 643.
Robertson, 1797, 1798,	Rouane, 1831.	Sandys, 1835.	Shanan. 1859.
1799.	Roughan, 1818.	Sargeant. 1836.	Shane, 965, 1478, 1866.
Robins. 1799.	Roughneen. 1801, 1809.	Sargent, 1836.	Shanessy, 1084, 1863.
Robinson. 1798, 1799.	Roulston, 1817.	Sargesson. 1853.	Shanihan, 1859.
Robison, 1799.	Roundtree, 1819.	Sargint, 1836.	Shannagh, 1860.
Robisson, 1799.	Rountree, 1819.	Sargisson. 1853.	Shannahan, 1859.
Robotham, 1813.	Rourke, 1682, 1820.	Sarseil, 1837.	Shannihan. 1859.
Robson, 1799.	Routh, 1828.	Sarsfield, 1837.	Shannon, 714, 1859,
Roche, 1800.	Routledge, 1830.	Saulisbury, 1833.	1860.
Rochefort. 1801.	Rowan, 1821.	Saulters, 1838.	Shanny, 1860.
Rochford, 1801.	Rowantree, 1819.	Saunders, 1839.	Shanon, 1860.
Rochfort, 1801.	Rowe, 1805.	Saunderson, 1839.	Sharket, 1861.
Rochneen, 1801.	Rowen, 1821.	Saurin, 1840. 1903.	Sharkey. 1861.
Rock, 248. 1802.	Rowlandson, 1808.	Sausheil, 1837.	Sharpe, 1862.
Rodan, 1804.	Rowlendson, 1770.	Savage, 1841.	Sharry, 635.
Rodaughan, 1779.	Rowlins, 1808.	Saway, 1842.	Sharvin, 1873.
Roddie, 1803.	Rowlston, 1817.	Sawer, 1843.	Shaughness, 1863.
Roddon, 1826.	Rowney, 1810.	Sawey, 1842.	Shaughnessy, 1684.
Roddy, 1778, 1803.	Roxberry, 1812.	Sawier, 1843.	1863.
Roden, 1804, 1826.	Roxborough, 1812.	Sawyer, 1843.	Shaughnesy, 1863.
Rodger, 1286, 1806.	Roy, 1309, 1384, 1824.	Sawyers, 1843.	Shaunessy, 1863.
Rodgers, 1286, 1366,	Royan, 1831.	Scally, 1844.	Shay, 1685.
1806.	Royce, 1823.	Scandlon, 1846.	Shea, 1685. 1864.
Rodin, 1804.	Roycraft, 1822.	Scanlan, 1845, 1846.	Sheahan, 1866.
Rodman, 1781.	Roycroft, 1822.	Scanlen, 1846.	Sheales, 1784.
Rodmont, 1781.	Roynane, 1809.	Scanlin, 1846.	Sheals, 1784.
Rody, 1803.	Royse, 1823.	Scanlon, 1845, 1846.	Shean, 1866.
Roe, 1805.	Royston, 1824.	Schoales, 1847.	Shearer, 1872.
Roger, 1806.	Ruan, 1821. 1831.	Schofield, 1848.	Shearhoon, 1737.
Rogers, 1286, 1366, 1806.	Ruane, 1825, 1831.	Scholefield, 1848.	Shearlock, 1871.
Rogerson, 1807.	Ruarke, 1820.	Scholes, 1847.	Sheckleton, 1858.
Rohan, 1818.	Ruddan, 1826	Schoules, 1847.	Shee, 1685.
Roice, 1791, 1823.	Rudden, 1804, 1826.	Schumacker, 1879.	Sheean, 1866.
Rolands, 1808.	Ruddin, 1826.	Scoales, 1847.	Sheedy, 1448, 1865.
Rolestone, 1817.	Ruddon, 1804.	Scofield, 1848.	Sheehan. 1866.
Rolfe, 1766.	Ruddy, 1803.	Scolefield, 1848.	Sheen. 1866.
Rollestone, 1817.	Rudican, 1779.	Scoles, 1847.	Sheenan, 1860.
Rollins, 1808.	Ruineen, 1810.	Scullion, 1849.	Sheera, 1869.
Rollstone, 1817.	Ruirk, 1820.	Scurlock, 1871.	Shehan, 1866.
Rolph, 1766.	Runey, 1810.	Seagrave, 1851.	Sheil, 1784.
Rolston, 1817.	Runian, 1810.	Seagrove, 1851.	Sheils, 1784.
Ronaghan, 1787.	Ruorke, 1820.	Searight, 1850.	Sheir, 1877.
Ronaldson, 1789.	Rurk, 1682.	Seaver, 1857.	Sheirdan, 1870.
Ronane, 1809.	Rushford, 1801.	Seawright, 1850.	Shekelton, 1858.
Ronayne, 1809.	Russboro, 1812.	Sedgwick, 264.	Shekleton, 1858.
Roney, 1810.	Russell, 1827.	Seerey, 650.	Sheles, 1874.
Roohan, 1810.	Russle, 1827.	Seery, 650.	Shelliday, 1875.
Roon, 1821.	Ruth, 1828.	Segrave, 1851, 1935.	Shelloe, 1867.
Rooneen, 1810.	Ruthven, 1829.	Segre, 1851.	Shelly, 1867.
Rooney, 1588, 1810.	Rutledge, 1830.	Selenger, 1927.	Shephard, 1868.
Roonoo, 1810.	Rutlege, 1830.	Sellinger, 1927.	Shepherd, 1868.
Roorke, 1820.	Ruttledge, 1830.	Semore, 1857.	Sheppard, 1868.
Roragh, 1682.	Ruttlege, 1830.	Semour, 1857.	Shepperd, 1868.
Rorison, 1807.	Ryall, 1790.	Semple, 1852.	Shera, 1869.
Rorke, 1682, 1820.	Ryan, 1825. 1231.	Sergeant, 1836.	Sherard, 1872.
Rosborough, 1812.	Rycroft, 1822.	Sergent, 1836.	Sherden, 1870.
Rosbottom, 1813.	Ryder, 1188, 1832.	Sergerson, 1853.	Sherdian, 1870.
Rosbrow, 1812.	Ryding, 1776.	Sergeson, 1853.	Sherdon, 1870.
Rosebery, 1812.	Ryely, 1785.	Sergesson, 1853.	Sheredan, 1870.
Rosebrough, 1812.	Ryle, 1790.	Sergison, 1853.	Shereden, 1870.
Roseingrave, 1811.	Ryley, 1785.	Sergisson, 1853.	Sheridan, 1870, 1875.
Rosey, 1811.	Rynard, 1786.	Serplice, 1940.	Sheriden, 1870.
Rositer, 1814.	Rynn, 2079.	Serplus, 1940.	Sherlock, 1871.
Rosmond, 1812.		Serrage, 1854.	Sherodan, 1870.
Rossboro, 1812.		Serridge, 1854.	Sherra, 1872.
Rossborough, 1812.	Sage, 1841.	Sewell, 1855.	Sherrar, 1872.
Rossbotham, 1813.	Salisberry. 1833.	Sexton, 1856.	Sherrard, 1872.
Rossbottam, 1813.	Salisbry, 1833.	Seymore, 1857.	Sherrerd, 1872.
Rossburrow, 1812.		Seymour, 1857.	Sherridan, 1870.

Surname and Reference No.	Surname and Reference No.	Surname and Reference No.	Surname and Reference No.
Sherwin, 1873.	Skehan, 1958.	Spalane, 1913.	Strachan, 1930.
Shiel, 1874.	Skellet, 1890.	Spear, 1910.	Straghan, 1930.
Shields, 1874.	Skelly, 1844.	Spears, 1910.	Strahan, 1930.
Shiells, 1874.	Skifenton, 1889.	Speed, 1945.	Strain, 1930.
Shiels, 1874.	Skiffington, 1889.	Speer, 1910.	Stratten, 1932.
Shier, 1877.	Skifington, 1889.	Speers, 1910.	Stratton, 1932.
Shiles, 1874.	Skillet, 1890.	Spelessy, 1913.	Strayhorn, 1931.
Shillady, 1875.	Skinnion, 438.	Spellane, 1913.	Streahorn, 1931.
Shilliady, 1875.	Skivington. 1889.	Spellman, 1911.	Streaton, 1932.
Shilliday, 1870, 1875.	Skoolin, 1849.	Spelman, 1911.	Streatton, 1932.
Shillidy, 1875.	Slamon, 1892.	Spence, 1912.	Streeten, 1932.
Shillitoe, 1876.	Slane, 1893.	Spense, 1912.	Stretton. 1932.
Shinagh, 643.	Slater, 1891.	Spilane, 1913.	Stuart, 1925. 1933.
Shine. 1866.	Slator, 1891.	Spillane, 1913.	Studdart, 1934.
Shinnagh, 643.	Slavin, 1892.	Spillessy. 1913.	Studdert, 1928, 1934.
Shinnahan, 1967.	Sleater, 1891.	Spince, 1912.	Suckley, 1908.
Shinnock, 643.	Sleator, 1891.	Splaine, 1913.	Suel. 1855.
Shirdan, 1870.	Sleavin, 1892.	Spollen, 1911.	Sughrue, 1935.
Shire, 1877.	Sleevin, 1892.	Sprool, 1914.	Sugrew, 1935.
Shirlock. 1871.	Sleigh, 1895.	Sproule. 1914.	Sugrue, 1851. 1925.
Shirra, 1869.	Slevan, 1892.	Sprowle. 1914.	Sulavan, 1936.
Shocknesy, 1863.	Slevin, 1892.	Sruffaun. 208.	Sulevan, 1936.
Shoebottom, 1878.	Sligh, 1895.	Stackpoole, 1915.	Sulivan, 1936.
Shoemaker. 1879.	Sloan, 1893.	Stacpole. 1915.	Sullavan, 1936.
Sholdice, 1882.	Sloane. 1893.	Stafford, 1916.	Sullevan, 1936.
Sholdies, 1882.	Sloey, 1536.	Stanton, 1919.	Sullivan, 1686, 1907,
Sholdise, 1882.	Slone, 1893.	Stapelton, 1917.	1936.
Shonahan, 965.	Slowey, 1536, 1894.	Stapleton, 1917.	Sumahean, 1904.
Shonogh, 643.	Slown, 1893.	Stapylton, 1917.	Sumeril, 1906.
Shorelahan, 1936.	Sloy, 1894.	Staratt, 1918.	Sumerly, 1906.
Short, 1346. 1880.	Sly, 1895.	Starrat, 1918.	Summerly, 1937.
Shortall, 1881.	Small, 1896.	Starret, 1918.	Summers, 1904.
Shortell, 1881.	Smallen, 1898.	Starrett, 1918.	1938.
Shorten, 1880.	Smalls, 1896.	Starritt, 1918	Summersett, 1905.
Shorthall. 1881.	Smallwoods, 2075.	Staunton, 1919.	Summerville. 1906.
Shortle, 1881.	Smeeth, 1897.	Stavely, 1920.	Sunderland, 1942.
Shoughnesey, 1863.	Smerle, 1900.	St. Clair, 1887.	Surgener, 1939.
Shoughnessy, 1863.	Smiley, 1899.	Stead, 1921.	Surgenor, 1939.
Shouldice, 1882.	Smillie, 1899.	Steads, 1921.	Surgeoner, 1939.
Shoye, 967.	Smily, 1899.	Steamson, 1923.	Surgeonor, 1939.
Shubottom, 1878.	Smirell, 1900.	Steavely. 1920.	Surgesson, 1853.
Shuell, 1855.	Smith, 728, 744, 1348,	Steed, 1921.	Surginer, 1939.
Shuiter, 1909.	1358, 1897, 1901.	Steen, 1923.	Surginor, 1939.
Shunagh, 643.	Smollan, 1898.	Steenson, 1923.	Surley, 1942.
Shunny, 643.	Smollen, 1898.	Steid, 1921.	Surplice, 1940.
Shurden, 1870.	Smullen, 1898.	Steinson, 1923.	Surtill, 1881.
Shuter, 1909.	Smurell. 1900.	Stenson, 1923.	Sutcliffe, 1941.
Sie, 1842.	Smylie, 1899.	Stenton, 1919.	Suter, 1909.
Silk, 1865.	Smyrl, 1900.	Stepenson, 1923.	Sutherland, 1942.
Sillitoe, 1876.	Smyrrell, 1900.	Stephens, 1922, 1923.	Suthhern, 1942.
Simcocks, 1883.	Smyth, 728, 1358, 1897,	Stephenson, 1922,	Sutliffe, 1941.
Simcox, 1883.	1901.	1923.	Sutor, 1909.
Simmon. 623.	Smythe, 1897.	Steritt, 1918.	Swanick, 1943.
Simmonds. 1884.	Snedden, 1902.	Sterling. 1924.	Swanwick, 1943.
Simmons. 623, 1884.	Snodden, 1902.	Stern, 1924.	Sweeny, 1483, 1485,
Simms, 1885, 1886.	Snoddon, 1902.	Sterritt, 1918.	1944. 1946.
Simon, 623.	Snoden, 1902.	Steuart. 1925.	Sweny, 1944.
Simonds, 1884.	Snodon, 1902	Stevely, 1920.	Swift, 634, 1945.
Simons, 623, 1884.	Snowden. 1902.	Steven, 1923.	Swine, 1946.
Simple, 1852.	Sodan, 1903.	Stevens, 1922.	Swiney, 1483, 1944,
Simpson, 1885, 1886.	Soden, 1840, 1903.	Stevenson, 1923.	1946.
Sims, 1885.	Sodin, 1840, 1903.	Stevinson, 1923.	Swords, 1947.
Simson, 1886.	Solesbury, 1833.	Steward, 1925.	Symcox. 1883.
Simvil, 1906.	Solisberry, 1833.	Stewart, 1925, 1933.	Symes, 1885.
Sinclair, 1887.	Sollsbury. 1833.	Stinson, 1923.	Symms, 1885.
Sinclare. 1887.	Somers, 1904. 1938.	Stinton, 1919.	Symonds, 1884.
Sincler, 1887.	Somerset, 1905.	Stirling, 1924.	Sympson, 1886.
Sinemon. 273.	Somerville. 1906.	Stirratt, 1918.	Syms, 1885.
Singen, 1926.	Sommers, 1904.	Stirrett, 1918.	Synnott, 1888.
Singin, 1926.	Sommersett, 1905.	Stirrit, 1918.	
Sinjohn, 1926.	Sommerville, 1906.	Stively, 1920.	
Sinjun, 1926.	Sonahaun, 1904.	St. John, 1926.	
Sinnamon, 273.	Soolivan, 1936	St. Ledger, 1927.	
Sinnott, 1888.	Soraghan, 1907, 1936.	St. Leger, 1927.	
Sinott, 1888.	Sorahan, 1907.	Stoakes, 1929.	
Sitcliff, 1941.	Soran, 1907.	Stoddart, 1928, 1934.	Taaffe, 1948.
Sitliff, 1941.	Soughley, 1908.	Stokes, 1929.	Tackney, 1856.
Size, 319.	Southerland, 1942.	Stothart, 1928.	Taff, 1948.
Skally, 1844.	Souttar, 1909.	Stotherg, 1928.	Tagart, 1949.
Skeffington, 1889.	Soy, 1842.	Stothers, 1928.	Tagert, 1949.

Surname and Reference No.	Surname and Reference No.	Surname and Reference No.	Surname and Reference No.
Taggart, 1949.	Topping, 1973.	Turk, 1993.	Vandeleur, 2014.
Taggert, 1949.	Torkington, 1993.	Turkington, 1993.	Vandelleur, 2014.
Tague, 1543, 1953.	Torley, 1974.	Turkinton, 1993.	Vargis, 599.
Taise, 1954.	Torpy, 1950.	Turley, 1974.	Vargus, 599.
Tait, 1951.	Torrance, 1975.	Turner, 1994.	Varily, 2015.
Taite, 1951.	Torrans, 1975	Turnor, 1994.	Varley, 2015.
Tally, 1989.	Torrence, 1975.	Turnour, 1994.	Varrelly, 585.
Tarpey, 1950.	Torrens, 1975.	Tuthill, 1995.	Varrilly, 2013, 2015.
Tarrant, 1958.	Torrins, 1975.	Tuttell, 1995.	Vaugh, 2035.
Tate, 1951.	Torry, 1975.	Tuttil, 1995.	Vaughan, 2016.
Tavey, 1147.	Tosh, 1152.	Tuttle, 1995.	Veakins, 2011.
Tayler, 1952.	Tothill, 1995.	Tutty, 1995.	Veasy, 2017.
Taylor, 1952.	Toughall, 2000	Twamley, 1996.	Veigh, 1489.
Taylour, 1952.	Toughill, 1968.	Tweedie, 1997.	Veldon, 2041.
Teague, 1543, 1953.	Touhy, 1992.	Tweedy, 1997.	Venton, 598.
Tease, 1954.	Tourisk, 2031.	Twigg, 1998.	Vesey, 2017.
Teaze, 1954.	Towell, 2000.	Twigley, 1751.	Vessey, 2017.
Tee, 1960.	Towhig, 1991.	Twinam, 1999.	Vezey, 2017.
Teerry, 1975.	Towill, 2000.	Twinem, 1999.	Vicars, 2018.
Teg, 1317.	Towmey, 2001.	Twinim, 1999.	Vickars, 2018.
Tegart, 1949.	Townsend, 1976, 1977.	Twohig, 1991.	Vickers, 2018.
Teggart, 1949.	Townshend, 1976.	Twohill, 2000.	Victory, 1441, 2019.
Teggarty, 1317.	Townsley, 1976, 1977.	Twohy, 1992.	Vikers, 2018.
Teigue, 1543.	Tracey, 1978.	Twomey, 2001.	Vincent, 2020.
Templeton, 1955.	Tracy, 1978.	Twomley, 1996.	Vulcougha, 1568.
Templetown, 1955.	Trainor, 1980.	Twoohy, 1992.	
Ternan, 1959.	Tranor, 1980.	Twoomy, 2001.	
Terney, 1959.	Travers, 1979.	Twynam, 1999.	
Terry, 1975.	Travors, 1979.	Twynem, 1999.	
Thompson, 1956.	Trayner, 1980.	Twynim, 1999.	
Thomson, 1956.	Traynor, 1980.	Tye, 1960.	
Thorn, 1958.	Treacy, 1978.	Tyghe, 1960.	
Thornberry, 1957.	Treanor, 1284, 1980.	Tyler, 1952.	Wachop, 2034.
Thornburgh, 1957.	Trehy, 1984.	Tymmany, 2002.	Wadden, 2021.
Thornton, 512, 1958.	Trenor, 1980.	Tymmins, 1961.	Waddick, 2036.
Tiernan, 1959.	Tressy, 1978.	Tymmons, 1961.	Wadding, 2021.
Tierney, 1959.	Trevors, 1979.	Tyndall, 2004.	Waddock, 2036.
Tiger, 1317.	Trim-Lavery, 38.	Tyndell, 2004.	Wade, 1469, 2022.
Tighe, 1487, 1960.	Trinlavery, 38.	Tynan, 2003.	Wadick, 2036.
Timmin, 2002.	Troland, 1983.	Tynnan, 2003.	Wadock, 2036.
Timmons, 1961.	Trolen, 1983.		Wadsworth, 2023.
Timothy, 1962, 1990.	Troosel, 1981.		Wadworth, 2023.
Tinckler, 1963.	Troughton, 1982.		Waid, 2022.
Tindal, 2004.	Trousdale, 1981.		Waide, 2022.
Tinin, 2003.	Trousdell, 1981.		Waite, 2024.
Tinkler, 1963.	Trouten, 1982.	Ubank, 2005.	Waites, 2024.
Tinsley, 1977.	Trouton, 1982.	Uiske, 2031.	Wallace, 2025, 2027.
Tipping, 1973.	Trower, 1979.	Ultagh, 1637.	Wallice, 2025.
Titterington, 1964.	Trowland, 1983.	Umphries, 934.	Wallis, 2025.
Titterton, 1964.	Trowtan, 1982.	Umphry, 934.	Wallsh, 2027.
Toal, 1687, 1965, 1968, 1972.	Troy, 1984.	Unckles, 2006.	Walmsley, 2026.
Toale, 1965.	Truesdall, 1981.	Uncles, 2006.	Walsh, 149, 2025, 2027.
Tobin, 1966.	Trusdale, 1981.	Unehan, 483.	Walwood, 2043.
Tobyn, 1966.	Trusdell, 1981.	Unkles, 2006.	Wamsley, 2026.
Todd, 1967.	Trusdill, 1981.	Uprichard, 2007.	Ward, 2028.
Toghill, 1968.	Trusill, 1981.	Urkuhart, 2008.	Warick, 2030.
Tohall, 1965.	Tryn-Lavery, 33.	Urquahart, 2008.	Waring, 2029.
Tohill, 1968.	Tubman, 1985.	Urquehart, 2008.	Warreck, 2030.
Tohull, 1968.	Tubridy, 1986.	Urquhart, 2008.	Warrell, 2076.
Tolan, 1969.	Tubrit, 1986.	Urrell, 2091.	Warren, 1192, 1599, 2029.
Toland, 1969.	Tugman, 1985.	Ushart, 2009.	Warrenne, 2029.
Tomilty, 1990.	Tuhill, 1972.	Usher, 2009.	Warrick, 2030.
Tomkin, 1970.	Tuhy, 1992.	Ussher, 880, 2009.	Warrin, 2029.
Tomkins, 1970.	Tuite, 1987.	Ustace, 565.	Warring, 2029.
Tomlinson, 1971.	Tuke, 1988.		Warton, 2045.
Tompson, 1956	Tully, 1989.		Warwick, 2030.
Tomson, 1956.	Tumalti, 1990.		Watch, 2032.
Tonson, 1956.	Tumbleton, 796.		Waters, 2031.
Tooey, 1992.	Tumblety, 1990.	Vahey, 572.	Waterson, 2031, 2033.
Toohig, 1991.	Tumblinson, 1971.	Vahy, 1489.	Watson, 2032.
Toohill, 2000.	Tumelty, 1962, 1990.	Vail, 2010.	Wattenson, 2033.
Toohy, 1992.	Tumiltey, 1990.	Vakins, 2011.	Watters, 2031.
Took, 1988.	Tumilty, 1990.	Valentine, 2012.	Wauchob, 2034.
Tooke, 1988.	Tummon, 1961.	Vallantine, 2012.	Wauchope, 2034.
Toole, 1687, 1965, 1972.	Tuohig, 1991.	Vallely, 2013, 2015.	Waugh, 2035.
Tooley, 1687.	Tuohill, 2000.	Vallentine, 2012.	Wauhope, 2034.
Toomey, 2000, 2001.	Tuohy, 1992.	Vallily, 2015.	Waytes, 2024.
Toompane, 1970.	Tuomy, 2001.	Vally, 2013.	Weadick, 2036.
Toorish, 2031.	Turbett, 440.	Vandaleur, 2014.	Weadock, 2036.
	Turish, 2031.		Weaks, 2039.
			Wear, 2040.
			Weatherhead, 2037.

94

Surname and Reference No.	Surname and Reference No.	Surname and Reference No.	Surname and Reference No.
Webber, 2038.	Whitaker, 2051.	Williams, 2062, 2063.	Wrafter, 1761.
Weber, 2038.	White, 666, 2049, 2057.	Williamson. 2062, 2063.	Wray, 1771, 2077.
Weekes, 2039.	Whiteacre, 2054.	Willison, 2066.	Wrayburn, 1775.
Weeks, 2039.	Whiteaker. 2054.	Willmott, 2065.	Wrayford. 2078.
Weere, 2046.	Whitegar, 2054.	Willson, 2066.	Wreford. 2078.
Weir, 2040.	Whitehead, 227, 2050.	Willoughby, 2064.	Wren, 1794.
Welch, 2027.	Whitely. 2051.	Wilmitt, 2065.	Wrenn, 1281, 1794, 2079.
Weldon, 2041.	Whiteman, 2059.	Wilmont. 2065.	Wright, 2080.
Wellesley. 2042.	Whiteside, 2052.	Wilmot, 2065.	Wrigley, 2081.
Wellwood, 2043.	Whitfield. 2053.	Wilson. 2066	Wrixon, 2082.
Welsh, 2027.	Whitla, 2051.	Wily. 2084.	Wrynn, 2079.
Welsley, 2042.	Whitley, 2051.	Wimbs, 2085	Wyber, 2038.
Welwood, 2043.	Whitly. 2016.	Winfield. 2067.	Wybrants, 2083.
Were, 2040.	Whitsitt, 2052.	Wingfield, 2067.	Wyer, 2040.
Werton, 2015.	Whittacre, 2051.	Winn, 2086.	Wyld, 2060.
Wesley, 2042	Whittaker, 2051.	Winnfield. 2067.	Wylde, 2060.
Wethered, 2037.	Whittegar, 2054.	Winter, 2068.	Wylie, 2084.
Whaite, 2024.	Whittley, 20.6.	Winters, 2068.	Wymbs, 2085.
Whalan, 2047.	Wholey, 925.	Winterson, 2033.	Wyn, 2086.
Whalen, 2047.	Wholihane, 905.	Winton, 1756.	Wynfield, 2067.
Whaley, 2044.	Wholy, 2055.	Wintour, 2068.	Wynn, 1158, 1335.
Whalley, 2044.	Whoolahan, 919.	Wire, 2040.	Wynne, 770, 1158. 1335:
Whammond, 797.	Whoolehan, 919.	Wise. 2087.	2086.
Whan, 1748.	Whooley, 513.	Wisehart, 2069.	Wynnfield, 2067.
Wharton, 2045.	Whoriskey, 2056.	Wiseheart. 2069.	Wynter. 2068.
Whately, 2046.	Whorriskey. 2031.	Wishart, 2069.	Wyse, 2087.
Whealan, 2047.	Whybron, 2083.	Withecomb, 2058.	
Whealon, 2047.	Whyte, 2049, 2057.	Wither. 2074.	
Whealy, 2044.	Wiber, 2038.	Wize, 2087.	
Wheately, 2046.	Wicks, 2039.	Wodsworth, 2023.	
Wheatly, 2046.	Widdecombe, 2058.	Wogan, 2070.	
Wheelahan, 2047.	Widdicomb, 2058.	Wolfe, 2071.	
Wheelan, 2047.	Wier, 2040.	Wolff, 2071.	Yates, 2088.
Whelahan. 2047.	Wigan, 1368	Wolseley, 2072.	Yeates, 2088.
Whelan, 944, 1719, 1721,	Wiggam, 2048.	Wolsey, 2072.	Yeats, 2088.
2047.	Wightman, 2059.	Wolsley, 2072.	Yeilding, 2089.
Wheleghan, 2047.	Wilby, 2064.	Woodroofe, 2073.	Yielding. 2089.
Whelehan. 2047.	Wild, 2060.	Woodrooffe, 2073.	Yonge, 2090.
Whelen, 2047.	Wilde, 2060.	Woodrow, 2074.	Young. 2090.
Whelon, 2047.	Wildes, 2060.	Woodruff, 2073.	Yourell, 2091.
Wherton, 2045.	Wiley, 2084.	Woods, 556. 2075.	
Whiffle, 2053.	Wilhair, 246.	Woolsey, 2072.	
Whigam, 2048.	Wilie, 2084.	Worald, 2076.	
Whigham, 2048.	Wilkie, 2061.	World, 2076.	
Whight, 2049.	Wilkinson, 2061.	Worrall, 20.6.	
Whin. 1755.	Wilkison, 2061.	Worrell, 2076.	
Whinn, 1755.	Wilkisson, 2061.	Woulfe, 2071.	Zorkin, 121.